Readings in Managerial Economics

Readings in

Managerial Economics

Edited by

Thomas Joseph Coyne
The University of Akron

1981

Third Edition

BUSINESS PUBLICATIONS, INC. Plano, Texas 75075
Irwin-Dorsey Limited   Georgetown, Ontario   L7G 4B3

338.5
R 287

© BUSINESS PUBLICATIONS, INC., 1973, 1977, and 1981

ISBN 0-256-02422-7

Library of Congress Catalog Card No. 80–70313

Printed in the United States of America

1 2 3 4 5 6 7 8 9 0 ML 8 7 6 5 4 3 2 1

Preface

An anthology is intended to improve student access to journal articles while allowing authors an outlet for somewhat wider dissemination of their views. Hopefully, this publication does not differ in that respect. This Third Edition retains those articles which reportedly appeal to economics scholars; in addition, it contains research of interest to skills-oriented students who must learn when, how, and why certain tools and techniques of the economist are applicable.

A few articles in the first two versions of this publication were too complicated for some students; a few articles were too easy. An attempt is made here to alter this condition. Professors wanting to maximize application of economic theory may welcome this slight change of emphasis.

The writings of the classical and socialistic economic theorists, which have contributed significantly to the literature, were not found in the first two versions and are *not* found in this third edition. Likewise, the unmistakable brilliance of the many economists who concerned themselves with the study and explanation of how an economy works and whether certain desirable goals such as full employment and price stability could be achieved are unnecessary in this kind of book. For the most part, those writers did not address themselves specifically to the price and output decisions that must be made daily by corporate executives, many of the tools for which *are* explained in this publication.

The purpose of this edition is to demonstrate that economic theory need not be confined to some ivory tower. Its objective is to supplement the reader's understanding of economic theory with enough knowledge of procedural technique(s) so that he or she will become a more effective decision maker, a more useful member of the management team.

Every economy, whether it be capitalistic, socialistic, or communistic, has little choice but to rely upon the subject matter of economics for meaningful decisions. Business executives as well as politicians will continue to lean heavily tomorrow on the "academic scribblers" of yesterday and today. In some small way, this publication should help them make significantly better decisions.

The price and output behavior of a firm operating in a mixed capitalistic system such as we have within the confines of the United States is, for the most part, the subject matter of this book. It has to do with economic methodology; demand; costs; production and productivity; pricing; capital budgeting; and economic forecasting. It is an exciting undertaking and one that will prove beneficial to students who pursue it seriously.

The astute student will find that *Readings in Managerial Economics* investigates the place a firm holds within an industry, the contribution it makes to society, and the impact it has upon international affairs.

As a separate subject, *managerial* economics is relatively new, its first serious treatment in textbook format being provided by Joel Dean in 1951. It applies concepts learned in the more traditional courses in micro-economic and/or macroeconomic theory—applies them in a manner useful in the daily operations of the firm. And why not? The last thing most organizations may need is an economist steeped in economic theory but unable to communicate with other executives employed by the firm. This readings book helps to put economic theory and practice in proper perspective.

One hesitates to guess at the number of articles that were reviewed in the selection process for this edition. Suffice it to say that many were called but few were chosen. And the probability is high that some mistakes were made. Naturally, I assume full responsibility for these errors, judgmental or otherwise.

Suggestions received from several colleagues almost caused adoption of a more uniform level of abstraction throughout the volume. The temptation was overcome; consequently, the user has abstract articles that develop important principles mixed with elementary ones that illustrate those principles clearly.

Constraints common to the practice continue with this third edition; namely, space, coverage, and balance. A self-imposed limitation of not reprinting materials from books is retained.

Whenever possible, footnotes are removed and, at times, textual material that does not contribute significantly to the overall aims of the book is omitted. To the greatest possible extent, editorial changes are minimal.

A matrix of cross-references between several leading textbooks and specific articles in this publication is provided for the user. In addition, these chapters are cross-referenced with specific articles in the Table of Contents.

Very sincere thanks is expressed to the authors and publishers who provided permission to reprint these articles.

I have benefited from helpful comments received from a number of students and colleagues. In particular, I would like to acknowledge the help of Ann N. P. Fisher, SUNY College at Fredonia; Oscar Jensen,

University of Connecticut at Storrs; Franklin E. Robeson, College of William and Mary; and Vishal C. Sabherwal, University of San Francisco. My research assistant at the The University of Akron, Glenn D. Weber, made more than his fair share of trips to the library.

I am particularly grateful to the students for feedback and suggestions concerning many of the articles considered but not used. Because of them, this publication should contribute to a better understanding of applied price theory; however, if this Third Edition does not accomplish everything for the student that I hope it will, I can be comforted by the fact that he who achieves everything he sets out to achieve probably doesn't set out to achieve enough in the first place.

THOMAS JOSEPH COYNE

Table of Contents

and

Text Cross-References[*]

PART ONE

The Scope and Method of Managerial Economics

---

* Textbooks referenced include:
Douglas, Evan J. *Managerial Economics*. Englewood Cliffs, N.J.: Prentice-Hall,
    1979.
Henry, William R., and Haynes, W. Warren. *Managerial Economics: Analysis and
    Cases,* 4th ed. Dallas, Texas: Business Publications, 1978.
McGuigan, James R., and Moyer, R. Charles. *Managerial Economics,* 2d ed. St. Paul,
    Minn.: West Publishing Co., 1979.
Pappas, James L., and Brigham, Eugene F. *Managerial Economics,* 3d ed. Hinsdale,
    Ill.: The Dryden Press, 1979.
Seo, K. K., and Winger, Bernard J. *Managerial Economics: Text, Problems and
    Short Cases,* 5th ed. Homewood, Ill.: Irwin, 1979.
Stokes, Charles J. *Economics for Managers*. New York: McGraw-Hill, 1979.
Webb, Samuel C. *Managerial Economics*. Boston: Houghton Mifflin, 1976.
Wilson, J. Holton, and Darr, Steven H. *Managerial Economics: Concepts, Applica-
    tions and Cases*. New York: Harper & Row, 1979.
Zudak, Lawrence S. *Managerial Economics*. New York: Harper & Row, 1980.

PART THREE

Costs, Production, and Productivity

PART FOUR

Pricing

PART FIVE

Capital Budgeting

PART SIX

Forecasting

TEXT CROSS-REFERENCES

	Part and Chapter Numbers					
Readings in This Book	Part One Scope and Method of Managerial Economics	Part Two Demand	Part Three Costs, Production, and Productivity	Part Four Pricing	Part Five Capital Budgeting	Part Six Forecasting
Douglas	1, 2	3, 4, 5	6, 7, 8, 12	9, 10, 11, 12	5, 7, 15	5, 8
Henry	1	3, 4, 5	6, 7, 8, 13	11, 12	14, 15	4, 5
McGuigan and Moyer	1, 6	4, 5, 6, 8	2, 10, 11, 18	12, 13, 14, 18, 19	10, 12, 15	4, 6, 7
Pappas and Brigham	1	4, 5	6, 8, 9, 14	10, 11-A, 12	8, 13, 14	App. B
Seo and Winger ..	1, 2	4, 5	6, 7, 9	7, 9, 11	13, 14	3
Stokes	1	3, 4	5, 6	4, 7, 8	4, 7, 15	10
Webb	1	6, 10, 11	12, 15, 16, 26	21	15, 24, 25	18
Wilson and Darr	1	5	7, 8, 11	9, 10, 14	8, 12, 13	4, 6
Zudak	1	2, 3	4, 5, 8, 9	9, 14	8, 9, 14	4, 6, App. 3

part ONE
The Scope and Method of Managerial Economics

INTRODUCTION

Managerial economics is economics applied to managerial decision making. It is a branch of economics bringing abstract theory into closer harmony with managerial practice. Its stress is on the use of the tools of economic analysis in clarifying problems, in organizing and evaluating information, and in comparing alternative courses of action. Its methods and point of view are applicable to business institutions, hospitals, government(s), universities, nonprofit foundations, and so forth, which allocate resources.

Economics is defined sometimes as the study of the allocation of scarce resources among unlimited wants. It follows that managerial economics is the study of the allocation of resources available to a firm or other decision-making institution. Thus, like all economics, managerial economics is concerned with choice; but, among the various branches of economics, it is supremely pragmatic. It cuts through many of the refinements of theory. While it seems to avoid some of the most difficult issues of abstract economic theory, it inevitably faces complications that are ignored in pure theory, for it must deal with the total situation in which decisions are made.

Managerial economics is therefore manifestly different from microeconomic theory, but it is somehow related. Just what this relation is has been a lively topic of debate. The extreme positions are, on the one hand, a naïve belief that the most abstract economic theories are applicable to the most complex of managerial problems; on the other, an equally repugnant belief that no part of economic theory is applicable to even the simplest of them. From a large and admirable literature covering the question from one extreme to the other, one article (Baumol's) has been selected to express some of the more tenable views. Another research

1

piece (Simon's) warns the reader against believing economic theories
and "laws" can stand alone.

The well-known paper by William Baumol establishes a point of view
for managerial economics; namely, that a managerial economist can
make significant contributions as a member of the management group
simply because he or she is an effective model builder. The economist's
analytic tools and techniques help that person deal with problems facing
an organization in a very rigorous and revealing manner. Managerial
economists tend to probe deeper into complex problems than do persons
without such training and these problems, once solved, are often presented in a simplified manner for all to see.

Herbert Simon wants the managerial economist to look beyond the
concepts found in economics. He argues for recognition of the numerous
instances where applied price theory overlaps the areas of psychology and
sociology. He wants one to realize the consumer as well as the entrepreneur is a compassionate person who hopes to gain and maintain a variety
of objectives—only one of which might be profit.

How closely one chooses to weave other disciplines into economics
depends primarily upon the range of questions being answered and the
confidence placed by the economist in assumptions dealing with such
things as static equilibrium.

Assumptions made by economists dealing with the behavior of consumers and entrepreneurs leans heavily upon psychology; assumptions
concerning their lifestyle, number of persons in the family, education,
and ethnic background are rooted in sociology. Surveys of consumer
and managerial behavior often rely upon theories of statistical induction,
stochastic learning, and concept formation. The manager of scarce and
costly resources, namely, the managerial economist, should consider
these variables; otherwise, he or she may be overlooking a significant
and very helpful managerial tool.

1. What Can Economic Theory Contribute to Managerial Economics?*

WILLIAM J. BAUMOL

What to me is one of the most significant aspects of economic theory for management science was brought out very clearly in a talk I had some time ago with a biologist friend of mine. This biologist is an eminent authority on clock mechanisms in animals. There is a remarkable and well-known periodicity in the behavior of a large variety of animal species—in fact, probably among all of them. To illustrate the point, the emergence of adult fruit flies from their pupae usually occurs shortly after dawn. Even if the flies are placed in a darkened room whose temperature, humidity, and other evidences of passage of time are carefully controlled, they will continue to emerge from the pupae at just about the same time day after day. However, if after being kept under these controlled laboratory conditions they are suddenly shown some light in order to produce the effect of a false dawn, there is a permanent shift of phase and, after some transient behavior, they will change the time at which they emerge from the pupae to that corresponding to the dawn which they were last shown. This suggests that there is a very definite way in which these animals can tell the time; that is to say, in which they can recognize when twenty-four hours are over, even though there is nothing conscious about it.

Of course a clock mechanism suggests periodicity, and periodicity, to any good cycle theorist, suggests difference or differential equations. And in fact, after this biologist had been working on the subject for some time, he became aware of this possibility and set out to find a mathematician who could help him to determine an appropriate equation. This was done, a relationship was fitted by statistical methods, and it turned out that it was appropriate to use a nonlinear differential equation. It was found that one such equation could fit a great variety of the data which this man had available. Not only could it do that,

* *American Economic Review*, vol. 51, no. 2 (May 1961), pp. 142-46.

but with the aid of the equation he was able to make a number of interesting predictions which were subsequently very closely confirmed by data which he was able to collect.

Here is where we come to the point of the story—the contrast between the situation of the biologist and that of the economic theorist—for the biologist who had obtained a very nice relationship on the basis of empirical data was totally unable to give any sort of analytical explanation of what he had. He had absolutely no model on which he could base a derivation of his mathematical relationship. We may, perhaps, generalize by remarking that biologists, with some notable exceptions, have data without models, whereas we in economic theory have models which usually are created without data. And in this way we have summarized one of the economic theorist's greatest weaknesses and one of his greatest strengths.

I would now like to emphasize the latter, the more pleasant, side: the fact that the economist is an expert model builder. Indeed, there are very few disciplines which produce model builders with such practice and such skill. This, I think, is one of the most important things which the economic theorist can contribute to the work of management science. In management science it is important—in fact, absolutely essential—to be able to recognize the structure of a managerial problem. In order to be able to analyze it at all and to be able to do so systematically, it is necessary to do several things: first of all, to undertake a judicious simplification—an elimination of minor details which are peripheral to the problem and which, if included in the model, would prevent any successful and systematic analysis. Second, it is important to capture in a formal statement the essence of all the interrelationships which characterize the situation, because it is only after stating these interrelationships so explicitly that we can hope to use the powerful techniques of rigorous analysis in the investigation of a managerial problem. It is the model which incorporates both these features; it is the central focus of the entire analysis which must capture the essence of the situation which is being investigated.

Thus, in any of the complex situations which are encountered in the systematic analysis of management problems, model building is a critical part of the investigation. Problems as diverse as the optimal size and composition of a department store product line or the location of a company's warehouses have one thing in common: their complexity—which arises to a large extent out of the network of interrelationships among their elements. An increase in the number of items carried in a store reduces the capacity for carrying stocks of other items: on the one hand it makes it more likely that the customer will find what she wants when she enters the store; on the other she may find more often that although the store usually carries what she desires, it happens to be out of it temporarily. The length of time a customer must search for an item is affected by a change in product line; the likelihood of "impulse" purchases is also affected, etc. The drawing together of such a diversity of strands is the major function of the model, without which most of our tools will not function. Moreover, in my experience it is not atypical that nearly half of the time spent in the investigation of such a problem is devoted to model building—to capturing the essence of the situation in a set of explicit relationships. For there are no cut and dried rules in model building. It is essentially a matter of discovery, involving all of the intangibles of discovery—hunch, insight, and intuition, and no holds are barred. Only after the model has been built can the problem sometimes be reduced to a routine by use of standard rules of calculation.

To my knowledge there are few classroom courses in this critical skill of model building, and, because it has no rules, it cannot be taught like trigonometry or chemistry. But apparently it can be learned by experience. And, as I have said, the economic theorist has had a great deal of experience in the construction and use of such models. When he employs some differential equations, you can almost be certain that he has derived them from a model which he built, not, like the biologist, from some data which he has collected.

This, then, is one of the major contributions which the economic theorist can, in my opinion, make to managerial analysis. It is, however, a skill and a predisposition that he brings with him, not a series of specific results.

This takes me to the second major point that I wish to make: the other way in which I think economic theory can be helpful to management science. I believe the most important thing a managerial economics student can get out of a course in economic analysis is not a series of theorems but rather a set of analytical methods. And for that reason I think it is far more important for him to learn the basis of these theorems, their assumption and their methods of derivation, than to end up with a group of conclusions. I can say quite categorically that I have never encountered a business problem in which my investigation was helped by any specific economic theorem, nor, may I add, have I ever met a practical problem in which I failed to be helped by the method of reasoning involved in the derivation of some economic theorem.

One of the major reasons that the propositions of economic theory are not directly applicable to management problems is that the theory does not deal with the major concerns of the businessman. Product line, advertising, budgeting, sales force allocation, inventory levels, new product introduction are all relative strangers to the idealized firm of value theory whose major concern is price-output policy. Certainly there is little in the theoretical literature which refers directly to the warehouse location or the department store product line problems which were mentioned previously.

Even where more familiar theoretical matters, such as pricing problems, arise in practice, the results of the theory provide only limited help. This is because theorems in economic analysis deal with rather general abstract entities, with firms which have the peculiar and most interesting characteristics of actual companies eliminated from them in order to enable the analyst to draw conclusions which apply to the entire economy and not just to one or several particular firms. As a result, when attempting to apply these theorems, one finds that they have abstracted some of the features it is most essential to retain in order to analyze the specific situation with which one is faced in the market. The theory offers us fairly general admonitions, like the one which tells us that marginal cost must equal marginal revenue if we are to maximize profits—surely a statement which is not very much of a guide in application. I repeat that in my applied work I have never found any occasion to use either this theorem or any other such specific proposition of economic analysis.

But I have often found it absolutely essential to use the techniques of marginal analysis as it occurs in the theory of the firm, the theory of production, and in welfare economics. Several times I have even found it helpful to use the techniques and derivations of some of the elasticity theorems. This last illustration perhaps merits a little expansion. It may appear extraordinary that the elasticity theorems were of any use in application at all for they would seem to provide the ultimate illustration of tools whose use requires the availability of extensive data. However, the point I am making is that it was not the theorems but the methods of analysis and derivation which were employed. For example, an analogue of the elementary proposition that unit elasticity is the borderline between increasing and decreasing total revenue in response to a decrease in price can be applied in other situations. In fact, it is precisely because of the lack of data that it often becomes necessary to decide just where such break-even points occur, and in a number of cases I have found that the ability to prove that this critical point is sufficiently beyond what may reasonably be expected is an adequate substitute for the availability of data. Thus knowledge of the method of derivation of the theorems—and, indeed, of the spirit of the theorems themselves—often enables one to do things without data which otherwise would be pretty much out of the question.

But this is not the major point. If it is true—and it certainly has been true in my experience—that every firm and every managerial situation requires a model which is more or less unique, none of the standard theorems is going to fit in with it. It will be necessary, in effect, to derive special theorems which enable one to deal with that specific situation. Here one is helped, then, not by the generalized propositions which have been developed by the theorist, but by the methods which have enabled him to achieve his results which show us how analogous conclusions or analogous analyses can be conducted for the problems at hand. It is for this reason that I make my plea about the teaching of economics and economic theory to the managerial economist. This plea is not only that economic theory should be taught to the business student but that it should be presented to him pretty much as it is taught to the liberal arts student, with the emphasis not on a series of canned conclusions but on the methods of investigation on the derivations behind the results—on the analytic tools and methods.

There is a third way in which economic theory can help in managerial analysis—and, perhaps strangely, here the more elementary concepts of economics are primarily involved or, rather, concepts which though relatively sophisticated are used in a very elementary way. These elementary concepts can imbue the economist with habits of thought which enable him to avoid some significant pitfalls. For example, consider the case of external economies and diseconomies. How much can familiarity with this concept tell us about the dangers involved in directing one branch of an enterprise to maximize its profits in disregard of the effects of its actions on other parts of the firm! Similarly, we economists are made very sensitive by marginal analysis to the perils of resource allocation by average cost and profit—resource allocation rules of thumb which are so frequently encountered in business practice. Such bits of reasoning once led one of my colleagues, who was reviewing some of the cases cited in the literature of managerial analysis, to remark that he was amazed at how often this reading had forced him to recall his sophomore economics!

To summarize, then, I have suggested very little by way of concrete contribution from economic theory to managerial economics. With some exceptions, I have not said that this particular result or that particular body of discussion is essential or even particularly helpful for the managerial economist. I have been able to offer no illustrations of managerial problems in which I was able to use very specific pieces of the body of economic analysis. But this is right in line with the very nature of my major point: the assertion that a managerial economist can become a far more helpful member of a management group by virtue of his studies of economic analysis, primarily because there he learns to become an effective model builder and because there he acquires a very rich body of tools and techniques which can help him to deal with the problems of the firm in a far more rigorous, a far more probing, and a far deeper manner.

2. Theories of Decision Making in Economics and Behavioral Science*

HERBERT A. SIMON

Recent years have seen important new explorations along the boundaries between economics and psychology. For the economist, the immediate question about these developments is whether they include new advances in psychology that can fruitfully be applied to economics. But the psychologist will also raise the converse question—whether there are developments in economic theory and observation that have implications for the central core of psychology. If economics is able to find verifiable and verified generalizations about human economic behavior, then these generalizations must have a place in the more general theories of human behavior to which psychology and sociology aspire. Influence will run both ways.

I. HOW MUCH PSYCHOLOGY DOES ECONOMICS NEED?

How have psychology and economics gotten along with little relation in the past? The explanation rests on an understanding of the goals toward which economics, viewed as a science and a discipline, has usually aimed.

Broadly speaking, economics can be defined as the science that describes and predicts the behavior of several kinds of economic man—notably the consumer and the entrepreneur. While perhaps literally correct, this definition does not reflect the principal focus in the literature of economics. We usually classify work in economics along two dimensions: (a) whether it is concerned with industries and the whole economy (macroeconomics) or with individual economic actors (microeconomics); and (b) whether it strives to describe and explain economic behavior (descriptive economics), or to guide decisions either at the level of public policy (normative macroeconomics) or at the level of the individual consumer or businessman (normative microeconomics).

The profession and literature of economics have been largely preoc-

* *American Economic Review*, vol. 49, no. 3 (June 1959), pp. 253–80.

cupied with normative macroeconomics. Although descriptive macroeconomics provides the scientific base for policy prescription, research emphases have been determined in large part by relevance to policy (e.g., business cycle theory). Normative microeconomics, carried forward under such labels as "management science," "engineering economics," and "operations research," is now a flourishing area of work having an uneasy and ill-defined relation with the profession of economics, traditionally defined. Much of the work is being done by mathematicians, statisticians, engineers, and physical scientists (although many mathematical economists have also been active in it).

This new area, like the old, is normative in orientation. Economists have been relatively uninterested in descriptive microeconomics—understanding the behavior of individual economic agents—except as this is necessary to provide a foundation for macroeconomics. The normative microeconomist "obviously" doesn't need a theory of human behavior: he wants to know how people *ought* to behave, not how they *do* behave. On the other hand, the macroeconomist's lack of concern with individual behavior stems from different considerations. First, he assumes that the economic actor is rational, and hence he makes strong predictions about human behavior without performing the hard work of observing people. Second, he often assumes competition, which carries with it the implication that only the rational survive. Thus, the classical economic theory of markets with perfect competition and rational agents is deductive theory that requires almost no contact with empirical data once its assumptions are accepted.

Undoubtedly there is an area of human behavior that fits these assumptions to a reasonable approximation, where the classical theory with its assumptions of rationality is a powerful and useful tool. Without denying the existence of this area, or its importance, I may observe that it fails to include some of the central problems of conflict and dynamics with which economics has become more and more concerned. A metaphor will help to show the reason for this failure.

Suppose we were pouring some viscous liquid—molasses—into a bowl of very irregular shape. What would we need in order to make a theory of the form the molasses would take in the bowl? How much would we have to know about the properties of molasses to predict its behavior under the circumstances? If the bowl were held motionless, and if we wanted only to predict behavior in equilibrium, we would have to know little, indeed, about molasses. The single essential assumption would be that the molasses, under the force of gravity, would minimize the height of its center of gravity. With this assumption, which would apply as well to any other liquid, and a complete knowledge of the environment—in this case the shape of the bowl—the equilibrium is completely determined. Just so, the equilibrium behavior of a perfectly adapting organism depends only on its goal and its environment; it is otherwise completely independent of the internal properties of the organism.

If the bowl into which we were pouring the molasses were jiggled rapidly, or if we wanted to know about the behavior before equilibrium was reached, prediction would require much more information. It would require, in particular, more information about the properties of molasses: its viscosity, the rapidity with which it "adapted" itself to the containing vessel and moved towards its "goal" of lowering its center of gravity. Likewise, to predict the short-run behavior of an adaptive organism, or its behavior in a complex and rapidly changing environment, it is not enough to know its goals. We must know also a great deal about its internal structure and particularly its mechanisms of adaptation.

If, to carry the metaphor a step farther, new forces, in addition to gravitational force, were brought to bear on the liquid, we would have to know still more about it even to predict behavior in equilibrium. Now its tendency to lower its center of gravity might be countered by a force to minimize an electrical or magnetic potential operating in some lateral direction. We would have to know its relative susceptibility to gravitational and electrical or magnetic force to determine its equilibrium position. Similarly, in an organism having a multiplicity of goals, or afflicted with some kind of internal goal conflict, behavior could be predicted only from information about the relative strengths of the several goals and the ways in which the adaptive processes responded to them.

Economics has been moving steadily into new areas where the power of the classical equilibrium model has never been demonstrated, and where its adequacy must be considered anew. Labor economics is such an area, oligopoly or imperfect competition theory another, decision making under uncertainty a third, and the theory of economic development a fourth. In all of these areas the complexity and instability of his environment becomes a central feature of the choices that economic man faces. To explain his behavior in the face of this complexity, the theory must describe him as something more than a featureless, adaptive organism; it must incorporate at least some description of the processes and mechanisms through which the adaptation takes place. Let us list a little more concretely some specific problems of this kind:

(a) The classical theory postulates that the consumer maximizes utility. Recent advances in the theory of rational consumer choice have shown that the existence of a utility function, and its characteristics, if it exists, can be studied empirically.

(b) The growing separation between ownership and management has directed attention to the motivations of managers and the adequacy of the profit-maximization assumption for business firms. So-called human relations research has raised a variety of issues about the motivation of both executives and employees.

(c) When, in extending the classical theory, the assumptions of perfect competition were removed, even the definition of rationality became ambiguous. New definitions had to be constructed, by no means as "obvious" intuitively as simple maximization, to extend the theory of rational behavior to bilateral monopoly and to other bargaining and out-guessing situations.

(d) When the assumptions of perfect foresight were removed, to handle uncertainty about the environment, the definition of rationality had to be extended in another direction to take into account prediction and the formation of expectations.

(e) Broadening the definition of rationality to encompass goal conflict and uncertainty made it hard to ignore the distinction between the objective environment in which the economic actor "really" lives and the subjective environment that he perceives and to which he responds. When this distinction is made, we can no longer predict his behavior—even if he behaves rationally—from the characteristics of the objective environment; we also need to know something about his perceptual and cognitive processes.

We shall use these five problem areas as a basis for sorting out some recent explorations in theory, model building, and empirical testing. In section II, we will examine developments in the theory of utility and consumer choice. In section III, we will consider somewhat parallel issues relating to the motivation of managers. In section IV, we will deal with conflict of goals and the phenomena of bargaining. In section V, we will survey some of the work that has been done on uncertainty and the formation of expectations. In section VI, we will explore recent developments in the theory of human problem solving and other higher mental processes, and see what implications these have for economic decision making.

II. THE UTILITY FUNCTION

The story of the reestablishment of cardinal utility, as a consequence of the introduction of uncertainty into the theory of choice, is well known. When Pareto and Slutsky had shown that the theory of consumer demand could be derived from the properties of indifference curves, without postulating a cardinal utility function underlying these curves, it became fashionable to regard utility as an ordinal measure—a ranking of alternatives by preference. Indeed, it could be shown that only ordinal utility had operational status—that the experiments that had been proposed, and even tried in a couple of instances, to measure an individual's utilities by asking him to choose among alternatives could never distinguish between two cardinal utility functions that were ordinally equivalent—that differed only by stretchings and contractions of the unit of measurement.

It was shown by von Neumann and Morgenstern, as a by-product of their development of the theory of games, that if the choice situation were extended to include choices among uncertain prospects—among lottery tickets, say—cardinal utilities could be assigned to the outcomes in an unequivocal way. Under these conditions, if the subject's behavior was consistent, it was possible to measure cardinally the utilities that different outcomes had for him.

A person who behaved in a manner consistent with the axioms of choice of von Neumann and Morgenstern would act so as to maximize the expected value—the average, weighted by the probabilities of the alternative outcomes of a choice—of his utility. The theory could be tested empirically, however, only on the assumption that the probabilities assigned to the alternatives by the subject were identical with the "objective" probabilities of these events as known to the experimenter. For example, if a subject believed in the gamblers' fallacy, that after a run of heads an unbiased coin would be more likely to fall tails, his choices might appear inconsistent with his utility function, while the real difficulty would lie in his method of assigning probabilities. This difficulty of "subjective" versus "objective" probability soon came to light when attempts were made to test experimentally whether people behaved in accordance with the predictions of the new utility theory. At the same time, it was discovered that the problem had been raised and solved thirty years earlier by the English philosopher and mathematician Frank Ramsey. Ramsey had shown that, by an appropriate series of experiments, the utilities and subjective probabilities assigned by a subject to a set of uncertain alternatives could be measured simultaneously.

Empirical Studies

The new axiomatic foundations of the theory of utility, which show that it is possible, at least in principle, to determine empirically whether people "have" utility functions of the appropriate kind, have led to a rash of choice experiments. An experimenter who wants to measure utilities, not merely in principle but in fact, faces innumerable difficulties. Because of these difficulties, most experiments have been limited to confronting the subjects with alternative lottery tickets, at various odds, for small amounts of money. The weight of evidence is that, under these conditions, most persons choose in a way that is reasonably consistent with the axioms of the theory—they behave as though they were maximizing the expected value of utility and as though the utilities of the several alternatives can be measured.

When these experiments are extended to more "realistic" choices—choices that are more obviously relevant to real-life situations—difficulties multiply. In the few extensions that have been made, it is not at all clear that the subjects behave in accordance with the utility axioms. There is some indication that when the situation is very simple and transparent, so that the subject can easily see and remember when he is being consistent, he behaves like a utility maximizer. But as the choices become a little more complicated—choices, for example, among phonograph records instead of sums of money—he becomes much less consistent.

We can interpret these results in either of two ways. We can say that consumers "want" to maximize utility, and that if we present them with clear and simple choices that they understand they will do so. Or we can say that the real world is so complicated that the theory of utility maximization has little relevance to real choices. The former interpretation has generally appeared more attractive to economists trained in classical utility theory and to management scientists seeking rules of behavior for normative microeconomics; the latter to behavioral scientists interested in the description of behavior.

Normative Applications

The new utility theory has provided the formal framework for much recent work in mathematical statistics—i.e., statistical decision theory. Similarly (it would be accurate to say "synonymously"), this framework provides the basis for most of the normative models of management science and operations research designed for actual application to the decision-making problems of the firm.[1] Except for some very recent developments, linear programming has been limited to decision making under certainty, but there have been far-reaching developments of dynamic programming dealing with the maximization of expected values of outcomes (usually monetary outcomes) in situations where future events can be predicted only in terms of probability distributions.

Again, there are at least two distinct interpretations that can be placed on these developments. On the one hand, it can be argued: "Firms would like to maximize profits if they could. They have been limited in doing so by the conceptual and computational difficulties of finding the optimal courses of action. By providing powerful new mathematical tools and computing machines, we now enable them to behave in the manner predicted by Alfred Marshall, even if they haven't been able to in the

---

[1] This work relates, of course, to profit maximization and cost minimization rather than utility maximization, but it is convenient to mention it at this point.

past." Nature will imitate art and economic man will become as real (and as artificial) as radios and atomic piles.

The alternative interpretation rests on the observation that, even with the powerful new tools and machines, most real-life choices still lie beyond the reach of maximizing techniques—unless the situations are heroically simplified by drastic approximations. If man, according to this interpretation, makes decisions and choices that have some appearance of rationality, rationality in real life must involve something simpler than maximization of utility or profit. In section VI, we will see where this alternative interpretation leads.

The Binary Choice Experiment

Much recent discussion about utility has centered around a particularly simple choice experiment. This experiment, in numerous variants, has been used by both economists and psychologists to test the most diverse kinds of hypotheses. We will describe it so that we can use it as a common standard of comparison for a whole range of theories and empirical studies.

We will call the situation we are about to describe the *binary choice* experiment. It is better known to most game theorists—particularly those located not far from Nevada—as a two-armed bandit; and to most psychologists as a partial reinforcement experiment. The subject is required, in each of a series of trials, to choose one or the other of two symbols—say, plus or minus. When he has chosen, he is told whether his choice was "right" or "wrong," and he may also receive a reward (in psychologist's language, a reinforcement) for "right" choices. The experimenter can arrange the schedule of correct responses in a variety of ways. There may be a definite pattern, or they may be randomized. It is not essential that one and only one response be correct on a given trial: the experimenter may determine that both or neither will be correct. In the latter case the subject may or may not be informed whether the response he did not choose would have been correct.

How would a utility-maximizing subject behave in the binary choice experiment? Suppose that the experimenter rewarded "plus" on one third of the trials, determined at random, and "minus" on the remaining two thirds. Then a subject, provided that he believed the sequence was random and observed that minus was rewarded twice as often as plus, should always, rationally, choose minus. He would find the correct answer two thirds of the time, and more often than with any other strategy.

Unfortunately for the classical theory of utility in its simplest form, few subjects behave in this way. The most commonly observed behavior is what is called *event matching*. The subject chooses the two alternatives (not necessarily at random) with relative frequencies roughly proportional to the relative frequencies with which they are rewarded. Thus, in the example given, two thirds of the time he would choose minus, and as a result would make a correct response, on the average, in five trials out of nine (on two thirds of the trials in which he chooses minus, and one third of those in which he chooses plus).[2]

All sorts of explanations have been offered for the event-matching behavior. The simplest is that the subject just doesn't understand what strategy would maximize his expected utility; but with adult subjects in a situation as transparent as this one, this explanation seems far-fetched. The alternative explanations imply either that the subject regards himself as being engaged in a competitive game with the experimenter (or with "nature" if he accepts the experimenter's explanation that the stimulus is random), or that his responses are the outcome of certain kinds of learning processes. We will examine these two types of explanation further in sections IV and V respectively. The important conclusion at this point is that even in an extremely simple situation, subjects do not behave in the way predicted by a straightforward application of utility theory.

Probabilistic Preferences

Before we leave the subject of utility, we should mention one recent important development. In the formalizations mentioned up to this point, probabilities enter only into the estimation of the consequences that will follow one alternative or another. Given any two alternatives, the first is definitely preferable to the second (in terms of expected utility), or the second to the first, or they are strictly indifferent. If the same pair of alternatives is presented to the subject more than once, he should always prefer the same member of the pair.

One might think this requirement too strict—that, particularly if the utility attached to one alternative were only slightly greater or less than that attached to the other, the subject might vacillate in his choice. An empirical precedent for such vacillation comes not only from casual observation of indecision but from analogous phenomena in the psycho-physical laboratory. When subjects are asked to decide which of two weights is heavier, the objectively heavier one is chosen more often than the lighter one, but the relative frequency of choosing the heaviest approaches one half as the two weights approach equality. The probability that a subject will choose the objectively heavier weight depends, in general, on the ratio of the two weights.

Following several earlier attempts, a rigorous and complete axiom

---

[2] Subjects tend to choose the more highly rewarded alternative slightly more frequently than is called for by event matching. Hence, the actual behavior tends to be some kind of average between event matching and the optimal behavior.

system for a utility theory incorporating probabilistic preferences has been constructed recently by Duncan Luce. Although the theory weakens the requirements of consistency in preference, it is empirically testable, at least in principle. Conceptually, it provides a more plausible interpretation of the notion of "indifference" than does the classical theory.

III. THE GOALS OF FIRMS

Just as the central assumption in the theory of consumption is that the consumer strives to maximize his utility, so the crucial assumption in the theory of the firm is that the entrepreneur strives to maximize his residual share—his profit. Attacks on this hypothesis have been frequent. We may classify the most important of these as follows:

(a) The theory leaves ambiguous whether it is short-run or long-run profit that is to be maximized.

(b) The entrepreneur may obtain all kinds of "psychic income" from the firm, quite apart from monetary rewards. If he is to maximize his utility, then he will sometimes balance a loss of profits against an increase in psychic income. But if we allow "psychic income," the criterion of profit maximization loses all of its definiteness.

(c) The entrepreneur may not care to maximize, but may simply want to earn a return that he regards as satisfactory. By sophistry and adept use of the concept of psychic income, the notion of seeking a satisfactory return can be translated into utility maximizing, but not in any operational way. We shall see in a moment that "satisfactory profits" is a concept more meaningfully related to the psychological notion of aspiration levels than to maximization.

(d) It is often observed that under modern conditions the equity owners and the active managers of an enterprise are separate and distinct groups of people, so that the latter may not be motivated to maximize profits.

(e) Where there is imperfect competition among firms, maximizing is an ambiguous goal, for what action is optimal for one firm depends on the actions of the other firms.

In the present section we shall deal only with the third of these five issues. The fifth will be treated in the following section; the first, second, and fourth are purely empirical questions that have been discussed at length in the literature; they will be considered here only for their bearing on the question of satisfactory profits.

Satisficing versus Maximizing

The notion of satiation plays no role in classical economic theory, while it enters rather prominently into the treatment of motivation in psychology. In most psychological theories the motive to act stems from *drives,* and action terminates when the drive is satisfied. Moreover, the conditions for satisfying a drive are not necessarily fixed, but may be specified by an aspiration level that itself adjusts upward or downward on the basis of experience.

If we seek to explain business behavior in the terms of this theory, we must expect the firm's goals to be not maximizing profit, but attaining a certain level or rate of profit, holding a certain share of the market or a certain level of sales. Firms would try to "satisfice" rather than to maximize.

It has sometimes been argued that the distinction between satisficing and maximizing is not important to economic theory. For in the first place, the psychological evidence on individual behavior shows that aspirations tend to adjust to the attainable. Hence in the long run, the argument runs, the level of aspiration and the attainable maximum will be very close together. Second, even if some firms satisficed, they would gradually lose out to the maximizing firms, which would make larger profits and grow more rapidly than the others.

These are, of course, precisely the arguments of our molasses metaphor, and we may answer them in the same way that we answered them earlier. The economic environment of the firm is complex, and it changes rapidly; there is no a priori reason to assume the attainment of long-run equilibrium. Indeed, the empirical evidence on the distribution of firms by size suggests that the observed regularities in size distribution stem from the statistical equilibrium of a population of adaptive systems rather than the static equilibrium of a population of maximizers.

Models of satisficing behavior are richer than models of maximizing behavior, because they treat not only of equilibrium but of the method of reaching it as well. Psychological studies of the formation and change of aspiration levels support propositions of the following kinds: (a) When performance falls short of the level of aspiration, search behavior (particularly search for new alternatives of action) is induced. (b) At the same time, the level of aspiration begins to adjust itself downward until goals reach levels that are practically attainable. (c) If the two mechanisms just listed operate too slowly to adapt aspirations to performance, emotional behavior—apathy or aggression, for example—will replace rational adaptive behavior.

The aspiration level defines a natural zero point in the scale of utility—whereas in most classical theories the zero point is arbitrary. When the firm has alternatives open to it that are at or above its aspiration level, the theory predicts that it will choose the best of those known to be available. When none of the available alternatives satisfies current aspirations, the theory predicts qualitatively different behavior: in the short run, search behavior and the revision of targets; in the longer run, what we have called above emotional behavior, and what the psychologist would be inclined to call neurosis.[3]

Studies of Business Behavior

There is some empirical evidence that business goals are, in fact, stated in satisficing terms. First, there is the series of studies stemming from the pioneering work of Hall and Hitch that indicates that businessmen often set prices by applying a standard markup to costs. Some economists have sought to refute this fact, others to reconcile it—if it is a fact—with marginalist principles. The study of Earley belongs to the former category, but its evidence is suspect because the questions asked of businessmen are leading ones—no one likes to admit that he would accept less profit if he could have more. Earley did not ask his respondents how they determined marginal cost and marginal revenue, how, for example, they estimated demand elasticities.

Another series of studies derived from the debate over the Keynesian doctrine that the amount of investment was insensitive to changes in the rate of interest. The general finding in these studies has been that the rate of interest is not an important factor in investment decisions.

More recently, my colleagues Cyert and March have attempted to test the satisficing model in a more direct way. They found in one industry some evidence that firms with a declining share of market strove more vigorously to increase their sales than firms whose shares of the market were steady or increasing.

Aspirations in the Binary Choice Experiment

Although to my knowledge this has not been done, it would be easy to look for aspiration-level phenomena in the binary choice experiment. By changing the probabilities of reward in different ways for different groups of subjects, we could measure the effects of these changes on search behavior—where amount of search would be measured by changes in the pattern of responses.

Economic Implications

It has sometimes been argued that, however realistic the classical theory of the firm as a profit maximizer, it is an adequate theory for

---

[3] Lest this last term appear fanciful, I should like to call attention to the phenomena of panic and broken morale, which are well known to observers of the stock market and of organizations but which have no reasonable interpretation in classical utility theory. I may also mention that psychologists use the theory described here in a straightforward way to produce experimental neurosis in animal and human subjects.

purposes of normative macroeconomics. Mason, for example, in commenting on Papandreou's essay on "Problems in the Theory of the Firm" says, "The writer of this critique must confess a lack of confidence in the marked superiority, *for purposes of economic analysis*, of this newer concept of the firm over the older conception of the entrepreneur." The italics are Mason's.

The theory of the firm is important for welfare economics—e.g., for determining under what circumstances the behavior of the firm will lead to efficient allocation of resources. The satisficing model vitiates all the conclusions about resource allocation that are derivable from the maximizing model when perfect competition is assumed. Similarly, a dynamic theory of firm sizes, like that mentioned above, has quite different implications for public policies dealing with concentration than a theory that assumes firms to be in static equilibrium. Hence, welfare economists are justified in adhering to the classical theory only if: (a) the theory is empirically correct as a description of the decision-making process; or (b) it is safe to assume that the system operates in the neighborhood of the static equilibrium. What evidence we have mostly contradicts both assumptions.

IV. CONFLICT OF INTEREST

Leaving aside the problem of the motivations of hired managers, conflict of interest among economic actors creates no difficulty for classical economic theory—indeed, it lies at the very core of the theory—so long as each actor treats the other actors as parts of his "given" environment, and doesn't try to predict their behavior and anticipate it. But when this restriction is removed, when it is assumed that a seller takes into account the reactions of buyers to his actions, or that each manufacturer predicts the behaviors of his competitors—all the familiar difficulties of imperfect competition and oligopoly arise.[4]

The very assumptions of omniscient rationality that provide the basis for deductive prediction in economics when competition is present lead to ambiguity when they are applied to competition among the few. The central difficulty is that rationality requires one to outguess one's opponents, but not to be outguessed by them, and this is clearly not a consistent requirement if applied to all the actors.

Game Theory

Modern game theory is a vigorous and extensive exploration of ways of extending the concept of rational behavior to situations involving

---

[4] There is by now a voluminous literature on the problem.

struggle, outguessing, and bargaining. Since Luce and Raiffa have recently provided us with an excellent survey and evaluation of game theory, I shall not cover the same ground here. I concur in their general evaluation that, while game theory has greatly clarified the issues involved, it has not provided satisfactory solutions. Not only does it leave the definition of rational conduct ambiguous in all cases save the zero-sum two-person game, but it requires of economic man even more fantastic reasoning powers than does classical economic theory.

Power and Bargaining

A number of exploratory proposals have been put forth as alternatives to game theory—among them Galbraith's notion of countervailing power and Schelling's bargaining theory. These analyses draw at least as heavily upon theories of power and bargaining developed initially to explain political phenomena as upon economic theory. They do not lead to any more specific predictions of behavior than do game-theoretic approaches, but place a greater emphasis upon description and actual observation, and are modest in their attempt to derive predictions by deductive reasoning from a few "plausible" premises about human behavior.

At least four important areas of social science and social policy, two of them in economics and two more closely related to political science, have as their central concern the phenomena of power and the processes of bargaining: the theory of political parties, labor-management relations, international politics, and oligopoly theory. Any progress in the basic theory applicable to one of these is certain to be of almost equal importance to the others. A growing recognition of their common concern is evidenced by the initiation of a new cross-disciplinary journal, *Journal of Conflict Resolution*.

Games against Nature

While the binary choice experiment is basically a one-person game, it is possible to interpret it as a "game against nature," and hence to try to explain it in game-theoretic terms. According to game theory, the subject, if he believes in a malevolent nature that manipulates the dice against him, should "minimax" his expected utility instead of maximizing it. That is, he should adopt the course of action that will maximize his expected utility under the assumption that nature will do her worst to him.

Minimaxing expected utility would lead the subject to call plus or minus at random and with equal probability, regardless of what the history of rewards has been. This is something that subjects demonstrably do not do.

However, it has been suggested by Savage and others that people are not as interested in maximizing utility as they are in minimizing regret. "Regret" means the difference between the reward actually obtained and the reward that could have been obtained with perfect foresight (actually, with perfect hindsight!). It turns out that minimaxing regret in the binary choice experiment leads to event-matching behavior. Hence, the empirical evidence is at least crudely consistent with the hypothesis that people play against nature by minimaxing regret. We shall see, however, that event matching is also consistent with a number of other rules of behavior that seem more plausible on their face; hence we need not take the present explanation too seriously—at least I am not inclined to do so.

V. THE FORMATION OF EXPECTATIONS

While the future cannot enter into the determination of the present, expectations about the future can and do. In trying to gain an understanding of the saving, spending, and investment behavior of both consumers and firms, and to make short-term predictions of this behavior for purposes of policy making, economists have done substantial empirical work as well as theorizing on the formation of expectations.

Empirical Studies

A considerable body of data has been accumulated on consumers' plans and expectations from the Survey of Consumer Finances, conducted for the Board of Governors of the Federal Reserve System by the Survey Research Center of the University of Michigan. These data, and similar data obtained by others, begin to give us some information on the expectations of consumers about their own incomes, and the predictive value of their expenditure plans for their actual subsequent behavior. Some large-scale attempts have been made, notably by Modigliani and Brumberg and, a little later, by Friedman to relate these empirical findings to classical utility theory. The current empirical research on businessmen's expectations is of two main kinds:

1. Surveys of businessmen's own forecasts of business and business conditions in the economy and in their own industries. These are obtained by straightforward questionnaire methods that assume, implicitly, that businessmen can and do make such forecasts. In some uses to which the data are put, it is also assumed that the forecasts are used as one basis for businessmen's actions.

2. Studies of business decisions and the role of expectations in these decisions—particularly investment and pricing decisions. We have already referred to studies of business decisions in our discussion of the goals of the firm.

Expectations and Probability

The classical way to incorporate expectations into economic theory is to assume that the decision maker estimates the joint probability distribution of future events. He can then act so as to maximize the expected value of utility or profit, as the case may be. However satisfying this approach may be conceptually, it poses awkward problems when we ask how the decision maker actually estimates the parameters of the joint probability distribution. Common sense tells us that people don't make such estimates, nor can we find evidence that they do by examining actual business forecasting methods. The surveys of businessmen's expectations have never attempted to secure such estimates, but have contended themselves with asking for point predictions—which, at best, might be interpreted as predictions of the means of the distributions.

It has been shown that under certain special circumstances the mean of the probability distribution is the only parameter that is relevant for decision—that even if the variance and higher moments were known to the rational decision maker, he would have no use for them. In these cases, the arithmetic mean is actually a certainty equivalent, the optimal decision turns out to be the same as if the future were known with certainty. But the situations where the mean is a certainty equivalent are, as we have said, very special ones, and there is no indication that businessmen ever ask whether the necessary conditions for this equivalence are actually met in practice. They somehow make forecasts in the form of point predictions and act upon them in one way or another.

The "somehow" poses questions that are important for business cycle theory, and perhaps for other problems in economics. The way in which expectations are formed may affect the dynamic stability of the economy, and the extent to which cycles will be amplified or damped. Some light, both empirical and theoretical, has recently been cast on these questions. On the empirical side, attempts have been made: (a) to compare businessmen's forecasts with various "naïve" models that assume the future will be some simple function of the recent past, and (b) to use such naïve models themselves as forecasting devices.

The simplest naïve model is one that assumes the next period will be exactly like the present. Another assumes that the change from present to next period will equal the change from last period to present; a third, somewhat more general, assumes that the next period will be a weighted average of recent past periods. The term "naïve model" has been applied loosely to various forecasting formulae of these general kinds. There is some affirmative evidence that business forecasts fit such models. There is also evidence that elaboration of the models beyond the first few steps of refinement does not much improve prediction. Arrow and his colleagues have explored some of the conditions under which forecasting formulae will, and will not, introduce dynamic instability into an economic system that is otherwise stable. They have shown, for example, that if a system of multiple markets is stable under static expectations, it is stable when expectations are based on a moving average of past values.

The work on the formation of expectations represents a significant extension of classical theory. For, instead of taking the environment as a "given," known to the economic decision maker, it incorporates in the theory the processes of acquiring knowledge about that environment. In doing so, it forces us to include in our model of economic man some of his properties as a learning, estimating, searching, information-processing organism.

The Cost of Information

There is one way in which the formation of expectations might be reincorporated in the body of economic theory: by treating information gathering as one of the processes of production, so to speak, and applying to it the usual rules of marginal analysis. Information, says price theory, should be gathered up to the point where the incremental cost of additional information is equal to the incremental profit that can be earned by having it. Such an approach can lead to propositions about optimal amounts of information-gathering activity and about the relative merits of alternative information-gathering and estimating schemes.

This line of investigation has, in fact, been followed in statistical decision theory. In sampling theory we are concerned with the optimal size of sample (and in the special and ingenious case of sequential sampling theory, with knowing when to stop sampling), and we wish to evaluate the efficiencies of alternative sampling procedures. The latter problem is the simpler, since it is possible to compare the relative costs of alternative schemes that have the same sampling error, and hence to avoid estimating the value of the information. However, some progress has been made also toward estimating the value of improved forecast accuracy in situations where the forecasts are to be used in applying formal decision rules to choice situations.

The theory of teams developed by Marschak and Radner is concerned with the same problem. It considers situations involving decentralized and interdependent decision making by two or more persons who share a common goal and who, at a cost, can transmit information to each other about their own actions or about the parts of the environment with which they are in contact. The problem then is to discover the optimal communication strategy under specified assumptions about communication costs and payoffs.

The cost of communication in the theory of teams, like the cost of observations in sampling theory, is a parameter that characterizes the economic actor, or the relation of the actor to his environment. Hence, while these theories retain, in one sense, a classical picture of economic man as a maximizer, they clearly require considerable information about the characteristics of the actor, and not merely about his environment. They take a long stride toward bridging the gap between the traditional concerns of economics and the concern of psychology.

Expectations in the Binary Choice Experiment

I should like to return again to the binary choice experiment, to see what light it casts on the formation of expectations. If the subject is told by the experimenter that the rewards are assigned at random, if he is told what the odds are for each alternative, *and if he believes the experimenter*, the situation poses no forecasting problem. We have seen, however, that the behavior of most subjects is not consistent with these assumptions.

How would sequential sampling theory handle the problem? Each choice the subject makes now has two consequences: the immediate reward he obtains from it, and the increment of information it provides for predicting the future rewards. If he thinks only of the latter consequences, he is faced with the classical problem of induction: to estimate the probability that an event will occur in the future on the basis of its frequency of occurrence in the past. Almost any rule of induction would require a rational (maximizing) subject to behave in the following general manner: to sample the two alternatives in some proportion to estimate the probability of reward associated with each; after the error of estimate had been reduced below some bound, always to choose the alternative with the higher probability of reward. Unfortunately, this does not appear to be what most subjects do.

If we give up the idea of maximization, we can make the weaker assumption that the subject is adaptive—or learns—but not necessarily in any optimal fashion. What do we mean by adaptation or learning? We mean, gradually and on the basis of experience responding more frequently with the choice that, in the past, has been most frequently rewarded. There is a whole host of rules of behavior possessing this characteristic. Postulate, for example, that at each trial the subject has a certain probability of responding "plus," and the complementary probability of responding "minus." Postulate further that when he makes a particular response the probability of making the same response on the next trial is increased if the response is rewarded and decreased if the response is not rewarded. The amount of increment in the response probability is a parameter characterizing the learning rate of the particular subject. Almost all schemes of this kind produce asymptotic behaviors, as the number of trials increases, that are approximately event matching in character.

Stochastic learning models, as the processes just described are usually called, were introduced into psychology in the early 1950s by W. K. Estes and Bush and Mosteller and have been investigated extensively since that time. The models fit some of the gross features of the observed behaviors—most strikingly the asymptotic probabilities—but do not explain very satisfactorily the fine structure of the observations.

Observation of subjects in the binary choice experiment reveals that usually they not only refuse to believe that (or even to act as if) the reward series were random, but in fact persist over many trials in searching for systematic patterns in the series. To account for such behavior, we might again postulate a learning model, but in this case a model in which the subject does not react probabilistically to his environment, but forms and tests definite hypotheses about systematic patterns in it. Man, in this view, is not only a learning animal; he is a pattern-finding and concept-forming animal. Julian Feldman has constructed theories of this kind to explain the behavior of subjects in the binary choice experiment, and while the tests of the theories are not yet completed, his findings look exceedingly promising.

As we move from maximizing theories, through simple stochastic learning theories, to theories involving pattern recognition, our model of the expectation-forming processes and the organism that performs it increases in complexity. If we follow this route, we reach a point where a theory of behavior requires a rather elaborate and detailed picture of the rational actor's cognitive processes.

VI. HUMAN COGNITION AND ECONOMICS

All the developments we have examined in the preceding four sections have a common theme: they all involve important modifications in the concept of economic man and, for the reasons we have stated, modifications in the direction of providing a fuller description of his characteristics. The classical theory is a theory of a man choosing among fixed and known alternatives, to each of which is attached known consequences. But when perception and cognition intervene between the decision maker and his objective environment, this model no longer proves adequate. We need a description of the choice process that recognizes that alternatives are not given but must be sought; and a description

that takes into account the arduous task of determining what consequences will follow on each alternative.

The decision maker's information about his environment is much less
than an approximation to the real environment. The term "approximation" implies that the subjective world of the decision maker resembles
the external environment closely, but lacks, perhaps, some fineness of
detail. In actual fact the perceived world is fantastically different from
the "real" world. The differences involve both omissions and distortions,
and arise in both perception and inference. The sins of omission in perception are more important than the sins of commission. The decision
maker's model of the world encompasses only a minute fraction of all
the relevant characteristics of the real environment, and his inferences
extract only a minute fraction of all the information that is present
even in his model.

Perception is sometimes referred to as a "filter." This term is as
misleading as "approximation," and for the same reason: it implies that
what comes through into the central nervous system is really quite a
bit like what is "out there." In fact, the filtering is not merely a passive
selection of some part of a presented whole, but an active process involving attention to a very small part of the whole and exclusion, from
the outset, of almost all that is not within the scope of attention.

Every human organism lives in an environment that generates millions
of bits of new information each second, but the bottleneck of the perceptual apparatus certainly do's not admit more than 1,000 bits per
second, and probably much less. Equally significant omissions occur in
the processing that takes place when information reaches the brain. As
every mathematician knows, it is one thing to have a set of differential
equations, and another thing to have their solutions. Yet the solutions
are logically implied by the equations—they are "all there," if we only
knew how to get to them! By the same token, there are hosts of inferences that *might* be drawn from the information stored in the brain
that are not in fact drawn. The consequences implied by information
in the memory become known only through active information processing, and hence through active selection of particular problem-solving
paths from the myriad that might have been followed.

In this section we shall examine some theories of decision making
that take the limitations of the decision maker and the complexity of
the environment as central concerns. These theories incorporate some
mechanisms we have already discussed—for example, aspiration levels
and forecasting processes—but go beyond them in providing a detailed
picture of the choice process.

A real-life decision involves some goals or values, some facts about
the environment, and some inferences drawn from the values and facts.
The goals and values may be simple or complex, consistent or contra-

dictory; the facts may be real or supposed, based on observation or the reports of others; the inferences may be valid or spurious. The whole process may be viewed, metaphorically, as a process of "reasoning," where the values and facts serve as premises, and the decision that is finally reached is inferred from these premises. The resemblance of decision making to logical reasoning is only metaphorical, because there are quite different rules in the two cases to determine what constitute "valid" premises and admissible modes of inference. The metaphor is useful because it leads us to take the individual *decision premise* as the unit of description, hence to deal with the whole interwoven fabric of influences that bear on a single decision—but without being bound by the assumptions of rationality that limit the classical theory of choice.

Rational Behavior and Role Theory

We can find common ground to relate the economist's theory of decision making with that of the social psychologist. The latter is particularly interested, of course, in social influences on choice, which determine the *role* of the actor. In our present terms, a role is a social prescription of some, but not all, of the premises that enter into an individual's choices of behavior. Any particular concrete behavior is the resultant of a large number of premises, only some of which are prescribed by the role. In addition to role premises there will be premises about the state of the environment based directly on perception, premises representing beliefs and knowledge, and idiosyncratic premises that characterize the personality. Within this framework we can accommodate both the rational elements in choice, so much emphasized by economics, and the nonrational elements to which psychologists and sociologists often prefer to call attention.

Decision Premises and Computer Programs

The analysis of choice in terms of decision premises gives us a conceptual framework for describing and explaining the process of deciding. But so complex is the process that our explanations of it would have remained schematic and hypothetical for a long time to come had not the modern digital computer appeared on the scene. The notion of decision premise can be translated into computer terminology, and when this translation has been accomplished, the digital computer provides us with an instrument for stimulating human decision processes—even very complex ones—and hence for testing empirically our explanations of those processes.

A fanciful (but only slightly fanciful) example will illustrate how this might be done. Some actual examples will be cited presently. Suppose we were to construct a robot incorporating a modern digital computer, and to program (i.e., to instruct) the robot to take the role of a business executive in a specified company. What would the program look like? Since no one has yet done this, we cannot say with certainty, but several points are fairly clear. The program would not consist of a list of prescribed and proscribed behaviors, since what an executive does is highly contingent on information about a wide variety of circumstances. Instead, the program would consist of a large number of *criteria* to be applied to possible and proposed courses of action, of routines for *generating* possible courses of action, of computational procedures for *assessing* the state of the environment and its implications for action, and the like. Hence, the program—in fact, a role prescription—would interact with information to produce concrete behavior adapted to the situation. The elements of such a program take the form of what we have called decision premises, and what the computer specialists would call instructions.

The promise of constructing actual detailed descriptions of concrete roles and decision processes is no longer, with the computer, a mere prospectus to be realized at some undefined future date. We can already provide actual examples, some of them in the area of economics.

1. *Management Science.* In the paragraphs on normative applications in section II, we have already referred to the use of such mathematical techniques as linear programming and dynamic programming to construct formal decision processes for actual situations. The relevance of these decision models to the present discussion is that they are not merely abstract "theories" of the firm, but actual decision-making devices. We can think of any such device as a simulation of the corresponding human decision maker, in which the equations and other assumptions that enter into the formal decision-making procedure correspond to the decision premises—including the role prescription—of the decision maker.

The actual application of such models to concrete business situations brings to light the information-processing tasks that are concealed in the assumptions of the more abstract classical models.

(1) The models must be formulated so as to require for their application only data that are obtainable. If one of the penalties, for example, of holding too small inventories is the loss of sales, a decision model that proposes to determine optimal inventory levels must incorporate a procedure for putting a dollar value on this loss.

(2) The models must call only for practicable computations. For example, several proposals for applying linear programming to certain factory scheduling problems have been shown to be impracticable because, even with computers, the computation time is too great. The task of decision theory (whether normative or descriptive) is to find alterna-

tive techniques—probably only approximate—that demand much less computation.

(3) The models must not demand unobtainable forecast information. A procedure that would require a sales department to estimate the third moment of next month's sales distribution would not have wide application, as either description or prescription, to business decision making.

These models, then, provide us with concrete examples of roles for a decision maker described in terms of the premises he is expected to apply to the decision—the data and the rules of computation.

2. *Engineering Design.* Computers have been used for some years to carry out some of the analytic computations required in engineering design—computing the stresses, for example, in a proposed bridge design. Within the past two years, ways have been found to program computers to carry out synthesis as well as analysis—to evolve the design itself. A number of companies in the electrical industry now use computers to design electric motors, transformers, and generators, going from customer specifications to factory design without human intervention. The significance of this for our purpose here is that the synthesis programs appear to simulate rather closely the processes that had previously been used by college-trained engineers in the same design work. It has proved possible to write down the engineers' decision premises and inference processes in sufficient detail to produce workable computer programs.

3. *Human Problem Solving.* The management science and engineering design programs already provide examples of simulation of human decision making by computer. It may be thought that, since in both instances the processes are highly arithmetical, these examples are relevant to only a very narrow range of human problem-solving activity. We generally think of a digital computer as a device which, if instructed in painful detail by its operator, can be induced to perform rather complicated and tedious arithmetical operations. More recent developments require us to revise these conceptions of the computer, for they enable it to carry out tasks that, if performed by humans, we would certainly call "thinking" and "learning."

Discovering the proof of a theorem of Euclid—a task we all remember from our high school geometry course—requires thinking and usually insight and imagination. A computer is now being programmed to perform this task (in a manner closely simulating the human geometer), and another computer has been successfully performing a highly similar task in symbolic logic for the past two years. The latter computer is programmed to learn—that is to improve its performance on the basis of successful problem-solving experience—to use something akin to imagery or metaphor in planning its proofs, and to transfer some of its skills to other tasks—for example, solving trigonometric identities—involving completely distinct subject matter. These programs, it should be observed, do not involve the computer in rapid arithmetic—or any arithmetic for that matter. They are basically nonnumerical, involving the manipulation of all kinds of symbolic material, including words.

Still other computer programs have been written to enable a computer to play chess. Not all of these programs, or those previously mentioned, are close simulations of the processes humans use. However, in some direct attempts to investigate the human processes by thinking-aloud techniques and to reproduce in computer programs the processes observed in human subjects, several striking simulations have been achieved. These experiments have been described elsewhere and can't be reviewed here in detail.

4. *Business Games.* Business games, like those developed by the American Management Association, International Business Machines Corporation, and several universities, represent a parallel development. In the business game, the decisions of the business firms are still made by the human players, but the economic environment of these firms, including their markets, are represented by computer programs that calculate the environment's responses to the actions of the players. As the games develop in detail and realism, their programs will represent more and more concrete descriptions of the decision processes of various economic actors—for example, consumers.

The games that have been developed so far are restricted to numerical magnitudes like prices and quantities of goods, and hence resemble the management science and engineering design programs more closely than they do those we have described under the heading of human problem solving. There is no reason, however, to expect this restriction to remain very long.

Implications for Economics

Apart from normative applications (e.g., substituting computers for humans in certain decision-making tasks) we are not interested so much in the detailed descriptions of roles as in broader questions: (1) What general characteristics do the roles of economic actors have? (2) How do roles come to be structured in the particular ways they do? (3) What bearing does this version of role theory have for macroeconomics and other large-scale social phenomena?

Characterizing Role Structure. Here we are concerned with generalizations about thought processes, particularly those generalizations that are relatively independent of the substantive content of the role. A classical example is Dewey's description of stages in the problem-solving process. Another example, of particular interest to economics, is the hypothesis we have already discussed at length: that economic man is a *satisficing* animal whose problem solving is based on search activity to meet certain aspiration levels rather than a *maximizing* animal whose problem solving involves finding the best alternatives in terms of specified criteria. A third hypothesis is that operative goals (those associated with an observable criterion of success, and relatively definite means of attainment) play a much larger part in governing choice than nonoperative goals (those lacking a concrete measure of success or a program for attainment).

Understanding How Roles Emerge. Within almost any single business firm, certain characteristic types of roles will be represented: selling roles, production roles, accounting roles, and so on. Partly, this consistency may be explained in functional terms—that a model that views the firm as producing a product, selling it, and accounting for its assets and liabilities is an effective simplification of the real world, and provides the members of the organization with a workable frame of reference. Imitation within the culture provides an alternative explanation. It is exceedingly difficult to test hypotheses as to the origins and causal conditions for roles as universal in the society as these, but the underlying mechanisms could probably be explored effectively by the study of less common roles—safety director, quality control inspector, or the like—that are to be found in some firms, but not in all.

With our present definition of role, we can also speak meaningfully of the role of an entire business firm—of decision premises that underlie its basic policies. In a particular industry we find some firms that specialize in adapting the product to individual customers' specifications; others that specialize in product innovation. The common interest of economics and psychology includes not only the study of individual roles, but also the explanation of organizational roles of these sorts.

Tracing the Implications for Macroeconomics. If basic professional goals remain as they are, the interest of the psychologist and the economist in role theory will stem from somewhat different ultimate aims. The former will use various economic and organizational phenomena as data for the study of the structure and determinants of roles; the latter will be primarily interested in the implications of role theory for the model of economic man, and indirectly, for macroeconomics.

The first applications will be to those topics in economics where the assumption of static equilibrium is least tenable. Innovation, technological change, and economic development are examples of areas to which a good empirically tested theory of the processes of human adaptation and problem solving could make a major contribution. For instance, we know very little at present about how the rate of innovation depends on the amounts of resources allocated to various kinds of research and development activity. Nor do we understand very well the nature of "know-how," the costs of transferring technology from one firm or economy to another, or the effects of various kinds and amounts of education upon national product. These are difficult questions to answer from aggregative data and gross observation, with the result that our views have been formed more by armchair theorizing than by testing hypotheses with solid facts.

VII. CONCLUSION

In exploring the areas in which economics has common interests with the other behavioral sciences, we have been guided by the metaphor we elaborated in section I. In simple, slow-moving situations, where the actor has a single, operational goal, the assumption of maximization relieves us of any need to construct a detailed picture of economic man or his processes of adaptation. As the complexity of the environment increases, or its speed of change, we need to know more and more about the mechanisms and processes that economic man uses to relate himself to that environment and achieve his goals.

How closely we wish to interweave economics with psychology depends, then, both on the range of questions we wish to answer and on our assessment of how far we may trust the assumptions of static equilibrium as approximations. In considerable part, the demand for a fuller picture of economic man has been coming from the profession of economics itself, as new areas of theory and application have emerged in which complexity and change are central facts. The revived interest in the theory of utility, and its application to choice under uncertainty, and to consumer saving and spending is one such area. The needs of normative macroeconomics and management science for a fuller theory of the firm have led to a number of attempts to understand the actual processes of making business decisions. In both these areas, notions of adaptive and satisficing behavior, drawn largely from psychology, are challenging sharply the classical picture of the maximizing entrepreneur.

The area of imperfect competition and oligopoly has been equally active, although the activity has thus far perhaps raised more problems than it has solved. On the positive side, it has revealed a community of interest among a variety of social scientists concerned with bargaining as a part of political and economic processes. Prediction of the future is another element common to many decision processes, and particularly important to explaining business cycle phenomena. Psychologists and economists have been applying a wide variety of approaches, empirical and theoretical, to the study of the formation of expectations. Surveys of consumer and business behavior, theories of statistical induction, stochastic learning theories, and theories of concept formation have all been converging on this problem area.

The very complexity that has made a theory of the decision-making process essential has made its construction exceedingly difficult. Most approaches have been piecemeal—now focused on the criteria of choice, now on conflict of interest, now on the formation of expectations. It seemed almost utopian to suppose that we could put together a model of adaptive man that would compare in completeness with the simple model of classical economic man. The sketchiness and incompleteness of the newer proposals has been urged as a compelling reason for clinging to the older theories, however inadequate they are admitted to be.

The modern digital computer has changed the situation radically. It provides us with a tool of research—for formulating and testing theories—whose power is commensurate with the complexity of the phenomena we seek to understand. Although the use of computers to build theories of human behavior is very recent, it has already led to concrete results in the simulation of higher mental processes. As economics finds it more and more necessary to understand and explain disequilibrium as well as equilibrium, it will find an increasing use for this new tool and for communication with its sister sciences of psychology and sociology.

part TWO
Demand

INTRODUCTION

An understanding of demand for a firm's product requires identification of those factors which determine or influence existing sales volume. After a firm or industry defines as precisely as possible why its product is selling at current levels, it may be in a better position to consider certain changes; consequently, this chapter dealing with demand is a necessary prelude to the one on forecasting, Part Six.

Demand analysis is important to decision making in two ways: (1) it provides the basis for analyzing market influences on the firm's products and thus helps the firm to adapt to the influences; and (2) it provides guidance to the manipulation of demand itself. Some decisions require a passive adaptation to market forces while others require the active shifting of those forces.

If the theoretical foundations of demand analysis are useful to the managerial economist, it would seem that empirical studies of demand are, too. Unfortunately, however, the results of very few empirical demand studies have stood up. The classic article by E. J. Working tells why. In empirical studies, a demand curve, once estimated, quite likely will not hold true for periods of time other than the one being studied. Such being the case, empirical curves cannot always be treated as corresponding to the demand curves of economic theory.

The desire of some consumers to be "in style," attempts by others to attain exclusiveness, and the persistent existence of Veblen's "conspicuous consumption" are incorporated into the theory of consumers' demand by H. Leibenstein. This is a very unique and interesting approach to determination of a demand curve.

To provide reliable estimates of elasticities, an empirical study must follow a simultaneous equations approach and deal with such well-known econometric problems as identification and multicollinearity; but even all the trimmings of grand econometric method are only necessary, not sufficient, conditions for reliable demand estimates, as experience sadly shows. Nevertheless, the subject is important. The brief note by Hogarty and Elzinga estimates price and income elasticities for a rather popular beverage: beer. Careful reading and understanding of their article may allow inclusion of its methodology in the student's tool kit.

The nature of the demand for various products often is demonstrated by economists to prove a point. Glenn Nelson and Tom Robinson reveal an acceptable methodology for presenting the demand and marketing order policy for fresh navel oranges. Their "Chicago" and "New York" models provide the kind of analysis upon which policy decisions are made.

A much broader study of demand is undertaken by Rodney L. Carlson. Expressed in terms of submarket segments, Carlson shows how to develop a multiequation linear model. He uses the automobile market for this purpose and identifies the demand for full-size, intermediate, compact, subcompact, and luxury cars. He estimates the price elasticity coefficients for each segment and interprets the model as to its implications for future demand.

As in all parts throughout the book, the articles in this Part Two may perhaps be read more for their exemplary use of a particular method than for substantive results. There is no particular reason to doubt any results presented herein. But even good results can become dated; good methods do not.

Good methods of estimating demand are mandatory if demand studies are to be useful in predicting the effects of changes in independent variables. But, a frequently used alternative to the statistical and other approaches surveyed here is one or more of the traditional forecasting methods. The material in Part Six, (Forecasting), therefore, is pertinent to this part as well.

3. What Do Statistical "Demand Curves" Show?*

E. J. WORKING

Many questions of practical importance hinge upon the elasticity of demand, or of demand and supply. The economist can answer them only in a vague and indefinite manner, because he does not know the nature of the demand curve. What will be the effect of a five-million-bushel increase in the corn crop upon the price of corn and of hogs? What will be the effect of a tariff on imports and prices; on the protected industry; on the balance of international payments? How large an indemnity can Germany pay? The answers all depend in greater or less measure upon the elasticity of demand of the various commodities in question.

Such are the needs of the theorist, and in recent years a great deal of attention has been turned to the construction of statistical demand curves. Beef, corn, cotton, hay, hogs, pig iron, oats, potatoes, sweet potatoes, sugar, and wheat are on the list of commodities for which we have statements of the "law of demand." Many economists have been skeptical, while others have been enthusiastic, on the significance of such demand curves. In consequence of this divergence of opinion, it may be well to consider some of the theoretical aspects of what the demand curves constructed by our statistical experts may be expected to show. Do they correspond to the demand curves of economic theory? If so, it would seem that they represent something tangible by which our theories may be tested and turned to better account.

Among the statistical studies of demand that have been made, there are cases in which the same commodity has been studied by more than one investigator, and their results indicate varying degrees of elasticity of demand. But despite this, in all but one of the cases the demand curves have been negatively inclined—they have been in accord with Marshall's "one general *law of demand*."

In the case of pig iron, however, Professor H. L. Moore finds a "law

---

* *The Quarterly Journal of Economics,* vol. 41, no. 2 (February 1927), pp. 212–35.

of demand" which is not in accord with Marshall's universal rule. He finds that the greater the quantity of pig iron sold, the higher will be the prices. If this is the nature of the statistical demand curve for pig iron, surely statistical demand curves must be of a very different sort from the demand curves of traditional economic theory!

Professor Moore holds that the statistical "law of demand" at which he arrives is a *dynamic* law, while that of theory is a *static* law. He says in part: "The doctrine of the uniformity of the demand function is an idol of the static state—the method of *cæteris paribus*—which has stood in the way of the successful treatment of dynamic problems." If it be true that statistical demand curves and the demand curves of theory differ so utterly from each other, of what value is statistical analysis to the theorist—of what value is economic theory to the statistical analyst? It would seem that so far as the study of demand is concerned, the statistical analyst and the economic theorist are on paths so divergent as to be wholly out of touch with each other. Before we accede to such a discouraging thought, let us examine a little more closely the nature of statistical demand curves as they may be viewed in the light of economic theory.

Let us first consider in what way statistical demand curves are constructed. While both the nature of the data used and the technique of analysis vary, the basic data consist of corresponding prices and quantities. That is, if a given quantity refers to the amount of a commodity sold, produced, or consumed in the year 1910, the corresponding price is the price which is taken to be typical of the year 1910. These corresponding quantities and prices may be for a period of a month, a year, or any other length of time which is feasible; and, as has already been indicated, the quantities may refer to amounts produced, sold, or consumed. The technique of analysis consists of such operations as fitting the demand curve, and adjusting the original data to remove, in so far as is possible, the effect of disturbing influences. For a preliminary understanding of the way in which curves are constructed, we need not be concerned with the differences in technique; but whether the quantities used are the amounts produced, sold, or consumed is a matter of greater significance, which must be kept in mind.

For the present, let us confine our attention to the type of study which uses for its data the quantities which have been sold in the market. In general, the method of constructing demand curves of this sort is to take corresponding prices and quantities, plot them, and draw a curve which will fit as nearly as possible all the plotted points. Suppose, for example, we wish to determine the demand curve for beef. First, we find out how many pounds of beef were sold in a given month and what was the average price. We do the same for all the other months of the period over which our study is to extend, and plot our data with quantities as abscissas and corresponding prices as ordinates. Next we draw a curve to fit the points. This is our demand curve.

In the actual construction of demand curves, certain refinements necessary in order to get satisfactory results are introduced. The purpose of these is to correct the data so as to remove the effect of various extraneous and complicating factors. For example, adjustments are usually made for changes in the purchasing power of money, and for changes in population and in consumption habits. Corrections may be made directly by such means as dividing all original price data by "an index of the general level of prices." They may be made indirectly by correction for trends of the two time series of prices and of quantities. Whatever the corrections and refinements, however, the essence of the method is that certain prices are taken as representing the prices at which certain quantities of the product in question were sold.

With this in mind, we may now turn to the theory of the demand-and-supply curve analysis of market prices. The conventional theory runs in terms substantially as follows. At any given time, all individuals within the scope of the market may be considered as being within two groups—potential buyers and potential sellers. The higher the price, the more the sellers will be ready to sell and the less the buyers will be willing to take. We may assume a demand schedule of the potential buyers and a supply schedule of the potential sellers which express the amounts that these groups are ready to buy and sell at different prices. From these schedules supply and demand curves may be made. Thus we have our supply and demand curves showing the market situation at any given time, and the price which results from this situation will be represented by the height of the point where the curves intersect.

This, however, represents the situation as it obtains at any given moment only. It may change; indeed, it is almost certain to change. The supply and demand curves which accurately represent the market situation of today will not represent that of a week hence. The curves which represent the average or aggregate of conditions this month will not hold true for the corresponding month of next year. In the case of the wheat market, for example, the effect of news that wheat which is growing in Kansas has been damaged by rust will cause a shift in both demand and supply schedules of the traders in the grain markets. The same amount of wheat, or a greater, will command a higher price than would have been the case if the news had failed to reach the traders. Since much of the buying and selling is speculative, changes in the market price itself may result in shifts of the demand and supply schedules.

If, then, our market demand-and-supply curves are to indicate conditions which extend over a period of time, we must represent them as shifting. A diagram such as the following, Figure 1, may be used to indicate them. The demand and supply curves may meet at any point within the area *a, b, c, d,* and over a period of time points of equilibrium will occur at many different places within it.

FIGURE 1
Utility and Demands

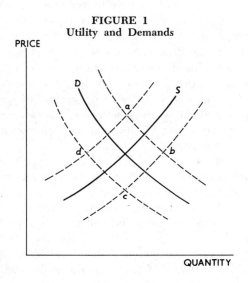

But what of statistical demand curves in the light of this analysis? If we construct a statistical demand curve from data of quantities sold and corresponding prices, our original data consist, in effect, of observations of points at which the demand and supply curves have met. Although we may wish to reduce our data to static conditions, we must remember that they originate in the market itself. The market is dynamic and our data extend over a period of time; consequently our data are of changing conditions and must be considered as the result of shifting demand and supply schedules.

Let us assume that conditions are such as those illustrated in Figure 2, the demand curve shifting from D_1 to D_2 and the supply curve shifting in similar manner from S_1 to S_2. It is to be noted that the chart shows approximately equal shifting of the demand and supply curves.

Under such conditions there will result a series of prices which may be graphically represented in Figure 3. It is from data such as those represented by the dots that we are to construct a demand curve, but evidently no satisfactory fit can be obtained. A line of one slope will give substantially as good a fit as will a line of any other slope.

But what happens if we alter our assumptions as to the relative shift-

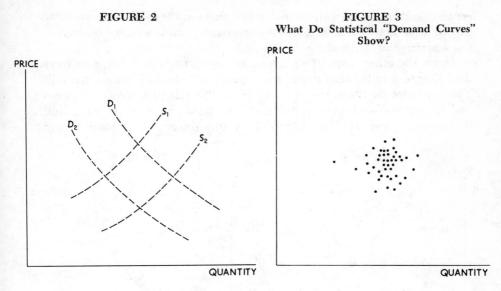

FIGURE 2

FIGURE 3
What Do Statistical "Demand Curves" Show?

ing of the demand and supply curves? Suppose the supply curve shifts in some such manner as is indicated by Figure 4, that is, so that the shifting of the supply curve is greater than the shifting of the demand

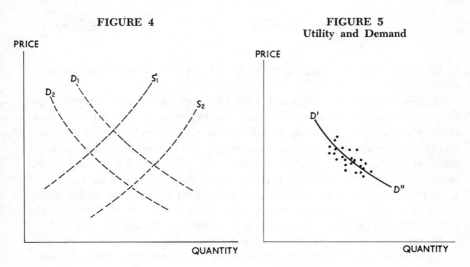

FIGURE 4

FIGURE 5
Utility and Demand

curve. We shall then obtain a very different set of observations—a set which may be represented by the dots of Figure 5. To these points we may fit a curve which will have the elasticity of the demand curve that we originally assumed, and whose position will approximate the central position about which the demand curve shifted. We may consider this to be a sort of typical demand curve, and from it we may determine the elasticity of demand.

If, on the other hand, the demand schedules of buyers fluctuate more than do the supply schedules of sellers, we shall obtain a different result. This situation is illustrated by Figure 6. The resulting array of prices and quantities is of a very different sort from the previous case, and its nature is indicated by Figure 7. A line drawn so as most nearly

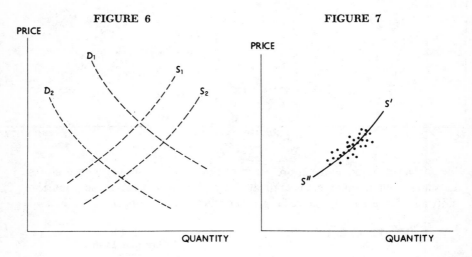

FIGURE 6   FIGURE 7

to fit these points will approximate a supply curve instead of a demand curve.

If this analysis is in accord with the facts, is it not evident that Professor Moore's "law of demand" for pig iron is in reality a "law of supply" instead? The original observations of prices and corresponding quantities are the resultant of both supply and demand. Consequently, they do not necessarily reflect the influence of demand any more than that of supply. The methods used in constructing demand curves (particularly if the quantity data are of quantities sold) may, under some conditions, yield a demand curve, under others, a supply curve, and, under still different conditions, no satisfactory result may be obtained.

In the case of agricultural commodities, where production for any given year is largely influenced by weather conditions, and where farmers sell practically their entire crop regardless of price, there is likely to be a much greater shifting of the supply schedules of sellers than of the demand schedules of buyers. This is particularly true of perishable commodities, which cannot be withheld from the market without spoilage, and in any case the farmers themselves can under no conditions use more than a very small proportion of their entire production. Such a condition results in the supply curve shifting within very wide limits. The demand curve, on the other hand, may shift but little. The quantities which are consumed may be dependent almost entirely upon price, so that the only way to have a much larger amount taken off the market is to reduce the price, and any considerable curtailment of supply is sure to result in a higher price.

With other commodities, the situation may be entirely different. Where a manufacturer has complete control over the supply of the article which he produces, the price at which he sells may be quite definitely fixed, and the amount of his production will vary, depending upon how large an amount of the article is bought at the fixed price. The extent to which there is a similar tendency to adjust sales to the shifts of demand varies with different commodities, depending upon how large overhead costs are and upon the extent to which trade agreements or other means are used to limit competition between different manufacturers. In general, however, there is a marked tendency for the prices of manufactured articles to conform to their expenses of production, the amount of articles sold varying with the intensity of demand at that price which equals the expenses of production. Under such conditions, the supply curve does not shift greatly, but rather approximates an expenses-of-production curve, which does not vary much from month to month or from year to year. If this condition is combined with a fluctuating demand for the product, we shall have a situation such as that shown in Figures 6 and 7, where the demand curves shift widely and the supply curves only a little.

From this, it would seem that, whether we obtain a demand curve or a supply curve, by fitting a curve to a series of points which represent the quantities of an article sold at various prices, depends upon the fundamental nature of the supply and demand conditions. It implies the need of some term in addition to that of elasticity in order to describe the nature of supply and demand. The term "variability" may be used for this purpose. For example, the demand for an article may be said to be "elastic" if, at a given time a small reduction in price would result in a much greater quantity being sold, while it may be said to be "variable" if the demand curve shows a tendency to shift markedly. To be called variable, the demand curve should have the tendency to shift back and forth, and not merely to shift gradually and consistently to the right or left because of changes of population or consuming habits.

Whether a demand or a supply curve is obtained may also be affected by the nature of the corrections applied to the original data. The corrections may be such as to reduce the effect of the shifting of the demand schedules without reducing the effect of the shifting of the supply schedules. In such a case the curve obtained will approximate a demand curve, even though the original demand schedules fluctuated fully as much as did the supply schedules.

By intelligently applying proper refinements, and making corrections to eliminate separately those factors which cause demand curves to shift and those factors which cause supply curves to shift, it may be possible even to obtain both a demand curve and a supply curve for the same product and from the same original data. Certainly it may be possible, in many cases where satisfactory demand curves have not been obtained, to find instead the supply curves of the articles in question. The supply curve obtained by such methods, it is to be noted, would be a market supply curve rather than a normal supply curve.

Thus far it has been assumed that the supply and demand curves shift quite independently and at random; but such need not be the case. It is altogether possible that a shift of the demand curve to the right may, as a rule, be accompanied by a shift of the supply curve to the left, and vice versa. Let us see what result is to be expected under such conditions. If successive positions of the demand curve are represented by the curves D_1, D_2 D_3, D_4, and D_5 of Figure 8, while

FIGURE 8
Utility and Demand

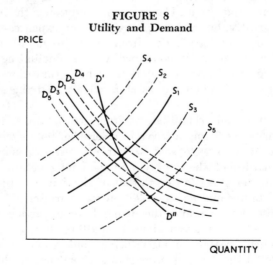

the curves S_1, S_2, S_3, S_4, and S_5 represent corresponding positions of the supply curves, then a series of prices will result from the intersection of D_1 with S_1, D_2 with S_2, and so on. If a curve be fitted to these points, it will not conform to the theoretical demand curve. It will have a smaller elasticity, as is shown by $D'D''$ of Figure 8. If, on the other hand, a shift of the demand curve to the right is accompanied by a shift of the supply curve to the right, we shall obtain a result such as that indicated by D′D″ in Figure 9. The fitted curve again fails to conform to the theoretical one, but in this case it is more elastic.

Without carrying the illustrations further, it will be apparent that similar reasoning applies to the fitted "supply curve" in case conditions are such that the demand curve shifts more than does the supply curve.

FIGURE 9

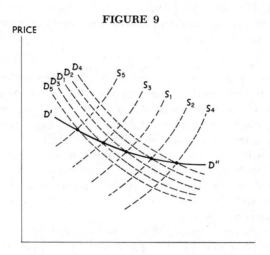

PRICE

If there is a change in the range through which the supply curve shifts, as might occur through the imposition of a tariff on an imported good, a new fitted curve will result, which will not be a continuation of the former one—this because the fitted curve does not correspond to the true demand curve. In case, then, of correlated shifts of the demand and supply curves, a fitted curve cannot be considered to be the demand curve for the article. It cannot be used, for example, to estimate what change in price would result from the levying of a tariff upon the commodity.

Perhaps a word of caution is needed here. It does not follow from the foregoing analysis that, when conditions are such that shifts of the supply and demand curves are correlated, an attempt to construct a demand curve will give a result which will be useless. Even though shifts of the supply and demand curves are correlated, a curve which is fitted to the points of intersection will be useful for purposes of price forecasting, provided no new factors are introduced which did not affect the price during the period of the study. Thus, so long as the shifts of the supply and demand curves remain correlated in the same way, and so long as they shift through approximately the same range, the curve of regression of price upon quantity can be used as a means of estimating price from quantity.

In cases where it is impossible to show that the shifts of the demand and supply curves are not correlated, much confusion would probably be avoided if the fitted curves were not called demand curves (or supply curves), but if, instead, they were called merely lines of regression. Such curves may be useful, but we must be extremely careful in our interpretation of them. We must also make every effort to discover whether the shifts of the supply and demand curves are correlated before interpreting the results of any fitted curve.

. . . . .

In assuming that we are dealing with quantities actually sold in the market, and in disregarding the fact that for many commodities there is a whole series of markets at various points in the marketing chain, we have simplified our problem. But it has been more than mere simplification, for the interpretation which is to be placed on statistical demand curves depends in large measure upon these matters. Whether the demand curve is a "particular" or a "general" demand curve, depends upon whether or not we use quantities sold. Whether it represents consumer or dealer demand, depends upon the point in the marketing chain to which the quantities sold refer.

Most theorists are acquainted with the concept of the general demand curve as it is presented by Wicksteed and Davenport. Briefly, the idea is that demand should be considered as including not merely the quantities that are bought, but rather all those in existence. The general demand curve, then, includes the possessors of a commodity as having a demand for it at any price below their reservation price, even if they are prospective sellers. Instead of showing the amounts that will be bought at various prices, it shows the marginal money valuation which will be placed upon varying quantities of an existing supply.

Wicksteed even indicates that the supply curve ought not to be considered at all. The following gives an intimation of his viewpoint:

But what about the "supply curve" that usually figures as a determinant of price, coördinate with the demand curve? I say it boldly and baldly: There is no such thing. When we are speaking of a marketable commodity, what is usually called a supply curve is in reality a demand curve of those who possess the commodity; for it shows the exact place which every successive unit of the commodity holds in their relative scale of estimates. The so-called supply curve, therefore, is simply a part of the total demand curve.[1]

Thus the general demand curve is an expression of the relation between the supply of a commodity and its valuation.

. . . . .

---

[1] P. H. Wicksteed, "The Scope and Method of Political Economy in the Light of the 'Marginal Theory of Value,' " *Economic Journal* (March, 1914) p. 1.

The amount of a commodity sold at one point in the marketing chain may differ from that sold at another in much the same way that the amount produced may differ from the amount sold. This is particularly true if monthly data are used. A case in point would be the demand for eggs. The amount of eggs sold by farmers in the spring of the year is greatly in excess of the amount sold by retail dealers, while in the winter months it is much less. Since differentials between the prices received by farmers and those received by retail dealers remain fairly constant, very different demand curves would be obtained. The consumers' demand curve would be very much less elastic than that of thè dealers who buy from farmers.

Differences between dealer demand and consumer demand are largely dependent upon whether we are considering short or long periods. Over long periods of time, dealer demand tends to conform to consumer demand. This difference, however, is not a thing which depends upon the length of period over which the data extend, but of the length of period to which the individual observations of prices and quantities refer. In the case of eggs, if yearly data were used, the principal difference which would be found between the elasticity of consumer and dealer demands would be due to price differentials alone.

The question whether statistical demand curves are static or dynamic is a perplexing one and rather difficult to deal with. This is largely due to uncertainty as to just what is meant by the terms "static" and "dynamic." Moore holds that his "laws of demand" are dynamic, and that this is an eminently desirable feature. Schultz, while considering it most desirable to obtain both a static and a dynamic law by means of multiple correlation, holds that the statistical devices of relative changes and of trend ratios give a static "law of demand."

Conditions are often defined as being static or dynamic on two different grounds. They may be called static if they refer to a point of time; or else they may be said to be static if all other things are held equal. Statements such as these, however, lack much in clarity and accuracy. How can a statement be made as to prices at which different quantities of a commodity will sell at a *point* of time? Is it really supposed that *all* other things must be held equal in order to study the demand of the commodity? Rather, the real supposition, though it may not be accurately expressed, is that the relationships between the various economic factors should be the same as those which exist at a given point of time, or that the relationships between these factors should remain constant.

The data used in a statistical study of demand must, of course, extend over a period of time, but they may in effect conform to conditions at a point of time if trend is removed and if there is no other change in the relationship between quantity and price. Of course, the shifting of the demand and supply curves constitutes a change in the relationship between the quantity and price, but the process of curve fitting corresponds to that of averaging. Consequently, the fitted curve may be considered to depict the average relationship between quantity and price. This amounts to the same thing as representing the relationship at a point of time which is typical for the period studied. In this sense, then, of relating to a point of time, Moore's "laws of demand" are static instead of dynamic.

Holding "all other things equal," however, is a different matter. Schultz states the difficulty in the following manner:

In *theory* the law of demand for any one commodity is given only on the assumption that the prices of all other commodities remain constant (the old *ceteris paribus* assumption). This postulate fails in the case of commodities for which substitutes are available. Thus when the price of beef is changed markedly, the prices of such rival commodities as mutton, veal, and pork cannot be supposed to remain constant. Likewise, the price of sugar cannot be increased beyond a certain point without affecting the prices of glucose, corn sugar, and honey.[2]

Marshall makes similar restrictions as to the need for other things to be held equal, and suggests that in some cases it may be best to "group together commodities as distinct as beef and mutton," in order to obtain a demand curve which will not be too restricted because of other things being equal.

The question arises, however, whether it is desirable to hold all other things equal in any case. Is it not better to have a demand curve for beef which expresses the relation between the price and quantity of beef while the prices of pork, mutton, and veal, vary as they normally do, with different prices of beef? Furthermore, may not this be called a static condition? The point can perhaps be made clearer if we take an extreme example. If we are studying the demand for wheat, it would be almost meaningless to get the demand curve for No. 2 Winter wheat while holding the price of all other grades of wheat constant. Other grades of wheat can be so readily substituted that the demand would be almost completely elastic. The difference between this and holding the prices of pork, mutton, and veal constant, while the price of beef varies, is only one of degree—a difference which depends upon the ease with which substitutes can be used in place of the article whose demand is being studied.

All other things being held equal is not a condition represented by a statistical law of demand or, strictly interpreted, of any useful demand curve theory. Some of the things that are correlated with the price of the commodity in question may be held equal, but it is impossible for

---

[2] Henry Schultz, "The Statistical Law of Demand," *The Journal of Political Economy* (October and December 1925). See pp. 498–502 of October issue.

all things to be held equal. However, a statistical law of demand represents a condition under which the relationships between factors may be considered to have remained the same, or, to put it more accurately, a condition which is an average of the relationships during the period studied.

In conclusion, then, it is evident that the mere statement that the demand for a commodity has a given elasticity is meaningless. As with the results of all other statistical analysis, statistical demand curves must be interpreted in the light of the nature of the original data and of the methods of analysis used. There are four questions, the answers to which it is particularly important to know. They concern (1) whether the supply or demand curve is more variable, (2) the market to which the price and quantity data refer, (3) the extent to which "other things are held equal," and (4) whether the shifting of the supply and demand curves is correlated or random.

For precision, it is preferable that the data of price and quantity should refer to the same market. Yet this may be out of the question. In a study of the demand for wheat, for example, if we want to obtain a demand curve of the quantity demanded by the entire country, we cannot use prices for all different points and for all different grades. Instead, the price at one market and for one grade may be used as representative, and the demand of the entire country determined for various prices at the one marketplace. If the price at any other market or for any other grade were used, the elasticity of demand might be different.

Furthermore, the point in the market chain must be specified and the results interpreted accordingly. As is the case with geographical points, it is preferable that the quantities and prices should refer to the same stage in the marketing process. If this is not the case, the interpretation should be made with the situation in view.

It is to be expected that the methods used in constructing statistical demand curves should be such as to give a demand curve which represents a point of time, that is, that trends in both quantities and prices are removed, or else multiple correlation is used to effect the same result. If, in addition to this, other things are held constant, the fact should be noted and the elasticity of demand should be stated as referring to a condition where these other things are held constant.

The matter of correlation between shifts of the demand and supply curves is a more difficult problem to deal with. Every effort should be made to discover whether there is a tendency for the shifting of these to be interdependent. In case it is impossible to determine this, it should be carefully noted that the demand curve which is obtained is quite likely not to hold true for periods other than the one studied, and cannot be treated as corresponding to the demand curve of economic theory.

4. Bandwagon, Snob, and Veblen Effects in the Theory of Consumers' Demand*

H. LEIBENSTEIN

I. THE NATURE OF THE PROBLEM

The desire of some consumers to be "in style," the attempts by others to attain exclusiveness, and the phenomena of "conspicuous consumption," have as yet not been incorporated into the current theory of consumers' demand. My purpose, in this paper, is to take a step or two in that direction.

1. "Non-additivity" in Consumers' Demand Theory

This enquiry was suggested by some provocative observations made by Professor Oskar Morgenstern in his article, "Demand Theory Reconsidered." After examining various aspects of the relationship between individual demand curves and collective market demand curves Professor Morgenstern points out that in some cases the market demand curve is not the lateral summation of the individual demand curves. The following brief quotation may indicate the nature of what he calls "non-additivity" and gives some indication of the problem involved. "Non-additivity in this simple sense is given, for example, in the case of fashions, where one person buys because another is buying the same thing, or vice versa. The collective demand curve of snobs is most likely not additive. But the phenomenon of non-additivity is in fact much deeper; since virtually all collective supply curves are non-additive it follows that the demand of the firms for their labor, raw materials, etc. is also non-additive. This expands the field of non-additivity enormously."

Since the purpose of Professor Morgenstern's article is immanent criticism he does not present solutions to the problems he raises. He does clearly imply, however, that since coalitions are bound to be important

---

* *Quarterly Journal of Economics,* vol. 64 (February 1950), pp. 183–207.

in this area only the "Theory of Games" . . . is likely to give an adequate solution to this problem. The present writer is not competent to judge whether this is or is not the case, but he does believe that there are many markets where coalitions among consumers are not widespread or of significance, and hence abstracting from the possibility of such coalitions may not be unreasonable. Should this be the case we may be able to make some headway through the use of conventional analytical methods.

What we shall therefore be concerned with substantially is a reformulation of some aspects of the static theory of consumers' demand while permitting the relaxation of one of the basic implicit assumptions of the current theory—namely, that the consumption behaviour of any individual is independent of the consumption of others. This will permit us to take account of consumers' motivations not heretofore incorporated into the theory. To be more specific, the proposed analysis is designed to take account of the desire of people to wear, buy, do, consume, and behave like their fellows; the desire to join the crowd, be "one of the boys," etc.—phenomena of mob motivations and mass psychology either in their grosser or more delicate aspects. This is the type of behaviour involved in what we shall call the "bandwagon effect." On the other hand, we shall also attempt to take account of the search for exclusiveness by individuals through the purchase of distinctive clothing, foods, automobiles, houses, or anything else that individuals may believe will in some way set them off from the mass of mankind—or add to their prestige, dignity, and social status. In other words, we shall be concerned with the impact on the theory created by the potential nonfunctional utilities inherent in many commodities.

2. The Past Literature

The past literature on the interpersonal aspects of utility and demand can be divided into three categories: sociology, welfare economics, and pure theory. The sociological writings deal with the phenomena of fashions and conspicuous consumption and their relationship to social status and human behaviour. This treatment of the subject was made famous by Veblen—although Veblen, contrary to the notions of many, was neither the discoverer nor the first to elaborate upon the theory of conspicuous consumption. John Rae, writing before 1834, has quite an extensive treatment of conspicuous consumption, fashions, and related matters pretty much along Veblenian lines. Rae attributes many of these ideas to earlier writers, going so far as to find the notion of conspicuous consumption in the Roman poet Horace; and a clear statement of the "keeping up with the Joneses" idea in the verse of Alexander Pope. An excellent account of how eighteenth and nineteenth century philosophers and economists handled the problem of fashion is given in Norine Foley's article "Fashion." For the most part, these treatments are of a "sociological" nature.

The economist concerned with public policy will probably find the "economic welfare" treatment of the problem most interesting. Here, if we examine the more recent contributions first and then go backward, we find examples of current writers believing they have stumbled upon something new, although they had only rediscovered what had been said many years before. Thus, Professor Melvin Reder in his treatment of the theory of welfare economics claims that ". . . there is another type of external repercussion which is rarely, *if ever*, recognized in discussions of welfare economics. It occurs where the utility function of one individual contains, as variables, the quantities of goods consumed by other persons." It can only be lack of awareness of the past literature that causes Reder to imply that this consideration has not been taken up before. Among those who considered the problem earlier are J. E. Meade, A. C. Pigou, Henry Cunynghame, and John Rae.

The similarity in the treatment of this matter by Reder and Rae is at times striking. For example, Reder suggests that legislation forbidding "invidious expenditure" may result in an increase in welfare by freeing resources from "competitive consumption" to other uses. In a similar vein Rae argued that restrictions on the trade of "pure luxuries" can only be a gain to some and a loss to none, in view of the labor saved in avoiding the production of "pure luxuries." It is quite clear from the context that what Rae calls "pure luxuries" is exactly the same as Reder's commodities that enter into "competitive consumption."

One reason why the interpersonal effects on demand have been ignored in current texts may be the fact that Marshall did not consider the matter in his *Principles*. We know, however, from Marshall's correspondence, that he was aware of the problem. Both Cunynghame and Pigou pointed out that Marshall's treatment of consumers' surplus did not take into account interpersonal effects on utility. Marshall seemed to feel that this would make the diagrammatical treatment too complex. Recently, Reder and Samuelson noticed that external economies and diseconomies of consumption may vitiate (or, at best, greatly complicate) their "new" welfare analysis, and hence, in true academic fashion, they assume the problem away. This, however, is not the place to examine the question in detail.

The only attack on the problem from the point of view of pure theory that the writer could find is a short article by Professor Pigou. In this article Pigou sets out to inquire under what circumstances the assumption of the additivity of the individual demand curves "adequately conforms to the facts, and, when it does not so conform, what alternative assumption ought to be substituted for it." It is obvious that the particular choice of alternative assumptions will determine (*a*) whether a solution can, given the existing analytical tools, be obtained, and (*b*) whether such a solution is relevant to the real world. Pigou's treatment of the problem is, unfortunately, exceedingly brief. He attempts to deal with non-additivity in both supply and demand curves within the confines of six pages. In examining the additivity assumption he points out that it is warranted when (1) the demand for the commodity is wholly for the direct satisfaction yielded by it or (2) where disturbances to equilibrium are so small that aggregate output is not greatly changed. After briefly suggesting some of the complexities of non-additivity he concludes that the ". . . problems, for the investigation of which it is necessary to go behind the demand schedule of the market as a whole, are still, theoretically, soluble; there are a sufficient number of equations to determine the unknowns." This last point, which is not demonstrated in Pigou's article, is hardly satisfying since it has been shown that the equality of equations and unknowns is not a sufficient condition for a determinate solution, or indeed for any solution, to exist.

3. The Approach and Limits of the Ensuing Analysis

It should, perhaps, be pointed out at the outset that the ensuing exposition is limited to statics. In all probability, the most interesting parts of the problem, and also those most relevant to real problems, are its dynamic aspects. However, a static analysis is probably necessary, and may be of significance, in order to lay a foundation for a dynamic analysis. In view of the limitations to be set on the following analysis, it becomes necessary to demarcate clearly the conceptual borderline between statics and dynamics.

There are, unfortunately, numerous definitions of statics and there seems to be some confusion on the matter. In view of this it will not be possible to give *the* definition of statics. All that we can hope to do is to choose *a* definition that will be consistent with and useful for our purposes—and also one that at the same time does not stray too far from some of the generally accepted notions about statics. Because of the fact that we live in a dynamic world most definitions of statics will imply a state of affairs that contradicts our general experience. But this is of necessity the case. What we must insist on is internal consistency but we need not, at this stage, require "realism."

Our task, then, is to define a static situation—a situation in which static economics is applicable. Ordinarily, it is thought that statics is in some way "timeless." This need not be the case. For our purposes, a static situation is not a "timeless" situation, nor is static economics timeless economics. It is, however, "temporally orderless" economics. That is, we shall define a static situation as one in which the order of events is of no significance. We, therefore, abstract from the consequences of the temporal order of events. The above definition is similar to, but perhaps on a slightly higher level of generality than, Hicks's notion that static deals with "those parts of economic theory where we do not have to trouble about dating."

In order to preserve internal consistency, it is necessary to assume that the period of reference is one in which the consumer's income and expenditure pattern is synchronized. And, we have to assume also that this holds true for all consumers. In other words, we assume that both the income patterns and the expenditure patterns repeat themselves *every* period. There is thus no overlapping of expenditures from one period into the next. This implies, of course, that the demand curve reconstitutes itself every period. The above implies also that only one price can exist during any unit period and that price can change only from period to period. A disequilibrium can, therefore, be corrected only over two or more periods.

II. FUNCTIONAL AND NONFUNCTIONAL DEMAND

At the outset it is probably best to define clearly some of the basic terms we are going to use and to indicate those aspects of demand that we are going to treat. The demand for consumers' goods and services may be classified according to motivation. The following classification, which we shall find useful, is on a level of abstraction which, it is hoped, includes most of the motivations behind consumers' demand.

A. Functional
B. Nonfunctional
    1. External effects on utility
        a. Bandwagon effect
        b. Snob effect
        c. Veblen effect
    2. Speculative
    3. Irrational

By functional demand is meant that part of the demand for a commodity which is due to the qualities inherent in the commodity itself. By nonfunctional demand is meant that portion of the demand for a consumers' good which is due to factors other than the qualities inherent in the commodity. Probably the most important kind of nonfunctional demand is due to external effects on utility. That is, the utility derived from the commodity is enhanced or decreased owing to the fact that others are purchasing and consuming the same commodity, or owing to the fact that the commodity bears a higher rather than a lower price tag. We differentiate this type of demand into what we shall call the "bandwagon" effect, the "snob" effect, and the "Veblen" effect. By the bandwagon effect, we refer to the extent to which the demand for a commodity is *increased* due to the fact that others are also consuming the same commodity. It represents the desire of people to purchase a commodity in order to get into "the swim of things"; in order to conform with the people they wish to be associated with; in order to be fashionable or stylish; or, in order to appear to be "one of the boys." By the snob effect we refer to the extent to which the demand for a consumers' good is *decreased* owing to the fact that others are also consuming the same commodity (or that others are increasing their consumption of that commodity). This represents the desire of people to be exclusive; to be different; to dissociate themselves from the "common herd." By the Veblen effect we refer to the phenomenon of conspicuous consumption; to the extent to which the demand for a consumers' good is increased because it bears a higher rather than a lower price. We should perhaps emphasize the distinction between the snob and the Veblen effect—the former is a function of the consumption of others, the latter is a function of price. This paper will deal almost exclusively with these three types of nonfunctional demand.

For the sake of completeness there should perhaps be some explanation as to what is meant by speculative and irrational demand. Speculative demand refers to the fact that people will often "lay in" a supply of a commodity because they expect its price to rise. Irrational demand is, in a sense, a catchall category. It refers to purchases that are neither planned nor calculated but are due to sudden urges, whims, and so forth, and that serve no rational purpose but that of satisfying sudden whims and desires.

In the above it was assumed throughout that income is a parameter. If income is not given but allowed to vary, then the income effect on demand may in most cases be the most important effect of all. Also, it may be well to point out that the above is only one of a large number of possible classifications of the types of consumers' demand—classifications that for some purposes may be superior to the one here employed. We therefore suggest the above classification only for the purposes at hand and make no claims about its desirableness, or effectiveness, in any other use.

III. THE BANDWAGON EFFECT

1. A Conceptual Experiment

Our immediate task is to obtain aggregate demand curves of various kinds in those cases where the individual demand curves are non-additive. First we shall examine the case where the bandwagon effect is important. In its pure form this is the case where an individual will demand more (less) of a commodity at a given price because some or all other individuals in the market also demand more (less) of the commodity.

One of the difficulties in analyzing this type of demand involves the choice of assumptions about the knowledge that each individual possesses. This implies that everyone knows the quantity that will be demanded by every individual separately, or the quantity demanded by all individuals collectively at any given price—after all the reactions and adjustments that individuals make to each other's demand has taken place. On the other hand, if we assume ignorance on the part of consumers about the demand of others, we have to make assumptions as to the nature and extent of the ignorance—ignorance is a relative concept. A third possibility, and the one that will be employed at first, is to devise some mechanism whereby the consumers obtain accurate information.

Another problem involves the choice of assumptions to be made about the demand behaviour of individual consumers. Three possibilities suggest themselves: (1) The demand of consumer A (at given prices) may be a function of the total demand of all others in the market collectively. Or, (2) the demand of consumer A may be a function of the demand of all other consumers both separately and collectively. In other words, A's demand may be more influenced by the demand of some than by the demand of others. (3) A third possibility is that A's demand is a function of the number of people that demand the commodity rather than the number of units demanded. More complex demand behaviour patterns that combine some of the elements of the above are conceivable. For present purposes it is best that we assume the simplest one as a first approximation. Initially, therefore, we assume that A's demand is a function of the units demanded by all others collectively. This is the same as saying that A's demand is a function of total market demand at given prices, since A always knows his own demand, and he could always subtract his own demand from the total market demand to get the quantity demanded by all others.

In order to bring out the central principle involved in the ensuing analysis, consider the following *gedankenexperiment*. A known product is to be introduced into a well-defined market at a certain date. The nature of the product is such that its demand depends partially on the functional qualities of the commodity, and partially on whether many or few units are demanded. Our technical problem is to compound the non-additive individual demand curves into a total market demand curve, given sufficient information about the individual demand functions. Now, suppose that it is possible to obtain an accurate knowledge of the demand function of an individual through a series of questionnaires. Since an individual's demand is, in part, a function of the total market demand, it is necessary to take care of this difficulty in our questionnaires. We can have a potential consumer fill out the first questionnaire by having him assume that the total market demand, at all prices, is a given very small amount—say 400 units. On the basis of this assumption the consumer would tell us the quantities he demands over a reasonable range of prices. Subjecting every consumer to the same questionnaire, we add the results across and obtain a market demand curve that would reflect the demand situation if every consumer believed the total demand were only 400 units. This, however, is not the real market demand function under the assumption of the possession of accurate market information by consumers, since the total demand (at each price) upon which consumers based their replies was not the actual market demand (at each price) as revealed by the results of the survey. Let us call the results of the first survey "schedule No. 1."

We can now carry out a second survey, that is, subject each consumer to a second questionnaire in which each one is told that schedule No. 1 reflects the total quantities demanded, at each price. Aggregating the replies we obtain schedule No. 2. Schedule No. 1 then becomes a parameter upon which schedule No. 2 is based. In a similar manner we can obtain schedules No. 3, No. 4, . . . , No. n in which each schedule is the result of adding the quantities demanded by each consumer (at each price), *if each consumer believes that the total quantities demanded (at each price) are shown by the previous schedule.* Now, the quantities demanded in schedule No. 2 will be greater than or equal to the quantities demanded in schedule No. 1 for the same prices. Some consumers may increase the quantity they demand when they note that the total quantity demanded, at given prices, is greater than they thought it would be. As long as some consumers or potential consumers continue to react positively to increases in the total quantity demanded the results of successive survey will be different. That is, some or all of the quantities demanded in schedule No. 1 will be less than the quantities demanded at the same prices, in schedule No. 2, which in turn will be equal to or less than the quantities demanded, at the same prices, in schedule No. 3, and so on.

At this point it is appropriate to introduce a new principle with the intention of showing that this process cannot go on indefinitely. Sooner or later two successive schedules will be identical. If two successive surveys yield the same market demand schedules, then an equilibrium situation exists since the total quantities demanded, at each price, upon which individual consumers based their demand, turns out to be correct. Thus, if schedule No. n is identical with schedule No. n-1, then schedule No. n is the actual market demand function for the product on the assumption that consumers have accurate information of market conditions.

The question that arises is whether there is any reason to suppose that sooner or later two successive surveys will yield exactly the same result. This would indeed be the case if we could find good reason to posit a principle to the effect that for every individual there is some point at which he will cease to increase the quantities demanded for a commodity, at given prices, in response to incremental increases in total market demand. Such a principle would imply that beyond a point incremental increases in the demand for the commodity by others have a decreasing influence on a consumer's own demand; and, further, that a point is reached at which these increases in demand by others have no influence whatsoever on his own demand. It would, of course, also be necessary to establish that such a principle holds true for every consumer. It would not be inappropriate to call this the principle of diminishing marginal consumption effect. Does such a principle really exist? There are some good reasons for believing that it does. First, the reader may note that the principle is analogous to the principle of diminishing marginal utility. As the total market demand grows larger, incremental increases in total demand become smaller and smaller proportions of the demand. It sounds reasonable, and probably appeals to us intuitively that an individual would be less influenced, and indeed take less notice of, a 1 percent increase in total demand, than of a 10 percent increase in total demand, though these percentage increases be the same in absolute amount. Second, we can probably appeal effectively to general experience. There are no cases in which an individual's demand for a consumers' good increases endlessly with increases in total demand. If there were two or more such individuals in a market then the demand for the commodity would increase in an endless spiral. Last but not least, the income constraint is sufficient to establish that there must be a point at which increases in a consumer's demand must fail to respond to increases in demand by others. Since every consumer is subject to the income constraint, it must follow that the principle holds for all consumers.

Now, to get back to our conceptual experiment, we would find that after administering a sufficient number of surveys, we would sooner or later get two surveys that yield identical demand schedules. The result of the last survey would then represent the true demand situation that would manifest itself on the market when the commodity was offered for sale. We may perhaps justly call such a demand function the equilibrium demand function—or demand curve. The equilibrium demand curve is the curve that exists when the marginal external consumption effect for every consumer, but one, at all alternate prices is equal to zero. All other demand curves may be conceived as disequilibrium curves that can exist only because of temporarily imperfect knowledge by consumers of other people's demand. Once the errors in market information were discovered such a curve would move to a new position.

2. The Bandwagon Effect—Diagrammatical Method

The major purpose of going through the conceptual experiment with its successive surveys was to illustrate the diminishing marginal external consumption effect and to indicate its role in obtaining a determinate demand curve. There is, however, a relatively simple method for obtaining the market demand function in those cases where external consumption effects are significant. This method will allow us to compare some of the properties of the "bandwagon demand curve" with the usual "functional" demand curve; and, it will also allow us to separate the extent to which a change in demand is due to a change in price, and the extent to which it is due to the bandwagon effect.

Given a certain total demand for a commodity as a parameter, every individual will have a demand function based on this total market demand. Let the alternative total market demands that will serve as parameters for alternate individual demand functions be indicated as superscripts $a, b, \ldots n$ (where $a < b < \ldots < n$). Let the individual demand functions be $d_1, d_2, \ldots d_n$; where every subscript indicates a different consumer. Thus d_3^a is the individual demand curve for consumer 3 if the consumer believes that the total market demand is a units. Similarly d_{500}^m is the individual demand curve for the 500th consumer if he believes that the total market demand will be m units. We could now add across $d_1^a, d_2^a, d_3^a, \ldots, d_n^a$ which will give us the market demand curve D^a, which indicates the quantities demanded at alternate prices if all consumers believed that the total demand was a units. In the same manner we can obtain $D^b, D^c, \ldots, D^n$. These hypothetical market demand curves $D^a, D^b, D^c, \ldots, D^n$ are shown in Figure 1. Now, if we assume that buyers have accurate knowledge of market conditions (i.e., of the total quantities demanded at every price) then only one point on any of the curves $D^a, D^b, \ldots, D^n$ could be on the real or equilibrium demand curve. These are the points on each curve $D^a, D^b, \ldots, D^n$ that represent the amounts on which the consumers based their individual demand curves; that is, the amounts that consumers expected to be the total market demand. These points are labeled in Figure 1 as $E^a, E^b, \ldots, E^n$. They are a series of virtual equilibrium points. Given that consumers possess accurate market information, $E^a, E^b, \ldots, E^n$, are the only points that can become actual quantities demanded. The locus of all these points D_B is therefore the actual demand curve for the commodity.

It may be of interest, at this point, to break up changes in the quantity demanded due to changes in price into a price effect and a bandwagon effect; that is, the extent of the change that is due to the change in price, and the extent of the change in demand that is due to consumers adjusting to each other's changed consumption. With an eye on Figure 1 consider the effects of a reduction in price from P_2 to P_1. The increase in

FIGURE 1

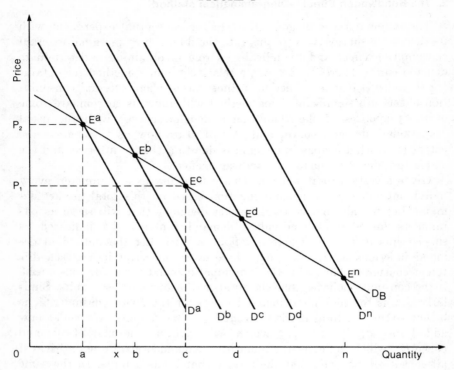

demand after the change in price is ac. Only part of that increase, however, is due to the reduction in price. To measure the amount due to the reduction in price we go along the demand curve D^a to P_1 which tells us the quantity that would be demanded at P_1 if consumers did not adjust to each other's demands. This would result in an increase in demand of ax. Due to the bandwagon effect, however, an additional number of consumers are induced to enter the market or to increase their demands. There is now an additional increase in demand of xc after consumers have adjusted to each other's increases in consumption. Exactly the same type of analysis can, of course, be carried out for increases as well as for decreases in price.

We may note another thing from Figure 1. The demand curve D_B is more elastic than any of the other demand curves shown in the diagram. This would suggest that other things being equal, the demand curve will be more elastic if there is a bandwagon effect than if the demand is based only on the functional attributes of the commodity.

This, of course, follows from the fact that reactions to price changes are followed by additional reactions, *in the same direction*, to each other's changed consumption.

3. Social Taboos and the Bandwagon Effect

Social taboos, to the extent that they affect consumption, are, in a sense, bandwagon effects in reverse gear. That is to say, some people will not buy and consume certain things because other people are not buying and consuming these things. Thus, there may not be any demand for a commodity even though it has a functional utility, although, apart from the taboo, it would be purchased. Individual A will not buy the commodity because individuals B, C, and D do not, while individuals B, C, and D may refrain from consumption for the same reasons. It is not within the competence of the economist to investigate the psychology of this kind of behaviour. For our purposes we need only note that such behaviour exists and attempt to analyze how such behaviour affects the demand function.

We can proceed as follows. Let d_1^x be the demand curve of the least inhibited individual in the market, where the superscript x is the total quantity demanded in the market upon which he bases his individual demand. Suppose that at market demand x consumer 1 will demand at some range of prices one unit of the commodity, but at no price will he demand more. If he believes, however, that the total market demand is less than x units he will refrain from making any purchases. Since, *ex hypothesi*, consumer 1 is the least inhibited consumer, he will, at best, be the only one who will demand one unit of the commodity if consumers expect the total market demand to be x units. It must be clear, then, that x units cannot be a virtual equilibrium point, since only points where the total expected quantity demanded is equal to the actual quantity demanded can be points on the real demand curve, and the quantity x cannot at any price be a point where expected total demand is equal to actual total demand. Now, if the total expected demand were $x + 1$ the actual demand might increase, say, to 2 units. At expected total demands $x + 2$ and $x + 3$, more would enter the market and the actual demand would be still greater since the fear of being different is considerably reduced as the expected demand is increased. With given increases in the expected total demand there must, at some point, be more than equal increases in the actual demand, because, if a real demand curve exists at all, there must be some point where the expected demand is equal to the actual demand. That point may exist, say, at $x + 10$. That is, at an expected total demand of $x + 10$ units a sufficient number of people have overcome their inhibitions to being different so that, at some prices, they will actually demand $x + 10$ units of the commodity. Let us call this point "T"—it is really the "taboo breaking point." The maximum bid (the point T^1 in Figure 2) of the marginal unit demanded if the total demand were T units now give us the first point on the real demand curve (the curve D_B).

How social taboos may affect the demand curve is shown in Figure 2. It will be noted that the price axis shows both positive and negative "prices." A negative price may be thought of as the price it would be necessary to *pay* individuals in order to induce them to consume in public a given amount of the commodity; that is, the price that it would be necessary to pay the consumers in order to induce them to disregard their aversion to be looked upon as odd or peculiar.

As we have already indicated, the point T in Figure 2 is the "taboo breaking point." T represents the number of units at which an *expected* total quantity demanded of T units would result in an *actual* quantity

FIGURE 2

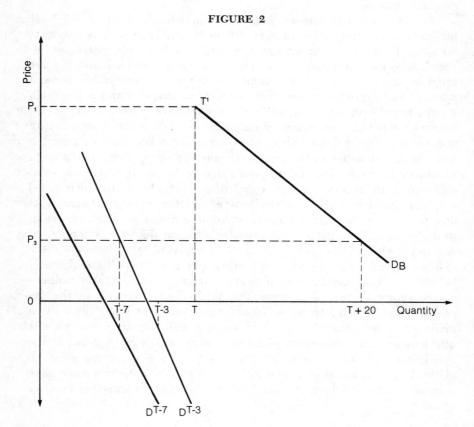

demanded of T units at some *real* price. Now, what has to be explained is why an expected demand of less than T units, say $T - 3$ units, would not yield an actual demand of $T - 3$ units at a positive price but only at a "negative price." Let the curve D^{T-3} be the demand curve that would exist if consumers thought the total demand was $T - 3$. Now, at any positive price, say P_3, the amount demanded would be less than $T - 3$, say $T - 7$. The price P_3 can therefore exist only if there is inaccurate information of the total quantity demanded. Once consumers discovered that at P_3 only $T - 7$ was purchased, and believed that this was the demand that would be sustained, their demand would shift to the D^{T-7} curve. At P_3 the amount purchased would now be less than $T - 7$ and demand would now shift to a curve to the left of the D^{T-7} curve. This procedure would go on until the demand was zero at P_3. We thus introduce a gap into our demand function and focus attention on an interesting psychological phenomenon that may affect demand. What we are suggesting, essentially, is that given "accurate expectations" of the total quantity demanded at any real price. In other words, this is a case in which a commodity will either "go over big" or not "go over" at all. It will be noted that at P_3 zero units or $T + 20$ units (Figure 2) may be taken off the market given "accurate expectations" of the total quantity demanded. It would seem, therefore, that "accurate expectations" of the total quantity demanded at P_3 can have two values depending upon whether people are generally pessimistic or optimistic about other consumers' demands for the commodity in question. If everybody expects that everybody else would not care much for the commodity, then zero units would be the accurate expectation of the total quantity demanded; if everybody, on the other hand, expects others to take up the commodity with some degree of enthusiasm, then $T + 20$ units would be the accurate expectation of the total quantity demanded. The factors that would determine one set of expectations rather than the other are matters of empirical investigation in the field of social psychology. The factors involved may be the history of the community, the people's conservatism or lack of conservatism, the type and quantity of advertising about the commodity under consideration, etc.

The really significant point in Figure 2 is T^1, the first point on the real demand curve D_B. As already indicated, it is the point at which the maximum bid of the marginal unit demanded is P_t and the total market demand is T units. If the price were higher than P_t, the Tth unit would not be demanded and all buyers would leave the market because of the effect of the taboo at less than a consumption of T units. By way of summary we might say that the whole point of this section is an attempt to show that in cases where social taboos affect demand the real demand curve may not start at the price-axis but that the smallest possible quantity demanded may be some distance to the right of the price-axis.

IV. THE SNOB EFFECT

Thus far, in our conceptual experiment and diagrammatic analysis, we have considered only the bandwagon effect. We now consider the reverse effect—the demand behaviour for those commodities with regard to which the individual consumer acts like a snob. Here, too, we assume at first that the quantity demanded by a consumer is a function of price and of the total market demand, but that the individual consumer's demand is negatively correlated with the total market demand. In the snob case it is rather obvious that the external consumption effect must reach a limit although the limit may be where one snob constitutes the only buyer. For most commodities and most buyers, however, the motivation for exclusiveness is not that great; hence the marginal external consumption effect reaches zero before that point. If the commodity is to be purchased at all, the external consumption effect must reach a limit, at some price, where the quantity demanded has a positive value. From this it follows that after a point the principle of the diminishing marginal external consumption effect must manifest itself. We thus have in the snob effect an opposite but completely symmetrical relationship to the bandwagon effect.

The analysis of markets in which all consumers behave as snobs follows along the same lines as our analysis of the bandwagon effect. Because of the similarity we will be able to get through our analysis of the snob effect in short order. We begin, as before, by letting the alternate total market demands that serve as parameters for alternate individual demand curves be indicated by the superscripts $a, b, \ldots, n$ (where $a < b < n$). Let the individual demand functions be $d_1, d_2, \ldots d_n$, where there are n consumers in the market. Again, d_3^a signifies the individual demand curve for consumer 3 on the assumption that he expects the total market demand to be "a" units. By adding

$$d_1^a + d_2^a + \ldots + d_n^a = D^a$$
$$d_1^b + d_2^b + \ldots + d_n^b = D^b$$

$$\cdot \qquad \cdot$$
$$\cdot \qquad \cdot$$
$$\cdot \qquad \cdot$$

$$d_1^n + d_2^n + \ldots + d_n^n = D^n$$

we obtain the market demand functions on the alternate assumptions of consumers expecting the total market demands to be $a, b, \ldots, n$. Due to snob behaviour the curves $D^a, D^b, \ldots, D^n$ move to the left as the expected total market demand increases. This is shown in Figure 3. Using the same procedure as before we obtain the virtual equilibrium points $E^a, E^b, \ldots, E^n$. They represent the only points on the curves $D^a, D^b, \ldots, D^n$ that are consistent with consumers' expectations (and hence with the assumption of accurate information). The locus of these virtual equilibrium points is the demand curve D_s.

Now, given a price change from P_2 to P_1 we can separate the effect of the price change into a price effect and a snob effect. In Figure 3 we see that the net increase in the quantity demanded due to the reduction in price is ab. The price effect, however, is ax. That is, if every consumer expected no increase in the total quantity demanded then the total quantity demanded at P_1 would be Ox. The more extreme snobs will react to this increase in the total quantity demanded and will leave the market. The total quantity demanded will hence be reduced by bx. The net result is therefore an increase in demand of only ab.

It may be of interest to examine some of the characteristics of the curves in Figure 3. First we may note that all the points on the curves other than D_s (except $E^a, E^b, \ldots, E^n$) are theoretical points that have significance only under conditions of imperfect knowledge. Second, we may note from the diagram that the demand curve for snobs is less

FIGURE 3

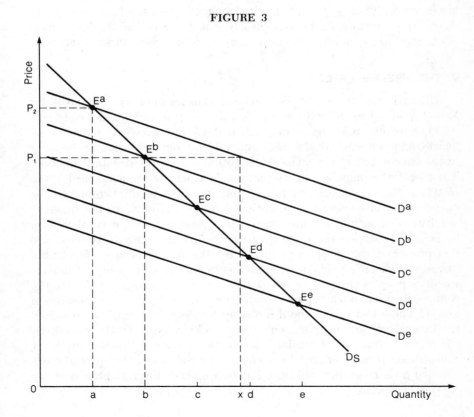

elastic than the demand curves where there are no snob effects. The reason for this, of course, is that the increase in demand due to a reduction in price is counterbalanced, in part, by some snobs leaving the market because of the increase in total consumption (i.e., the decrease in the snob value of the commodity). It should be clear, however, that the snob effect, as defined, can never be in excess of the price effect since this would lead to a basic contradiction. If the snob effect were greater than the price effect, then the quantity demanded at a lower price would be less than the quantity demanded at a higher price. This implies that some of the snobs in the market at the higher price leave the market when there is a reduction in the total quantity demanded; which, of course, is patently inconsistent with our definition of snob behaviour. It therefore follows that the snob effect is never greater than the price effect. It follows, also, that D_s is monotonically decreasing if $D^a, D^b, \ldots,$ D^n are monotonically decreasing.

Finally, it may be interesting to note another difference between the usual functional demand curve and the D_s curve. In the usual demand curve the buyers at higher prices always remain in the market at lower prices. That is, from the price point of view, the bids to buy are cumulative downward. This is clearly not the case in the D_s curve. Such terms as intramarginal buyers may be meaningless in snob markets.

V. THE VEBLEN EFFECT

Although the theory of conspicuous consumption as developed by Veblen and others is quite a complex and subtle sociological construct we can, for our purposes, quite legitimately abstract from the psychological and sociological elements and address our attention exclusively to the effects that conspicuous consumption has on the demand function. The essential economic characteristic with which we are concerned is the fact that the utility derived from a unit of a commodity employed for purposes of conspicuous consumption depends not only on the inherent qualities of that unit, but also on the price paid for it. It may, therefore, be helpful to divide the price of a commodity into two categories; the real price and the conspicuous price. By the real price we refer to the price the consumer paid for the commodity in terms of money. The conspicuous price is the price other people think the consumer paid for the commodity and which therefore determines its conspicuous consumption utility. These two prices would probably be identical in highly organized markets where price information is common knowledge. In other markets, where some can get "bargains" or special discounts the real price or conspicuous price need not be identical. In any case, the quantity demanded by a consumer will be a function of both the real price and the conspicuous price.

The market demand curve for commodities subject to conspicuous consumption can be derived through a similar diagrammatical method (summarized in Figure 4). This time we let the superscripts $1, 2, \ldots, n$

FIGURE 4

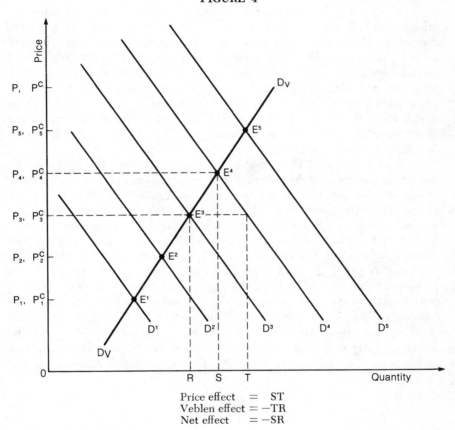

Price effect $=$ ST
Veblen effect $= -$TR
Net effect $= -$SR

stand for the expected conspicuous prices. The real prices are $P_1, P_2, \ldots, P_n$. The individual demand functions are $d_1, d_2, \ldots, d_n$. In this way d_6^3 stands for the demand curve of consumer number 6 if he expects a conspicuous price of P_3^c. We can now add across $d_1^1, d_2^1, \ldots, d_n^1$ and get the market demand curve D^1 which indicates the quantities demanded at alternate prices if all consumers expected a conspicuous price of P_1^c. In a similar manner we obtain $D^2, D^3, \ldots, D^n$. The market demand curves will, of course, up to a point, shift to the right as the expected conspicuous price increases. Now on every curve $D^1, D^2, \ldots, D^n$ in Figure 4 only one point can be a virtual equilibrium point if we assume that consumers possess accurate market information—the point where the real price is equal to the conspicuous price (that is, where $P_1 = P_1^c, P_2 = P_2^c, \ldots, P_n = P_n^c$). The locus of these virtual equilibrium points $E^1, E^2, \ldots, E^n$ gives us the demand curve D_V.

As before, we can separate the effects of a change in price into two effects—the price effect, and, what we shall call for want of a better term, the Veblen effect. In Figure 4 it will be seen that a change in price from P_4 to P_3 will reduce the quantity demanded by RS. The price effect is to increase the quantity demanded by ST; that is, the amount that would be demanded if there were no change in the expected conspicuous price would be OT. However, at the lower price a number of buyers would leave the market because of the reduced utility derived from the commodity at that lower conspicuous price. The Veblen effect is therefore RT.

It should be noted that unlike the D_S curve, the D_V curve can be positively inclined, negatively inclined or a mixture of both. It all depends on whether at alternate price changes the Veblen effect is greater or less than the price effect. It is possible that in one portion of the curve one effect may predominate while in another portion another may predominate. It is to be expected, however, that in most cases, if the curve is not monotonically decreasing it will be shaped like a backward S, as illustrated in Figure 5A. The reasons for this are as follows: First, there must be a price so high that no units of the commodity will be purchased at that price owing to the income constraint (among other reasons). This is the price P_n in Figure 5A, and it implies that there must be some point at which the curve shifts from being positively inclined to being negatively inclined as price increases. Second, there must be some point of satiety for the good. This is the point T in Figure 5A.

FIGURE 5

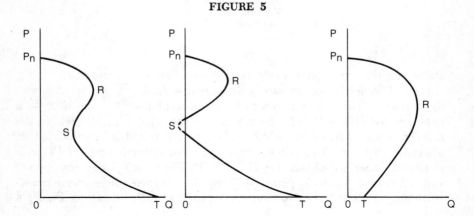

It therefore follows that some portion of the curve must be monotonically decreasing to reach T if there exists some minimum price at which the Veblen effect is zero. It is of course reasonable to assume that there is some low price at which the commodity would cease to have any value for purposes of conspicuous consumption. If this last assumption does not hold, which is unlikely, then the curve could have the shape indicated in Figure 5C. Otherwise, it would have the general shape indicated in Figure 5A, or it might be in two segments as illustrated in Figure 5B.

VI. MIXED EFFECTS

Any real market for semidurable or durable goods will most likely contain consumers that are subject to one or a combination of the effects discussed heretofore. Combining these effects presents no new formal difficulties with respect to the determination of the market demand curve, although it complicates the diagrammatic analysis considerably. The major principle, however, still holds. For any price there is a quantity demanded such that the marginal external consumption effect (or the marginal Veblen effect) for all buyers but one, is zero. This implies that for every price change there is a point at which people cease reacting to each other's quantity changes, regardless of the direction of these reactions. If this is so, then for every price there is a determinate quantity demanded, and hence the demand curve is determinate.

Now, for every price change we have distinguished between the price effect and some other, such as the snob, the Veblen, or the bandwagon effect. In markets where all four effects are present we should be able to separate out and indicate the direction of each of them that will result from a price change. That is, every price change will result in two positive and two negative effects—two which, other things being equal, will increase the quantity demanded, and two which, other things being equal, will decrease it. Which effects will be positive and which will be negative will depend on the relative strength of the Veblen effect as against the price effect. The Veblen and the price effects will depend directly on the direction of the price change. An increase in price will therefore result in price and bandwagon effects that are negative, and Veblen and snob effects that are positive, provided that the price effect is greater than the Veblen effect; that is, if the net result is a decrease in the quantity demanded at the higher price. If, on the other hand, the Veblen effect is more powerful than the price effect, given a price increase, then the bandwagon effect would be positive and the snob effect negative. The reverse would of course be true for price declines.

The market demand curve for a commodity where different consumers are subject to different types of effects can be obtained diagrammatically through employing the methods developed above—although the diagrams would be quite complicated. There is no point in adding still more diagrams to illustrate this. Briefly, the method would be somewhat as follows: (1) Given the demand curves for every individual, in which the expected total quantity demanded is a parameter for each curve, we can add these curves laterally and obtain a map of aggregate demand curves, in which each aggregate curve is based on a given total quantity demanded. (2) The locus of the equilibrium points on each aggregate demand curve (as derived in Figure 1) gives us a market demand curve that accounts for both bandwagon and snob effects. This last curve assumes that only one conspicuous price exists. For every conspicuous price there exists a separate map of aggregate demand curves from which different market demand curves are obtained. (3) This procedure yields a map of market demand curves in which each curve is based on a different conspicuous price. Employing the method used in Figure 4 we obtain our final market demand curve which accounts for bandwagon, snob, and Veblen effects simultaneously.

VII. CONCLUSION

It is not unusual for a writer in pure theory to end his treatise by pointing out that the science is really very young; that there is a great deal more to be done; that the formulations presented are really of a very tentative nature; and that the best that can be hoped for is that his treatise may in some small way pave the road for future formulations that are more directly applicable to problems in the real world. This is another way of saying that work in pure theory is an investment in the future state of the science where the returns in terms of applications to real problems are really very uncertain. This is probably especially true of value theory where the investment in time and effort is more akin to the purchase of highly speculative stocks rather than the purchase of government bonds. Since this was only a brief essay on one aspect of value theory, the reader will hardly be surprised if the conclusions reached are somewhat less than revolutionary.

Essentially, we have attempted to do two things. First, we have tried to demonstrate that non-additivity is not necessarily an insurmountable obstacle in effecting a transition from individual to collective demand curves. Second, we attempted to take a step or two in the direction of incorporating various kinds of external consumption effects into the theory of consumers' demand. In order to solve our problem, we have introduced what we have called the principle of the diminishing marginal external consumption effect. We indicated some reasons for believing that for every individual, there is some point at which the marginal external consumption effect is zero. We have attempted to show that if this principle is admitted, then there are various ways of effecting a transition from individual to collective demand curves. The major conclusion reached is that under conditions of perfect knowledge (or accurate expectations) any point on the demand curve, for any given price, will be at that total quantity demanded where the marginal external consumption effect for all consumers but one, is equal to zero.

In comparing the demand curve in those situations where external consumption effects are present with the demand curve as it would be where these external consumption effects are absent, we made three basic points. (1) If the bandwagon effect is the most significant effect, the demand curve is more elastic than it would be if this external consumption effect were absent. (2) If the snob effect is the predominant effect, the demand curve is less elastic than otherwise. (3) If the Veblen effect is the predominant one, the demand curve is less elastic than otherwise, and some portions of it may even be positively inclined; whereas, if the Veblen effect is absent, the curve will be negatively inclined regardless of the importance of the snob effect in the market.

5. The Demand for Beer[*]

THOMAS F. HOGARTY and KENNETH G. ELZINGA

I. INTRODUCTION

This note presents estimates of the price and income elasticities of beer. Aside from the usual academic and commercial interest in learning of demand characteristics, knowledge of the demand for beer also has public policy implications due to the heavy taxation of the product. About 35 percent of the price of a glass of beer represents tax revenue with federal and state taxes on beer currently generating more than 1.5 billion dollars in revenue.

In what follows, we first summarize available knowledge on the demand for beer. Then we discuss the methodology and data employed in the present study. Finally, we present our findings and their implications.

II. PREVIOUS STUDIES

William Niskanen analyzed the markets for alcoholic beverages with aggregate time series data for the 22 years 1934–1941 and 1947–1960. Wholesale price indexes (including taxes) for spirits and wine were prepared specially for his study from data provided by the Washington State Liquor Control Board. The beer price indexes were derived from a (now discontinued) Census series by Niskanen on total expenditures for beer. The results of his study, as they apply to the demand for beer, were that: (1) the price elasticity of beer was about —0.7; (2) the income elasticity of beer was about —0.4; (3) spirits and beer were weak substitutes while the relations between the beer and wine markets were highly unstable.

Ira and Ann Horowitz, as part of their overall study of the beer industry, estimated the price and income elasticity of demand for beer with combined cross-section and time series data. Lacking specific data on beer prices, they used state excise tax levels as proxies. They found a weak, negative correlation between beer consumption and excise taxes on beer for 9 of the 13 years (1949–1961) studied. Their estimates of

[*] *The Review of Economics and Statistics,* vol. 54, no. 2 (May 1972), pp. 195–198.

income elasticity were uniformly positive, but not significantly different from zero after 1956.

III. THE PRESENT STUDY

Sample Data

The price indexes used in this study are based primarily on the FOB mill prices of "Blatz Pilsner" and "Pabst Blue Ribbon" beers for 48 states and the District of Columbia for the years 1956–1959. In raw form these price data consisted of FOB mill prices for cases of twenty-four 12-ounce returnable bottles, exclusive of state excise taxes and bottle deposits. We made the following adjustments:

1. Where prices changed during the year, we computed an average price, weighted in terms of the relative number of months the new price was in effect.

2. States vary enormously in terms of consumption of packaged and draft beer, e.g., in Alabama in 1956–1959 virtually all beer consumed was packaged beer; while in Wisconsin draught beer comprised some 40 percent of consumption. Niskanen calculated from 1947, 1954, and 1958 Census of Manufactures data that the average wholesale value of packaged beer, exclusive of all excise taxes, was about 1.8 times the average value of draught beer in each year. We used this relation to calculate approximate FOB prices (in case equivalents) for draught beer. After adding appropriate federal and state excise taxes to both the packaged and draught FOB prices, we computed for each state a weighted average price for each brand of beer, the weights then consisting of the relative proportions of packaged and draught beer consumed in the various states (U.S. Brewers Association).

3. These first three adjustments produced approximate retail prices for each of the two brands of beer. Our price index was then calculated as a simple average of these two brand prices.

4. Data on transport rates from Milwaukee for 1957 only were used in conjunction with the 1957 Blatz price data to estimate the impact of excluding transport rates from other years. These and other data on distances show this source of bias to be relatively minor.

5. A final insoluble problem was lack of reliable data on retail markups. Fortunately, in view of our results (see Section IV below), this defect causes modest concern.

6. As a final adjustment, the price indexes were expressed in real terms by means of the Bureau of Labor Statistics Consumer Price Index for 1956–1959.

Data on quantity (U.S. Brewers Association (USBA)), consisted of apparent consumption (in cases) per adult. Estimates of the *adult* population in each state consisted of interpolated Census data (1950, 1960). Estimates of state *per capita* income, also expressed in real terms, were derived from a special Census estimate (1966).

Methodological Issues and Data Problems

Two potential difficulties confront our attempt to estimate demand elasticities for beer. The first is the standard identification problem; the second results from our use of individual brand prices.

The first problem appears inconsequential. The period 1956–1959 was one of excess capacity in the beer industry.[1] Hence, the assumption of perfectly elastic supply appears appropriate.

The second problem appears almost as minor. To begin with, the brand structure of prices in the beer industry is (or at least was) relatively stable:

"Anheuser-Busch once conducted a survey involving 113,305 price comparisons in 78 areas. In over 100,000 comparisons, a differential of 5 cents per can or per 12-ounce bottle existed between Budweiser and the popular priced beers. In over 90 percent of the comparisons a 10 cent differential existed over local beers."

In addition, the nationwide market shares of Pabst and Blatz were relatively stable during 1956–1959, as were the shares of premium, popular, and local beers in three states during 1957–1960.[2] Finally, the prices of Pabst and Blatz can be considered representative of premium and popular priced beers, respectively. Unfortunately, price data for local beers are unavailable.

Ideally, of course, we should like to use a weighted index of prices, with the weights corresponding to the relative market shares of premium, popular, and local beers in the various states. Fortunately, however, our lack of data on prices of local beers and relative market shares does not seriously distort our price elasticity estimates.

---

[1] During 1956–1959, United States breweries, on the average, operated at about 64 percent of capacity.

[2] For Blatz, the correlations between market share in 1956 and market shares in 1957–1959 were 0.97, 0.87, and 0.81, respectively; for Pabst, the corresponding correlations were 0.99, 0.95, and 0.90, respectively.

For the three-state area comprised of Illinois, Michigan, and Wisconsin, the following market shares prevailed during 1957–1960.

Year	Premium Beers	Popular Priced Beers	Local Beers
1957	27.86	51.80	20.34
1958	28.54	50.13	21.33
1959	29.05	51.02	19.93
1960	29.51	50.22	20.27

Procedure

Our mode of analysis consisted of ordinary least squares with, at least initially, all variables expressed in logarithmic form, as in

$$\ln Q_{it} = b_0 + b_1 \ln P_{it} + b_2 \ln Y_{it} \tag{1}$$

where

Q_i = apparent consumption (in cases) of beer *per adult* in i^{th} state in year t

P_i = real price of case of beer in i^{th} state in year t

Y_i = real, *per capita* income in i^{th} state in year t

$i = 1, 2, \ldots, 45$

$t = 1, 2, 3, 4$

Estimates of the coefficients of equation (1) were made for each of the years 1956–1959 individually ($n = 45$) and for a combined sample consisting of data for the entire period ($n = 180$). A test for overall homogeneity indicated that all four cross-sections could be regarded as coming from the same population and hence only estimates for the entire period are presented.[3]

IV. RESULTS

As indicated in equation (1), our initial estimates presumed constant price and income elasticities. The estimates obtained are presented in table 1 (line 1).

With respect to price elasticity, our estimate of unity plus accords approximately with those of Niskanen in that neither Niskanen's esti-

---

[3] The test for overall homogeneity is:

$$F = \frac{\left[S_d{}^2 - \sum_{t-6} S_{at}{}^2 \right] \Big/ (T-1)(K+1)}{\sum_{t-6} S_{at}{}^2 \Big/ [N - T(K+1)]}$$

where

$S_d{}^2$ = residual sums of squares from grand regression ($n = 180$)

$S_{at}{}^2$ = residual sums of squares from cross-section regression t ($t = 1956, 57, 58, 59$) ($n = 45$)

T = number of years (sub-samples)

K = number of independent variables.

For our sample

$$F = \frac{[7.715 - 7.309]/9}{(7.309)/168} = 1.025$$

which is not statistically significant at the 0.05 level.

TABLE 1

**Estimates of Price and Income Elasticity[a] of Beer Based on Sample Excluding
States with Substantial Local Excise Taxation of Beer[b] ($n = 180$)**

	b_0	b_1	b_2	b_3[c]	b_4	$\bar{R}2$
(1)	−2.935	−1.128	0.926			.666
(2)	4.823	−0.992		0.942		.687
(3)	3.539	−0.889		0.430[d]	0.174[d]	.759

Entry identification:

b_0 = intercept.
b_1 = price elasticity.
b_2 = (constant) income elasticity.
b_3 = (median) income elasticity.
b_4 = elasticity of beer consumption with respect to national origin.
   [a] Unless otherwise indicated, all coefficients are significantly different from zero at the 0.01 level or better; however, unless otherwise indicated, none of the coefficients are significantly different from unity at the 0.10 level or better.
   [b] These states were Alabama, Georgia, Louisiana, and Tennessee.
   [c] The income elasticities in this column were calculated at the income level prevailing in the median income state.
   [d] Significantly different from unity at 0.01 level.

mates nor ours differed significantly from unity. The estimate of income elasticity was more surprising inasmuch as the Horowitzes found beer consumption to be unrelated to income while Niskanen found beer to be an inferior good. Experimentation with subsamples of high and low income states[4] demonstrated a tendency for the income elasticity of beer to vary inversely with the level of income.

Accordingly, we reformulated equation (1) to read:[5]

$$\ln Q_{it} = b_0 + b_1 \ln P_{it} - b_3 (1/Y_{it}) \tag{2}$$

The results of fitting equation (2) to our data are contained in table 1 (line 2). The estimate of income elasticity presented is calculated at the median level of real, *per capita* income.

Our next step consisted of adding as independent variables indexes of

---

   [4] The states were classified as high or low income according to whether or not their *per capita* income for 1956–1959 was above or below that for the *median* state.
   [5] The income elasticity for equation (2) is

$$I_E = e^{b_0 - b_3/Y} \cdot \frac{b_3}{QY}$$

$$= \frac{b_3}{Y} \text{ since } Q = \frac{e^{b_0 - b_3}}{Y}$$

$$= 2 \text{ when } Y = \frac{b_3}{2}.$$

Hence, income elasticity varies inversely with income and asymptotically approaches zero as income increases.

spirits and wine prices.[6] Unfortunately, these attempts were unsuccessful.[7] On the other hand, we were able to account, at least in part, for differences in taste. On the presumption that immigrants were more prone to beer drinking than native Anglo-Saxons, we introduced as a proxy variable the percent of each state's population that was foreign born. The results are presented in table 1 (line 3).

Thus, our final estimates of price and income elasticity for beer are —0.9 and 0.4, respectively. In addition, we estimate the beer-drinking capacity of the United States as a little more than two cans (12 ounces per adult per day).[8]

V.   CONCLUDING REMARKS

Although lack of price data on beer for the past decade makes prediction impossible, we note that from 1962 to 1969 per adult beer consumption increased by 16 percent while real, *per capita* income rose by 27 percent. Assuming stable real prices for beer, the implied income elasticity is 0.59. Average *per capita* income (1958 dollars) during 1962–1969 was approximately $2,250. At this level we estimate income elasticity as 0.37. Since average state taxes on beer increased about 7 percent in real terms during 1962–1969 our estimate appears sufficiently close to warrant confidence in its reliability.

Regarding implications for the future, it appears that the beer industry can anticipate moderate increases in consumption, assuming the price of beer remains relatively stable. Moreover, it further appears that excise taxes on beer could be reduced considerably with only modest losses in tax revenues. The desirability of such reductions might be questioned on noneconomic grounds; however, there appears little doubt that beer excise taxes are regressive.

---

[6] Our initial step consisted of using excise taxes on spirits and wine as proxies for price. This procedure produced cross elasticity estimates of zero for both spirits and wine. Our second attempt consisted of using the retail price of Seagram's 7 Crown (fifth) as an index of retail prices in general.

[7] The estimates of cross elasticity between beer consumption and the price of spirits were statistically significant, but negative. These results persisted despite use of subsamples which excluded dry, moonshine, and transient liquor traffic states. We rejected these results on the grounds that beer and spirits were unlikely complements. Nonetheless, these results, insofar as they applied to the estimates of price and income elasticity for beer, were roughly in accord with those presented in table 1.

[8] Ignoring price effects, the drinking capacity of the United States is that level of consumption which would prevail at infinitely high levels of income. In our formulation this is $e^b{}_0$ cases per adult per year or, as noted, approximately two cans per adult per day.

6. Retail and Wholesale Demand and Marketing Order Policy for Fresh Navel Oranges*

GLENN NELSON and TOM H. ROBINSON

The nature of the demand for fresh navel oranges was the subject of considerable controversy in early 1974. Navel oranges are marketed under the provisions of a federal marketing order authorized by the Agricultural Marketing Agreement Act of 1937, as amended. Fresh shipments of oranges to domestic and Canadian markets are controlled by means of prorates on a weekly basis. In early 1974 the Naval Orange Administrative Committee (NOAC), U.S. Department of Agricultural (USDA), Cost of Living Council (CLC), and elected officials became collected by the Bureau of Labor Statistics (BLS) and reported by weekly shipments.

The CLC became concerned when, despite a projected increase of 14 percent in 1973–74 navel orange production, prorates were below 1972–73 levels and prices were above a year earlier. The CLC concluded that the NOAC was acting to enhance the price of fresh shipments by restricting the amounts reaching the market. Acting through the CLC Food Committee chaired by George P. Shultz, secretary of the treasury, the secretary of agriculture was requested to raise the weekly prorates above the shipping schedule proposed by the NOAC. USDA and NOAC resisted, but prorates moved above year earlier levels in the last week of January. Fresh market shipments increased in February and March and prices declined, after a short lag in some cases. Orange growers were angry and continued to seek lower prorates.

On March 28 representatives of growers, retailers, USDA, Department of Justice (to ensure that antitrust laws were not violated), and CLC met at the invitation of CLC. CLC urged retailers to feature navel oranges so consumers would be aware of the large supply and reasonable prices; growers were urged to continue to ship all fruit of adequate

* *American Journal of Agricultural Economics,* vol. 60, no. 3 (August 1978), pp. 502–9.

quality to the fresh market. The position of John T. Dunlop, director of CLC, and Kenneth J. Fedor, director of the Office of Food, CLC, as reported in the *New York Times*, was: "increased shipments at lower prices might mean lower total revenues for navel orange growers, who are concentrated in California and Arizona. But, . . . supermarket "specials"—combinations of price cuts and heavy advertising—could generate extra volume and revenues."

The uproar from growers continued. They successfully marshalled influential congressional support for their position. In early April, CLC lost the support of the White House. The lower prorates recommended by NOAC were approved by USDA. Fresh shipments declined and prices rose. The NOAC position is stated clearly in its 1973–74 *Annual Report:*

> Interference with the Marketing Order by the Cost of Living Council caused needless loss to navel orange growers estimated by some industry sources to be $3 to $4 million. . . .
> The Cost of Living Council's interference began when it forced its influence on the secretary, and in 10 of 12 consecutive weeks beginning the week ending January 10, compelled weekly allotments higher than recommended by the Committee with little or no regard for consequences to the industry. . . .
> The chaos and market instability caused by actions of the Council resulted in average f.o.b. prices dropping from about $3.86 a carton to $3.25 a carton during the 10-week period. With excellent fruit quality and favorable marketing conditions then existing, such purposeless price deterioration would not have occurred had the Committee been permitted to fulfill its responsibility and the industry been able to market the oranges under orderly marketing conditions. Ironically, trade surveys during the period revealed practically no reduction in retail prices of navel oranges—a fact that belies the justification given by the Cost of Living Council for its unconscionable intervention in the industry's business (p. 4).

The purpose of this article is to examine the merits of the opposing positions. The critical economic factors are the elasticity of wholesale demand and the behavior of the wholesale-retail price spread as wholesale prices fall. A model of the retail and wholesale demand for fresh navel oranges is specified and estimated in order to ascertain the underlying economic behavior.

Model and Parameter Estimates

Consumer demand is specified as

$$PR = f(QN, QF, QA, QG, M), \tag{1}$$

where PR is real retail price (1967 dollars), QN is per capita quantity of fresh navel oranges; QF, per capita quantity of other fresh oranges; QA, per capita quantity of apples; QG, per capita quantity of fresh grapefruit; and M, a monthly binary variable included to account for systematic seasonal variation in product quality and consumer tastes. Monthly supply of fresh navel oranges is assumed to be predetermined by natural processes and the decisions of the NOAC.

Wholesale demand is specified as

$$PW = g(PR, TQN, W), \tag{2}$$

where PW is real wholesale price (1967 dollars) PR, is real retail price as in (1), TQN is total quantity of navel oranges, and W is the real wage (1967 dollars) of grocery employees. Note that QN equals TQN divided by population.

The data include the months of December through May in the 1967–68 through 1975–76 seasons. The retail price of fresh navel oranges is collected by the Bureau of Labor Statistics (BLS) and reported by USDA on a dollars-per-carton basis. The quantity data for shipments of fresh oranges and grapefruit and the wholesale price of navel oranges are found in the reports of the NOAC and the Growers Administrative Committee of the Florida Citrus Industry. The weekly quantity data were first aggregated into figures on million cartons per month, and then the actual monthly totals were converted to a standard 30-day month by multiplying by the appropriate fraction, for example, 30/28 or 30/31. The monthly wholesale price in dollars per carton was computed from a weighted average of weekly f.o.b. shipping point prices.

The quantity of apples is the U.S. commercial crop in billion pounds as reported by USDA. The annual apple crop figure is used for each monthly observation. While crude, this approximation is deemed adequate for the six-month period, especially in the presence of the monthly binary variables. Wage is measured by the monthly BLS reports on the average hourly earnings of employees of grocery, meat, and vegetable stores. The consumer price index (1974 = 100) was used to convert all prices and wages to real values. Population refers to total resident U.S. population. Finally, the February 1972 observation was eliminated from the analysis because of the very high retail price recorded in Chicago, which was inconsistent with observations on all other variables including retail prices in other cities, and which could not be explained by any known factor.

The model represented by equations (1) and (2) was applied to two major retail markets, New York and Chicago, and a common wholesale market. The results are displayed in Table 1. Several pre-tests with respect to included variables and functional form were performed on the 1967–68 through 1974–75 data. After these were complete and the functional forms in Table 1 were hypothesized, the regression analysis was extended through 1975–76 as a test structural validity. The computed (asymptotic) F-statistics for the equations in columns (1) through (4) of Table 1 were 1.2, 0.7, 1.5, and 0.4, respectively, which are encouraging.

TABLE 1
Retail and Wholesale Demand Equations for Fresh Navel Oranges in New York, Chicago, and Shipping Points

Explanatory Variables[a]	Retail[b] New York	Retail[b] Chicago	Wholesale: Shipping Point Destined For: Structural[b] New York	Structural[b] Chicago	Restricted Reduced Form[c] New York	Restricted Reduced Form[c] Chicago
Quantity of navels						
QN_t	−.179 (.264)[d]	−.095 (.259)	−	−	−	−
QN_{t-1}	−.580 (.299)	−.296 (.286)	−	−	−	−
QN_{t-2}	−.232 (.279)	−.372 (.272)	−	−	−	−
TQN_t	−	−	−.234 (.099)	−.195 (.121)	−.266	−.215
$(TQN)_t^2$	−	−	.0239 (.0127)	.0183 (.0158)	.0239	.0183
TQN_{t-1}	−	−	−	−	−.103	−.064
TQN_{t-2}	−	−	−	−	−.041	−.080
Other fresh oranges						
QF_t	.292 (.333)	.314 (.320)	−	−	.110	.143
QF_{t-1}	.086 (.354)	.447 (.345)	−	−	.032	.203
QU_{t-2}	−.445 (.403)	−.685 (.393)	−	−	−.167	−.311
Other substitutes						
QA_t	−1.309 (.355)	−.936 (.342)	−	−	−.491	−.426
QG_t	−.728 (.188)	−.318 (.183)	−	−	−.273	−.144
Monthly binaries						
DEC_t	−1.802 (.821)	−1.893 (.812)	−	−	−.676	−.861
JAN_t	−.543 (.600)	−.993 (.587)	−	−	−.204	−.452
MAR_t	−.262 (.506)	−.570 (.489)	−	−	−.098	−.259
APR_t	−.657 (.445)	−.763 (.431)	−	−	−.247	−.347
MAY_t	−1.575 (.520)	−1.246 (.507)	−	−	−.591	−.567
Grocery wages						
W_t	−	−	−1.757 (.593)	−2.171 (.647)	−1.757	−2.171
Navel retail price						
PR_t	−	−	.375 (.068)	.455 (.647)	−	−
Intercept	16.279 (1.531)	12.647 (1.494)	4.653 (1.823)	5.369 (1.911)	10.758	11.123
F-statistic	13.5 [13,39][e]	5.9 [13,39]	38.4 [4,48]	24.3 [4,48]	−	−
R^2	.82	.66	.76[f]	.67[f]	−	−

a See text for detailed definitions.

b Estimated by three-stage-least squares.

c Constructed by substituting the retail equation into the structural wholesale equation. A population figure of 210.8 million (February 1974) was used in adjusting the coefficients of QN from a per capita to a total quantity basis.

d The figures in parentheses are the appropriate standard errors (adjusted for degrees of freedom).

e The figures in brackets are the degrees of freedom for the (asymptotic) F-statistic.

f Based upon residuals computed from the original observations on the explanatory variables.

Interpretation of Results

The total retail price flexibilities for New York and Chicago, evaluated at the mean, are $-.26$ and $-.22$, respectively. As per capita shipments vary seasonally from low to high levels, the flexibilities vary in range of about $-.13$ to $-.45$. The statistical significance of the coefficients of the individual quantity variables is generally low and some coefficients possess unexpected signs, as is common in lagged formulations due to multicollinearity problems. While the individual coefficients are unbiased estimates of the interim impacts in each month, conclusions based upon the total influence of a variable entering with several lags (i.e., the sum of the individual coefficients) have a stronger basis than those based upon individual coefficients of lagged variables. The retail demand for navel oranges alone is considerably more elastic than the demand for all fresh oranges, as is expected. Matthews, Womack, and Huang estimated a price flexibility for all fresh oranges of $-.83$ from annual data. George and King found a retail price elasticity of $-.66$ for all fresh oranges.

The fresh fruit substitutes of apples and grapefruit exhibit considerably more statistical significance than shown in prior studies. Rausser experimented with these and other fresh fruit substitutes but deleted them from his final model estimated from 1954–67 data due to insignificance and other undesirable features. Matthews, Womack, and Huang included apples and bananas with encouraging but less statistically significant results.

The failure of orange concentrate product prices to enter into retail demand is consistent with most, but not all, other studies. Matthews, Womack, and Huang did not include orange concentrate prices. Prato, as reported by Rausser, found that the demands for fresh oranges and concentrate are independent in the winter season that is the subject of this analysis. A series of studies at the University of Florida of the demand for processed orange products has not included fresh oranges as a substitute. Rausser included frozen orange concentrate and chilled orange juice in his study of the demand for fresh oranges.

Income was deleted from the retail demand equation despite the strong theoretical basis because of the unexpected, negative sign. The omission of income is consistent with Rausser's model. However, George and King found a substantial income response for oranges. Matthews, Womack, and Huang included income, but they also included a time trend. The negative impact of the time trend nearly neutralizes the positive impact of income. Since the two variables are highly correlated and not statistically significant, the results may be spurious.

The monthly binary variables were included to account for systematic seasonal influences not contained in other explanatory variables. The smooth pattern assumed by the coefficients is a reflection of product quality reaching a peak in midseason.

The structural wholesale demand equations are similar to the function estimated by Matthews, Womack, and Huang. The results are also similar, with increased quantity showing a negative impact on wholesale prices over the full range in Matthews, Womack, and Huang, and over much of the relevant range in this study. The restricted reduced form equations, also shown in Table 1, are useful for further analysis of wholesale prices. (The restricted reduced form estimates differ from direct estimates of the reduced form due to the inclusion of more structural information in the former.) The total wholesale price flexibility, evaluated at the mean, is $-.32$ in both restricted reduced form equations. As discussed for retail demand, the seasonal variation of quantities yields a variation of flexibilities over a range of about $-.1$ to $-.45$. These estimates exhibit the same seasonal pattern as found by Rausser, but his flexibilities tend to be about double these estimates in absolute value.

The price impact multipliers associated with changes in fresh navel shipments are displayed in Table 2. The larger total multiplier for the New York retail price as compared to the Chicago retail price may be partially a result of New York prices averaging about 11 percent higher than Chicago prices. The total multipliers for the wholesale price developed from the two models are very similar, which, of course, is reassuring. While the distribution of the interim multipliers does vary between New York and Chicago, the maximum price impact of an increase in shipments consistently occurs in the second or third ensuing month rather than the current month.

The results in Table 2 contrast sharply with those of Heien for all fresh oranges. Heien regresses retail prices on a distributed lag of whole-

TABLE 2
Price Impacts of a One Million Carton Increase in Fresh Navel Shipments

Month	Retail Price		Wholesale Price Based Upon	
	New York	Chicago	New York	Chicago
1	−8.6	−4.6	−3.6	−4.0
2	−28.0	−14.3	−10.3	−6.4
3	−11.2	−17.9	−4.1	−8.0
Total	−47.8	−36.8	−18.1	−18.4

sale prices and wage rates in a "price equation." His conclusion is that a 1.0 percent change in wholesale price is associated with a 0.4 percent change in retail price and that the maximum impact of wholesale price on retail price occurs in the current month. Since retail and wholesale prices are both endogenous in the model presented in this paper, an expression describing the elasticity of retail prices with respect to whole-sale prices has no analytic content beyond its value as a descriptive statistic. However, comparisons among total multipliers such as those in Table 2 are useful and analytically sound. Comparing the total multi-pliers with the sample means for prices, we find that the percentage change in retail prices in response to a change in shipments equals about 80–95 percent of the percentage change in wholesale prices. (The total multipliers as a percentage of the sample mean prices are: New York retail, 6.2 percent; Chicago retail, 5.4 percent; wholesale based upon New York, 6.6 percent; and wholesale based upon Chicago, 6.8 percent.) Furthermore, while the interim multipliers for retail and wholesale prices show similar distributions, this study makes it clear that both prices lag underlying causal shifters by two or three months. Thus, the structural approach followed in this paper that systematically accounts for simul-taneity and exogenous factors yields quite different results than the simpler theory and "common sense" approach of Heien.

Prior to using the model to analyze the controversy between NOAC and CLC in early 1974, the ability of the model to explain the period must be examined. Comparisons of actual and predicted retail and whole-

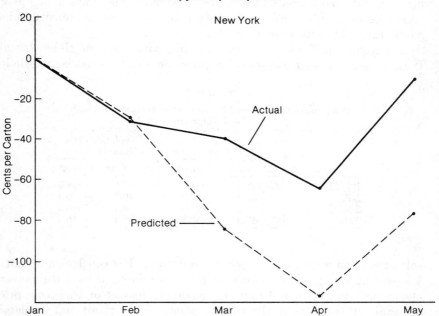

FIGURE 1A

Actual and Predicted Retail Price Changes from a January Base, January–May 1974

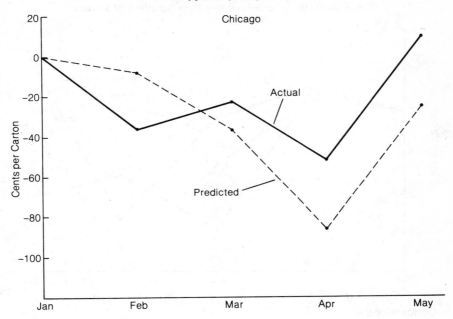

FIGURE 1B
Actual and Predicted Retail Price Changes from a January
Base, January–May 1974

sale price changes are presented in Figures 1 and 2, respectively. The retail price equation for New York overestimates the decline in prices as fresh shipments rose, but the equation does catch the turning point. While merely conjecture, the unexpected strength of prices might have been a reflection of unusual stimulation of demand through extensive advertising in response to CLC jawboning. The retail price equation for Chicago gives a better representation of actual changes in prices, but also overestimates the April low point. The predictions of wholesale price changes are less satisfactory than the retail estimates. The models predict a trough in April and a marked rise in May. Actual wholesale price reached a low point in March and declined slightly from April to May. The large decline observed from February to March may be a reflection of a major strike by independent truckers in February as they were subjected to a financial squeeze growing out of the OPEC instigated petroleum crisis. The resulting strain on the transportation system and abrupt shift in trucking rates may have appeared with a brief lag. Ending on a more positive note, the wholesale models accurately predict a small rise in February prices as shipments rose followed by lower prices in March and April as higher levels of shipments were maintained.

FIGURE 2

**Actual and Predicted Wholesale Price Changes from a
January Base, January–May 1974
(based upon the restricted reduced form equations in Table 1)**

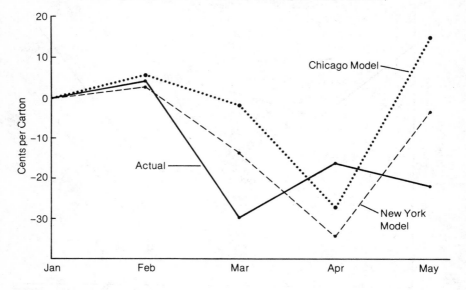

Conclusions

An examination of the data and the analytic results leads to several
conclusions. The NOAC appears to have limited shipments with the
results that (a) quantities available to consumers were lower, (b) retail
prices were higher, and (c) grower and packer total receipts were lower.
This third conclusion is surprising in view of whom NOAC represents,
and we return to it at the end of this section.

Actual retail prices of navel oranges fell significantly as shipments
increased in early 1975, contrary to NOAC assertions. New York retail
prices, measured in current dollars, declined 63 cents per carton or 6.2
percent from January to April. Current dollar Chicago retail prices declined 48 cents per carton or 5.2 percent over this same period. While
the fall in New York prices was less than predicted by the model, the
analytic results in this paper support the CLC position that retail prices
of fresh navels respond to shipments, that is, the observed price decline
was not a "fluke" but consistent with general behavioral patterns of consumers, retailers, and other middlemen. The estimated retail price flexibility consistent with the early 1974 context is −.4. Thus, consumers
increased their total expenditures on fresh navels as shipments rose and
prices declined.

The actual wholesale price (current dollars) fell 23 cents per carton or 6.2 percent from January to the March–April average. This decline was comparable in percentage terms to the drop in retail prices. The actual spread between wholesale and retail prices shrank over this period, which is consistent with the predictions of the models. There is no indication that "middlemen" were able to maintain retail prices at high levels while depressing shipping point prices as shipments rose. To the contrary, there is some evidence that wholesale-retail price spreads narrow at high levels of shipments.

Fresh navel shipments in February, March, and April were 54 percent, 55 percent, and 22 percent greater, respectively, than January shipments. The much smaller percentage decline in wholesale prices would seem to confirm the analytic results that NOAC was operating in the elastic portion of the demand curve. Comparing actual 1974 figures with actual 1973 figures, fresh navel shipments in February–April, 1974 were 130 percent greater than in February–April 1973. Wholesale prices in March–May 1974 were 15 percent below those of the same period in 1973. Even recalling that production of other fresh oranges declined from 1973 to 1974, the year-to-year comparison also is evidence of an elastic demand curve. Thus, there is little reason to believe the CLC action to increase shipments led to lower receipts for growers, as NOAC claimed, even if one were to account explicitly for packer charges. These results support the conclusion that total receipts to growers and packers increased.

We are puzzled by the actions of the NOAC with respect to its members' total receipts, assuming the analytic results are accepted. The following three hypotheses are suggested as a basis for further thought and analysis by others. First, restricting supply to the domestic fresh market was advantageous from an industry viewpoint because the demands faced in other outlets (primarily exports and processing) were even more elastic. Relative elasticities are the crucial factor in short-term marketing decisions. Second, restricting supply to the domestic fresh market was advantageous from an industry viewpoint of all producers of oranges. As noted earlier, the demand for all fresh oranges is less elastic than the demand for fresh navel oranges—and perhaps the former demand was inelastic. Third, the NOAC may simply have made a mistake, or borne a short-term economic cost, in the heat of an intense political battle. The objective of reducing the role of CLC in the food sector may have been so overriding that NOAC and USDA inadvertently or purposely ignored other objectives.

7. Seemingly Unrelated Regression and the Demand for Automobiles of Different Sizes, 1965—75: A Disaggregate Approach[*]

RODNEY L. CARLSON

I. INTRODUCTION

The automobile industry exerts substantial impact on the level of economic activity in the United States. In fact, the importance of automobile production to the American economy needs little emphasis—almost 200 million cars have been purchased since World War II and one business in six is automotive in nature. While significant research has been done on the total demand for automobiles, little study has been made of the demand for automobiles of different sizes. Also, the literature is void of any analysis on (1) how increasing car prices, the recessionary economy, and the energy crisis (higher gasoline prices and/or possible shortages) are affecting sales of different size automobiles and (2) the relative importance of these factors in the present automobile market.

Possibly the most elaborate study ever made of automobile demand was by Roos and Szeliski. Their guiding premise, that consumers do not buy new cars but transportation service that is continually changing, was used in many later studies. Two such researchers were Chow and Nerlove; their resulting formulations, however, were considerably different. Suits was the first to consider consumer credit in his demand model, while Houthakker and Taylor were the first to derive the demand relationship from a first-order differential equation in order to build a more dynamic model. Atkinson, interested in analyzing post–World War II demand, fitted a log-linear model while Huang, working later, used a hybrid form of probit analysis and multiple regression to find the probability of auto purchase given certain income, social, and demo-

* *Journal of Business,* vol. 51, no. 2 (1978), pp. 243–62.

graphic variables. Probably the most recent study on automobiles has been done by Smith. By using time series of cross-sectional data he was able to investigate the effects of changes in the distribution of income on auto sales.

These previous studies of automobile demand all explained auto purchase by using highly aggregative techniques. This research assumes that as little aggregation as possible is desirable in a model of the new car market. This can be done by breaking the auto market into segments, where each submarket would have less variation in the reasons for automobile purchase.

This study will disaggregate total automobile sales according to manufacturer's classification—subcompact, compact, intermediate, full size, and luxury—for several reasons. First, data are available which make such classification possible. And second, car size is a reasonably good proxy for gasoline consumption, a classification useful for examining sales trends in light of the energy crisis.

The growth of automobile sales in the late 1960s and early 1970s was caused primarily by the emergence of the small car market. In 1968, small car sales accounted for 10 percent of the market; however, by 1973, domestic and imported small cars accounted for 50 percent of total sales. This shift in demand to smaller cars (subcompacts and compacts) has been mainly at the expense of the full-size automobile. Figure 1 shows

FIGURE 1
Automobile Sales in the United States by Quarter, 1965

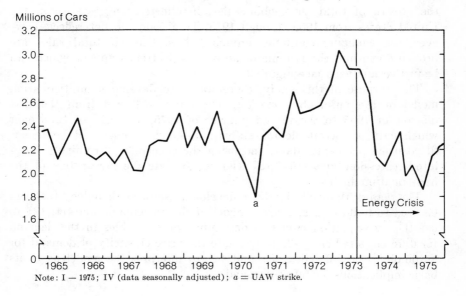

Note: I — 1975; IV (data seasonally adjusted); a = UAW strike.

FIGURE 2

Automobile Sales in the United States by Quarter, Classified by Size, 1965

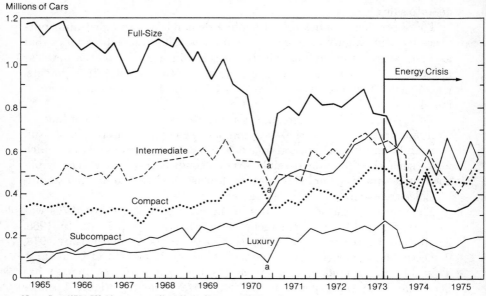

Note: I — 1975; IV (data seasonally adjusted); a = UAW strike.
Source: Information derived from R. L. Polk & Co. data.

the growth of total automobile sales, in quarterly aggregates, in the United States from 1965 through 1975. Total sales do not reflect, however, the changing consumer buying habits. Only if total sales are broken down into the five major auto sizes do trends appear which can be further analyzed (see Figure 2).

The purpose of this study, therefore, is to develop a multiequation model of the automobile market. The study will run from the first quarter of 1965 to the second quarter of 1975, a period of time over which data are available for all variables. The model will be linear, fitted using per capita data, and using the concept of "seemingly unrelated regression equations" (SURE) to estimate the parameters of the five-equation model.

The plan of the study is (1) to develop a useful methodology that can be used to build a disaggregate model of the automobile market, (2) to use the five-equation model to determine key variables in the demand for different sized cars, (3) to estimate the price elasticity of demand for automobiles of different sizes, and (4) to interpret the model as to its basic implications for future demand.

II. METHODOLOGY AND MODEL

A Conceptual Model

A dynamic approach called the stock-adjustment concept will be used to build a general model for automobile demand. Fundamental to this concept is the explicit assumption that there exists an equilibrium or desired level of durable-goods stock toward which adjustment is made from an initial stock. Thus, the investment in stock in time period t is in direct proportion to (1) the difference between this desired level of stock (S^*) in time period t and the actual level (S) in time period $t-1$, and (2) the amount of stock that depreciates in time period $t-1$. Assuming a rate of depreciation, d, the demand for automobiles can be written as

$$D_t^A = f(S_t^{A*} - S_{t-1}^A) + d(S_{t-1}^A) \qquad (1)$$

where d is between zero and one inclusive.

The desired stock (S_t^{A*}) of automobiles for any size can be hypothesized to depend on such factors as expected purchasing power (Y^E), purchase price (P), price of substitute automobiles (P^S), population (PP), consumer attitudes (C), and used car prices (P^U). In addition, consumer demand has been heavily influenced by the increasing cost of automobile operation and the energy shortage. These factors will be included in the model by using (1) gasoline price (G) to account for the general increase in costs and (2) dummy variables (Z^E) to account for shifts in the demand functions brought about by gasoline shortage in the first and second quarter of 1974. Assuming a linear model the best functional form, the result is

$$S_t^{A*} = b_0 + b_1 Y_t^E + b_2 P_t + b_3 P_t^S + b_4 PP_t + b_5 C_t + b_6 P^U + b_7 G_7 + b_8 Z_t^E + e_t \qquad (2)$$

where e_t is the error term.

When equation (2) is substituted into equation (1), similar terms combined, and uppercase symbols used for the coefficients, the model becomes

$$D_t^A = B_0 + B_1 Y_t^E + B_2 P_t + B_3 P_t^S + B_4 PP_t + B_5 C_t + B_6 P^U + B_7 G_t + B_8 Z_t^E + B_9 S_{t-1}^S + e_t. \qquad (3)$$

A preliminary study at this point indicated that the model should be fitted using per capita data which would eliminate the effect of population change on automobile demand. The preliminary study showed that equations fitted to per capita data had R^2 values that were in the same range as the equations fitted to non-per capita data and t-values that were in many cases superior. This suggests that the use of per capita data reduces multicollinearity between certain variables in the model and leads to smaller standard errors. It also suggests that the true model of automobile demand is better reflected using per capita demand as previous studies had indicated.

The preliminary study also indicated that to include the purchase price of every car size in each equation resulted in coefficients significant at less than the .10 level for all price variables as well as many other variables in the model. With similar trends in many of the variables (some equations had 12 variables) multicollinearity was certainly the result. The choice was to drop either (1) the prices of other size automobiles or (2) the energy, stock, and consumer attitude variables. The price variables were dropped because (1) there is higher correlation among these variables and (2) this study is interested in the effects of energy on auto demand. In addition, because no information is available on used car prices (P^U) for different sized automobiles, this variable was omitted from the model.

Expression (4) will be used as the basic model for developing the empirical formulations in each of the market segments. All demand, income, and stock variables will be used in per capita form and labeled by the subscript p to differentiate from non-per capita variables. The model can now be written as

$$D_{p,t}^i = B_0 + B_1 Y_{p,t}^E + B_2 P_t^i + B_3 G_t + B_4 C_t \\ + B_5 S_{p,t-1}^i + B_6 Z_f^E + E_t \qquad (4)$$

where

$D_{p,t}^i$ = Demand per capita for car size $i, i = 1$ (subcompact), 2 (compact), 3 (intermediate), 4 (full size), and 5 (luxury).

$Y_{p,t}^E$ = Expected purchasing power per capita adjusted to constant dollars.

P_t^i = An average of car prices for size $i, i = 1, 2, 3, 4, 5$; adjusted to constant dollars.

G_t = Gasoline price (or RG_t, gasoline price adjusted to constant dollars).

$S_{p,t-1}^i$ = Stock per capita for car size $i, i = 1, 2, 3, 4, 5$.

Z_f^E = $\begin{cases} 1, \text{1st and 2d quarter, 1974.} \\ 0, \text{otherwise.} \end{cases}$

E_t = The disturbance term.

Additional work is necessary, however, before the model can be estimated. Expected purchasing power (Y^E) and consumer attitudes (C), are not observable and must be replaced with proxy variables. Some of the techniques tested will be (1) the use of distributed-lag schemes, and (2) the use of disposable income as expected income and the *Index of Consumer Sentiment* published by the Survey Research Center of the University of Michigan as indicating consumer attitudes.

Seemingly Unrelated Regression Estimation

When estimating a set of regression equations whose disturbances are correlated SURE should be used since OLS estimators will not be efficient. Examples of such sets of equations would be demand functions for various commodities or for different industries. In this study the disturbance in the demand function for one automobile size may be correlated with the disturbances for the other automobile sizes. In using the SURE concept, the mathematical form and list of regressors for each equation is specified using OLS, after which the SURE procedure is used to estimate the parameters of the entire model. While there are alternative estimation procedures for SURE, Zellner's two-stage Aitken, which uses a generalized least squares approach, is used in this study.

III. THE DATA PROBLEM

While much information is available on automobiles in general, there is little published on automobiles classified by size. This part of the paper explains how (1) sales for each size of automobile, (2) average sale price for each size of automobile, and (3) automobile stock of different sizes in the hands of consumers were derived from raw automobile data.

Deriving Key Variables

Automobile Demand. After all automobiles sold from 1965 to 1975 were classified as one of the five sizes, automobile sales for each size of car were aggregated using

$$D_t^i = \sum_{n=1}^{k} d_{n,t}^i \,; t = 1, 2, \ldots, 42, \text{ and } i = 1, 2, 3, 4, 5 \qquad (5)$$

where D_b^i is the demand for car size i in time period t, $d_{n,t}^i$ is the demand for car size i, model n, in time period t, and n is the model index number for each size for each time period (k differed between time period and car size). (Figure 2 is derived from equation [5].) For example, the demand for the 18 compact cars in the first quarter of 1975 was aggregated using

$$D_{41}^2 = \sum_{n=1}^{18} d_{n,41}^2 .$$

Automobile Selling Price. The fundamental difficulty in deriving this variable is that "the actual sales price" between dealer and consumer is an unknown quantity. Chow used the price in the used car market of cars of the current model year. Suits used the wholesale price index for automobiles published by the Bureau of Labor Statistics multiplied by estimated dealer markup to obtain sales price. Roos and von Szeliski used the average delivered price of the lowest-priced cars freely available in volume.

This study will develop a proxy variable by analyzing the sales transaction between dealer and consumer. In payment for a new car a dealer generally receives a used car (as a trade-in) and cash. Then, in order to obtain the retail price of this automobile the dealer will normally sell the used car to another auto dealer for the wholesale price, withholding only cars in excellent condition to sell himself. Thus, automobile dealers seldom have trouble attaining the retail price even though no single buyer normally pays this amount. This means that the dealer can set a target value (a full retail price that includes a trade-in plus cash) and then try to obtain that amount in selling a certain model to a customer. It is an estimate of this target price that this study will use as a price variable.

This full retail price will be estimated using equation (6):

$$p_{n,t}^i = (M_{n,t}^i + O_{n,t}^i) \ (1 - Q_t^i/2) \ R_{n,t}^i \qquad (6)$$

where $p_{n,t}^i$ is the sales price of the nth model in time period t for car size i, $M_{n,t}^i$ the manufacturer's retail base price of the nth model in time period t for car size i, $O_{n,t}^i$ the retail price of all optional equipment on the nth model in time period t for car size i, $R_{n,t}^i$ the rebate available on the nth model in time period t for car size i, and Q_t^i the estimated dealer markup in time period t for car size i.

The equation states that the full retail price which the dealer tries to obtain is equal to the manufacturer's base price, plus price of included options, modified by a discount which the dealer will give depending on (1) the size of the car and (2) how good the consumer is at making a good deal, minus rebates (1974 and 1975 only). Using information obtained from *Consumer Reports* and a survey of local auto dealers, this markup of sticker price $(M_{n,t}^i + O_{n,t}^i)$ above dealer cost was estimated for the different sized cars as 12 percent (subcompact), 14 percent (compact), 18 percent (intermediate), 22 percent (full), and 25 percent (luxury). It will be assumed that the average dealer will lose half his markup in negotiations with consumers.

Once the prices for all makes and models were calculated, they were aggregated into a composite price for each size of car for each quarter. The easiest and most feasible method was to use a weighted average procedure. Using the price information developed for each model (equation [6]) and the corresponding sales of that model for the same time period (equation [5]), the average selling price for each size of car for each time period was estimated using equation (7):

$$P_t^i = \frac{\sum_{n=1}^{k} P_{n,t}^i \cdot D_{n,t}^i}{\sum_{n=1}^{k} D_{n,t}^i} \qquad \begin{array}{l} t = 1, 2, \ldots, 42, \text{ and} \\ i = 1, 2, 3, 4, 5 \end{array} \tag{7}$$

where k is the number of models available that quarter. For example, the average sales price for the 18 compact cars sold in the first quarter of 1975 was estimated using

$$P_{41}^2 = \frac{\sum_{n=1}^{18} P_{n,41}^2 \cdot D_{n,41}^2}{\sum_{n=1}^{18} D_{n,41}^2}.$$

Constant-dollar auto prices, a better reflection of the change in car prices over the period of the study, were then found by dividing the values of equation (7) by the Consumer Price Index. The constant-dollar prices of subcompacts, compacts, intermediates, and luxury automobiles showed a general decrease until mid-1973, a time period in which the demand for these automobiles increased. Moreover, there has been a great decrease in demand for full-size cars since the late 1960s, the only size of automobile that had a general increase in relative price throughout the entire time period. This inverse relationship, also found by Smith over the same time period, is important to this study since economic theory suggests this relationship, *ceteris paribus*, in demand functions.

Automobile Stock. It was postulated that the level of automobile demand over and above replacement demand depends on the gap between desired and existing stock levels. The simplest solution was to define existing auto stock (S_t) as the sum total of all automobiles in use at the end of time period t, or

$$S_t = D_t + (1-s)S_{t-1}; t = 2, 3, \ldots, 42, \tag{8}$$

where D_t is the demand for automobiles in time period t and s the scrappage rate. Use of this formulation in the preliminary study, however, led to poor results.

Another approach, more often used, was to define auto stock as the number of new cars and new car equivalents on the road. Chow was the first to use this assumption; however, this concept was also used by Nerlove in his research and by Suits and Sparks in the Brookings Model.

This method uses the rate of depreciation and not scrappage rates in its calculation procedure. It is common knowledge that cars depreciate rapidly the first few years and more slowly thereafter. This suggests the concept of constant percentage depreciation. Chow reached this conclusion in a study of used car prices and estimated the depreciation rate at 25 percent.

Assuming a constant percentage rate of depreciation, d, the total stock of automobiles, adjusted for age composition, can be derived from the past purchase of new cars. If S_t is the stock of equivalent automobiles at the end of period t, D_t the new car demand in period t, and so on, then it is possible to write after n periods

$$S_t = D_t + (1-d)D_{t-1} + (1-d)^2 D_{t-2} + \ldots + (1-d)^n D_{t-n}. \quad (9)$$

If this equation is lagged one period, solved for D_{t-1}, and substituted in equation (9), the result is

$$S_t = D_t + (1-d)S_{t-1} + (1-d)^n D_{t-n} - (1-d)^{n+1}D_{t-(n+1)}. \quad (10)$$

When n is large (in this study n could theoretically reach 41), the difference between the last two terms approaches zero and expression (10) can be shortened with little error involved. Modifying the formulation for different sizes of cars and assuming a depreciation rate of 6.25 percent per quarter gives

$$S_t^i = D_t^i + .9375\, S_{t-1}^i;\, t = 1, 2, \ldots, 42,\, \text{and}$$
$$i = 1, 2, 3, 4, 5 \quad (11)$$

where S_t^i is the stock of new cars and equivalent new cars of size i in the market at the end of period t, and D_t^i is the sale of new cars of size i in time period t. Equivalent stock can now be calculated by using data from equation (5).

Other Variables

Since expected income is a measure of purchasing power that cannot be observed, disposable income and Friedman's permanent-income variable will be used as proxies. Every equation contained one of the following structures to represent the effect of expected income in the model:

  (i) $D_{p,t}^i = f(Y_{p,t}^D, \overline{X})$ ... a static relationship.
  (ii) $D_{p,t}^i = f(Y_{p,t}^D, D_{p,t-1}^i, \overline{X})$ ... a Koyck transformation.
  (iii) $D_{p,t}^i = f(Y_{p,t}^D, \Delta Y_{p,t}^D, \overline{X})$ ... including a first-difference term.
  (iv) $D_{p,t}^i = f(Y_{p,t-1}^D, \overline{X})$ ... a one-period lag.
  (v) $D_{p,t}^i = f(Y_{p,t}^E, \overline{X})$ ... the permanent-income hypothesis.

where $\overline{X}$ represents the other variables in the model. A dummy variable (Z) will also be necessary to account for the effects of a United Auto

Workers strike in the fall of 1970. The effects of this strike on automobile sales can be seen by looking at Figures 1 and 2.

IV. EMPIRICAL FINDINGS

Table 1 indicates that the best methods to represent the effect of expected income per capita are illustrated by structures i and v. The use of the Koyck transformation, the first-difference term in income, or a one-period lag resulted in income variables that were not significant at even the .10 level. However, the use of current disposable income or Friedman's permanent income gives much better results which are very similar. If past income or wealth is more important in influencing auto demand, then the use of pertinent income is preferable. However, research on consumer attitudes has usually suggested that consumers look at expected future income as a major factor in buying a new car. If this is true, then current disposable income should be used in the model since it is the best indicator of future income. Also, equations using current disposable income per capita have higher R^2 values.

While studies have shown that consumer attitudes do play a role in automobile demand, the *Index of Consumer Sentiment* used to represent these attitudes has been on a downward trend since 1966, and the result was a negative sign in all equations except for full-sized cars. A reverse result occurred in this same equation with the structures used to represent expected income. Since sales of full-sized cars have been decreasing since the late 1960s, all income variables had negative signs, the result of conflicting trends in the variables. These results, in the use of the attitude and income variables, are hard to justify. Not only does economic theory not suggest these results, *ceteris paribus*, but to include these variables with negative signs would make the equations worthless in forecasting. Thus, the attitude variable will be retained in, and the income variable will be omitted from, the full-size-car equation only. It is possible, however, that because of the correlation of attitudes with expected income, the attitude variable will serve two functions in this equation.

The SURE Model

With Table 1 as a guide, the functional relationships selected for the different demand equations were as follows:

$$D_{p,t}^1 = f(P_t^1, Y_{p,t}^D, G_t, Z_f^E) - \text{subcompact}$$
$$D_{p,t}^2 = f(P_t^2, Y_{p,t}^D, G_t, S_{p,t-1}^2, Z_f^E) - \text{compact.}$$
$$D_{p,t}^3 = f(P_t^3, Y_{p,t}^D, G_t, Z_f^E, Z_t) - \text{intermediate.}$$
$$D_{p,t}^4 = f(P_t^4, C_t, G_t, Z_f^E, Z_t) - \text{full.}$$
$$D_{p,t}^5 = f(P_t^5, Y_{p,t}^D, RG_t^5, S_{p,t-1}, Z_f^E, Z_t) - \text{luxury.}$$

TABLE 1

Summary Results of Testing Different Formulations for the Five Sizes of Automobile Using OLS (constant term, not included in table)

Equation Number	Dependent Variable	$Y^D_{p,t}$	$Y^D_{p,t-1}$	$D^i_{p,t-1}$	$\Delta Y^D_{p,t}$	$Y^E_{p,t}$	P_t	G_t	RG_t	C_t	$S_{p,t-i}$	Z^E_t	Z_t	R^2	S	d
1 ..	$D^1_{p,t}$ (Sub)	.144 (.723)	…	…	…p	…	−.982 (.449)	30.2 (15.6)	…	…	.114 (.021)	312** (233)	…	.90	300	1.17 A
2 ..	$D^1_{p,t}$ (Sub)	…	…	…	…	3.401 (.741)	−.656* (.401)	15.4** (11.9)	…	…	.139 (.05)	308** (249)	…	.89	312	.87 A
3 ..	$D^1_{p,t}$ (Sub)	1.070** (1.780)	…	.639 (.163)	…	…	−.501* (.350)	7.24** (10.4)	…	…	.151 (1.07)	351** (201)	…	.88	306	2.40 I
4 ..	$D^1_{p,t}$ (Sub)	3.400 (.650)	…	…	−.504** (.610)	…	−.814 (.422)	19.1* (12.1)	…	…	.171 (.07)	342** (241)	…	.89	305	1.10 A
5 ..	$D^1_{p,t}$ (Sub)	…	.0687** (.161)	…	…	…	−2.58 (.326)	63.8 (10.1)	…	…	…	…	…	.86	315	1.19 A
6 ..	$D^1_{p,t}$ (Sub)	3.347 (.742)	…	…	…	…	−.841 (.401)	20.0** (14.5)	…	…	…	380* (240)	…	.91	301	1.15 A
7 ..	$D^1_{p,t}$ (Sub)	3.201 (.702)	…	…	…	…	−.875** (.390)	…	−21.4** (20.1)	…	.121 (.03)	…	…	.90	302	1.20 A
8 ..	$D^2_{p,t}$ (Comp)	1.654 (.547)	…	…	…	…	−1.11 (.247)	43.0 (11.3)	…	…	−.1362 (.042)	−228* (130)	…	.74	172	1.68 I
9 ..	$D^2_{p,t}$ (Comp)	…	…	…	…	1.583 (.791)	−1.16 (.27)	45.2 (14.9)	…	…	−.1288 (.621)	−256* (157)	…	.73	175	1.32 A
10 ..	$D^2_{p,t}$ (Comp)	.017** (.377)	…	.0496** (.103)	…	…	−.868 (.26)	20.5 (6.4)	…	…	−.1302** (.402)	−230* (140)	…	.70	189	1.41 I
11 ..	$D^2_{p,t}$ (Comp)	…	−.096** (.073)	…	…	…	−1.00 (.16)	13.4 (4.8)	…	…	−.1411** (.501)	−241* (147)	…	.71	190	1.40 I
12 ..	$D^2_{p,t}$ (Comp)	.225** (.359)	…	…	.130** (.082)	…	−.819 (.26)	10.0** (6.2)	…	…	…	−270 (130)	…	.70	192	1.51 I
13 ..	$D^2_{p,t}$ (Comp)	…	.0539 (.005)	.0354** (.130)	…	…	−.76 (.29)	…	−16.2 (8.1)	…	−.1401** (.521)	−266* (140)	…	.68	195	1.41 I
14 ..	$D^3_{p,t}$ (Int.)	…	…	…	…	.816 (.427)	−1.27* (.711)	−27.0 (8.4)	…	…	.0306** (.031)	−507 (197)	−595 (252)	.56	246	1.42 I
15 ..	$D^3_{p,t}$ (Int.)	.864 (.391)	…	…	…	…	−1.16* (.63)	−28.2 (8.2)	…	…	…	−495 (195)	−584 (247)	.60	243	1.44 I

												R^2	N	d
16 .. $D_{p,t}^3$ (Int.)	...	.0347** (.109)	...	...	−2.02 (.57)	−23.3 (7.0)	...	...	.0247** (.0410)	−510 (210)	−602 (291)	.54	250	1.51 I
17 .. $D_{p,t}^3$ (Int.)	.487** (.383)	...	.0017* (.0010)	...	−2.18 (.81)	...	...	...	.0417** (.035)	−498 (218)	−571 (239)	.53	260	1.49 I
18 .. $D_{p,t}^3$ (Int.)	.901 (.450)	...	...	.066** (.116)	−1.14* (.77)	−34.1 (8.7)	...	...	.0395** (.029)	−521 (201)	−588 (241)	.58	251	1.52 I
19 .. $D_{p,t}^4$ (Full)	...	...	...	...	−1.64 (.68)	...	...	99.3 (8.5)	...	−805 (401)	−929 (450)	.87	460	1.84
20 .. $D_{p,t}^4$ (Full)	...	...	...	...	−2.01 (.549)	−67.1 (19.3)	...	58.8 (11.3)	...	−794 (340)	−923 (445)	.93	425	1.91
21 .. $D_{p,t}^4$ (Full)	...	...	...	...	−3.10 (.92)	...	−114 (51)	87.1 (9.8)	.008** (.010)	−906 (420)	−940 (491)	.89	450	1.87
22 .. $D_{p,t}^4$ (Full)	...	.019** (.062)	−.252** (.793)	...	−2.51 (.71)	−50.1 (21)	...	50.8 (12.6)	.007** (.009)	−842 (491)	−951 (502)	.92	429	1.87
23 .. $D_{p,t}^5$ (Lux)	...	...	...	...	−.588 (.16)	...	−21.2* (13.6)	...	.026 (.010)	−197 (83)	−391 (101)	.84	101	1.71
24 .. $D_{p,t}^5$ (Lux)	.839 (.130)	...	...	...	−.347 (.124)	...	−34.4 (9.5)	...	.0382 (.013)	−194 (81)	−382 (99)	.86	95	1.66
25 .. $D_{p,t}^5$ (Lux)	.340** (.240)	...	.0026* (.0014)	...	−.216** (.157)	...	−21.9* (12.4)	...	.0361 (.014)	−182 (87)	−367 (104)	.81	102	1.72
26 .. $D_{p,t}^5$ (Lux)	.627 (.161)	...	...	.072** (.060)	−.213** (.162)	...	−29.1 (11.7)	...	...	−210 (91)	−371 (104)	.74	130	1.40 I
27 .. $D_{p,t}^5$ (Lux)	...	...	...	.993 (.139)	.310 (.110)	...	−37.5 (9.1)	...	.0463 (.011)	−223 (78)	−387 (94)	.86	94	1.70

Note: The values in parentheses are standard errors, the R^2 values are unadjusted, and the Durbin–Watson statistic d (at the .05 level), is labeled A for autocorrelation and I for in-conclusive. All coefficients are significant at the .05 level except those with one asterisk, the .10 level, and two, less than the .10 level.

A basic assumption has been that an interrelationship exists between the demand functions of different sizes of automobiles and that this correlation between residuals is due primarily to interaction between demand forces in the market. The correlation coefficients existing between the residuals of these selected equations (fitted in Table 1) are shown in the unnumbered table below. When the correlation between residuals is in the range exhibited here, SUR) should be 10 percent–?0 percent more efficient than OLS.

The estimation of seemingly unrelated regressions with autoregressive disturbances was necessary since all subcompact demand functions of Table 1 exhibited this violation of OLS. This problem was corrected by estimating the autocorrelation coefficient $\hat{p}$ and transforming the original observations to remove the autoregressive scheme from the variables. This regression equation can be represented as

$$(Y_t - \hat{p}Y_{t-1}) = B_0(1-\hat{p}) + B_{1,t} - \hat{p}X_{1,t-1})$$
$$+ \ldots + B_k(X_{k,t} - \hat{p}X_{k,t-1}) + u_t$$

where $t = 2, 3, \ldots, 42$, and k is the number of variables in the equation.

Table 2 shows the results of estimating the parameters of the model using SURE and compares it with the results obtained from using OLS. A comparison of the two procedures indicates that SURE is more efficient, resulting in lower standard errors of up to 20 percent.

Calculating Elasticities

Price elasticity coefficients were computed using two procedures. The SURE model was used and then, in an attempt to evaluate whether or not the mathematical form of the model would change these estimates, the exponential model fitted to the logarithms of the data was tested as an alternative. The variables used in the exponential model were the same as the linear model with the exception of the dummy variables.

Table 3 shows the resulting price elasticity coefficients for the different sizes of automobile using the different mathematical formulations. A comparison of the elasticities of this and previous studies shows that they are very similar. Price elasticities calculated in this study are a little higher (more elastic) than those of other studies; however, the elasticities are not directly comparable.

Correlation Coefficients between Residuals of Selected Demand Equations

	Subcompact	Compact	Intermediate	Full	Luxury
Subcompact	1.000	.105	.301	.176	−.025
Compact	.105	1.000	.364	.386	−.076
Intermediate	.301	.364	1.000	.331	.361
Full	.176	.386	.331	1.000	.437
Luxury	−.025	−.076	.361	.437	1.000

TABLE 2

Demand Functions for Different Sizes of Automobile Using OLS and Seemingly Unrelated Regressions

Dependent Variable	Constant	P_t^i	$Y_{p,t}^D$	G_t	RG_t	$S_{p,t-1}^i$	C_t	Z_t^E	Z_t	Estimation Techniques
$D_{p,t}^1$	−6,782 (1,367)	−.827 (.431)	3.259 (.707)	15.21* (9.3)	…	…	…	121.7 (62)	…	SURE
(Sub)	−6,175 (2,630)	−.841 (.401)	3.347 (.742)	20.0** (14.5)	…	…	…	308.4** (240)	…	OLS
$D_{p,t}^2$	1,198** (1,150)	−.994 (.200)	1.517 (.431)	34.3 (9.3)	…	−.1078 (.031)	…	−203.3* (107)	…	SURE
(Comp.)	1,453** (1,371)	−1.11 (.247)	1.654 (.547)	43.0 (11.3)	…	−.1362 (.042)	…	−228.9* (130)	…	OLS
$D_{p,t}^3$	4,309gl (2,476)	−1.30 (.64)	.985 (.385)	−29.7 (8.21)	…	…	…	−521.5 (197.1)	−443.1 (232.7)	SURE
(Int.)	4,252* (2,636)	−1.16 (.63)	.864 (.391)	−28.2 (8.23)	…	…	…	−495.1 (195)	−584.2 (247)	OLS
$D_{p,t}^4$	8,721 (2,029)	−2.03 (.455)	…	−72.8 (15.4)	…	…	53.5 (8.5)	−820.8 (323)	−793.1 (386)	SURE
(Full)	8,014 (2,667)	−2.01 (.549)	…	−67.1 (19.3)	…	…	58.8 (11.3)	−794.1 (340)	−923.6 (445)	OLS
$D_{p,t}^5$	5,990** (703)	−.341 (.103)	.878 (.117)	…	−38.8 (8.9)	.0396 (.0089)	…	−188.4 (80.5)	−410.9 (94.9)	SURE
(Lux)	625.4** (807.1)	−.347 (.124)	.839 (.130)	…	−34.4 (9.52)	.0382 (.0113)	…	−194.2 (81.1)	−381.6 (99.3)	OLS

Note: All coefficients significant at the .05 level with the following exceptions: one asterisk = significant at the .10 level, and two = significant at less than the .10 level; OLS equations are 6, 8, 15, 20, and 24 from Table 1; standard errors in parentheses.

TABLE 3
Price Elasticities Calculated for the Different Sizes of Automobile Using Alternative Estimating Procedures and Their Comparison to the Results of Other Studies

	Subcompact	Compact	Inter-mediate	Full	Luxury
SURE	.817	1.21	1.30	1.54	2.07
Exponential ...	.951	1.21	1.34	1.39	2.38
Chow	0.74–1.11				
Nerlove	1.00–1.50				
Roos and Szeliski	1.00–2.50	(probably 1.5)*			
Atkinson	1.31				
Suits	0.50–1.50	(probably 1.0)*			

Note: (1) There have been more studies on automobile demand; however, none computed elasticity coefficients.

(2) Elasticities computed using $E = \dfrac{dD^i}{dP} \cdot \dfrac{\overline{P}}{\overline{D^i}}$.

* This was the researcher's best estimate.

V. SUMMARY AND CONCLUSIONS

Interpreting the Model

To better interpret the meaning and magnitudes of the variables in the different equations, the regression coefficients were transformed into beta-coefficients which can be compared from equation to equation for the same variable and which, within a given equation, reflect the relative importance of the variables. Thus transformed, the model becomes

$$D^S_{p,t} = -.267\, P^S_f + .755\, Y^D_{p,t} + .154 G_t - .044\, Z^E_f;$$
$$D^C_{p,t} = -.677\, P^C_f + .881\, Y^D_{p,t} + .669 G_t - .671\, S^C_{p,t-1} - .137\, Z^E_f;$$
$$D^I_{p,t} = -.377\, P^I_f + .502\, Y^D_{p,t} - .551 G_t - .318\, Z^E_f - .213\, Z_t;$$
$$D^F_{p,t} = -.422\, P^F_f + .410\, C_t - .481\, G_t - .120\, Z^E - .101 Z_t;$$
$$D^L_{p,t} = -.307\, P^L_f + .741\, Y^D_{p,t} - .360\, RG_t + .405\, S^L_{p,t-1} - .177\, Z^E_f.$$

The variables in the model are not surprising. With the exception of gasoline price and the energy dummy all others have been found to be related to auto demand by researchers working at different points in time. It is obvious that disposable income (Y^D) is the variable of greatest impact in the model. This is to be expected since no consumer purchasing power is the primary determinant of expenditures on durable goods. The beta-coefficients also suggest that sales price (P) is a powerful variable which is in contrast to many previous studies: however, auto stock (S) was not found significant in all equations, and its relative importance in the model appears to be minor. This conclusion could be the result of the disaggregation procedure. One possible explanation is that the higher degree of aggregation in previous studies dampened the effect of price while magnifying that of stock. Aggregate price is developed through an averaging procedure that could eliminate trends, while stock is computed by an additive method that would only magnify trends in data.

Furthermore, sales price appears to have a lesser import on subcompact and luxury cars than on compact, intermediate, and full-sized automobiles. On the other hand, income seems to be a relatively more important factor in the subcompact and luxury markets. While it is certainly possible that income influences luxury demand more than sales price, this effect is not as apparent for subcompacts. One possible explanation is that subcompact automobiles became popular as a second car, an event made possible by increasing standards of living and the economy of these small cars. Thus, the model supports the proposition that income, not sales price or gasoline economy, caused the growth (or at least at the onset) of the small-car market.

An analysis of the compact-, intermediate-, and full-size-car equations shows that sales price is a prime determinant in the purchase of one of these cars. The model also suggests that sales of intermediate and full-sized autos are strongly affected in an adverse manner by the price of gasoline and supports the claim that poor fuel economy has been a prime reason for these cars losing sales in recent years. As expected, however, the model indicates that higher gas prices caused increased demand for subcompact and compact cars. In addition, the coefficients of the shortage dummies (Z^E) show that the gasoline shortage increased the demand for subcompacts, but decreased the demand for all other automobiles. This result would seem to indicate that consumers felt that only subcompacts were real gas economy cars.

Analyzing Elasticities

Table 3 shows that the price elasticity coefficients, in general, follow a pattern. Subcompact demand is seen to be inelastic, with that of compact, intermediate, and full-sized automobiles being slightly elastic. It is possible to suggest some possible explanations for this pattern. First, while automobiles are deemed to be necessities, the larger cars must be regarded as a greater luxury item than the smaller ones. Also, the larger cars command a greater price and a greater share of the consumer's budget. Moreover, larger cars would seem to have more substitutes than the smaller cars in that small cars are usually purchased for their performance (even if a second car). If this is true, larger cars would make poor substitutes. That the demand for smaller cars is more inelastic than that of larger cars is not surprising since increasing gasoline and maintenance costs have made smaller cars more of a necessity to a large segment of the population and have decreased the substitutability between the large- and small-car markets. While people have substituted smaller cars for full sized cars especially (see Figure 2), it must be noted that the demand for luxury cars, while large automobiles, did not decline but even increased over the period of the study. Because the owner of a luxury car would not seem concerned with price, its elasticity coefficient seems high (around 2.0); however, it is possible that luxury cars have more substitutes than generally thought. This result could also suggest that there are substantial numbers of fringe buyers of luxury cars who are responsive to price.

The exponential model exhibits results similar to the SURE model; thus there seems to be some justification for declaring that a pattern does exist. While it is impossible to know for sure what part elasticity plays in the pricing policy of automobile firms, it would seem no coincidence that the smaller cars, especially subcompacts, have increased in price more (as a percentage) than the larger cars over the time period of the study.

Forecasting Implications

The main purpose of this research is not to predict future sales; however, the model can be used to derive demand implications, given assumptions about energy and economic conditions.

Because the level of disposable income is clearly the most important determinant of automobile demand, the model suggests that, unless real disposable income increases at rates equal to prerecessionary levels (around 5 percent between 1965 and 1973), long-run demand could stagnate at less than pre-1974 levels of 11.5 million, even under favorable assumptions about energy and automobile prices. For example, if disposable income is increased at a 5 percent quarterly rate and all other variables extrapolated by simple trend, the model projects sales for 10.3 million for 1977 and no higher than 11 million for any year before 1980. Only if greater increases in income are used or the other variables kept at very favorable levels (little change in the constant-dollar price of automobiles, a less than 5 cents per year increase in gasoline price, no shortage, and so forth) does the model indicate demand exceeding 1972 and 1973 levels. While sales of 1977 autos are currently at a record pace, this could be only a short-run spurt caused by the obvious backlog in demand built up in 1974–76.

In addition, a redistribution of demand to smaller cars will be inevitable if the energy crisis happens again (government intervention may cause it to happen anyway). The model indicates that gasoline shortage and/or higher gasoline prices will cause a redistribution of demand; however, there is one apparent reason why this could take time—habit. People like to drive large cars; in fact, the American love affair with the large automobile is more than fiction. A good example is in the sales of larger automobiles in 1976 and 1977. With the memory of gasoline shortages vanishing and gasoline prices remaining stable, consumers returned to buying full-sized and luxury cars at pre-1974 levels.

In summary, the model indicates that the total demand for automobiles depends on income levels, while the distribution of demand is a function of price levels and energy considerations. Since it is almost impossible to make definite short-run projections about a commodity as volatile as auto sales, these forecasts are meant only to be indications of future trends.

part THREE
Costs, Production, and Productivity

INTRODUCTION

The word *cost* means different things to different people. Business people in general and accountants in particular are prone, at times, to overwork this word. *Production* and *productivity* appear no less susceptible to the same problem. With almost no exaggeration, the cost of a student's education is repaid if he or she goes from a course in *managerial economics* with a deep respect for and an understanding of cost, production, and productivity. Unfortunately, the literature in the field doesn't help much in explaining that in a price-oriented economy, nothing of substance gets produced without incurring costs; moreover, even with the payment of fixed, variable, financial, real, opportunity, short-run, long-run, sunk, empirical, and/or other costs, production levels may not be high enough to allow an organization to break even.

The literature on empirical cost studies has become increasingly technical. Severe data and econometric problems have forced investigators into more sophisticated methods and armed their critics with more powerful weapons. But, what is "cost" and how do we know? Robert N. Anthony tells why the word is confusing; moreover, he suggests certain definitions, standards, and approaches necessary for better cost measurement.

Armen A. Alchian and Harold Demsetz explain how productivity is increased through cooperative specialization between resource owners and factors of production. They explain how proper structure of the organization contributes to increased output.

Classical methods of statistical estimation are not used by all cost analysts. George J. Stigler applies the "survivor" principle to the investigation of economies of scale; fundamental to problems associated with this approach is acquisition of reliable raw data with which to work.

A primary reason for owning and/or operating a business may be to generate a profit. If profit is measured on an incremental basis, by function, very detailed pieces of information are necessary regarding costs by function. Using commercial banks as an example the article by Thomas Joseph Coyne reveals a method of cost of funds calculation and utilization that may be useful in analyzing costs for nonfinancial as well as financial corporations.

Statistical cost functions are useful devices (1) for describing the relationships which exist currently between various measurable variables and (2) for forecasting the effects of changes in one or more of these variables. Using the Federal Reserve System's functional cost analysis data, William A. Longbrake applies this technique to the commercial banking industry.

8.   What Should "Cost" Mean?*

ROBERT N. ANTHONY

Suppose the president of a widget company says, "Last year our cost of manufacturing widgets was $1.80 each." The ordinary person may think he has learned a concrete piece of information from this statement.

Anyone who understands the vagaries of cost accounting knows differently. He knows that "cost" in this context has no generally accepted meaning, that two manufacturers of physically identical widgets who use different, but acceptable, methods of measuring cost could differ in their reported costs of making widgets by 100 percent or more. The informed person therefore realizes that he cannot understand a number that purports to be the cost of a widget unless he knows a great deal about the particular cost accounting system from which it was derived.

Some persons say this situation is inevitable, in view of the complicated nature of business. Others say it is desirable: manufacturers should be encouraged to exercise their own best judgment in measuring cost. Still others, including me, find it neither inevitable nor desirable. They find it deplorable.

The increasing number of responsible persons who find it deplorable has generated activity on several fronts to develop cost standards. The activity involves accounting groups, the General Accounting Office, and the Senate Banking and Currency Committee, which plans hearings on the subject. (Later, I shall offer some ideas as to how cost concepts can best be formulated.)

CORRECTION OF INADEQUACIES

For reasons discussed in the next section, I shall limit myself here to the meaning of "cost" in this situation:

Two parties facing each other across a table are negotiating a contract. Mr. A has agreed to manufacture some articles or perform some services for Mr. B. They have agreed on the specifications and delivery schedule of the articles or services. They also have agreed that the purchaser (B) will pay the supplier (A) for the cost of manufacturing

---

* Reprinted by permission of the *Harvard Business Review* "What Should 'Cost' Mean?" by Robert N. Anthony (May–June 1970). Copyright © 1970 by the President and Fellows of Harvard College; all rights reserved.

the articles or providing the services, plus a profit. The problem is: What should "cost" mean in this situation?

There are several conceivable ways of answering this question, but in most situations only one way is both fair and practical. Let us look at the possibilities:

1. The parties could leave "cost" undefined, in the belief that there exists a body of generally accepted cost accounting principles defining it. They would be wrong.

2. At the opposite extreme, they could try to imagine all the cost accounting problems that might arise in the course of manufacturing the articles or providing the services, and agree on how each of them is to be resolved. The end product of such an approach would be a cost accounting manual.

But it is not generally practical to write a manual for a specific contract, except for a very simple job; the circumstances, and the possible ways of treating each circumstance, are too numerous. Moreover, the negotiations would be extraordinarily time-consuming.

3. The buyer could permit the manufacturer to define cost to mean what the manufacturer says it means, no more and no less. Even Alice would not accept this White Queen approach, and it is preposterous to expect that a hardheaded buyer would agree to it.

It is, nevertheless, an approach advocated by a number of people for contracts in which they sit on one side of the negotiating table and a government representative sits on the other side, as indicated by this excerpt from a letter written to the General Accounting Office by a trade association representative: "We do not believe that the adoption of Uniform Cost Accounting Standards would be practical for government or industry. Each industry already has developed, and is utilizing, the most appropriate accounting systems and procedures for its needs."

4. They could negotiate *de novo* a set of standards that would provide at least the general direction of solutions that arose in measuring the cost of the contract. This would be very inefficient. Since most problems that arise in measuring costs have arisen thousands of times before, working out solutions from scratch for each new contract is a waste of everyone's time.

5. They could agree to use a set of standards that has been developed by someone else for contracts of the type being negotiated, or perhaps a set of standards for contracts in general. This is the only fair and practical solution. Neither the first nor the third alternative is fair to the purchaser, and neither the second nor the fourth is practical.

An agreed-on definition of cost that is applicable to a number of situations is what is meant by the term "cost standards." (Incidentally, the phrase "cost standards" should not be confused with "standard costs." Standard costs are a device used for internal control, which is intended to express what costs *should be*, not what they *are*.)

Several such definitions already exist. Section XV of the Armed Services Procurement Regulations (ASPR) is one; it helps to define cost in negotiations when one of the participants is the government. Many trade associations have developed standards for defining costs applicable to their industries.

But these existing sets of standards have serious deficiencies, and the time has come to attempt the construction of a set of standards that will define cost whenever one party to a contract agrees to pay to the other party an amount based on the cost of performing the contract.

The time is propitious because of the interest in this problem that has been generated by a study conducted by the General Accounting Office (GAO) as required by Public Law 370 of the 90th Congress. This law only required the GAO to report on the "feasibility" of applying "uniform cost accounting standards" to negotiated defense contracts. (In the quoted phrase, "uniform" is clearly redundant, and I shall omit it henceforth. Can anyone give an example of a nonuniform cost standard?)

The comptroller general made his report on January 19, 1970. He stated that it is feasible to develop and use cost standards for defense contracts. He could scarcely have concluded otherwise, for it is inconceivable that the two parties to a contract could communicate with one another in the absence of such standards. They communicate now, and have for years, using the previously mentioned ASPR standards.

These standards are inadequate, however. The comptroller general summarized their inadequacies this way: (*a*) in some crucial matters, ASPR instructs the parties to use "generally accepted accounting principles," whereas relevant principles do not exist; (*b*) in other matters, ASPR is silent or vague as to which of several possible cost constructions may be used in a given set of circumstances.

Admittedly, some persons oppose any effort to develop better cost standards. Analysis of their arguments shows that they are not questioning the desirability of standards per se. What they are really worried about is that the standards may be *bad* standards; that is, that the group responsible for developing them will not do a good job.

This, it seems to me, is an untenable position, for such a possibility exists in any proposal to change the status quo. Instead of merely expressing opposition, these critics could make a constructive contribution if they focused their energies on ensuring that the effort to develop standards is well conceived, well organized, and well manned.

HOW BROAD THE STANDARDS?

The first question to be resolved is how broad the standards should be. There are two extremes:

They could define "cost" in whatever context it is used.

They could define cost as used in "all negotiated prime contract and subcontract defense procurements of $100,000 or more," which is the language of P.L. 90-370.

In my view, one extreme is unmanageably broad and the other is unnecessarily narrow. That is why the question at the beginning of this article was framed in such a way that it applies to all negotiated contracts where the payment is in part based on cost, but only to such contracts.

Problem Categories

If the group concerned set out to develop all-inclusive cost standards, it would have to cover at least these five contexts:

1. There is the situation I described, where the problem is to measure the total (i.e., "full") costs incurred in performing a contract.

2. There is the problem of defining the costs that company management should weigh in deciding between proposed alternative courses of action. These are often labeled "decision-making" costs. In contrast with the first type, these are not incurred costs, but estimates of future costs. Neither are they necessarily full costs, but differential or incremental costs.

3. There are the costs considered in setting selling prices for other than cost-type contracts. Some persons regard pricing as one type of decision-making problem, while others regard it as a special case in the measurement of costs incurred. In view of this disagreement it would be arbitrary to classify the costs relevant for pricing as coming within either the costs-incurred or the decision-making categories.

4. There are the costs involved in measuring inventory amounts on the balance sheet and cost of sales on the income statement. Perhaps the principles governing measurement of costs for financial statements are so similar to those in the first category that this is not really a separate category. Such a conclusion is, however, premature.

5. There are the costs used as a basis for influencing the actions of managers and measuring their performance. They may be called "management control" costs. They properly involve motivational considerations, so they differ in some respects from those in the other categories. As with the previous category, further analysis may show that these differences are not significant enough to warrant the creation of a separate category.

To summarize this list, there are at least two quite different kinds of costs: total, incurred costs and differential, future costs. There may also be other important categories, depending on whether the principles relevant to costs for pricing, costs for financial statements, and costs for management control are essentially the same as those in one or the other of the categories listed.

Some very broad comments about cost can be made that apply to all these categories. This, for example, is the approach taken in William J. Vatter's *Standards of Cost Analysis*. A study of this excellent report shows, however, that statements made at this level of generality provide only what Vatter himself describes as "first steps" in approaching any of the classes of problems I described.

The cost concepts study sponsored by the American Institute of Certified Public Accountants (AICPA)—described in the February 1969 issue of *The Journal of Accountancy*—appears to take the same broad approach as does Vatter.

Choosing a Category

If the contexts in which cost is used are too diverse to allow tackling them simultaneously, which one should be selected as the focus for a program to develop standards? Of the two main categories—a focus on total costs that have been incurred versus a focus on estimates of differential costs *to be* incurred—the former is clearly the more desirable.

In internal decision making, company management can specify the definition of cost it thinks best. Some cost constructions are more useful than others, and management should welcome advice on what constructions are most useful for purposes of decision making. But it should be free to accept or reject this advice; there is no compelling reason why some outside agency should impose its views on the company in the guise of a set of standards.

On the other hand, A and B, the negotiators in the episode at the beginning of this article, *must* have some standards. Without them, A and B have no practicable way of reaching a meeting of minds as to what the contract means by the word "cost," once the parties have agreed that reimbursement is to be based in part on cost. This area is the one on which the standards-development effort should be focused.

The effort should not be limited to developing cost standards for defense contracts. Those responsible will render a greater service to the business community if they view their job as relating to all cost-type contracts. For what difference is there, in principle, between costs that are relevant to a defense contract and those relevant to a nondefense contract? The defense establishment consumes 8 percent of our gross national product, and its contracts cover nearly every conceivable kind of product and service.

Defense contracts do, however, have a few peculiarities. DOD has rules for reimbursing contractors for some items that may not fit within a general definition of costs incurred on a contract—principally those known as "independent research and development costs" and "bid and proposal costs." Provision in the standards for such items, if they indeed turn out to be exceptions (and it would be premature to so classify them before cost standards have been developed), could easily be treated as special cases, applying only to defense.

A set of standards is useful in most contracts involving payments based on cost. The standards would in no way prevent the parties, whether or not it is a government negotiation, from defining cost in a different way if they mutually agree to do so.

Many construction contracts, for instance, specify the use of $2'' \times 4''$ lumber. There is a standard for $2'' \times 4''$ lumber which, among other characteristics, defines it as having dimensions of at least $1\frac{1}{2}'' \times 3\frac{1}{2}''$ under certain circumstances and at least $1\frac{9}{16}'' \times 3\frac{9}{16}''$ under other circumstances. It is normally not done, but the parties can, if they wish, change this definition and require that the lumber actually measure $2'' \times 4''$, or any other dimension they specify.

The problem of defining cost obviously is vastly more complicated than that of defining the dimensions of lumber. Cost standards would therefore not be anywhere near as specific as those for lumber or those for similar criteria worked out by the U.S.A. Standards Institute. I stress this point because many persons have a mistaken impression about it.

Parameters of Analysis. The question posed in the "A and B negotiate" episode was worded so as to restrict the analysis in certain dimensions. For one, it is deliberately limited to the problem of reimbursable costs.

Costs are used for other purposes in connection with contract work, such as measuring performance while the work is going on. But performance measurement involves several problems that need not be faced in measuring the costs to be reimbursed. For example, in the Defense Department a controversy currently goes on as to the proper timing of material charges for performance measurement purposes: Should they be reported when material is acquired or when it is consumed? This question of timing does not even arise in the cost reimbursement area; if an item of material is used on a contract, it is unquestionably a cost of that contract, regardless of when it is acquired or used.

The question early in the article was stated so as to exclude also the problem of developing standards for cost estimates that are often used by negotiating parties in deciding on the work to be done under a contract. They are important in negotiated fixed-price contracts as well as cost-type contracts.

These cost estimates should be influenced by the standards in the sense that the buyer ought to insist that the cost constructions used in the estimates are consistent with the standards applicable to the measurement of costs incurred. The job of making the estimates, however, involves certain considerations (some of them quite complicated) that are not present in the measurement of costs incurred.

For example, the standards for measuring costs incurred should indicate what kind of effort constitutes direct labor, and what, if any, fringe benefits should be included in the price of each hour of direct labor. *Estimates* of this labor cost should ordinarily be constructed in the same terms; but the estimator must also make certain assumptions about future wage rates, future labor productivity, and the number of hours required to produce the article. It does not appear feasible, as a part of the initial effort to develop standards, to work out standards governing the choice of these assumptions.

The contracting parties may also be involved in change orders, repricing formulas, renegotiation provisions, termination costs, and similar complications. All involve the measurement of costs actually incurred, as distinguished from estimates of costs to be incurred, and therefore the standards should apply to them.

For these reasons, then, the approach suggested at the beginning of this article seems to be the most feasible and the most useful. By limiting the focus to developing standards for costs incurred, we can avoid the complications involved in developing standards for other kinds of cost. By broadening it from defense contracts to all negotiated contracts, we gain in breadth of coverage with no significant increase in effort.

FIRST THINGS FIRST

The formulation of cost standards resembles the efforts of the Accountting Principles Board (APB) of the American Institute of Certified Public Accountants to develop standards for financial accounting. Its experience teaches an important lesson; namely, that the undertaking should consist of two sequential stages:

The development of a few underlying, basic concepts.

The development of standards based on those concepts.

(A third possible stage, the development of detailed rules and procedures, is not properly a part of the effort, of course.)

When the APB began its work in 1959, it decided that its opinions should rest on a foundation of broad principles. It therefore encouraged research that could be used as a basis for formulating principles. The work culminated in "A Tentative Set of Broad Accounting Principles for Business Enterprises."

The APB did not accept the principles proposed in that study, but neither could its members agree on any alternative set of principles. So the APB proceeded to formulate standards for specific topics, without the conceptual underpinning that a statement of broad principles would have provided. There was some justification for this approach; certain problems required immediate resolution, and it may not have been feasible to hold up action on them until an agreement on broad principles could be reached.

Whatever justification there was at the time, we know by hindsight that the subsequent APB opinions, and the discussions leading to them, have suffered greatly from the absence of an agreed-on conceptual foundation. As a leading practitioner comments:

The APB . . . has been so busy "putting out fires" and dealing with a large and ever-increasing backlog of current problems that it has never established an adequate basis upon which to build. This deficiency results not only in the waste of a great deal of time in debating each subject on a more-or-less isolated basis but also in makeshift conclusions which could in the end defeat the entire effort to improve accounting principles. . . . This approach can be compared to building a room for a house without having either a foundation or plans for the house.

In 1968, the APB began another effort to decide on broad concepts, so the importance of doing so is still recognized. In the meantime, whoever is responsible for developing cost accounting standards can learn from the experience. The individual standards must be derived from a conceptual foundation, and the first task is to build it.

BUILDING THE FOUNDATION

What should the conceptual foundation look like? Its general nature is, I believe, quite easy to sketch out. Cost measures the use of resources. To return to my original example:

When B agrees to pay A an amount based on cost incurred, he has in mind that A will use certain resources in the time period covered by the contract, and that this use will be measured by a dollar amount known as cost.

Some of this use of resources can be directly related to the contract, and B expects to pay the cost of these resources. Some are used jointly for contract work and noncontract work, and B expects to pay a "fair share" of the cost of these resources. The sum of these two elements he regards as the cost of performing the contract. (He may specify that he will pay for these costs only to the extent that they are reasonable.)

This suggests that the conceptual foundation should spell out in broad terms the answers to two questions:

1. What are the total costs incurred by an organization in an accounting period?

2. How should this total be divided among the several cost objectives of that period? (A cost objective is anything to which costs are assigned. We are here interested in a contract as one cost objective.)

Costs Incurred in a Period

The concepts governing measurement of the total costs incurred in an accounting period are financial accounting concepts. If the APB had adopted a complete and acceptable set of broad principles, the cost accounting effort would require no further work with respect to this question. It seems highly unlikely that the APB will answer this question in the near future. If it does not, the new group must develop these concepts.

This job involves wrestling with only a relatively few topics. A measure of agreement already exists on at least some of them, and the task is therefore to find words to express the concepts unambiguously. There is general agreement, for example, that the accrual concept should govern measurement of costs, but no generally accepted unambiguous statement exists on what should be meant by the accrual concept. For writing such a statement, the literature can be used as a basis for discussion.

The principal aspects of the main question to be considered are:

The types of resources that are properly included in the costs of an accounting period.

How these resources should be priced.

In regard to resources that provide services to more than one accounting period, how the amount applicable to a single period should be measured.

In addition, attention should be given to the terms "materiality" and "consistency." Moreover, since most cost-type contracts contemplate that reimbursement will be limited to "reasonable" cost, rather than cost in an unqualified sense, "reasonable" needs to be defined.

There is, finally, the special problem of the cost of capital. Although capital has a cost, it is not recognized as such under currently accepted financial accounting principles. Interest, which is the cost of *debt* capital, is recognized for some purposes, but there is no formal recognition in the accounts of the cost of *equity* capital.

This situation has led to confusion and inequity in contract costing. Under ASPR (paragraph 15-305.17), interest is an unallowable cost. If, however, a contractor leases an asset, the lease payment generally includes an allowance for the cost of capital—both debt capital and equity capital—and such a lease payment is often an allowable cost.

The cost of a building constructed by a contractor's own work force may include an allowance for interest, but it rarely includes an allowance for the cost of equity capital. If a third party constructed the building for the contractor's account, the cost would normally include the cost of capital.

It is inappropriate here to suggest a solution to this problem, but it surely is one to which special attention must be given.

Assignment of Costs

The second question, the assignment of total costs to cost objectives, is the province of cost accounting. In this area APB opinions give no substantial guidance. The closest authoritative precedent is ASPR, and this is useful in providing a structure for the conceptual problem. In rough outline this structure is:

Costs are divided into direct costs and indirect costs.

Direct costs are assigned to cost objectives.

Each cost objective is assigned a "fair share" of the indirect costs.

This structure suggests two main considerations, investigation of which can provide the conceptual foundation necessary for the construction of individual standards:

The *first* consideration has to do with how direct costs should be defined. The definition should, I believe, encompass more costs than those that clearly can be traced to a cost objective, because they exclude most kinds of fringe benefits, overtime, labor that is closely but not unequivocally related to a cost objective, many aspects of material cost, and many services.

Some of these cost elements should be included within the definition of direct costs, leaving the indirect cost category as small as possible, for the more costs that reasonably can be assigned directly, the more confidence that the total costs are indeed equitable. So the answer to this question is by no means as simple as it may appear.

The way to approach this problem, I believe, is to break it into: (a) What physical inputs should be costed as direct? (b) How are these inputs to be priced?

The latter is the more difficult. Consider, for example, two pieces of timber of identical size which required an identical amount of effort to grow, harvest, and transport to where they are to be used. Log X is in some significant sense "better" than Log Y; it has fewer defects or a better grain. If Log X is used on Contract A and Log Y on Contract B, it seems reasonable to some persons that more than half the cost of the two logs should be assigned to Contract A. Others believe that the same amount of cost should be assigned to each contract.

This is a basic conceptual disagreement that must be resolved. The treatment of overtime and material waste and spoilage are other topics that have this same characteristic.

The *second* consideration has to do with the concepts governing the assignment of indirect costs to contracts. Although some persons find the idea of "fair share" or "equity" a less than satisfactory basis for approaching this question, no one, as far as I know, has proposed a better one.

If those responsible cannot come up with a better approach (and I doubt that they can), they will presumably use the foundation that is already familiar to cost accountants: costs are initially collected in relatively homogeneous pools, and the total of each of these pools is then divided among the cost objectives on some equitable basis. So there needs to be one set of criteria for specifying what is meant by a "homogeneous pool" and another set for deciding among the possible ways of allocating the total of each pool to cost objectives.

In the report to the comptroller general which I mentioned, Vatter classifies cost pools as people-oriented, payroll-oriented, materials-oriented, machine-oriented, or uncorrelated with any of the others. This classification provides a good starting point in approaching the question of homogeneity. It should not be difficult to frame a general concept of the meaning of homogeneity, together with a *de minimis* qualification that limits the creation of separate pools in situations where the effort to do so is not worthwhile.

A decision on the concepts governing the method of allocating the total cost accumulated in a pool to the relevant cost objectives is much more difficult to reach. The literature suggests a number of alternatives, including benefits received, correlation with individual input elements, correlation with total input cost, correlation with outputs, relative use of facilities, and degree of control by cost objective. These must in some way be sorted out.

There are several possible ways of doing this. One is to arrange the methods of allocation in a hierarchy according to their conceptual desirability and specify that a particular method should be used only when a more desirable one is not feasible.

The concept might state, for example, that the costs in a pool should be allocated to cost objectives in proportion to the benefits received, if it is feasible to do so. If this is not feasible, another criterion should govern, then another, until one is left with a pool of costs for which no logical basis for allocation exists. (Such a pool would contain at least part of the element often labeled "general and administrative costs.")

In the absence of a logical basis for allocating such costs, the method of allocation is necessarily arbitrary. The relevant concept is therefore also arbitrary. But this is nothing to be concealed or be ashamed of; it is simply inherent in the situation.

The set of basic concepts emerging from this analysis should be relatively brief, a few thousand words at most (which is much shorter than Section XV of ASPR). There will nevertheless be much sweat, some tears, and possibly even some blood shed by members of the group responsible for this effort. The job of selecting the best ideas is a formidable exercise in logic tempered by the realities of practice, and the job of expressing those ideas in unambiguous language is almost as difficult.

But unless this job is completed before the work of setting standards on individual elements of cost begins, the undertaking is likely to be a patchwork of loosely related, sometimes conflicting, statements, which is one of the troubles with the present state of affairs.

Approach to Procedure

This is what I have in mind by the term "concepts": they are broad, they are few in number, and they govern the standards to be developed for individual elements of cost—but they do not themselves deal with those elements. Once these concepts have been agreed to, the task of developing cost standards can begin. Probably this work could be divided according to the principal elements of cost, although other methods of breaking it down may turn out to be preferable.

Whatever the basis for selecting topics, the research and analysis leading to a recommendation on each topic should seek to:

Define alternative circumstances that warrant different methods of cost assignment.

State the method (or methods) that is appropriate under each of these circumstances.

Take one of the most difficult problems as an example: the amount of depreciation cost assigned to an accounting period can be determined on a straight-line basis, or an annuity basis. The standard on depreciation should spell out either the circumstances under which each of these methods is appropriate, or, as a minimum, the circumstances under which each is inappropriate.

At best, cost accounting standards are guides to practice; they cannot provide detailed solutions to all problems. They can and must narrow the choice of alternatives, but they cannot eliminate the necessity for making judgments among alternatives according to the circumstances in a specific situation. The real world is too complicated for that.

ORGANIZING FOR THE TASK

Next, there is the question of how to go about it. In other words, what organization should be responsible, and what procedures should it follow? Here are some considerations bearing on these questions:

The organization must be a continuing one, for the formidable task has no foreseeable end. While results in development of the broad cost concepts can be produced in two years or so, devising standards consistent with those concepts is a much more time-consuming job. It has no foreseeable end because any set of standards will doubtless require modification as circumstances change.

One organization should be responsible for both aspects of the undertaking. Otherwise, human nature is such that the standards-setting group would probably start by a reexamination of the cost concepts, which might well take as much time as the concepts formulation in the first place.

The organization must be authoritative. Experience has demonstrated that recommendations of an individual or an ad hoc committee, however brilliant or logical they may be, have little practical impact. Authority can be derived either from legislative fiat or from the prestige of the organization, although each of these sources of authority offers disadvantages.

Authority, incidentally, is a necessary, but not a sufficient, condition. A poor set of standards is unlikely to gain permanent acceptance even though it is promulgated with substantial authority.

Standards can be developed for contracts in general, in which case they could be applied to government contracts as a special case, or to defense contracts as an even more special case. Alternatively, standards can be developed for defense contracts, or for government contracts, and then extended to other types of contracts.

I have given the argument for the first approach: essentially the same standards should apply to most contracts, and it is therefore artificial to select a special category for attention. The argument for the second approach is the practical one that congressional interest, and hence public interest, is aroused about the problem of defense contracts, and this interest might dissipate if the problem were tackled in broader terms.

With respect to defense contracts, there is a basic conflict of interest between the parties. The contractor wants the standards to be few and general, giving him the maximum amount of latitude in choosing the most advantageous cost alternative in a particular circumstance. The government, on the other hand, wants the standards to be specific in order to minimize the judgments required in auditing cost reimbursements.

(Some, by the way, deny the existence of this conflict. They assert that a contractor, even in the absence of standards, will voluntarily measure costs according to what is fair, even when this is inconsistent with his interests. This is a naive point of view, and it is surprising that knowledgeable men appear to expect that other knowledgeable men will give credence to it.)

The task of devising standards is expensive. Counting the work done in the public accounting firms and the salaries of those who spend a substantial amount of time on the effort, the work of the APB costs more than a million dollars a year. The cost concepts effort should be even more expensive per year than that unless it is strung out over an unacceptably long period of time.

The organization must be able to attract competent people. The task requires experts who have a profound understanding not only of accounting, but also of the realities of business—plus an ability to think conceptually and write precisely. Such people are scarce and are well paid in their current jobs. Much thought needs to be given to the inducements that would lead them to undertake this novel and potentially frustrating effort.

If the job of developing standards is carried out under the aegis of a professional organization, it may take a long time. The standard for 2″ × 4″ lumber I mentioned took 7 years to develop. The APB has issued only 15 opinions in the 10 years of its existence. Some of them supersede others, and it has not yet covered all the important topics even once.

Some persons fear that standards developed unilaterally by a government agency might be more restrictive than the situation warrants. The accounting standards developed by the Interstate Commerce Commission, the Civil Aeronautics Board, the Federal Power Commission, and the state public utility regulatory agencies are examples of overly restrictive standards. On the other hand, those of the Securities and Exchange Commission are by no means too restrictive; and the regulations of the Internal Revenue Service, though restrictive, are in my view not *overly* restrictive. This concern is therefore not necessarily justified.

Private or Public?

With these considerations in mind, we are in a better position to weigh the decision whether the work should be carried out under private or public auspices.

A Private-Sector Effort. The business community undoubtedly would like to see this effort undertaken by a group in the private sector analogous to the APB. But the considerations of authoritativeness, permanence, and financing lead me to the reluctant conclusion that such an approach is unlikely to succeed.

The APB, in its work on financial accounting principles, has had two great advantages that no other private organization seems likely to match in developing cost accounting standards: .

1. The APB is authoritative. It can enforce its pronouncements through sanctions applicable to all members of the AICPA. The other leading organizations—the National Association of Accountants, the Financial Executives Institute, and the American Accounting Association—have no way whatsoever of ensuring compliance with their pronouncements.

2. The APB can raise substantial sums of money from the profession, since the development of financial accounting standards is now recognized by the public accounting firms to be very much in their own interest. No other private group has corresponding sources of support for the development of cost concepts and standards.

As for the AICPA itself, it is unlikely that it could succeed in this endeavor. It would have no way of obtaining adherence to cost standards comparable to the sanctions it can apply to information on published financial statements, and it has no obvious new source of financial support that would at least double the money it now raises.

Congress, moreover, which will undoubtedly have the final say on how the job gets done, would be unwilling to rely on a private organization unless it was convinced that the group would be permanent, well financed, and authoritative; that it adequately represented the interests of both government and business; and that it had safeguards against dilatory tactics.

I cannot visualize a private-sector effort that would satisfy these conditions. Indeed, the generally negative testimony of trade association representatives before the Senate Banking and Currency Committee in 1968 and negative responses to the General Accounting Office's request for comments on the feasibility of cost standards indicate that substantial segments of the business community are unwilling to meet these conditions.

A Government Effort. It seems likely, therefore, that the organization will be set up within the framework of the federal government. This can be done in either of two ways:

1. Congress could direct the comptroller general to undertake the task. (The Bureau of the Budget, the other possibility among existing organizations, has not been as close to the problem, nor does it have the nucleus of a staff.) The comptroller general might then set up a cost standards board, similar to the APB. He probably would obtain nominations for membership on this board from the accounting profession, business organizations, government organizations, and the academic community.

The board would specify the research that should be undertaken, and it would eventually make recommendations on cost concepts and standards to the comptroller general. The ground rule might be that the comptroller general would normally accept these recommendations, but he could modify or reject them for substantial cause.

2. An independent organization could be created, consisting of a small group of commissioners supported by an appropriate staff. It would be appointed by the president (probably in consultation with the comptroller general as the representative of the legislative branch in these matters) and financed with appropriated funds. Its pronouncements on standards would be authoritative since they presumably would be binding for government contracts, and might well be made applicable to the cost-measurement systems prescribed by various regulatory agencies.

Such a body could easily evolve into the "accounting court" which Leonard Spacek, chairman of Arthur Andersen & Company, has long advocated. After cost standards are developed, questions of interpretation will arise, and the board would provide a logical mechanism for resolving such questions. With such a procedure, there would also be a greater likelihood that the standards are kept in tune with changing circumstances.

The choice between these alternatives is by no means clearcut. An independent commission would give greater status to the effort, and it also would be more acceptable to those segments of the business community that are worried about the impartiality of an effort lodged within the General Accounting Office.

On the other hand, a commission is an unknown quantity. With appointees of the right caliber, it could do a better job than an existing organization, but if its members are second-rate, nothing useful would happen. It will not be easy to find high-salaried men who are willing to risk their careers in a much lower-paying job. Perhaps a part-time commission is the answer, though this device is rarely used in the federal government.

However established, the organization needs an adequate staff both to undertake research and to arrange for outside parties to do research. Such a staff would also operate the mechanism for circulating drafts of proposed concepts and standards for comment, and it would analyze and summarize the comments for the board or commission.

CONCLUDING NOTE

Too often, as I have tried to show, the word "cost" has a vague and ill-defined meaning, which can be troublesome particularly in contracts where cost is part of the reimbursement. An increasing number of persons for whom the meaning of cost is important have come to realize that standardization of meanings is a feasible goal.

These persons—in the business sector, in government agencies, and in Congress—understand that what must be done is to establish an authoritative, well-financed group which is charged with development of cost concepts and standards. So far the activity is just talk, but in the not-distant future the creation by the mutually interested parties of such a body may become a reality.

Inaction would be very disadvantageous to business. Congress might be persuaded to take no action, either on the false premise that there is no problem or on the promise that the business community will do the job in some unspecified way.

If Congress does not act, and if the subsequent voluntary effort is half-hearted and dilatory, in a few years the problem will make the headlines once more, and we will then almost surely see a unilateral government effort, probably with only insignificant participation by business.

9. Production, Information Costs, and Economic Organization[*]

ARMEN A. ALCHIAN and HAROLD DEMSETZ

The mark of a capitalistic society is that resources are owned and allocated by such nongovernmental organizations as firms, households, and markets. Resource owners increase productivity through cooperative specialization and this leads to the demand for economic organizations which facilitate cooperation. When a lumber mill employs a cabinetmaker, cooperation between specialists is achieved within a firm, and when a cabinetmaker purchases wood from a lumberman, the cooperation takes place across markets (or between firms). Two important problems face a theory of economic organization—to explain the conditions that determine whether the gains from specialization and cooperative production can better be obtained within an organization like the firm, or across markets, and to explain the structure of the organization.

It is common to see the firm characterized by the power to settle issues by fiat, by authority, or by disciplinary action superior to that available in the conventional market. This is delusion. The firm does not own all its inputs. It has no power of fiat, no authority, no disciplinary action any different in the slightest degree from ordinary market contracting between any two people. I can "punish" you only by withholding future business or by seeking redress in the courts for any failure to honor our exchange agreement. That is exactly all that any employer can do. He can fire or sue, just as I can fire my grocer by stopping purchases from him or sue him for delivering faulty products. What then is the content of the presumed power to manage and assign workers to various tasks? Exactly the same as one little consumer's power to manage and assign his grocer to various tasks. The single consumer can assign his grocer to the task of obtaining whatever the customer can induce the grocer to provide at a price acceptable to both parties. That is precisely all that an employer can do to an employee. To speak of managing, directing, or assigning workers to various tasks is a deceptive way of noting

[*] *American Economic Review*, vol. 62, no. 5 (December 1972), pp. 777–95.

that the employer continually is involved in renegotiation of contracts on terms that must be acceptable to both parties. Telling an employee to type this letter rather than to file that document is like my telling a grocer to sell me this brand of tuna rather than that brand of bread. I have no contract to continue to purchase from the grocer and neither the employer nor the employee is bound by any contractual obligations to continue their relationship. Long-term contracts between employer and employee are not the essence of the organization we call a firm. My grocer can count on my returning day after day and purchasing his services and goods even with the prices not always marked on the goods —because I know what they are—and he adapts his activity to conform to my directions to him as to what I want each day . . . he is not my employee.

Wherein then is the relationship between a grocer and his employee different from that between a grocer and his customers? It is in a *team* use of inputs and a centralized position of some party in the contractual arrangements of *all* other inputs. It is the *centralized contractual agent in a team productive process*—not some superior authoritarian directive or disciplinary power. Exactly what is a team process and why does it induce the contractual form, called the firm? These problems motivate the inquiry of this paper.

I. THE METERING PROBLEM

The economic organization through which input owners cooperate will make better use of their comparative advantages to the extent that it facilitates the payment of rewards in accord with productivity. If rewards were random, and without reward to productive effort, no incentive to productive effort would be provided by the organization; and if rewards were negatively correlated with productivity the organization would be subect to sabotage. Two key demands are placed on an economic organization—metering input productivity and metering rewards.

Metering problems sometimes can be resolved well through the exchange of products across competitive markets, because in many situations markets yield a high correlation between rewards and productivity. If a farmer increases his output of wheat by 10 percent at the prevailing market price, his receipts also increase by 10 percent. This method of organizing economic activity meters the *output directly,* reveals the marginal product and apportions the *rewards* to resource owners in accord with that direct measurement of their outputs. The success of this decentralized, market exchange in promoting productive specialization requires that changes in market rewards fall on those responsible for changes in *output.*

The classic relationship in economics that runs from marginal productivity to the distribution of income implicitly *assumes* the existence of an organization, be it the market or the firm, that allocates rewards to resources in accord with their productivity. The problem of economic organization, the economical means of metering productivity and rewards, is not confronted directly in the classical analysis of production and distribution. Instead, that analysis tends to assume sufficiently economic—or zero cost—means, as if productivity automatically created its reward. We conjecture the direction of causation is the reverse—the specific system of rewarding which is relied upon stimulates a particular productivity response. If the economic organization meters poorly, with rewards and productivity only loosely correlated, then productivity will be smaller; but if the economic organization meters well productivity will be greater. What makes metering difficult and hence induces means of economizing on metering costs?

II. TEAM PRODUCTION

Two men jointly lift heavy cargo into trucks. Solely by observing the total weight loaded per day, it is impossible to determine each person's marginal productivity. With team production it is difficult, solely by observing total output, to either define or determine *each* individual's contribution to this output of the cooperating inputs. The output is yielded by a team, by definition, and it is not a *sum* of separable outputs of each of its members. Team production of Z involves at least two inputs, X_i and X_j, with $\partial^2 Z / \partial X_i \partial X_j \neq 0$. The production function is *not* separable into two functions each involving only inputs X_i or only inputs X_j. Consequently there is no *sum* of Z of two separable functions to treat as the Z of the team production function. (An example of a *separable* case is $Z = aX_i^2 + bX_j^2$ which is separable into $Z_i = aX_i^2$ and $Z_j = bX_j^2$, and $Z = Z_i + Z_j$. This is not team production.) There exists production techniques in which the Z obtained is greater than if X_i and X_j had produced separable Z. Team production will be used if it yields an output enough larger than the sum of separable production of Z to cover the costs of organizing and disciplining team members—the topics of this paper.

Usual explanations of the gains from cooperative behavior rely on exchange and production in accord with the comparative advantage specialization principle with separable additive production. However, as suggested above there is a source of gain from cooperative activity involving working as a *team*, wherein individual cooperating inputs do not yield identifiable, separate products which can be *summed* to measure the total output. For this cooperative productive activity, here called "team" production, measuring *marginal* productivity and making payments in accord therewith is more expensive by an order of magnitude than for separable production functions.

Team production, to repeat, is production in which (1) several types of resources are used and (2) the product is not a sum of separable outputs of each cooperating resource. An additional factor creates a team organization problem—(3) not all resources used in team production belong to one person.

We do not inquire into why all the jointly used resources are not owned by one person, but instead into the types of organization, contracts, and informational and payment procedures used among owners of teamed inputs. With respect to the one-owner case, perhaps it is sufficient merely to note that (*a*) slavery is prohibited, (*b*) one might assume risk aversion as a reason for one person's not borrowing enough to purchase all the assets or sources of services rather than renting them, and (*c*) the purchase-resale spread may be so large that costs of short-term ownership exceed rental costs. Our problem is viewed basically as one of organization among different people, not of the physical goods or services, however much there must be selection and choice of combination of the latter.

How can the members of a team be rewarded and induced to work efficiently? In team production, marginal products of cooperative team members are not so direct and separably (i.e., cheaply) observable. What a team offers to the market can be taken as the marginal product of the team but not of the team members. The costs of metering or ascertaining the marginal products of the team's members is what calls forth new organizations and procedures. Clues to each input's productivity can be secured by observing *behavior* of individual inputs. When lifting cargo into the truck, how rapidly does a man move to the next piece to be loaded, how many cigarette breaks does he take, does the item being lifted tilt downward toward his side?

If detecting such behavior were costless, neither party would have an incentive to shirk, because neither could impose the cost of his shirking on the other (if their cooperation was agreed to voluntarily). But since costs must be incurred to monitor each other, each input owner will have more incentive to shirk when he works as part of a team, than if his performance could be monitored easily or if he did not work as a team. If there is a net increase in productivity available by team production, net of the metering cost associated with disciplining the team, then team production will be relied upon rather than a multitude of bilateral exchange of separable individual outputs.

Both leisure and higher income enter a person's utility function. Hence, each person should adjust his work and realized reward so as to equate the marginal rate of substitution between leisure and production of real output to his marginal rate of substitution in consumption. That is, he would adjust his rate of work to bring his demand prices of leisure and output to equality with their true costs. However, with detection, policing, monitoring, measuring or metering costs, each person will be induced to take more leisure, because the effect of relaxing on *his realized* (reward) rate of substitution between output and leisure will be less than the effect on the *true* rate of substitution. His realized cost of leisure will fall more than the true cost of leisure, so he "buys" more leisure (i.e., more nonpecuniary reward).

If his relaxation cannot be detected perfectly at zero cost, part of its effects will be borne by others in the team, thus making *his* realized cost of relaxation less than the true total cost to the team. The difficulty of detecting such actions permits the private costs of his actions to be less than their full costs. Since each person responds to his private realizable rate of substitution (in production) rather than the true total (i.e., social) rate, and so long as there are costs for other people to detect his shift toward relaxation, it will not pay (them) to force him to readjust completely by making him realize the true cost. Only enough efforts will be made to equate the marginal gains of detection activity with the marginal costs of detection; and that implies a lower rate of productive effort and more shirking than in a costless monitoring, or measuring, world.

In a university, the faculty use office telephones, paper, and mail for personal uses beyond strict university productivity. The university administrators could stop such practices by identifying *the* responsible person in each case, but they can do so only at higher costs than administrators are willing to incur. The extra costs of identifying each party (rather than merely identifying the presence of such activity) would exceed the savings from diminished faculty "turpitudinal peccadilloes." So the faculty is allowed some degree of "privileges, perquisites, or fringe benefits." And the total of the pecuniary wages paid is lower because of this irreducible (at acceptable costs) degree of amenity-seizing activity. Pay is lower in pecuniary terms and higher in leisure, conveniences, and ease of work. But still every person would prefer to see detection made more effective (if it were somehow possible to monitor costlessly) so that he, as part of the now more effectively producing team, could thereby realize a higher pecuniary pay and less leisure. If everyone could, at zero cost, have his reward-realized rate brought to the true production possibility real rate, all could achieve a more preferred position. But detection of the responsible parties is costly; that cost acts like a tax on work rewards. Viable shirking is the result.

What forms of organizing team production will lower the cost of detecting "performance" (i.e., marginal productivity) and bring personally realized rates of substitution closer to true rates of substitution? Market competition, in principle, could monitor some team production. (It already *organizes* teams.) Input owners who are not team members can offer, in return for a smaller share of the team's rewards, to replace excessively (i.e., overpaid) shirking members. Market competition among potential team members would determine team membership and individual rewards. There would be no team leader, manager, organizer, owner, or employer. For such decentralized organizational control to work, outsiders, possibly after observing each team's total output, can speculate about their capabilities as team members and, by a market competitive process, revised teams with greater productive ability will be formed and sustained. Incumbent members will be constrained by threats of replacement by outsiders offering services for lower reward shares or offering greater rewards to the other members of the team. Any team member who shirked in the expectation that the reduced output effect would not be attributed to him will be displaced if his activity is detected. Teams of productive inputs, like business units, would evolve in apparent spontaneity in the market—without any central organizing agent, team manager, or boss.

But completely effective control cannot be expected from individualized market competition for two reasons. First, for this competition to be completely effective, new challengers for team membership must know where, and to what extent, shirking is a serious problem, that is, know they can increase net output as compared with the inputs they replace. To the extent that this is true it is probably possible for existing fellow team members to recognize the shirking. But, by definition, the detection of shirking by observing team output is costly for team production. Secondly, assume the presence of detection costs, and assume that in order to secure a place on the team a new input owner must accept a smaller share of rewards (or a promise to produce more). Then his incentive to shirk would still be at least as great as the incentives of the inputs replaced, because he still bears less than the entire reduction in team output for which he is responsible.

III. THE CLASSICAL FIRM

One method of reducing shirking is for someone to specialize as a monitor to check the input performance of team members. But who will monitor the monitor? One constraint on the monitor is the aforesaid market competition offered by other monitors, but for reasons already given, that is not perfectly effective. Another constraint can be imposed on the monitor: give him title to the net earnings of the team, net of payments to other inputs. If owners of cooperating inputs agree with the monitor that he is to receive any residual product above prescribed amounts (hopefully, the marginal value products of the other inputs), the monitor will have an added incentive not to shirk as a monitor. Specialization in monitoring plus reliance on a residual claimant status will reduce shirking; but additional links are needed to forge the firm of classical economic theory. How will the residual claimant monitor the other inputs?

We use the term *monitor* to connote several activities in addition to its disciplinary connotation. It connotes measuring output performance, apportioning rewards, observing the input behavior of inputs as means of detecting or estimating their marginal productivity and giving assignments or instructions in what to do and how to do it. (It also includes, as we shall show later, authority to terminate or revise contracts.) Perhaps the contrast between a football coach and team captain is helpful. The coach selects strategies and tactics and sends in instructions about what plays to utilize. The captain is essentially an observer and reporter of the performance at close hand of the members. The latter is an inspector-steward and the former a supervisor manager. For the present all these activities are included in the rubric "monitoring." All these tasks are, in principle, negotiable across markets, but we are presuming that such market measurement of marginal productivities and job reassignments are not so cheaply performed for team production. And in particular our analysis suggests that it is not so much the costs of spontaneously negotiating contracts in the markets among groups for team production as it is the detection of the performance of individual members of the team that calls for the organization noted here.

The specialist *who receives the residual rewards* will be the monitor of the members of the team (i.e., will manage the use of cooperative inputs). The monitor earns his residual through the reduction in shirking that he brings about, not only by the prices that he agrees to pay the owners of the inputs, but also by observing and directing the actions or uses of these inputs. *Managing or examining the ways to which inputs are used in team production is a method of metering the marginal productivity of individual inputs to the team's output.*

To discipline team members and reduce shirking, the residual claimant must have power to revise the contract terms and incentives of *individual* members without having to terminate or alter every other input's contract. Hence, team members who seek to increase their productivity will assign to the monitor not only the residual claimant right but also the right to alter individual membership and performance on the team. Each team member, of course, can terminate his own membership (i.e., quit the team), but only the monitor may unilaterally terminate the membership of any of the other members without necessarily terminating the team itself or his association with the team; and he alone can expand or reduce membership, alter the mix of membership, or sell the right to be the residual claimant-monitor of the team. It is this entire bundle of rights: (1) to be a residual claimant; (2) to observe input behavior; (3) to be the central party common to all contracts with inputs; (4) to alter the membership of the team; and (5) to sell these rights, that defines the *ownership* (or the employer) of the *classical* (capitalist, free-enterprise) firm. The coalescing of these rights has arisen, our analysis asserts, because it resolves the shirking-information problem of team production better than does the noncentralized contractual arrangement.

The relationship of each team member to the *owner* of the firm (i.e, the party common to all input contracts *and* the residual claimant) is simply a "quid pro quo" contract. Each makes a purchase and sale. The employee "orders" the owner of the team to pay him money in the same sense that the employer directs the team member to perform certain acts. The employee can terminate the contract as readily as can the employer, and long-term contracts, therefore, are not an essential attribute of the firm. Nor are "authoritarian," "dictational," or "fiat" attributes relevant to the conception of the firm or its efficiency.

In summary, two necessary conditions exist for the emergence of the firm on the prior assumption that more than pecuniary wealth enter utility functions: (1) It is possible to increase productivity through team-oriented production, a production technique for which it is costly to directly measure the marginal outputs of the cooperating inputs. This makes it more difficult to restrict shirking through simple market exchange between cooperating inputs. (2) It is economical to estimate marginal productivity by observing or specifying input behavior. The simultaneous occurrence of both these preconditions leads to the contractual organization of inputs, known as the *classical capitalist firms* with (a) joint input production, (b) several input owners, (c) one party who is common to all the contracts of the joint inputs, (d) who has rights to renegotiate any input's contract independently of contracts with other input owners, (e) who holds the residual claim, and (f) who has the right to sell his central contractual residual status.

Other Theories of the Firm

At this juncture, as an aside, we briefly place this theory of the firm in the contexts of those offered by Ronald Coase and Frank Knight. Our view of the firm is not necessarily inconsistent with Coase's; we attempt to go further and identify refutable implications. Coase's penetrating insight is to make more of the fact that markets do not operate costlessly, and he relies on the cost of using markets to *form* contracts as his basic explanation for the existence of firms. We do not disagree with the proposition that, *ceteris paribus,* the higher is the cost of transacting across markets the greater will be the comparative advantage of organizing resources within the firm; it is a difficult proposition to disagree with or to refute. We could with equal ease subscribe to a theory of the firm based on the cost of managing, for surely it is true that, *ceteris paribus*, the lower is the cost of managing the greater will be the comparative advantage of organizing resources within the firm. To move the theory forward, it is necessary to know what is meant by a firm and to explain the circumstances under which the cost of "managing" resources is low relative to the cost of allocating resources through market transaction. The conception of and rationale for the classical firm that we propose takes a step down the path pointed out by Coase toward that goal. Consideration of team production, team organization, difficulty in metering outputs, and the problem of shirking are important to our explanation but, so far as we can ascertain, not in Coase's. Coase's analysis insofar as it had heretofore been developed would suggest open-ended contracts but does not appear to imply anything more—neither the residual claimant status nor the distinction between employee and subcontractor status (nor any of the implications indicated below). And it is not true that employees are generally employed on the basis of long-term contractual arrangements any more than on a series of short-term or indefinite length contracts.

The importance of our proposed additional elements is revealed, for example, by the explanation of why the person to whom the control monitor is responsible receives the residual, and also by our later discussion of the implications about the corporation, partnerships, and profit sharing. These alternative forms for organization of the firm are difficult to resolve on the basis of market transaction costs only. Our exposition also suggests a definition of the classical firm—something crucial that was heretofore absent.

In addition, sometimes a technological development will lower the cost of market transactions while, at the same time, it expands the role of the firm. When the "putting out" system was used for weaving, inputs were organized largely through market negotiations. With the development of efficient central sources of power, it became economical to perform weaving in proximity to the power source and to engage in team production. The bringing in of weavers surely must have resulted in a reduction in the cost of negotiating (forming) contracts. Yet, what we observe is the beginning of the factory system in which inputs are organized within a firm. Why? The weavers did not simply move to a common source of power that they could tap like an electric line, purchasing power while they used their own equipment. Now team production in the joint use of equipment became more important. The measurement of marginal productivity, which now involved interactions between workers, especially through their joint use of machines, became more difficult through contract negotiating cost was reduced, while managing the *behavior* of inputs became easier because of the increased centralization of activity. The firm as an organization expanded even though the cost of transactions was reduced by the advent of centralized power. The same could be said for modern assembly lines. Hence the emergence of central power sources expanded the scope of productive ability in which the firm enjoyed a comparative advantage as an organizational form.

Some economists, following Knight, have identified the bearing of risks of wealth changes with the director or central employer without explaining why that is a viable arrangement. Presumably, the more risk-averse inputs become employees rather than owners of the classical firm. Risk averseness and uncertainty *with regard to the firm's fortunes* have little, if anything, to do with our explanation although it helps to explain why all resources in a team are not owned by one person. That is, the role of risk taken in the sense of absorbing the windfalls that buffet the firm because of unforeseen competition, technological change, or fluctuations in demand are not central to our theory, although it is true that imperfect knowledge and, therefore, risk, in *this* sense of risk, underlie the problem of monitoring team behavior. We deduce the system of paying the manager with a residual claim (the equity) from the desire to have efficient means to reduce shirking so as to make team production economical and not from the smaller aversion to the risks of enterprise in a dynamic economy. We conjecture that "distribution-of-risk" is not a valid rationale for the *existence* and organization of the *classical* firm.

Although we have emphasized team production as creating a costly metering task and have treated team production as an essential (necessary?) condition for the firm, would not other obstacles to cheap metering also call forth the same kind of contractual arrangement here denoted as a firm? For example, suppose a farmer produces wheat in an easily ascertained quantity but with subtle and difficult to detect quality variations determined by how the farmer grew the wheat. A vertical integration could allow a purchaser to control the farmer's behavior in order to more economically estimate productivity. But this is not a case of joint or team production, unless "information" can be considered part of the product. (While a good case could be made for that broader conception of production, we shall ignore it here.) Instead of forming a firm, a buyer can contract to have his inspector on the site of production, just as home builders contract with architects to supervise building contracts; that arrangement is not a firm. Still, a firm might be organized in the production of many products wherein no team production or jointness of use of separately owned resources is involved.

This possibility rather clearly indicates a broader, or complementary, approach to that which we have chosen. (1) As we do in this paper, it can be argued that the firm is the particular policing device utilized when joint team production is present. If other sources of high policing costs arise, as in the wheat case just indicated, some other form of contractual arrangement will be used. Thus to each source of informational cost there may be a different type of policing and contractual arrangement. (2) On the other hand, one can say that where policing is difficult across markets, various forms of contractual arrangements are devised, but there is no reason for that known as the firm to be uniquely related or even highly correlated with team production, as defined here. It might be used equally probably and viably for other sources of high policing cost. We have not intensively analyzed other sources, and we can only note that our current and readily revisable conjecture is that (1) is valid, and has motivated us in our current endeavor. In any event, the test of the theory advanced here is to see whether the conditions we have identified are necessary for firms to have long-run viability rather than merely births with high infant mortality. Conglomerate firms or collections of separate production agencies into one owning organization can be interpreted as an investment trust or investment diversification device—probably along the lines that motivated Knight's interpretation. A holding company can be called a firm, because of the common association of the word firm with any ownership unit that owns income sources. The term *firm* as commonly used is so turgid of meaning that we can not hope to explain every entity to which the name is attached in common or even technical literature. Instead, we seek to identify and explain a particular contractual arrangement induced by the cost of information factors analyzed in this paper.

IV. TYPES OF FIRMS

A. Profit-Sharing Firms

Explicit in our explanation of the capitalist firm is the assumption that the cost of *managing* the team's inputs by a central monitor, who disciplines himself because he is a residual claimant, is low relative to the cost of metering the marginal outputs of team members.

If we look within a firm to see who monitors—hires, fires, changes, promotes, and renegotiates—we should find him being a residual claimant or, at least, one whose pay or reward is more than any others correlated with fluctuations in the residual value of the firm. They more likely will have options or rights or bonuses than will inputs with other tasks.

An implicit "auxiliary" assumption of our explanation of the firm is that the cost of team production is increased if the residual claim is not held entirely by the central monitor. That is, we assume that if profit sharing had to be relied upon for *all* team members, losses from the resulting increase in central monitor shirking would exceed the output gains from the increased incentives of other team members not to shirk. If the optimal team size is only two owners of inputs, then an equal division of profits and losses between them will leave each with stronger incentives to reduce shirking than if the optimal team size is large, for in the latter case only a smaller percentage of the losses occasioned by the shirker will be borne by him. Incentives to shirk are positively related to the optimal size of the team under an equal profit-sharing scheme.

The preceding does not imply that profit sharing is never viable. Profit sharing to encourage self-policing is more appropriate for small teams. And, indeed, where input owners are free to make whatever contractual arrangements suit them, as generally is true in capitalist economies, profit sharing seems largely limited to partnerships with a relatively small number of *active* partners. Another advantage of such arrangements for smaller teams is that it permits more effective reciprocal monitoring among inputs. Monitoring need not be entirely specialized.

Profit sharing is more viable if small team size is associated with situations where the cost of specialized management of inputs is large relative to the increased productivity potential in team effort. We conjecture that the cost of managing team inputs increases if the productivity of a team member is difficult to correlate with his behavior. In "artistic" or "professional" work, watching a man's activities is not a good clue to what he is actually thinking or doing with his mind. While it is relatively easy to manage or direct the loading of trucks by a team of dock workers where input activity is so highly related in an obvious way to output, it is more difficult to manage and direct a lawyer in the preparation and presentation of a case. Dock workers can be directed in detail without the monitor himself loading the truck, and assembly line workers can be monitored by varying the speed of the assembly line, but detailed direction in the preparation of a law case would require in much greater degree that the monitor prepare the case himself. As a result, artistic or professional inputs, such as lawyers, advertising specialists, and doctors, will be given relatively freer reign with regard to individual behavior. If the management of inputs is relatively costly, or ineffective, as it would seem to be in these cases, but, nonetheless if team effort is more productive than separable production with exchange across markets, then there will develop a tendency to use profit-sharing schemes to provide incentives to avoid shirking.

B. Socialist Firms

We have analyzed the classical proprietorship and the profit-sharing firms in the context of free association and choice of economic organization. Such organizations need not be the most viable when political constraints limit the forms of organization that can be chosen. It is one thing to have profit sharing when professional or artistic talents are used by small teams. But if political or tax or subsidy considerations induce profit-sharing techniques when these are not otherwise economically justified, then additional management techniques will be developed to help reduce the degree of shirking.

For example, most, if not all, firms in Jugoslavia are owned by the employees in the restricted sense that all share in the residual. This is true for large firms and for firms which employ nonartistic, or nonprofessional, workers as well. With a decay of political constraints, most of these firms could be expected to rely on paid wages rather than shares in the residual. This rests on our auxiliary assumption that general sharing in the residual results in losses from enhanced shirking by the monitor that exceed the gains from reduced shirking by residual-sharing employees. If this were not so, profit sharing with employees should have occurred more frequently in Western societies whre such organizations are neither banned nor preferred politically. Where residual sharing by employees is politically imposed, as in Jugoslavia, we are led to expect that some management technique will arise to reduce the shirking by the central monitor, a technique that will not be found frequently in Western societies since the monitor retains all (or much) of the residual in the West and profit sharing is largely confined to small, professional-artistic team production situations. We do find in the larger scale residual-sharing firms in Jugoslavia that there are employee committees that can recommend (to the state) the termination of a manager's contract (veto his continuance) with the enterprise. We conjecture that the workers' committee is given the right to recommend the termination of the manager's contract precisely because the general sharing of the residual increases "excessively" the manager's incentive to shirk.

C. The Corporation

All firms must initially acquire command over some resources. The corporation does so primarily by selling promises of future returns to those who (as creditors or owners) provide financial capital. In some situations resources can be acquired in advance from consumers by promises of future delivery (for example, advance sale of a proposed book). Or where the firm is a few artistic or professional persons, each can "chip in" with time and talent until the sale of services brings in revenues. For the most part, capital can be acquired more cheaply if many (risk-averse) investors contribute small portions to a large investment. The economies of raising large sums of equity capital in this way suggest that modifications in the relationship among corporate inputs are required to cope with the shirking problem that arises with profit sharing among large numbers of corporate stockholders. One modification is limited liability, especially for firms that are large relative to a stockholder's wealth. It serves to protect stockholders from large losses no matter how they are caused.

If every stock owner participated in each decision in a corporation, not only would large bureaucratic costs be incurred, but many would shirk the task of becoming well informed on the issue to be decided, since the losses associated with unexpectedly bad decisions will be borne in large part by the many other corporate shareholders. More effective control of corporate activity is achieved for most purposes by transferring decision authority to a smaller group, whose main function is to negotiate with and manage (renegotiate with) the other inputs of the team. The corporate stockholders retain the authority to revise the membership of the management group and over major decisions that affect the structure of the corporation or its dissolution.

As a result a new modification of partnerships is induced—the right to sale of corporate shares without approval of any other stockholders. Any shareholder can remove his wealth from control by those with whom he has differences of opinion. Rather than try to control the decisions of the management, which is harder to do with many stockholders than with only a few, unrestricted salability provides a more acceptable escape to each stockholder from continued policies with which he disagrees.

 Indeed, the policing of managerial shirking relies on across-market competition from new groups of would-be managers as well as competition from members within the firm who seek to displace existing management. In addition to competition from outside and inside managers, control is facilitated by the temporary congealing of share votes into voting blocs owned by one or a few contenders. Proxy battles or stock-purchases concentrate the votes required to displace the existing management or modify managerial policies. But it is more than a change in policy that is sought by the newly formed financial interests, whether of new stockholders or not. It is the capitalization of expected future benefits into stock prices that concentrates on the innovators the wealth gains of their actions if they own large numbers of shares. Without capitalization of future benefits, there would be less incentive to incur the costs required to exert informed decisive influence on the corporation's policies and managing personnel. Temporarily, the structure of ownership is reformed, moving away from diffused ownership into decisive power blocs, and this is a transient resurgence of the classical firm with power again concentrated in those who have title to the residual.

In assessing the significance of stockholders' power it is not the usual diffusion of voting power that is significant but instead the frequency with which voting congeals into decisive changes. Even a one-man-owned company may have a long term with just one manager—continuously being approved by the owner. Similarly a dispersed voting power corporation may be also characterized by a long-lived management. The question is the probability of replacement of the management if it behaves in ways not acceptable to a majority of the stockholders. The unrestricted salability of stock and the transfer of proxies enhances the probability of decisive action in the event current stockholders or any outsider believes that management is not doing a good job with the corporation. We are not comparing the corporate responsiveness to that of a single proprietorship; instead, we are indicating features of the corporate structure that are induced by the problem of delegated authority to manager-monitors.

D. Mutual and Nonprofit Firms

The benefits obtained by the new management are greater if the stock can be purchased and sold, because this enables *capitalization* of anticipated future improvements into present *wealth* of new managers who bought stock and created a larger capital by their management changes. But in nonprofit corporations, colleges, churches, country clubs, mutual savings banks, mutual insurance companies, and "coops," the future consequences of improved management are not capitalized into present wealth of stockholders. (As if to make more difficult that competition by new would-be monitors, multiple shares of ownership in those enterprises cannot be bought by one person.) One should, therefore, find greater shirking in nonprofit, mutually owned enterprises. (This suggests that nonprofit enterprises are especially appropriate in realms of endeavor where more shirking is desired and where redirected uses of the enterprise in response to market-revealed values is less desired.)

E. Partnerships

Team production in artistic or professional intellectual skills will more likely be by partnerships than other types of team production. This amounts to market-organized team activity and to a non-employed status. Self-monitoring partnerships, therefore, will be used rather than employer-employee contracts, and these organizations will be small to prevent an excessive dilution of efforts through shirking. Also, partnerships are more likely to occur among relatives or long-standing acquaintances, not necessarily because they share a common utility function, but also because each knows better the other's work characteristics and tendencies to shirk.

F. Employee Unions

Employee unions, whatever else they do, perform as monitors for employees. Employers monitor employees and similarly employees monitor an employer's performance. Are correct wages paid on time and in good currency? Usually, this is extremely easy to check. But some forms of employer performance are less easy to meter and are more subject to employer shirking. Fringe benefits often are in nonpecuniary, contingent form; medical, hospital, and accident insurance, and retirement pensions are contingent payments or performances partly in *kind* by employers to employees. Each employee cannot judge the character of such payments as easily as money wages. Insurance is a contingent payment—what the employee will get upon the contingent event may come as a disappointment. If he could easily determine what other employees had gotten upon such contingent events he could judge more accurately the performance by the employer. He could "trust" the employer not to shirk in such fringe contingent payments, but he would prefer an effective and economic monitor of those payments. We see a specialist monitor—the union employees' agent—hired by them and monitoring those aspects of employer payment most difficult for the employees to monitor. Employees should be willing to employ a specialist monitor to administer such hard-to-detect employer performance, even though their monitor has incentives to use pension and retirement funds not entirely for the benefit of employees.

V. TEAM SPIRIT AND LOYALTY

Every team member would prefer a team in which no one, not even himself, shirked. Then the true marginal costs and values could be equated to achieve more preferred positions. If one could enhance a common interest in nonshirking in the guise of a team loyalty or team spirit, the team would be more efficient. In those sports where team activity is most clearly exemplified, the sense of loyalty and team spirit is most strongly urged. Obviously the team is better, with team spirit and loyalty, because of the reduced shirking—not because of some other feature inherent in loyalty or spirit as such.

Corporations and business firms try to instill a spirit of loyalty. This should not be viewed simply as a device to increase profits by *over-*working or misleading the employees, nor as an adolescent urge for belonging. It promotes a closer approximation to the employees' potentially available true rates of substitution between production and leisure and enables each team member to achieve a more preferred situation. The difficulty, of course, is to create economically that team spirit and loyalty. It can be preached with an aura of moral code of conduct—a morality with literally the same basis as the ten commandments—to restrict our conduct toward what we would choose if we bore our full costs.

VI. KINDS OF INPUTS OWNED BY THE FIRM

To this point the discussion has examined why firms, as we have defined them, exist? That is, why is there an owner-employer who is the common party to contracts with other owners of inputs in team activity? The answer to that question should also indicate the kind of the jointly used resources likely to be owned by the central-owner-monitor and the kind likely to be hired from people who are not team owners. Can we identify characteristics or features of various inputs that lead to their being hired or to their being owned by the firm?

How can residual-claimant, central-employer-owner demonstrate ability to pay the other hired inputs the promised amount in the event of a loss? He can pay in advance or he can commit wealth sufficient to cover negative residuals. The latter will take the form of machines, land, buildings, or raw materials committed to the firm. Commitments of labor-wealth (i.e., human wealth) given the property rights in people, is less feasible. These considerations suggest that residual claimants—owners of the firm—will be investors of resalable capital equipment in the firm. The goods or inputs more likely to be invested, than rented, by the owners of the enterprise, will have higher resale values relative to the initial cost and will have longer expected use in a firm relative to the economic life of the good.

But beyond these factors are those developed above to explain the existence of the institution known as the firm—the costs of detecting output performance. When a durable resource is used it will have a marginal product and a depreciation. Its use requires payment to cover at least use-induced depreciation; unless that user cost is specifically detectable, payment for it will be demanded in accord with *expected* depreciation. And we can ascertain circumstances for each. An indestructible hammer with a readily detectable marginal product has zero user cost. But suppose the hammer were destructible and that careless (which is easier than careful) use is more abusive and causes greater depreciation of the hammer. Suppose in addition the abuse is easier to detect by observing the way it is used than by observing only the hammer after its use, or by measuring the output scored from a hammer by a laborer. If the hammer were rented and used in the absence of the owner, the depreciation would be greater than if the use were observed by the owner and the user charged in accord with the imposed depreciation. (Careless use is more likely than careful use—if one does not pay for the greater depreciation.) An absentee owner would therefore ask for a higher rental price because of the higher *expected* user cost than if the item were used by the owner. The expectation is higher because of the greater difficulty of observing specific user cost, by inspection of the hammer after use. Renting is therefore in this case more costly than owner use. This is the valid content of the misleading expressions about ownership being more economical than renting—ignoring all other factors that may work in the opposite direction, like tax provision, short-term occupancy and capital risk avoidance.

Better examples are tools of the trade. Watch repairers, engineers, and carpenters tend to own their own tools especially if they are portable. Trucks are more likely to be employee owned rather than other equally expensive team inputs because it is relatively cheap for the driver to police the care taken in using a truck. Policing the use of trucks by a nondriver owner is more likely to occur for trucks that are not specialized to one driver, like public transit busses.

The factor with which we are concerned here is one related to the costs of monitoring not only the gross product performance of an input but also the abuse or depreciation inflicted on the input in the course of its use. If depreciation or user cost is more cheaply detected when the owner can see its use than by only seeing the input before and after, there is a force toward owner use rather than renting. Resources whose user cost is harder to detect when used by someone else, tend on this count to be owner used. Absentee ownership, in the lay language, will be less likely. Assume momentarily that labor service cannot be performed in the absence of its owner. The labor owner can more cheaply monitor any abuse of himself than if somehow labor services could be provided without the labor owner observing its mode of use or knowing what was happening. Also his incentive to abuse himself is increased if he does not own himself.

The similarity between the preceding analysis and the question of absentee landlordism and of sharecropping arrangements is no accident. The same factors which explain the contractual arrangements known as a firm help to explain the incidence of tenancy, labor hiring or share-cropping.

VII. FIRMS AS A SPECIALIZED MARKET INSTITUTION FOR COLLECTING, COLLATING, AND SELLING INPUT INFORMATION

The firm serves as a highly specialized surrogate market. Any person contemplating a joint-input activity must search and detect the qualities of available joint inputs. He could contact an employment agency, but that agency in a small town would have little advantage over a large firm with many inputs. The employer, by virtue of monitoring many inputs, acquires special superior information about their productive talents. This aids his *directive* (i.e., market hiring) efficiency. He "sells" his information to employee inputs as he aids them in ascertaining good input combinations for team activity. Those who work as employees or who rent services to him are using him to discern superior combinations of inputs. Not only does the director-employer "decide" what each input will produce, he also estimates which heterogeneous inputs will work together jointly more efficiently, and he does this in the context of a privately owned market for forming teams. The department store is a firm and is a superior private market. People who shop and work in one town can as well shop and work in a privately owned firm.

This marketing function is obscured in the theoretical literature by the assumption of homogeneous factors. Or it is tacitly left for individuals to do themselves via personal market search, much as if a person had to search without benefit of specialist retailers. Whether or not the firm arose because of this efficient information service, it gives the director-employer more knowledge about the productive talents of the team's inputs, and a basis for superior decisions about efficient or profitable combinations of those heterogeneous resources.

In other words, opportunities for profitable team production by inputs already within the firm may be ascertained more economically and accurately than for resources outside the firm. Superior combinations of inputs can be more economically identified and formed from resources already used in the organization than by obtaining new resources (and knowledge of them) from the outside. Promotion and revision of employee assignments (contracts) will be preferred by a firm to the hiring of new inputs. To the extent that this occurs there is reason to expect the firm to be able to operate as a conglomerate rather than persist in producing a single product. Efficient production with heterogeneous resources is a result not of having *better* resources but in *knowing more accurately* the relative productive performances of those resources. Poorer resources can be paid less in accord with their inferiority; greater accuracy of knowledge of the potential and actual productive actions of inputs rather than having high productivity resources makes a firm (or an assignment of inputs) profitable.

VIII. SUMMARY

While ordinary contracts facilitate efficient specialization according to comparative advantage, a special class of contracts among a group of joint inputs to a team production process is commonly used for team production. Instead of multilateral contracts among all the joint inputs' owners, a central common party to a set of bilateral contracts facilitates efficient organization of the joint inputs in team production. The terms of the contracts form the basis of the entity called the firm—especially appropriate for organizing team production processes.

Team productive activity is that in which a union, or joint use, of inputs yields a larger output than the sum of the products of the separately used inputs. This team production requires—like all other production processes—an assessment of marginal productivities if efficient production is to be achieved. Nonseparability of the products of several differently owned joint inputs raises the cost of assessing the marginal productivities of those resources or services of each input owner. Monitoring or metering the productivities to match marginal productivities to costs of inputs and thereby to reduce shirking can be achieved more economically (than by across market bilateral negotiations among inputs) in a firm.

The essence of the classical firm is identified here as a contractual structure with: (1) joint input production; (2) several input owners; (3) one party who is common to all the contracts of the joint inputs; (4) who has rights to renegotiate any input's contract independently of contracts with other input owners; (5) who holds the residual claim; and (6) who has the right to sell his central contractual residual status. The central agent is called the firm's owner and the employer. No authoritarian control is involved; the arrangement is simply a contractual structure subject to continuous renegotiation with the central agent. The contractual structure arises as a means of enhancing efficient organization of team production. In particular, the ability to detect shirking among owners of jointly used inputs in team production is enhanced (detection costs are reduced) by this arrangement and the discipline (by revision of contracts) of input owners is made more economic.

Testable implications are suggested by the analysis of different types of organizations—nonprofit, proprietary for profit, unions, cooperatives, partnerships, and by the kinds of inputs that tend to be owned by the firm in contrast to those employed by the firm.

We conclude with a highly conjectural but possibly significant interpretation. As a consequence of the flow of information to the central party (employer), the firm takes on the characteristic of an efficient market in that information about the productive characteristics of a large set of specific inputs is now more cheaply available. Better recombinations or new uses of resources can be more efficiently ascertained than by the conventional search through the general market. In this sense inputs compete with each other within and via a firm rather than solely across markets as conventionally conceived. Emphasis on interfirm competition obscures intrafirm competition among inputs. Conceiving competition as the *revelation and exchange* of knowledge or information about qualities, potential uses of different inputs in different potential applications indicates that the firm is a device for enhancing competition among sets of input resources as well as a device for more efficiently rewarding the inputs. In contrast to markets and cities which can be viewed as publicly or nonowned marketplaces, the firm can be considered a privately owned market; if so, we could consider the firm and the ordinary market as competing types of markets, competition between private proprietary markets and public or communal markets. Could it be that the market suffers from the defects of communal property rights in organizing and influencing uses of valuable resources?

10. The Economies of Scale[*]

GEORGE J. STIGLER

The theory of the economies of scale is the theory of the relationship between the scale of use of a properly chosen combination of all productive services and the rate of output of the enterprise. In its broadest formulation this theory is a crucial element of the economic theory of social organization, for it underlies every question of market organization and the role (and locus) of governmental control over economic life. Let one ask himself how an economy would be organized if every economic activity were prohibitively inefficient upon alternately a small scale and a large scale, and the answer will convince him that here lies a basic element of the theory of economic organization.

The theory has limped along for a century, collecting large pieces of good reasoning and small chunks of empirical evidence but never achieving scientific prosperity. A large cause of its poverty is that the central concept of the theory—the firm of optimum size—has eluded confident measurement. We have been dangerously close to denying Lincoln, for all economists have been ignorant of the optimum size of firm in almost every industry all of the time, and this ignorance has been an insurmountable barrier between us and the understanding of the forces which govern optimum size. It is almost as if one were trying to measure the nutritive values of goods without knowing whether the consumers who ate them continued to live.

The central thesis of this paper is that the determination of the optimum size is not difficult if one formalizes the logic that sensible men have always employed to judge efficient size. This technique, which I am old-fashioned enough to call the survivor technique, reveals the optimum size in terms of private costs—that is, in terms of the environment in which the enterprise finds itself. After discussing the technique, we turn to the question of how the forces governing optimum size may be isolated.

* The Journal of Law and Economics, vol. 1 (October 1958), pp. 54–71.

I. THE SURVIVOR PRINCIPLE

The optimum size (or range of sizes) of enterprises in an industry is now ascertained empirically by one of three methods. The first is that of direct comparison of actual costs of firms of different sizes; the second is the comparison of rates of return on investment; and the third is the calculation of probable costs of enterprises of different sizes in the light of technological information. All three methods are practically objectionable in demanding data which are usually unobtainable and seldom up to date. But this cannot be the root of their difficulties, for there is up-to-date information on many economic concepts which are complex and even basically incapable of precise measurement (such as income). The plain fact is that we have not demanded the data because we have been unable to specify what we wanted.

The comparisons of both actual costs and rates of return are strongly influenced by the valuations which are put on productive services, so that an enterprise which over- or undervalues important productive services, will under- or overstate its efficiency. Historical cost valuations of resources, which are most commonly available, are in principle irrelevant under changed conditions. Valuations based upon expected earnings yield no information on the efficiency of an enterprise—in the limiting case where all resources are so valued, all firms would be of equal efficiency judged by either average costs or rates of return. The ascertainment on any scale of the maximum value of each resource in alternative uses is a task which only the unsophisticated would assume and only the omniscient would discharge. The host of valuation problems are accentuated by the variable role of the capital markets in effecting revaluations and the variable attitudes of the accountants toward the revaluations.

The technological studies of costs of different sizes of plant encounter equally formidable obstacles. These studies are compounded on some fairly precise (although not necessarily very relevant) technical information and some crude guesses on nontechnological aspects such as marketing costs, transportation rate changes, labor relations, etc.—that is, much of the problem is solved only in the unhappy sense of being delegated to a technologist. Even ideal results, moreover, do not tell us the optimum size of firm in industry A in 1958, but rather the optimum size of new plants in the industry, on the assumption that the industry starts *de novo* or that only a small increment of investment is being made.

The survivor technique avoids both the problems of valuation of resources and the hypothetical nature of the technological studies. Its fundamental postulate is that the competition of different sizes of firms sifts out the more efficient enterprises. In the words of Mill, who long ago proposed the technique:

Whether or not the advantages obtained by operating on a large scale preponderate in any particular case over the more watchful attention, and greater regard to minor gains and losses usually found in small establishments, can be ascertained, in a state of free competition, by an unfailing test. . . . Wherever there are large and small establishments in the same business, that one of the two which in existing circumstances carries on the production at the greater advantage will be able to undersell the other.[1]

Mill was wrong only in suggesting that the technique was inapplicable under oligopoly, for even under oligopoly the drive of maximum profits will lead to the disappearance of relatively inefficient sizes of firms.

The survivor technique proceeds to solve the problem of determining the optimum firm size as follows: Classify the firms in an industry by size, and calculate the share of industry output coming from each class over time. If the share of a given class falls, it is relatively inefficient, and in general is more inefficient the more rapidly the share falls.

An efficient size of firm, on this argument, is one that meets any and all problems the entrepreneur actually faces: strained labor relations, rapid innovation, government regulation, unstable foreign markets, and what not. This is, of course, the decisive meaning of efficiency from the viewpoint of the enterprise. Of course, social efficiency may be a very different thing: the most efficient firm size may arise from possession of monopoly power, undesirable labor practices, discriminatory legislation, etc. The survivor technique is not directly applicable to the determination of the socially optimum size of enterprise, and we do not enter into this question. The socially optimum firm is fundamentally an ethical concept, and we question neither its importance nor its elusiveness.

Not only is the survivor technique more direct and simpler than the alternative techniques for the determination of the optimum size of firm, it is also more authoritative. Suppose that the cost, rate of return, and technological studies all find that in a given industry the optimum size of firm is one which produces 500 to 600 units per day, and that costs per unit are much higher if one goes far outside this range. Suppose also that most of the firms in the industry are three times as large, and that those firms which are in the 500 to 600 unit class are rapidly failing or growing to a larger size. Would we believe that the optimum size was 500 to 600 units? Clearly not: an optimum size that cannot survive in rivalry with other sizes is a contradiction, and some error, we would all say, has been made in the traditional studies. Implicitly

---

[1] *Principles of Political Economy* (Ashley ed.), p. 134. Marshall states the same argument in Darwinian language: "For as a general rule the law of substitution—which is nothing more than a special and limited application of the law of survival of the fittest—tends to make one method of industrial organization supplant another when it offers a direct and immediate service at a lower price." *Principles of Economics*, p. 597 (8th ed., 1920).

all judgments on economies of scale have always been based directly upon, or at least verified by recourse to, the experience of survivorship.

This is not to say that the findings of the survivor technique are unequivocal. Entrepreneurs may make mistakes in their choice of firm size, and we must seek to eliminate the effects of such errors either by invoking large numbers of firms so errors tend to cancel or by utilizing time periods such that errors are revealed and corrected. Or the optimum size may be changing because of changes in factor prices or technology, so that perhaps the optimum size rises in one period and falls in another. This problem too calls for a close examination of the time periods which should be employed. We face these problems in our statistical work below.

We must also recognize that a single optimum size of firm will exist in an industry only if all firms have (access to) identical resources. Since various firms employ different kinds or qualities of resources, there will tend to develop a frequency distribution of optimum firm sizes. The survivor technique may allow us to estimate this distribution; in the application below we restrict ourselves to the range of optimum sizes.

The measure of the optimum size is only a first step toward the construction of a theory of economies of scale with substantive content, but it is the indispensable first step. We turn in later sections of this paper to the examination of the methods by which hypotheses concerning the determinants of optimum size may be tested.

II. ILLUSTRATIVE SURVIVORSHIP MEASURES

The survivor principle is very general in scope and very flexible in application, and these advantages can best be brought out by making concrete applications of the principle to individual industries. These applications will also serve to display a number of problems of data and interpretation which are encountered in the use of the survivor technique. We begin with the American steel industry.

In order that survivorship of firms of a given size be evidence of comparative efficiency, these firms must compete with firms of other sizes—all of the firms must sell in a common market. We have therefore restricted the analysis to firms making steel ingots by open-hearth or Bessemer processes. Size has perforce been measured by capacity, for production is not reported by individual companies, and capacity is expressed as a percentage of the industry total to eliminate the influence of the secular growth of industry and company size. The geographical extent of the market is especially difficult to determine in steel, for the shifting geographical pattern of consumption has created a linkage between the various regional markets. We treat the market as national, which exaggerates its extent, but probably does less violence to the facts than a sharp regional classification of firms. The basic data are given in table 1.

TABLE 1
Distribution of Output of Steel Ingot Capacity
by Relative Size of Company

Company Size (percent of industry total)	1930	1938	1951
1. Percent of Industry Capacity			
Under 0.5	7.16	6.11	4.65
0.5 to 1	5.94	5.08	5.37
1 to 2.5.	13.17	8.30	9.07
2.5 to 5	10.64	16.59	22.21
5 to 10	11.18	14.03	8.12
10 to 25	13.24	13.99	16.10
25 and over	38.67	35.91	34.50
2. Number of Companies			
Under 0.5	39	29	22
0.5 to 1	9	7	7
1 to 2.5.	9	6	6
2.5 to 5	3	4	5
5 to 10	2	2	1
10 to 25	1	1	1
25 and over	1	1	1

Sources: *Directory of Iron and Steel Works of the United States and Canada,* 1930, 1938; *Iron Age,* January 3, 1952.

Over two decades covered by table 1 (and, for that matter, over the last half century) there has been a persistent and fairly rapid decline in the share of the industry's capacity in firms with less than half a percent of the total, so that we may infer that this size of firm is subject to substantial diseconomies of scale.[2] The firms with 0.5 to 2.5 percent of industry capacity showed a moderate decline, and hence were subject to smaller diseconomies of scale. The one firm with more than one fourth of industry capacity declined moderately, so it too had diseconomies of scale. The intervening sizes, from 2.5 to 25 percent of industry capacity, grew or held their share so they constituted the range of optimum size.

The more rapid the rate at which a firm loses its share of the industry's output (or, here, capacity), the higher is its private cost of production relative to the cost of production of firms of the most efficient size. This interpretation should not be reversed, however, to infer that the size class whose share is growing more rapidly is more efficient than

[2] In 1930 the firm with 0.5 percent of the industry capacity had a capacity of 364,000 net tons; in 1951, 485,000 net tons. Of course, we could have employed absolute firm size classes, but they are less appropriate to many uses.

other classes whose shares are growing more slowly; the difference can merely represent differences in the quantities of various qualities of resources. In the light of these considerations we translate the data of table 1 into a long-run average cost curve for the production of steel ingots and display this curve in figure 1. Over a wide range of outputs there is no evidence of net economies or diseconomies of scale.

FIGURE 1

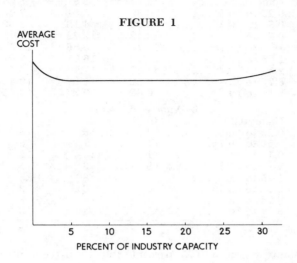

PERCENT OF INDUSTRY CAPACITY

Although the survivor test yields an estimate of the shape of the long-run cost curve, it does not allow an estimate of how much higher than the minimum are the costs of the firm sizes whose shares of industry output are declining. Costs are higher the more rapid the rate at which the firm size loses its share of industry output, but the rate at which a firm size loses a share of industry output will also vary with numerous other factors. This rate of loss of output will be larger, the less durable and specialized the productive resources of the firm, for then exit from the industry is easier. The rate of loss will also be larger, the more nearly perfect the capital and labor markets, so that resources can be obtained to grow quickly to more efficient size. The rate of loss will be smaller, given the degree of inefficiency, the more profitable the industry is, for then the rate of return of all sizes of firms is larger relative to other industries.

By a simple extension of this argument, we may also estimate the most efficient size of *plant* in the steel ingot industry during the same period (table 2). We again find that the smallest plants have a tendency to decline relative to the industry, and indeed this is implied by the company data. There is no systematic tendency toward decline in shares

TABLE 2
Distribution of Output of Steel Ingot Capacity

Plant Size (percent of industry total)	1930	1938	1951
1. Percent of Industry Capacity			
Under 0.25	3.74	3.81	3.25
0.25 to 0.5	6.39	5.81	7.20
0.5 to 0.75.	6.39	4.18	3.82
0.75 to 1	9.42	12.29	10.93
1 to 1.75.	21.78	15.56	20.67
1.75 to 2.5	13.13	16.73	17.01
2.5 to 3.75.	23.49	17.18	8.10
3.75 to 5	8.82	12.07	12.46
5 to 10	6.82	12.37	16.56
2. Number of Plants			
Under 0.25	40	29	23
0.25 to 0.5	20	16	18
0.5 to 0.75.	11	7	6
0.75 to 1	11	14	12
1 to 1.75.	18	13	15
1.75 to 2.5	6	8	8
2.5 to 3.75.	8	6	3
3.75 to 5	2	3	3
5 to 10	1	2	3

Source: Same as Table 1.

held by plants between 0.75 percent and 10 percent of the industry size. We may therefore infer that the tendency of very small plants and companies to decline relative to the industry is due to the diseconomy of a small plant, and the tendency of the largest company (U.S. Steel) to decline has been due to diseconomies of multiplant operation beyond a certain scale.

An equally important and interesting industry, passenger automobiles, uncovers different problems. Here we can use production data instead of capacity, and have no compunctions in treating the market as national in scope. The basic data for the individual firms are given in table 3.

A striking feature of the automobile industry is the small number of firms, and this poses a statistical problem we have glossed over in our discussion of steel: what confidence can be attached to changes in the share of industry output coming from a firm size when that size contains very few firms? For the automobile industry (unlike steel) we possess annual data, and can therefore take into account the steadiness of direction or magnitude of changes in shares of various firm sizes, and to this extent increase our confidence in the estimates. We may also extend the period which is surveyed, although at the risk of combining periods with different sizes of optimum firms. Aside from recourse to related data (the survivorship pattern of the industry in other

TABLE 3

Percentages of Passenger Automobiles Produced in United States
by Various Companies 1936–41 and 1946–55

Year	General Motors	Chrys-ler	Ford	Hudson	Nash	Kaiser	Willys Over-land	Packard	Stude-baker	Other
1936............	42.9	23.6	22.6	3.3	1.5	...	0.7	2.2	2.4	0.8
1937............	40.9	24.2	22.6	2.7	2.2	...	2.0	2.8	2.1	0.5
1938............	43.9	23.8	22.3	2.5	1.6	...	0.8	2.5	2.3	0.3
1939............	43.0	22.7	21.8	2.8	2.3	...	0.9	2.6	3.7	0.3
1940............	45.9	25.1	19.0	2.3	1.7	...	0.7	2.1	3.1	0.1
1941............	48.3	23.3	18.3	2.1	2.1	...	0.8	1.8	3.2	0.1
1946............	38.4	25.0	21.2	4.2	4.6	0.6	0.3	1.9	3.6	0.2
1947............	40.4	21.7	21.3	2.8	3.2	4.1	0.9	1.6	3.5	0.5
1948............	40.1	21.2	19.1	3.6	3.1	4.6	0.8	2.5	4.2	0.7
1949............	43.0	21.9	21.0	2.8	2.8	1.2	0.6	2.0	4.5	0.2
1950............	45.7	18.0	23.3	2.1	2.8	2.2	0.6	1.1	4.0	0.1
1951............	42.2	23.1	21.8	1.8	3.0	1.9	0.5	1.4	4.2	0.1
1952............	41.5	22.0	23.2	1.8	3.5	1.7	1.1	1.4	3.7	...
1953............	45.7	20.3	25.2	1.2	2.2	1.0		1.3	3.0	...
1954............	52.2	13.1	30.6	1.7		0.3		0.5	1.6	...
1955............	50.2	17.2	28.2	2.0		0.1			2.3	...

Source: Ward's Automotive Yearbook 1951, 1955, 1956.

countries, for example), there is no other method of reducing the uncertainty of findings for small number industries.

The survivorship record in automobiles (summarized in Table 4) is more complicated than that for steel. In the immediate prewar years there was already a tendency for the largest company to produce a rising share and for the 2.5 to 5 percent class to produce a sharply declining share; the smallest and next to largest sizes showed no clear tendency. In a longer span of time, however, the smallest companies reveal a fairly consistently declining share. In the immediate postwar period, the 2.5 to 5 percent size class was strongly favored by the larger companies' need to practice price control in a sensitive political atmosphere, and the same phenomenon reappeared less strongly in the first two years after the outbreak of Korean hostilities. From this record we would infer that there have been diseconomies of large size, at least for the largest size of firm, in inflationary periods with private or public price control, but substantial economies of large scale at other times. The long-run average cost curve is saucer shaped in inflationary times, but shows no tendency to rise at the largest outputs in other times.

TABLE 4

Percentage of Passenger Automobiles Produced by
Companies of Various Sizes

	Company Size (as percent of industry)				Number of Companies	
	Over 35	10-35	2.5-5	Under 2.5	2.5-5	Under 2.5
Year	Percent	Percent	Percent	Percent	Percent	Percent
1936.......	42.9	46.2	3.3	7.6	1	5*
1937.......	40.9	46.8	5.5	6.8	2	4*
1938.......	43.9	46.1	5.0	5.0	2	4*
1939.......	43.0	44.4	9.1	3.5	3	4*
1940.......	45.9	44.1	3.1	6.9	1	6*
1941.......	48.4	41.6	3.2	6.8	1	5
1946.......	38.4	46.2	12.4	3.0	3	4
1947.......	40.4	43.0	13.6	3.0	4	3
1948.......	40.1	40.3	18.0	1.5	5	2
1949.......	43.0	42.9	10.0	4.0	3	4
1950.......	45.7	41.3	6.8	6.1	2	5
1951.......	42.2	44.9	7.2	5.7	2	5
1952.......	41.5	45.2	7.2	6.1	2	5
1953.......	45.6	45.5	3.0	5.8	1	4
1954.......	52.2	43.7	0	4.1	0	4
1955.......	50.2	45.4	0	4.4	0	3

Source: Table 3.
* Or more.

The automobile example suggests the method by which we determine whether changing technology, factor prices, or consumer demands lead to a change in the optimum firm size. We infer an underlying stability in the optimum size in those periods in which the survivorship trends are stable. Indeed it is hard to conceive of an alternative test; one can judge the economic importance, in contrast to technological originality, of an innovation only by the impact it has upon the size distribution of firms.

Before we leave these applications of the survivorship technique we should indicate its flexibility in dealing with other problems which seem inappropriate to our particular examples. For example, a Marshallian may object that firms must begin small and grow to optimum size through time, so that the size structure of the industry in a given period will reflect this historical life pattern as well as the optimum size influences. In an industry such as retail trade this interpretation would be quite plausible. It can be met by studying the survivor experience of firm sizes in the light of the age or rate of growth of the firms. Again, one may argue that firms of different sizes have different comparative advantages at different stages of the business cycle. Such a hypothesis could be dealt with by comparing average survivorship patterns in given cycle stages with those calculated for full cycles.

Let us now turn to the methods by which one may test hypotheses on the determinants of optimum size.

III. INTER-INDUSTRY ANALYSES OF THE DETERMINANTS OF OPTIMUM SIZE

Once the optimum firm size has been ascertained for a variety of industries, the relationship between size and other variables can be explored. This is, in fact, the customary procedure for economists to employ, and the present investigation differs, aside from the method of determining optimum size, only in being more systematic than most such investigations. For example, numerous economists have asserted that advertising is a force making for large firms, and they usually illustrate this relationship by the cigarette industry. Will the relationship still hold when it is tested against a list of industries which has not been chosen to illustrate it? This is essentially the type of inquiry we make here.

Although the survivor method makes lesser demands of data than other methods to determine optimum firm size, it has equally exacting requirements of information on any other variable whose influence is to be studied. In the subsequent investigation of some 48 ("three-digit") manufacturing industries, whose optimum firm size is calculated from data in *Statistics of Income,* we have therefore been compelled to exclude some variables for lack of data and to measure others in a most imperfect manner. The industries we study, and the measures we contrive, are given in table 5; we describe their derivation below.

TABLE 5
Basic Data on Forty-eight Manufacturing Industries

Industry	Optimum Company Size (in thousand dollars of total assets) (1948–51)	Optimum Range Class Limits (in thousand dollars) From	Optimum Range Class Limits (in thousand dollars) To	Average Establishment Size (in thousand dollars of value added) (1947)	Number of Chemists and Engineers per 100 Employed (1950)	Advertising Expenditure as Percent of Gross Sales (1950)
Motor vehicles, incl. bodies and truck trailers	$827,828	$100,000	$open	$ 3,715	1.5879	0.4395
Petroleum refining	765,716	100,000	open	3,420	6.9171	0.4562
Blast furnaces, steel works, and rolling mills	525,485	100,000	open	8,310	2.0956	0.1321
Dairy products	446,483	100,000	open	110	0.7865	1.5221
Distilled, rectified, and blended liquors	248,424	100,000	open	2,090	0.9041	1.3674
Pulp, paper, and paperboard	203,794	100,000	open	1,645	1.4927	0.3357
Paints, varnishes, lacquers, etc.	175,404	100,000	open	394	6.0431	1.3539
Railroad equipment, incl. locomotives and streetcars	150,217	100,000	open	3,407	2.7171	0.3611
Tires and tubes	141,600	10,000	open	11,406	2.0974*	0.9453
Grain mill products ex. cereals preparations	128,363	100,000	open	210	1.0344	1.2492
Drugs and medicines	123,662	100,000	open	552	6.2599	8.3858
Smelting, refining, rolling, drawing, and alloying of nonferrous metals	100,398	10,000	open	1,658	2.9845†	0.4088
Office and store machines	65,914	10,000	open	1,411	2.5860	1.5812
Bakery products	58,960	50,000	100,000	192	0.2359	2.1335
Yarn and thread	44,375	10,000	open	687	0.4461	0.3238
Carpets and other floor coverings	37,337	10,000	100,000	1,119	1.2391	1.7295
Broadwoven fabrics (wool)	31,265	10,000	open	1,211	0.4461	0.3400
Watches, clocks, and clock work operated devices	31,025	10,000	50,000	705	1.2027	5.3238
Cement	29,554	10,000	100,000	1,600	2.1277‡	0.2726
Malt liquors and malt	28,922	10,000	open	1,750	0.9041	4.7962
Agricultural machinery and tractors	28,291	1,000	open	684	2.1816	0.8956
Structural clay products	24,001	10,000	100,000	253	1.6292	0.4552
Newspapers	23,428	10,000	100,000	168	0.1348§	0.1948
Knit goods	17,918	10,000	100,000	273	0.1244	0.8522
Confectionery	13,524	5,000	50,000	335	0.5950	2.6281
Commercial printing including lithographing	11,939	5,000	50,000	97	0.1348§	0.6474
Furniture—household, office, public building, and professional	11,378	5,000	50,000	209	0.3990‖	0.9152

* Rubber products.
† Primary nonferrous.
‡ Cement, and concrete, gypsum, and plaster products.

TABLE 5 (*continued*)

Industry	Optimum Company Size (in thousand dollars of total assets) (1948–51)	Optimum Range Class Limits (in thousand dollars)		Average Establishment Size (in thousand dollars of value added) (1947)	Number of Chemists and Engineers per 100 Employed (1950)	Advertising Expenditure as Percent of Gross Sales (1950)
		From	To			
Men's clothing	$ 10,077	$ 5,000	$ 50,000	$ 247	0.0456#	0.8795
Dyeing and finishing textiles, excl. knit goods	9,625	5,000	50,000	545	1.1223	0.3472
Canning fruit, vegetables, and seafood	6,536	1,000	open	240	0.9144	1.8462
Broadwoven fabrics (cotton)	5,847	50	open	2,595	0.4461**	0.2822
Footwear, exc. rubber	4,359	1,000	100,000	524	0.1474	1.1619
Paperbags, and paperboard containers and boxes	4,127	1,000	100,000	428	0.6939	0.1854
Cigars	3,753	250	50,000	174	0.2274††	2.3188
Meat products	2,665	500	100,000	322	0.5983	0.4264
Nonferrous foundries	2,365	500	50,000	172	2.9845†	0.2793
Fur goods	1,966	1,000	5,000	55	0.0456#	0.4119
Partitions, shelving, lockers, etc.	1,545	500	50,000	121	0.3990‖	0.8678
Narrow fabrics and other small wares	1,382	500	5,000	226	0.4461**	0.3212
Wines	1,304	500	5,000	227	0.9041‡‡	3.5854
Women's clothing	1,304	500	50,000	150	0.0456#	0.9150
Books	1,137	50	50,000	399	0.1348§	2.8796
Periodicals	1,117	250	10,000	307	0.1348§	0.5245
Leather—tanning, curring, and finishing	764	0	10,000	720	0.8140	0.1813
Concrete, gypsum, and plaster products	762	250	10,000	53	2.1277†	0.6855
Window and door screens, shades, and venetian blinds	667	100	10,000	110	0.3990‖	1.0581
Nonalcoholic beverages	546	100	50,000	75	0.9041‡‡	4.0740
Millinery	468	250	5,000	108	0.0456#	0.4438

§ Printing, publishing, and allied industries
‖ Furniture and fixtures.
†† Tobacco manufactures.
‡‡ Beverage industries.
# Apparel and accessories.
** Yarn, thread, and fabric mills.

1. *Size of Firm.* The optimum size of firm in each industry is determined by comparing the percentage of the industry's assets possessed by firms in each asset class in 1948 and 1951.[3] Those classes in which the share of the industry's assets was stable or rising were identified, and the average assets of the firms within these sizes was calculated. The range of optimum sizes is also given in Table 5. An industry was excluded if it had a very large noncorporate sector (for which we could not measure firm size) or gave strong evidence of heterogeneity by having two widely separated optimum sizes (as, for example, in "aircraft and parts").

2. *Advertising Expenditures.* We have already remarked that extensive advertising is often mentioned as an explanation for the growth of large firms, especially in consumer goods industries such as cigarettes, liquor, and cosmetics. The argument supporting this view can take one of three directions. First, national advertising may be viewed as more efficient than local advertising, in terms of sales per dollar of advertising at a given price. Second, long-continued advertising may have a cumulative impact. Finally, and closely related to the preceding point, the joint advertising of a series of related products may be more efficient than advertising them individually. We measure the variable by the ratio of advertising expenditures to sales, both taken from *Statistics of Income.*

3. *Technology and Research.* A host of explanations of firm size are related to technological characteristics and research. Complicated production processes may require large companies, or at least large plants. The economies of research are held to be substantial; the outcome of individual projects is uncertain, so small programs are more risky; a balanced research team may be fairly large; and much capital may be required to bring a new process to a commercial stage and to wait for a return upon the outlay.

At present there is no direct measure available for either the importance of research or the intricacy of technology. We use an index, chemists and engineers as a ratio to all employees, that may reflect both influences, but probably very imperfectly. When it becomes possible to make a division of these personnel between research and routine operation, a division which would be very valuable for other purposes also, the interpretation of an index of technical personnel will be less ambiguous.

4. *Plant Size.* Plant size normally sets a minimum to company size, and therefore exerts an obvious influence on the differences among indus-

---

[3] These particular dates were dictated by the data; there were large changes in industry classification in 1948, and no minor industry data were tabulated for 1952. A better, but more laborious, determination of optimum size could have been made if the data for intervening years were utilized.

tries in company size. We are compelled to resort to a measure of plant size—value added per establishment in 1947—which is not directly comparable to company size because the 1947 Census of Manufacturers did not report corporate establishments at the requisite level of detail.

Preliminary analysis revealed that there is no significant relationship between firm size and advertising expenditures, so this variable was omitted from the statistical calculations. The average ratio of advertising expenditures to sales was 1.97 percent in consumer goods industries and 0.57 percent in producer goods industries, but in neither group was there a significant relationship between the ratio and firm size.[4]

A regression analysis confirms the impression one gets from table 5 that the other variables we examine are positively related to optimum firm size:

$$X_1 = -5.092 + 34.6\ X_2 + 42.7\ X_3,$$
$$(10.8) \qquad (12.2)$$

where

X_1 is firm size, in millions of dollars of assets,
X_2 is plant size, in millions of dollars of value added,
X_3 is engineers and chemists per 100 employees.

The standard errors of the regression coefficients are given below the coefficients.

An examination of table 5 suggests that the correlation would be higher if the data were somewhat more precise. The size of plant is unduly low in motor vehicles, because of the inclusion of suppliers of parts. Moreover the plant sizes have not been estimated by the survivor technique. Technological personnel are exaggerated in nonferrous foundries because we are compelled to use the ratio for a broader class, and the same is true of concrete products. The relatively small size of company in footwear, as compared to plant size, is at least partially due to the fact that the machinery was usually leased, and hence not included in assets. Industries which are "out of line" have not been omitted, however, for similar considerations may have caused other industries to be "in line." Yet the general impression is that the correlation would rise substantially with improved measurements of the variables.

The range of optimum sizes is generally wide, although the width is exaggerated, and our measurements impaired, because the largest asset class (over $100 million) embraces numerous firms of very different sizes—growth and inflation are outmoding the size classes used in *Statistics of Income*. In ten industries only this largest size has had a rising share of industry assets, and in another nine industries it is included in the range of sizes with rising shares. When the upper limit of optimum

---

[4] The respective rank correlation coefficients were $-.187$ and $-.059$.

sizes is known, the range of optimum sizes is typically three or four times the average size of the firms in these sizes.

The results of this exploratory inter-industry study are at least suggestive—not only in their specific content but also in pointing out a line of attack on the economies of scale that escapes that confession of failure, the case method. The chief qualifications that attach to the findings are due to the imperfections of the data: the industry categories are rather wide; and the measure of technical personnel is seriously ambiguous. At least one finding—a wide range of optimum firm sizes in each industry—is so general as to deserve to be taken as the standard model in the theory of production.

IV. INTRAINDUSTRY ANALYSIS OF THE DETERMINANTS OF OPTIMUM SIZE

One may also examine the varying fates of individual firms within an industry in the search for explanations of optimum size. If, for example, firms moving to optimum size were vertically integrated and those moving to or remaining in nonoptimum size were not so integrated, we could infer that vertical integration was a requisite of the optimum firm in the industry. This approach has the advantage over the inter-industry approach of not requiring the assumption that a determinant such as advertising or integration works similarly in all industries.

The intraindustry analysis, however, has a heavy disadvantage; it can be applied only to those variables for which we can obtain information on each firm and in industries with numerous firms hardly any interesting variables survive this requirement. Because we could examine so few influences, and because the results were so consistently negative, we shall be very brief in describing our results in the industry—petroleum refining—in which this approach was tried.

The basic survivor experience for companies and plants in petroleum refining is given in tables 6 and 7, for the postwar period 1947–1954. In each case only operating plants are included, and asphalt plants and companies are excluded. Capacities are measured in terms of crude oil; as in the case of steel plants, actual outputs cannot be obtained for all companies.

There is a family resemblance between the data for petroleum and steel companies: in each case there has been a substantial reduction in the share of the largest company. In the petroleum refining industry, the size range from 0.5 percent to 10 percent has contained all the size classes which have stable or rising shares of industry capacity.

The plant survivor data suggest that the disappearance of the smaller companies has been due to the relative inefficiency of the smaller plants,

TABLE 6
Distribution of Petroleum Refining Capacity
by Relative Size of Company

Company Size (percent of industry capacity)	1947	1950	1954
1. Percent of Industry Capacity			
Under 0.1	5.30	4.57	3.89
0.1 to 0.2	4.86	3.57	3.00
0.2 to 0.3	2.67	2.16	2.74
0.3 to 0.4	2.95	2.92	1.65
0.4 to 0.5	2.20	0	.89
0.5 to 0.75	3.04	4.66	5.05
0.75 to 1.00	.94	0	1.58
1.0 to 2.5	11.70	12.17	10.53
2.5 to 5	9.57	16.70	14.26
5 to 10	45.11	42.15	45.69
10 to 15	11.65	11.06	10.72
2. Number of Companies			
Under 0.1	130	108	92
0.1 to 0.2	34	24	22
0.2 to 0.3	11	9	11
0.3 to 0.4	8	8	5
0.4 to 0.5	5	0	2
0.5 to 0.75	5	8	8
0.75 to 1.00	1	0	2
1.0 to 2.5	6	7	6
2.5 to 5.0	3	5	5
5.0 to 10.0	7	6	7
10.0 to 15.0	1	1	1
Total	211	176	161

Source: Bureau of Mines, Petroleum Refineries, including Cracking Plants in the United States, January 1, 1947, January 1, 1950, January 1, 1954, Information Circulars 7455 (March 1948), 7578 (August 1950), and 7693 (July 1954).

for all plant size classes with less than 0.5 percent of the industry's capacity have also declined substantially. The sizes between 0.5 percent and 2.5 percent of industry capacity have all grown relatively, and the top plant size has declined moderately, so that the growth of company sizes beyond 2.5 percent of industry capacity has presumably been due to the economies of multiple plant operation.

It has been claimed that backward integration into crude oil pipelines was necessary to successful operation of a petroleum refinery. We tabulate some of the material bearing on this hypothesis in table 8. There does not appear to be any large difference between the changes in market shares of firms with and without pipelines. Since all firms with more than 0.75 percent of industry refining capacity have some pipelines, a comparison (not reproduced here) was made between changes in their market shares and crude pipeline mileage per 1,000 barrels of daily refining capacity. There was no relationship between the two variables.

TABLE 7
Distribution of Petroleum Refining Capacity
by Relative Size of Plant

Plant Size	1947	1950	1954
1. Percent of Industry Capacity			
Under 0.1	8.22	7.39	6.06
0.1 to 0.2.	9.06	7.60	7.13
0.2 to 0.3.	6.86	4.95	3.95
0.3 to 0.4.	5.45	4.99	7.28
0.4 to 0.5.	4.53	6.56	4.06
0.5 to 0.75	9.95	10.47	11.82
0.75 to 1.0.	5.35	7.07	8.33
1.0 to 1.5.	12.11	10.36	13.38
1.5 to 2.5.	17.39	23.64	22.45
2.5 to 4.0.	21.08	16.96	15.54
2. Number of Plants			
Under 0.1	184	158	138
0.1 to 0.2.	64	53	51
0.2 to 0.3.	27	19	16
0.3 to 0.4.	15	14	21
0.4 to 0.5.	10	15	9
0.5 to 0.75	17	16	19
0.75 to 1.0.	6	8	10
1.0 to 1.5.	10	8	11
1.5 to 2.5.	9	12	12
2.5 to 4.0.	7	5	5
Total	349	308	292

Source: Same as table 6.

TABLE 8
Industry Shares of Petroleum Refining Companies with
and without Crude Pipelines in 1950

Company Size (average of 1947, 1950, and 1954 percentage of industry capacity)	Companies with Pipelines			Companies without Pipelines		
	Number 1950	Share 1947	Share 1954	Number 1950	Share 1947	Share 1954
Under 0.1	25	1.40	1.12	60	2.87	2.18
0.1 to 0.2.	17	2.19	2.50	5	0.77	0.77
0.2 to 0.3.	6	1.48	1.63	2	0.34	0.50
0.3 to 0.4.	5	1.90	1.63	0	. . . .	. . . .
0.4 to 0.5.	1	0.40	0.55	2	0.54	1.22
0.5 to 0.75	7	3.59	4.72	1	0.38	0.61
0.75 to 1.0.	0	. . . . .	. . . . .	0	. . . .	. . . .
1.0 to 2.5.	7	11.54	13.10	0	. . . .	. . . .
2.5 to 5.0.	4	11.11	11.69	0	. . . .	. . . .
5.0 to 10.0.	7	45.11	45.69	0	. . . .	. . . .
10.0 to 15.0.	1	11.65	10.72	0	. . . .	. . . .
Not in existence all years	16	2.30	0.05	79	2.43	1.33
Total	96	92.67	93.40	149	7.33	6.60

Source: *International Petroleum Register.*

The intraindustry analysis has its chief role, one may conjecture, in providing a systematic framework for the analysis of the data commonly employed in industry studies. A complete analysis of the plausible determinants of firm size requires such extensive information on the individual firms in the industry as to make this an unattractive method of attack on the general theory.

V. CONCLUSION

The survivor technique for determining the range of optimum sizes of a firm seems well adapted to lift the theory of economies of scale to a higher level of substantive content. Although it is prey to the usual frustrations of inadequate information, the determination of optimum sizes avoids the enormously difficult problem of valuing resources properly that is encountered by alternative methods.

Perhaps the most striking finding in our exploratory studies is that there is customarily a fairly wide range of optimum sizes—the long-run marginal and average cost curves of the firm are customarily horizontal over a long range of sizes. This finding could be corroborated, I suspect, by a related investigation: if there were a unique optimum size in an industry, increases in demand would normally be met primarily by near proportional increases in the number of firms, but it appears that much of the increase is usually met by expansion of the existing firms.

The survivor method can be used to test the numerous hypotheses on the factors determining the size of firm which abound in the literature. Our exploratory study suggests that advertising expenditures have no general tendency to lead to large firms, and another experiment (which is not reported above) indicates that fixed capital-sales ratio are also unrelated to the size of firms. The size of plant proves to be an important variable, as is to be expected, and the survivor method should be employed to determine the factors governing plant size. A rather ambiguous variable, the relative share of engineers and chemists in the labor force, also proves to be fairly important, and further data and work is necessary to disentangle research and routine technical operations. The determination of optimum size permits the investigator to examine any possible determinants which his imagination nominates and his data illuminate.

11. Commercial Bank Profitability by Function*

THOMAS J. COYNE

In studying the profitability of commercial banks by function it becomes obvious that they need to know much more about cost of funds and price output behavior if they are to expand service(s) profitably. With the possible exception of university administrators and church leaders, it is highly probable that commercial bankers know less about specific functions within their business than any similar group. Nonetheless, research into this troublesome area has been practically nonexisting. Bell and Murphy studied economies of scale by bank function, but relatively little has been published recently about the cost, price *and* profitability of commercial banks *by function*. Other profitability studies have been done but they overlook profit by function.

This paper is concerned with the cost, price, and profit by function. It estimates the profit for real estate, installment, commercial and agricultural loans, and investments for banks stratified by size of deposit.

Raw data were obtained from the Federal Reserve Bank of Cleveland's functional cost analysis of 41 banks. In addition, a questionnaire sent to the chief executive officer of 510 commerical banks provides insight into the manner in which commercial banks utilize: (1) the degree to which the average cost of funds by function is known to the bank and the method, if any, that is used to make that determination; (2) the degree to which the average price (interest rate) by function is known to the bank and, expressed by a percent, whether it is equal to or greater than the cost of funds by function; and (3) the degree to which the bank is able to determine its profit by function from 1 and 2.

Assuming that the results of the questionnaire are representative of the aggregate commercial banking community, the study concludes by applying cost of funds estimates to average balance sheet entries for the Representative Bank of America (RBA), a hypothetical company created from averages of 41 banks with deposits ranging from $8 million to $50 million.

---

* *Financial Management,* vol. 2, no. 1 (Spring 1973), pp. 64–73.

FUNCTIONAL COST ANALYSIS

The most serious effort to date to determine profitability by bank function has been made by the Federal Reserve System. Its work is concerned mostly with cost and is confined to relatively few banks, perhaps 1,000 or so.

The Fed's functional cost system is a major attempt to make comparative data available to banks of similar size in terms of total deposits. The data are presented in annual reports and are designed to serve as a basic management tool. These yearly reports are based upon annual data, and contain the usual shortcomings associated with such figures. Balance sheet averages vary, for example, as each institution determines for itself what date to select for calculations. Very few measures of dispersion about the mean are included. In addition, the report concentrates on earnings before taxes and does not calculate "below-the-line adjustments." These below-line adjustments are not included because the major purpose of the annual Functional Cost Analysis (FCA) report is to make possible performance comparisons through time and cross-sectionally.

The cost of funds section of the Fed's functional cost analysis does not include cost of capital statistics. In addition, differences in salaries or other expenses, such as depreciation practices, of the individual bank are not considered. Consequently, a small bank that leases the space that it occupies, for example, must consider this rental expense to be a cost for FCA purposes; but if that same bank owns its premises and is depreciating it over time, its cost of capital figure as presented annually in the FCA report would be distorted. Figures are presented for occupancy costs, of course, but each bank would have to adjust the data to make it usable. In other words, the FCA is not wholly valid without interpretation for comparative purposes.

FCA analyzes and presents explicit costs only. Implicit costs, such as the opportunity cost to the bank of not investing idle funds, are not considered.

Many bankers do not calculate their total costs and/or profits by function. The main object of this study is to determine the degree to which these costs are unknown to the banks and to suggest a method by which they could be determined.

Cost of Funds: Calculation

A survey of 510 commercial banks was conducted, stratifying all banks into five classes of total deposits at the end of 1971. This classification is more detailed than that used by the Fed because of the author's belief that for some analytical purposes FCA data stratifications are too broad.

Class	Deposit Size	Number of Banks
1	$ 1,000,000–$ 5,000,000	89
2	5,000,000– 15,000,000	194
3	15,000,000– 25,000,000	71
4	25,000,000– 50,000,000	79
5	50,000,000 and over	77
Total		510

The result of this survey reflects the degree to which costs and profits by function are unknown. As a percent of the total number of banks within a class size, Class 5 banks provided the greatest number of responses. The heavier response by Class 5 banks was not unexpected for they are the ones that are better able to employ a highly professional management group.

Exhibit 1 indicates that, when grouped by bank size, the larger banks are somewhat better informed concerning their costs of funds than are the smaller banks. None of the smaller banks, Class 1, had any indication of their cost of funds. When asked to explain specifically how these costs of funds are determined, most of the Class 2, 3 and 4 banks and many of the Class 5 banks responded by saying that they "participate in the Federal Reserve's Functional Cost program." The Fed's FCA program, it should be noted, is designed to produce a weighted rather than marginal or incremental cost-of-funds figure.

In addition to FCA, many of the Class 5 banks use a pool of funds concept of available funds. Therefore, the cost of funds to the using function, i.e., installment loans, is the average of the total costs of providing all functions. In addition, many of these larger banks tend to have their own unique method(s) of calculating the total cost of funds but these methods do not isolate necessarily all costs by type of function. These larger banks, however, do tend to be more "cost center," or "profit center" oriented than are banks that fall within Classes 1 through 4 in size of total deposits. This effort on the part of individual commercial banks that have total deposits of $50 million or more is encouraging but Class 5 banks represent only 15 percent of the total number of commercial banks surveyed. Also, as noted later in this study, even Class 5 banks when viewed in the aggregate have less than what some observers believe to be adequate information concerning their cost of funds.

Cost of Funds: Utilization

The results of the survey indicate that most banks do not have a method of determining their cost of funds. Moreover, a strong association

EXHIBIT 1

Tabulation of Results from Survey of Commercial Banks

Questions	Percent of Banks Responding "No," by Bank Class					
	Class 1	Class 2	Class 3	Class 4	Class 5	All Classes
(1) Bank has method of determining cost of funds by:						
(a) Demand deposits	100	82	87	59	43	74
(b) Time deposits	89	82	68	52	39	68
(c) Total capital accounts	100	82	79	54	47	73
(2) Bank considers cost of funds in determining the general level of interest rate(s) to charge in a given area, i.e., commercial lending	89	73	81	50	56	69
(3) Bank has method for determining operating expense(s) for each department	94	93	87	58	26	74
(4) Bank knows the total cost of operating each department (cost of funds plus operating costs)	100	88	87	62	45	77
(5) In determining the general level of interest rates to be charged in each department the bank considers:						
(a) Total costs	69	59	39	27	17	38
(b) Cost of funds only	100*	89	100*	66	57	79
(c) Operating costs only	100*	100	100*	79	55	83
(6) Bank can determine net income (gross income minus cost of funds and operating expenses) of each lending department?	94	86	81	65	39	73
Number of banks answering	22	50	18	29	30	149
Percent of total banks answering	24	25	25	36	38	29

* The absolute number of respondents was too small to consider this relative finding significant.

is revealed between banks that have no method of determining their costs of funds and banks that do not *consider* their costs of funds in determining what price (interest rate) must be charged in order to operate profitably. The question, then, becomes: How *does* a bank determine what interest rate(s) it will charge within a given functional area? The response of a Class 1 bank: "charge a higher rate of interest on loans than we are paying for (time deposit) funds used."

Virtually none of the banks queried appear to be following traditional pricing techniques other than, perhaps, the rigid adherence to full-cost pricing, however defined, as followed by some of the smallest firms in the industry. If the typical small bank deviates from this practice, it considers cost of funds on real estate loans only or cost of funds for *one* similar function, i.e., consumer installment loans, and then maintains a system of cost plus fixed markup pricing for that function. In some cases, if the bank knows that it is receiving a "proper" rate of interest in comparison to other portfolio investments available (an opportunity cost concept), plus consideration of the prime rate and compensating balances, it is satisfied.

A few of the Class 4 and most of the Class 5 banks indicate a higher degree of sophistication than implied by the comments above but even they consider cost of funds on a very cursory basis only. One Class 5 bank explained that this consideration amounts often "to little more than saying that interest costs and tax costs are so much, consequently our rates should be so much. We have no formula or formal plan."

Yet, the results reveal isolated examples of bankers who understand fully that the cost of funds should have a direct bearing on interest rates that are charged within a functional area, and as the cost of funds fluctuate the impact on a specific department should be measured in terms of the ultimate profitability that will be obtained from continuing that function. "Firm control over the cost of funds is the only way to predict profitability and establish corporate goals." (This is a quote from a Class 4 bank which acknowledges also that it neither knows nor considers its cost of funds.)

Pricing positions were volunteered by some respondents. Conspicuous by its absence, however, was any mention of full costs plus variable markups, pricing using programmed costs other than full costs, and pricing based upon incremental or marginal costs. No mention is made of first, second, or third degree price discrimination. None of the banks answering stated that they sought a certain target marketshare, nor did any bank say that they priced to achieve a target return on investment. Indeed, most banks establish prices (interest rates) with little reference to costs. They are interested mainly in matching or "meeting competition." Some observers would argue that this behavior is appropriate, and indeed it would be if these banks were operating in competitive product markets. In the words of one Class 5 respondent, not the same bank quoted above, "In these days of high competition and rapid monetary policy changes, less and less attention is paid to the cost of funds in determining rates to be charged for loans. Usually, rates are established in relation to what the market will bear. Cost of funds may indicate that loan rates should be a certain level, but monetary policy and competition can dictate otherwise, regardless of cost of funds."

Operating Expenses: Calculation

Quite clearly, the larger the bank the better the knowledge that it has concerning its total operating expenses. Most banks surveyed, regardless of size, recognize that with bank holding companies becoming a large competitive factor, and with more lenient banking laws a possibility, intelligent identification, planning, and control of operating expenses is mandatory. Yet, many small banks are not departmentalized; and, although salaries often are allocated on a time-study basis and total expenses are reviewed periodically, expenses incurred as a result of operating individual departments are "not real specific," according to a Class 4 bank. This shortcoming is serious because 85 percent of all commercial banks surveyed lie in size Classes 1 through 4.

Some banks in Class 5 are attempting to develop "responsibility accounting." The department(s) responsible for the expense is charged directly for the expense. The majority of explicit costs are coded by the accounting department at the time of payment, entered daily into the computer, printed and distributed to department heads and other members of upper middle management and top management. Other explicit costs, such as employee benefits, personal property tax, and so on, are allocated to applicable departments and are made known to management by the computer print-out. Some of these banks attempt also to assign indirect costs to specific departments. but with somewhat less success.

Two of these large banks assign direct charges to major departments and branches but make no attempt to allocate indirect charges, and another Class 5 bank states "we do not allocate in any manner, any type of expenses." And this observer found that none of the banks responding to the survey attempt to quantify and allocate implicit costs.

NET INCOME DETERMINATION

Commercial bankers seem to agree that they should be able to determine the net income generated by each lending department.

The Class 5 banks that determine net income of each lending department do so in a variety of ways, but the most prevalent method is to deduct total operating expenses from total departmental income and from this figure the cost of money (funds) is deducted to produce net income by function.

The net income figure by function, once obtained, is used in various departmental and branch operations, budgeting, personnel, and expansion proposals. This information is used also by some banks to determine which lending department is to receive the bulk of the available cash. In addition, of course, *ex post* rankings of departments according to profitability is possible, and bank management analyzes these rankings when making decisions that will affect the allocation of resources. It should be noted, however, that several Class 5 banks state that they can and do determine net income in each lending department but that they "do not utilize it very efficiently."

The cost of funds, of course, should be calculated by each bank, regardless of whether it participates in FCA, and the resulting figure(s) should be used by that bank when determining interest rates to be charged by bank function and when measuring net profit after taxes by function.

One approach to illustrate a solution to this problem is to start with the righthand side of a typical bank's balance sheet. Exhibit 2 presents the average balance sheet of 41 commercial banks. For purposes of this presentation, these figures are to be considered those of the Representative Bank of America.

Bank balance sheets must be adjusted in calculating the cost of funds. Two bank balance sheet definitions are: (1) "valuation reserves" and (2) "available funds." Respectively, they are those reserves created to cover potential losses on loans, securities, and other assets and the sum of cash and due from banks, loans, and investments.

Net capital for RBA is as follows:

Capital and valuation reserves	$2,768,312
Plus other liabilities and borrowings	339,688
Net capital subtotal	$3,108,000
Less fixed and other assets	837,679
Net capital funds available	$2,270,321

Net capital funds represents one of three major components of total financing available. The other two components of the bank are demand deposits and time deposits, which amount in the case of RBA to $10,042,581 and $15,149,431, respectively. Taken together, these three components amount to $27,462,333 and represent the total available for lending and investment purposes. This figure differs from total assets by the amount of money invested in bank premises, other real estate, and some miscellaneous assets as presented in exhibit 2. In other words, with reference to exhibit 2, the net capital figure of $2,270,321 is the summation of lines 28, 29, 30, and 31, minus lines 17, 18.

EXHIBIT 2
Representative Bank of America Balance Sheet (average of 41 banks having total
deposits ranging from $8 million to $50 million), 1970

1. Cash and due from banks			$ 2,762,199
2. U.S. securities, under 5 years	$3,780,146		
3. U.S. securities, 5 years and over	466,548		
4. Tax exempt loans and investments	4,874,269		
5. Other bonds and stocks	980,395		
6. Liquidity loans	936,990		
7. Subtotal, investments		$11,038,348	
8. Real estate mortgage loans		5,787,707	
9. Direct installment loans	$2,520,006		
10. Indirect installment loans	1,233,759		
11. Floor plan loans	110,193		
12. Subtotal installment loans		3,863,958	
13. Commercial and other loans	$3,798,936		
14. Agricultural loans	211,185		
15. Subtotal comm'l and agricul. loans		4,010,121	
16. Subtotal, loans and investments			24,700,134
17. Bank premises			530,257
18. Other real estate and other assets			307,422
19. Total Assets			$28,300,012
20. Regular checking accounts	$9,077,134		
21. Special checking accounts	393,698		
22. Other demand deposits	571,749		
23. Subtotal demand deposits		$10,042,581	
24. Regular savings accounts	$7,652,552		
25. Club accounts and school savings	103,812		
26. Certificates of deposit and other time	7,393,067		
27. Subtotal, time deposits		15,149,431	
28. Other liabilities and borrowed money		339,688	
29. Capital funds		2,413,959	
30. Valuation reserves		321,257	
31. Preferred stock, notes, and debentures		33,096	
32. Total Liabilities and Capital			$28,300,012

Capital cost includes two elements: one called "net capital expense,"
an internal cost, and the other, called "cost of common equity," an external cost. The calculation of net capital expense is presented below and
calculation of cost of common equity is explained in a subsequent section.

From exhibit 3 one is able to determine the before-tax dollar cost of
funds. These costs, of course, need to be compared with the aggregate
figures presented in the balance sheet, exhibit 2, as adjusted for changes
in net capital funds available, in order to obtain the before-tax cost of
funds rate. This before-tax cost of funds figure is simply the ratio of
the net cost of funds to total funds available, by component part. Using

EXHIBIT 3
Representative Bank of America Net Dollar Cost of Funds

	Net Capital	Demand Deposits	Time Deposits	Available Funds
Servicing costs and interest expense	$60,106	$308,106	$809,225	$1,177,437
Less service charge and other income	2,433	89,732	1,865	94,030
Net cost of funds	$57,673	$218,374	$807,360	$1,083,407

RBA's component parts, as presented in exhibit 2 and 3, and as elaborated upon in exhibit 5, this calculation reveals before-tax cost of funds rates of 2.54 percent, 2.17 percent, 5.33 percent, and 3.95 percent for net capital, demand deposits, time deposits, and total available funds, respectively. Assuming a 48 percent tax rate, the after-tax equivalents, as revealed in exhibit 5, would be 1.32 percent for net capital; 1.13 percent for demand deposits; 2.77 percent for time deposits; and 2.05 percent for total available funds.

The total cost of net capital expense, $60,106 in exhibit 3, is the summation of officers' salaries, processing salaries and wages, fringe benefits, directors' fees, examinations and audits, fees, legal and so on, and "other" expenses, plus federal fund and borrowing costs, and capital note and debenture interest. All of these costs are deductible for income tax purposes.

The total demand deposit expense, $308,106 in exhibit 3, is the summation of tellers' salaries and wages, transit and bookkeeping wages, fringe benefits, furniture and equipment, computer service expenses, printing and stationery supplies, postage, freight and deliveries, telephone and telegraph, legal and other fees, officers' salaries and supplemental benefits, publicity and advertising, F.D.I.C. insurance, lease (occupancy) costs, and "other" expenses. All of these costs are deductible for income tax purposes.

The composition of the total time deposit costs of $809,225 in exhibit 3 is virtually identical to that of demand deposits and capital funds and, of course, these costs also are tax deductible.

To these cost figures, however, the bank should add the cost of two additional components: (1) the cost of common equity; and (2) implicit cost of holding cash in excess of required reserves.

One method of determining the cost of equity capital is to determine the rate of return that stockholders expect to earn on the bank's common stock. In other words, the bank should solve for k, where k equals the cost of equity capital: $k = D/P_0 + g$, where D equals average 1970 dividends paid of $1.89, g equals the required or anticipated growth rate assumed arbitrarily to be 5 percent and P_0 equals the average price of the bank's common stock in 1970, $54.21. The price per share of RBA is equal to the mean of the 1970 prices of seven banks chosen from the 41 banks comprising RBA's balance sheet. Consequently, the cost of equity capital is 8.5 percent.

The total market value of RBA's stock is equal to $54.21 times the average number of shares outstanding, 45,908, or $2,488,673. At 8.5 percent the dollar cost of RBA's equity capital on this market value is $211,537. The after-tax equivalent of the cost of available funds shown in exhibit 3 is $563,372. When equity cost is added the total is $774,909. The combined after-tax cost of funds rate for RBA is then 2.82 percent, $774,909 divided by total capital, $27,462,333.

The cost of holding cash reserves in excess of required reserves is, of course, an opportunity cost. Required reserves of national banks at the end of 1970 amounted to about 15 percent of demand deposits and 3 percent of time deposits. In total dollars for the RBA that required reserve amounted on average to $1,960,871, as depicted in exhibit 4. There is, of course, an implicit cost associated with required reserves over which the bank has no control. The bank, however, *can* control the use of excess reserves.

Had the excess reserves shown in exhibit 4 been invested in 1970 at a 6 percent federal fund rate, about $48,079 would have been generated. Since the bank chose instead to hold this $801,328 as idle cash and due from banks, this foregone income of $48,079 may be considered as an opportunity cost to the bank.

One could argue that the $801,328 excess cash held by RBA is not all "excess." Since the total dollar reserve figure from RBA, column 5 of exhibit 4, is the average "cash and due from banks" entry for the year 1970, and inasmuch as certain levels of cash must be retained for daily operations, there is no way of determining precisely how much of this

EXHIBIT 4
Excess Reserves, Representative Bank of America, December 1970

	(1) Total Deposits*	(2) Re- quired Reserve Rate*	(3) Required Reserves	(4) Total Required Reserves	(5) Total Dollar Actual Reserves	(6) Excess Reserves
Demand deposits	$10,042,584	15%	$1,506,388			
Time deposits	$15,149,431	3%	$ 454,483	$1,960,871	$2,762,199	$801,328

* Rounded for illustrative purposes. The actual calculation for demand deposits is made by subtracting cash and due from banks from demand deposits to arrive at net demand deposits. Against this net figure apply a 12.5 percent reserve for all deposits up to $5,000,000 and a 13 percent reserve for all net demand deposits in excess of $5,000,000; for time deposits apply a 3 percent required reserve against savings accounts. Three percent for all "other" time deposits up to $5,000,000 and a 5 percent reserve for all monies in excess of $5,000,000.

EXHIBIT 5
Total After-Tax Cost of Funds, Representative Bank of America, 1970
Part I

	(1) Dollar Cost	(2) Capital Component Available	(3) After- Tax Dollar Cost[a]	(4) Before- Tax Cost of Funds	(5) After-Tax Cost of Funds Rate (Col. 3 ÷ Col. 2)
Net capital	$ 57,673	$ 2,270,321	$ 29,990	2.54	1.32
Demand deposits	218,384	10,042,581	113,555	2.17	1.13
Time deposits	807,360	15,149,431	419,827	5.33	2.77
Total	$1,083,407	$27,462,333	$563,372	3.95	2.05

[a] Assumes a 48 percent tax rate.

Part II

	(1) Total Market Value of Equity Capital[b]	(2) Dollar Cost of Equity Capital	(3) Cost of Equity Capital Expressed as Percent[c]
Common stock........................	$2,488,673	$211,537	8.5

[b] Market value of RBA's stock is equal to its mean value, $54.21 times average number of shares outstanding, 45,908.
[c] The cost, 8.5 percent, represents a combination of dividend yield, 3.5% plus growth, 5%.

Part III

	(1) Excess Reserves	(2) Oppor- tunity Cost	(3) Implicit Dollar Cost	(4) After-Tax Cost of Funds Rate
"Excess cash"	$801,328	.06[d]	$48,079	3.12

[d] Assumed opportunity cost of hoarding excess cash.

Part IV

	(1) Total After-Tax Dollar Cost	(2) Total Available Funds	(3) After-Tax Cost of Funds Rate (Col. 1 ÷ Col. 2)
Summation of Parts I, II, and III	$822,988	$27,462,333	2.99

money is controllable excess. Consequently, this $48,079 opportunity cost of holding excess cash is the maximum. On the other hand, however, the federal funds rate during 1970 averaged over 7 percent. Consequently, this $48,079 opportunity cost might be a little low. Knowing the rationale behind its calculation, individual commercial banks should have no trouble in determining their own opportunity costs, if any, of idle cash.

Calculation of total weighted cost of funds is made by adding the after-tax dollar cost of net capital, demand deposits, and time deposits which total $563,372 to the dollar cost of equity capital, $211,537, and the implicit cost of excess cash reserves, $48,079. These costs are revealed in parts I, II and III, respectively, of exhibit 5. These figures total $822,988 and when divided by the total dollar amount of available funds, $27,462,333, a cost of funds rate of 2.99 percent results.

PROFITABILITY BY FUNCTION: REPRESENTATIVE
BANK OF AMERICA

Profitability by function for the RBA is determined by subtracting all direct and allocable indirect expenses from total gross revenue generated by that function. The resulting figure is the net revenue, or yield, exclusive of cost of funds. From the net yield, the cost of funds is subtracted to determine the net profit of the bank by function. For purposes of this presentation, four major leading functions are presented: investments, real estate mortgage loans, installment loans and commercial and agricultural loans. These four component parts amount to 87 percent of the RBA's total assets.

Profitability by function, expressed as percentage return on available funds, is presented in exhibit 6. Three different assumptions concerning cost of funds are used. The first assumption calculates the cost of funds by function using the after-tax rate on net capital, demand deposits, and time deposits. This after-tax cost of funds rate is 2.05 percent. The second assumption adds the cost of equity to net capital. This after-tax cost of funds is 2.82 percent. And assumption three makes the calculation based upon all of the components of assumption two plus the opportunity cost of holding idle cash. The third version is the total after-tax cost of funds. It amounts to 2.99 percent and is the most valid of the three for decision making purposes.

The advantage of this approach is obvious: the bank can determine its most profitable lending functions, rank them in descending order of profitability, and channel loanable funds into those functional areas that generate the highest percentage and/or dollar return(s) consistent with degree of risk. Of course, banks must attempt to lend in all areas even though some generate more deposits than others, for this lending is necessary to maintain total deposits. Consequently, so long as the rate of

EXHIBIT 6
After-Tax Profitability By Function,

	Installment Loan Function			Investment Function		
Total funds employed...................	$3,863,958			$11,038,348		
Gross revenue	$ 462,143			$ 798,870		
Minus expenses	163,795			15,835		
Income before taxes and cost of funds	$ 298,348			$ 783,035		
Minus tax-exempt securities				411,751		
Income before taxes and cost of funds				$ 371,284		
Minus taxes @ 48 percent	143,207			178,216		
Income after taxes and before cost of funds	$ 155,141			$ 193,068		
Add actual tax-exempt securities*				205,876		
Net income after tax and before cost of funds	$ 155,141	$155,141	$155,141	$ 398,944	$398,944	$398,944
Minus cost of funds	79,211[a]	108,964[b]	115,532[c]	226,286[a]	311,281[b]	330,047[c]
Net profit	$ 75,930	$ 46,177	$ 39,609	$ 172,658	$ 87,663	$ 68,897
After-tax return on funds employed under three assumptions regarding cost of funds:						
Assumption one:		1.96%		1.56%		
Assumption two:		1.19%		0.79%		
Assumption three:		1.02%		0.62%		

[a] assumption one; 2.05%
[b] assumption two; 2.82%
[c] assumption three; 2.99%
* Actual income received by the bank

return within a function is equal to or greater than the cost of funds for that function, loans can be made profitably by the bank. At a minimum, commercial bankers should know these costs and levels of profit by function within their own firms. In the case of RBA, this percentage return on available funds ranking would be: (1) installment loan function; (2) investment function; (3) commercial and agricultural loan function; and (4) real estate and mortgage function.

One could argue that the cost of funds is irrelevant when a pooling of funds is used because the cost is the same for each function. The author uses this method, however, for he is interested in revealing the total *dollar* cost of money allocated to a function and the total *dollar* after-tax profit of that function. Also, it is desirable to have a method of cost calculation for those commercial banks who neither know their total costs of operating each department (function) nor their overall cost of funds. The method is of use also to determine the resulting dollar profit if the gross yield for a function, any function, were high enough to justify allocation of funds but there was only limited absorptive capacity. In such a situation, it would be essential for the bank to know the total *dollar* after-tax yield of a function as well as its after-tax rate of return. Exhibit 6 reveals both pieces of information.

Representative Bank of America, 1970

Commercial and Agricultural Function			Real Estate Mortgage Function			Total Bank Functions		
$4,010,121			$5,787,707			$24,700,134		
$ 320,302			$ 397,501					
51,046			40,873					
$ 269,256			$ 356,628					
129,243			171,181					
$ 140,013			$ 185,447					
$ 140,013	$140,013	$140,013	$ 185,447	$185,447	$185,447			
82,207[a]	113,085[b]	119,903[c]	118,648[a]	163,213[b]	173,052[c]			
$ 57,806	$ 26,928	$ 20,110	$ 66,829	$ 22,234	$ 12,395	$ 373,223	$183,002	$141,011
1.44%			1.15%			1.51%		
0.67%			0.38%			0.74%		
0.50%			0.21%			0.57%		

CONCLUSION

This study is designed to provide a method of cost and profit calculation to the numerous small and medium-sized banks who indicated in
response to the author's survey that they knew little or nothing about
their costs by function. To the extent that the results of this survey in
general and the profitability of RBA in particular is representative of
the entire banking community, this study should be helpful to individual
banks as well as being of some value at the policy-making levels of
state and national government where questions concerning matters such
as usury laws and price (interest rate) controls appear to be taking a
disproportionately large amount of time and effort to resolve.

12. Statistical Cost Analysis*

WILLIAM A. LONGBRAKE

Statistical techniques provide information useful in making many types of business decisions. For several reasons, however, statistical analysis is seldom used in analyzing production and other costs. Standard costing procedures, such as time and motion studies and direct costing procedures based on past experience and modified by anticipated changes, are sufficient in many decision-making situations.

Data limitations frequently hinder the employment of statistical analysis. To use it, data concerning costs, output, and product characteristics must exist for a sufficient number of time periods in one business firm or, alternatively, these data must be available for one time period for several firms producing essentially the same product. Another impediment is the general lack of knowledge about statistical cost analysis.

This article will demonstrate the use of statistical analysis for product costing, incremental costing, and cost forecasting. While the illustrations are developed specifically for use by commercial banks in making decisions about demand deposit operations, the basic techniques could be modified for cost analysis of products in other industries or products of a single firm.

Detailed cost accounting and production data exist for a sample of nearly 1,000 banks that have voluntarily participated in the Federal Reserve Banks' Functional Cost Analysis (FCA) program. Development of uniform accounting classifications and methods of allocating costs by the FCA has enabled participating banks to compare their performance with the average performance of similarly-sized banks. As a result, the accuracy and consistency of FCA data is excellent. Hence, the data afford a good basis for demonstrating the use of statistical analysis.

METHODOLOGY

Before statistical analysis can take place, it is necessary to construct a cost function that describes accurately all relevant factors. First, cost categories must be defined. For example, three types of costs are incurred

---

* *Financial Management,* vol. 2, no. 1 (Spring 1973), pp. 49–55.

in providing services to demand deposit customers—fixed maintenance costs, variable maintenance costs, and transactions costs. Fixed maintenance costs arise from routine operations performed on a regular basis for every account, e.g., carrying a master record of an account on a ledger card and preparing and sending monthly statements. Variable maintenance costs, such as FDIC insurance and "free" services, vary with the size of an account. Transactions costs vary directly with the volume of transactions.

Second, measurable variables must be found that explain variations in each general cost category.

Third, other factors that may indirectly influence the costs of providing demand deposit services should be identified, and variables should be defined that explain their effects. For example, to the extent that common production costs exist and cannot be allocated precisely, the level of time deposit operations may have an influence on demand deposit costs. Other factors arise when the cost behavior of several firms is being analyzed. For instance, legal organizational form—unit, branch, or holding company affiliate—may influence the organization of demand deposit operations and, therefore, influence operating costs as well. In addition, wage rates prevailing in local labor markets will have an important effect on demand deposit costs because of the large amount of labor required.

It may be impossible to determine the separate effects of each of these factors because of their complex interrelationships. Moreover, if the volume of output affects the unit cost related to any one of these factors, the accountant's use of standard costs may overlook important variations that occur with changes in the level of output. Thus, a cost function may be a useful alternative to ordinary accounting practices.

Bell and Murphy and Longbrake have demonstrated that a log-linear cost function of the type defined in the following equation is appropriate for commercial banks and explains most of the variation in demand deposit operating costs among banks:

$$\log C = \log H + \delta_1 \log N + \delta_2 \log S + \psi_1 \log T_1 + \psi_2 \log T_2 \\ + \psi_3 \log T_3 + \psi_4 \log T_4 + \psi_5 \log T_5 + \psi_6 \log T_6 \\ + \alpha_1 \log B + \alpha_2 \log M + \alpha_3 \log w + \alpha_4 \log I,$$

where C is total *direct* operating costs allocated by a bank to the demand deposit function. A glossary of the symbols in the equation appears in the inset. The reader is asked to peruse them before proceeding, and refer to them as necessary in company with the following exposition.

Coefficients of the variables in the cost equation shown above—δ_i, ψ_i, and α_i—indicate that percentage change in total cost occurring when a particular variable changes by 1 percent, with all other variables unchanged. The effect on costs of the addition of a new account with characteristics *identical* to the existing "average" account is measured by the

---

Glossary of Symbols

C = total *direct* operating costs allocated by a bank to the demand deposit function

$\log H$ = cost function constant

N = average number of accounts per banking office

S = average dollar size of a demand deposit account

T_1 = average number of home debits (items posted to the debit column in the ledger for each account) per account

T_2 = average number of deposits per account

T_3 = average number of transit checks (checks written on banks other than the home bank) deposited per account

T_4 = average number of official checks issued per account

T_5 = average number of checks cashed per account

T_6 = average number of transit checks cashed per account

B = number of offices operated by a bank

M = ratio of the number of regular checking accounts to the sum of both regular and special accounts

w = average annual wage rate per demand deposit employee

I = ratio of the dollar volume of demand deposits to the dollar volume of demand and time deposits, measures the effects of time deposit production activities on demand deposit costs

$\delta_i, \psi_i, \alpha_i$ indicate that percentage change in total cost that occurs when a particular variable changes by 1 percent, given that all other variables remain unchanged.

---

coefficient of $\log N$. The indicated percentage change in costs will include additional fixed maintenance, variable maintenance, and transactions costs. The percentage change in costs caused by an increase in the average size of account S will indicate primarily increases in variable maintenance costs associated with account size. The percentage change in costs caused by an increase in T_1 will show the change in transactions costs due to a large number of home debits per account. Changes in the other transactions variables can be interpreted in a similar fashion.

If a regular account is substituted for a special account, the coefficient of $\log M$ will indicate whether costs increase or decrease. The change in costs may result from differences in either fixed maintenance, variable maintenance, or transactions costs for two accounts which are identical in all respects except that one is a special account and the other is a regular account. The coefficient of $\log w$ indicates the percentage change in costs which occurs when the wage rate changes. Differences in local

wage rates or differences in the mix of personnel engaged in demand
deposit operations could cause differences in total costs. Therefore, the
effects of maintenance, transactions, and other factors on demand deposit
costs are contained within the cost function. Although the cost of a specific
demand deposit production operation may not be identifiable, the
statistical cost function can be used to determine the costs which occur
for a given set of production relationships.

Data for estimating the coefficients of the cost equation shown above
were obtained from 964 banks that participated in the 1971 FCA program.
These banks ranged in size from $5 million to $6 billion in total
deposits. Regression analysis was used to estimate the coefficients; the
results are presented in exhibit 1. These results will serve as a base for

EXHIBIT 1
Regression Results for the 1971 Demand
Deposit Cost Function°

$$\log C = -1.7345 + .9503 \log N + .3936 \log S + .0467 \log T_1$$
$$(.1792) \quad (.0127) \quad\quad (.0248) \quad\quad\quad (.0268)$$
$$+ .1427 \log T_2 + .0742 \log T_3 + .0583 \log T_4 +$$
$$(.0348) \quad\quad (.0126) \quad\quad (.0111)$$
$$+ .0183 \log T_5 - .0046 \log T_6 + 1.0150 \log B +$$
$$(.0105) \quad\quad (.0124) \quad\quad (.0092)$$
$$- .0626 \log M + .4312 \log w + .0113 \log I$$
$$(.0251) \quad\quad (.0470) \quad\quad (.0311)$$

$\bar{R} = .9630$
Standard Error of Estimate = .0998
F-Ratio = 2087.5

* Numbers in parentheses are standard errors of the regression coefficients.

developing illustrations of product costing, incremental costing, and cost
forecasting below.

PRODUCT COSTING

Accountants generally recognize two methods of product costing—job
order costing and process costing. In job order costing, each job is an
accounting unit to which material, labor, and other costs are assigned.
However, in process costing, attention centers on total costs incurred by
a department for a given time period in relation to the units processed.
Dividing total costs by the quantity of units produced gives the average
unit cost. Process costing is usually more appropriate for mass production.

Statistical analysis of costs is more applicable in process than in job
order costing. Costs are accumulated over a period of time for a specific
department, and data concerning production activities in the department
are collected for the same time period. However, rather than employing

traditional accounting methods to ascertain average unit costs, average unit costs are estimated through a statistical analysis of the cost-output relationship as defined in a cost function. Traditional accounting methods must assume a rather uncomplicated relationship between output and costs (or various categories of costs); however, if complex interrelationships prevail among the various factors influencing total costs, statistical methods may be more appropriate. It must be remembered that data are required for several time periods or for several firms producing essentially the same product before statistical analysis is feasible. Traditional accounting methods do not have such a requirement.

In many respects, servicing demand deposits in a bank is similar to a continuous production process in manufacturing and thus will serve as a good general illustration. Tellers perform several operations including counting cash, verifying deposit amounts, and issuing receipts. The proof department sorts checks by type and identifies questionable checks. The bookkeeping department posts deposits and checks to appropriate accounts. Furthermore, many other activities, in addition to those mentioned above, occur on a regular and continuing basis.

Two kinds of demand deposit accounts—regular and special—customarily exist in most banks. Special accounts have no minimum balance requirement whereas regular accounts do. As a result of the no minimum balance feature, special accounts tend to be held by individuals rather than businesses and they tend to be less active and have smaller average balances than regular accounts. Thus, regular and special accounts are distinct products; however, production operations for both always occur simultaneously. Consequently, the cost of servicing each type of account is not easily separable.

In exhibit 2, it is shown how the total and average cost per $100 of an average regular and an average special account can be determined from the results of the statistical analysis shown in exhibit 1. For convenience, values of the various account characteristics and bank characteristics have been selected that are approximately equal to the sample geometric means of these characteristics. In the cost computations for regular accounts, it is assumed that no special accounts exist. However, in the cost computations for special accounts, it is assumed that 1 percent of the accounts are regular. This assumption is required because the log of the mix variable (M) is undefined when there are no regular accounts.

The average regular account in exhibit 2 is more than twice as costly to service as the average special account. However, the average regular account is only 29 percent as costly per *dollar* of deposits as the average special account. Product costs developed in this way can be used to develop pricing policy. In the case of banks, this kind of information is useful in establishing service charge schedules. It should be noted that the average unit cost of an account need not be the same for each set of

EXHIBIT 2
Computation of Average Unit Costs for Regular and Special Checking Accounts

	(1)	(2) Regular Account	(3)	(4)	(5)	(6) Special Account	(7)
	Value	Log of Value	Cost Function Coefficient	Product of Columns 2 and 3	Value	Log of Value	Product of Columns 3 and 6
Characteristics of average account							
S Account size	$2,100	3.32222	.3936	1.30763	$ 300	2.47712	.97499
T_1 Home debits/accounts	230	2.36173	.0467	.11029	100	2.00000	.09340
T_2 Deposits/accounts	40	1.60206	.1427	.22861	25	1.39794	.19949
T_3 Transit checks deposited/ accounts	180	2.25527	.0742	.16734	20	1.30103	.09654
T_4 Official checks/accounts	3	.47712	.0583	.02782	2	.30103	.01755
T_5 Checks cashed/accounts	30	1.47712	.0183	.02703	30	1.47712	.02703
T_6 Transit checks cashed/ accounts	14	1.14613	−.0046	−.00527	16	1.20412	−.00554
Bank characteristics							
N Number of accounts	3,250	3.51188	.9503	3.33734	3,250	3.51188	3.33734
B Number of offices	3	.47712	1.0150	.48428	3	.47712	.48428
M Regular accounts/all accounts	100%	.00000	−.0626	.00000	1%	−2.00000	.12520
w Annual wage rate	$5,700	3.75587	.4312	1.61953	$5,700	3.75587	1.61953
I Demand deposits/total deposits	40%	−.39794	.0113	−.00450	40%	−.39794	−.00450
H Cost function constant				−1.73447			−1.73447
Total cost (log)				5.53860			5.23084
(antilog)				$345,623.00			$170,054.00
Average cost per account				35.45			17.44
Average cost per $100				1.69			5.81

account characteristic and bank characteristic variables. Any bank which knows its values for the variables in exhibit 2 may determine its average unit costs by following the demonstrated computational procedure.

This method of product costing would be useful in any business enterprise that produces more than one product on a regular and continuing basis using essentially the same types of resources. For example, different types of telephone service—private, party, or commercial—could be costed using the methods described above. Other possible applications might include the manufacture of canned and processed foods, book publishing, manufacture of apparel, manufacture of consumer durable goods such as automobiles, refrigerators, television sets, appliances, lawn mowers, and so on.

INCREMENTAL COSTING

Incremental or differential costs are the increases or decreases in total costs, or the changes in specific elements of cost, that result from some variation in operations. An incremental costing approach to decision making is important when certain costs are fixed and, as such, are not influenced by changes in operations. Ordinarily such a situation occurs in the short run when scale of operations cannot be changed. When the decision is whether or not to accept another order or expand output from a given level, and certain costs are fixed or are relatively inflexible, use of standard costs or average unit costs may lead to the wrong decision. This could happen because the incremental cost of the additional output may differ from the change in total costs indicated by multiplying the additional output by the average unit cost.

Situations in which an incremental cost approach to decision making may be appropriate include: taking on new orders; increasing, decreasing, or eliminating production of certain products; replacing old equipment with new; and so forth. In commercial banks, it may be useful to know the incremental costs of a new demand deposit account, especially if it is tied to a loan arrangement, so that an appropriate pricing strategy can be developed. Incremental costs can also be developed for specific types of demand deposit accounts that differ in various respects from the average account.

The usual accounting approach to differential costing is to identify variable and fixed costs. Then, in a particular situation the affected variable costs can be used to determine the differential cost. However, if variable costs cannot be determined easily, or if variable costs do not remain constant per unit of output at various levels of output, the usual accounting techniques may prove to be insufficient.

Statistical cost analysis may improve the accuracy of incremental cost determination in such circumstances because estimates of incremental (marginal) costs can be derived directly from the cost function for every variation in the basic product that might exist. For example, incremental costs can be determined for each type of transaction that is identified in the demand deposit cost function. Thus, the incremental cost of one additional home debit per account is the change in total cost, C, which results from an increase in home debits per account, T_1, while all other variables in the cost equation shown above remain unchanged. This incremental cost is computed by taking the partial derivative of total cost, C, with respect to home debits per account, T_1. In the present instance, the incremental cost of one additional home debit per account is equal to the cost function coefficient of T_1 (Ψ_1) times total cost (C) divided by T_1. Thus, the incremental cost of an additional home debit per regular demand account is computed in column 3 of exhibit 3 by multiplying the appropriate cost function coefficient in column 1 (.0467) by total cost ($345,623) and then dividing by the number of home debits per regular account (230). Incremental cost per unit, shown in column 4, is obtained by dividing the incremental cost figure in column 3 by the number of regular accounts (9,750). Incremental costs for other variations in the product are calculated in a similar fashion and the results are shown in exhibit 3.

The incremental cost of an additional regular demand deposit account that is *identical* to the average regular account is $33.69. This is less than the average unit cost of $35.45 for an existing regular account as indicated in exhibit 2. However, the incremental cost of an additional special account is slightly larger than the average unit cost of a special account. Thus, increases in the number of regular accounts would reduce average unit cost, but increase in the number of special checking accounts would increase average unit cost. To the extent that unutilized capacity exists, management may wish to promote regular rather than special accounts.

An additional dollar in a special account is more than three times as costly to service as an additional dollar in a regular account. This indicates that the cost of providing extra services to small special checking accounts is greater per dollar than the cost of providing additional services to large regular checking accounts. This also implies that the incremental cost associated with an additional dollar of deposits most likely depends on the size of the deposit, i.e., fixed account maintenance costs can be spread over more dollars in large accounts. Home debits are associated with highly routinized operations which may explain why there is little difference in the incremental costs of home debits in regular and special checking accounts. With the exception of transit checks deposited, incremental costs of changes in other account characteristics are greater for regular accounts than they are for special accounts. There are only one ninth as many transit checks deposited annually in special accounts as in regular accounts. The difference in incremental costs for transit

EXHIBIT 3
Incremental Costs for Various Characteristics of Regular and Special Accounts

		(1)	(2) Regular Accounts	(3) Regular Accounts	(4) Regular Accounts	(5) Special Accounts	(6) Special Accounts	(7) Special Accounts
	Characteristics	Cost Function Coefficient	Value	Incremental Cost	Incremental Cost per Unit*	Value	Incremental Cost	Incremental Cost per Unit*
N†	Account	$\delta_1 = .9503$	9,750	$ 33.69	$33.6867	9,750	$ 17.67	$17.6664
S	Account size	$\delta_2 = .3936$	$ 2,100	64.78	.0066	$ 300	223.11	.0229
T_1	Home debits/accounts	$\psi_1 = .0467$	230	70.18	.0072	100	79.42	.0081
T_2	Deposits/accounts	$\psi_2 = .1427$	40	1,233.01	.1265	25	970.67	.0996
T_3	Transit checks deposited/accounts	$\psi_3 = .0742$	180	142.47	.0146	20	630.90	.0647
T_4	Official checks/accounts	$\psi_4 = .0583$	3	6,716.61	.6889	2	4,957.07	.5084
$(T_5 - T_6)$‡	Nontransit checks cashed/accounts	$\psi_5 = .0183$	16	210.83	.0216	14	103.73	.0106
T_6	Transit checks cashed/accounts	$\psi_6 = -.0046$ $\alpha_2 = -.0626$	14	97.27	.0100	16	54.84	.0056
C	Total costs			$345,623			$170,054	

* Incremental cost per unit is determined by dividing incremental cost by 9,750 accounts.

† The number of accounts variable (N) includes both regular and special accounts. However, the mix variable also contains both regular and special accounts. Let $N = (N_R + N_S)/B$ and $M = N_R/(N_R + N_S)$. Then, the incremental cost of another regular account $= (\delta_1 - \alpha_2)[C/N_R + N_S] + \alpha_2(C/N_R)$. The incremental cost of another special account $= (\delta_1 - \alpha_2)[C/N_R + N_S]$.

‡ Nontransit checks cashed per account equals $(T_5 - T_6)$ while transit checks cashed equals T_6. The sum of these two categories is total checks cashed (T_5). The incremental cost of nontransit checks cashed $= \psi_5(C/T_5)$. The incremental cost of transit checks cashed $= \psi_5(C/A_5) + \psi_6(C/T_6)$.

EXHIBIT 4
Computation of the Cost of a Regular Checking Account Which Differs from the Average Regular Checking Account

Characteristics	(1) Value Example Account	(2) Value Average Account	(3) Difference (1) − (2)	(4) Incremental Cost per Item	(5) Change in Average Cost per Account
S Account size	$5,000	$2,100	2,900	.0066	$19.14
T_1 Home debits/account	400	230	170	.0072	1.22
T_2 Deposits/account	50	40	10	.1265	1.26
T_3 Transit checks deposited/account	300	180	120	.0146	1.75
T_4 Official checks/account	5	3	2	.6889	1.38
$(T_5 - T_6)$ Nontransit checks cashed/account	20	16	4	.0216	.09
T_6 Transit checks cashed/account	20	14	6	.0100	.04
Total					$24.88
Cost of average regular account					+35.45
Cost of example regular account					$60.33
Cost per $100 of the example regular account					1.21

checks deposited in regular and special accounts may occur if the cost of handling the first few transit checks is high while the cost of handling each additional transit check declines.

Suppose management wishes to know the cost of a specific regular checking account that differs in identifiable ways from the average regular account. Incremental cost analysis can be used to help determine the cost of this *example* regular account. Characteristics of the example regular account to be costed are shown in column 1 of exhibit 4 and characteristics of the average account are contained in column 2. Column 3 is the difference of the first two columns. The incremental cost in column 5 is the product of the figure in column 3 and the incremental cost per item in column 4, which was computed in exhibit 3.

Although the cost of the example regular account in exhibit 4 is considerably greater than the cost of the average regular account, the cost per $100 is lower because of the larger balance. This result suggests that service charge rates should be based on account size and the number of various types of transactions. Knowledge of incremental costs can be used to establish variable rate service charge schedules which reflect the actual cost incurred in servicing a particular account more accurately than using average unit costs or some kind of standard costing procedure.

Such an approach to pricing may be useful in nonfinancial firms that produce a product or service capable of being differentiated or varied in several ways. For example, the incremental costing method may be useful in establishing the cost of selling particular types of merchandise in retailing firms or in determining the cost of handling particular types of customer credit accounts.

COST FORECASTING

When management contemplates or expects some change in operations at a future date, it is important to forecast the effects of this change on costs. The use of statistical analysis in forecasting, especially for forecasting sales, is well established. However, cost forecasts ordinarily are based on a nonstatistical evaluation of the production facilities, equipment, labor, and materials required to produce enough to meet the sales forecast. When statistical methods are used to forecast costs, it usually involves either a simple regression analysis of volume and cost or, in rare cases, a multiple regression analysis.

The principal danger inherent in statistical cost forecasting is that future behavior may differ substantially from past cost behavior, thus making forecasts unreliable. Changes in plant and equipment, materials, products, production techniques, personnel, internal organization, prices paid for materials and labor, and many other factors will tend to impair the reliability of statistical cost forecasts. Nevertheless, in some circumstances statistical cost forecasting may provide helpful information. For example, if prices of materials and labor have varied in the past, this information can be included in the statistical cost function. Then, the effect of expected future changes in these prices on costs can be determined. In a firm that operates several plants or branches, all producing and selling the same product, statistical cost analysis may prove useful in forecasting the costs of *operating* a new plant or branch. Statistical analysis is not as likely to be useful in determining the cost of constructing a new plant. Several illustrations of cost forecasting are given below.

Turning to the banking example, suppose a branch bank is operating three offices with an average of 3,250 demand deposit accounts per office. It is considering opening a new office that it expects to be able to attract 3,250 new demand deposit accounts having characteristics essentially similar to those of existing demand deposits. Management is concerned about the effect of this expansion on its costs of operation for demand deposits. The change in costs can be forecast by making appropriate changes in the statistical cost function shown in the cost equation above:

$$\log C_1 = \log C_0 + \alpha_1 (\log B_1 - \log B_0)$$
$$= 5.53860 + 1.0150 \, (.60206 - .47712)$$
$$= 5.53860 + .12681$$
$$= 5.66541$$

Total costs are \$345,623 before the addition of the new branch and will be \$462,820 afterwards, an increase of \$117,197. Average unit cost before expansion is \$35.45, but after expansion it will be \$35.60. The \$.15 increase in average unit cost reflects added costs of coordination associated with the operation of the new branch.

Suppose that this branch bank is not considering opening a new branch but expects the number of demand deposits handled by each branch to increase from 3,250 to 4,333. The change in costs that occurs when 1,083 new demand accounts are added to each of the three existing branches can be computed in the same manner as described above: $5.53860 + .9503(3.63682 - 3.51188) = 5.65733$. Total costs will be \$454,289 and average cost per account will be \$34.95, a decline of \$.50 per account. In both of the cost forecasting examples given here, there will be 13,000 accounts and \$27.3 million in deposits (assuming that average account size is \$2,100). In one example, though, there are four offices while in the other there are only three. Having one more branch for the same number of accounts and the same amount of deposits causes a difference of \$7,531 or nearly 2 percent in total operating costs.

Management can also forecast the effect of an increase in the average annual wage paid per employee. Suppose management expects wages to rise by 10 percent from \$5,700 to \$6,270. Total costs will be: $5.53860 +$

.4312 (3.79727 — 3.75587) = 5.55645 or $360,125. Average unit costs will be $36.94, an increase of $1.49 per account.

The effects of other anticipated changes, in addition to those illustrated above, can be determined in the same way. In fact, the effects of all expected changes on total costs can be forecast simultaneously.

Any business firm able to construct its own cost function can use it to forecast the effects of changes in any or all of its variables. This procedure is legitimate so long as there is no significant change in the production-cost relationship.

CONCLUDING REMARKS

These uses of statistical cost analysis were demonstrated for commercial banks. However, any business enterprise which produces its products on a relatively regular and continuing basis and which maintains detailed records about output, resource prices, product characteristics, and costs can construct its own statistical cost function and use it for product costing, incremental costing, or cost forecasting. Thus, a host of business enterprises have the potential to use some kind of management-oriented statistical cost analysis.

If the production-cost relationship is more complex than that presumed in break-even analysis or variable budgeting, statistical cost analysis may provide useful supplemental information that these more conventional cost accounting techniques are incapable of providing. It is not suggested that information derived from employing statistical techniques should supplant other types of information; rather, it is urged that statistical cost information be used in conjunction with other cost accounting information to help *improve* decision making.

part FOUR
Pricing

INTRODUCTION

The relative place of demand and cost in the pricing decisions of firms of the real world—as opposed, presumably, to those of theory—was once a likely topic of debate in the economic journals. The participants arranged themselves mainly into two camps, the "marginalists" and the "full costers," the latter denying virtually any role to demand and some of the former coming dangerously close to denying any role to costs. A little less is heard about the question nowadays, partly because interest in it may have run its course (economics being no less prey to fashion than most disciplines) but mostly because we are coming to realize that the marginalists were talking primarily about *determinants* and the full costers mainly about *mechanics*. But each new generation of students begins with a clean slate and must be convinced of the practical importance of demand.

Business firms, presumably, are attempting to maximize something. It may be profits, total revenue, position in the community; nonetheless, all firms must sell their product at some price. How is and/or how should that price be determined? The survey by Aubrey Silberston is a classic presentation dealing with pricing developments and their impact on the overall theory of the firm. Pricing decisions represent only one of the decisions a firm must make but they are very important ones, by any standard of measurement.

A vice president in charge of pricing does not exist in the corporate structure of most organizations; also conspicuous by its absence is an office for the vice president in charge of profits. Seemingly, decisions regarding prices and profits are determined by a committee, the membership of which is often unknown. The article by Thomas Joseph Coyne provides a method of determining when a firm or industry is charging too high (low) a price or making too much (little) profit.

Joel Dean's classic article treats the separate issue of transfer pricing and the impact it has on profits. It is the standard introduction to this subject and directs attention to the main principles of rational pricing policy in any context. This subject is as disturbing as it is important, for Dean states that to be economically effective autonomous divisions of most large companies must establish transfer prices. Most existing transfer price systems are inadequate, and huge quantities of time and patience are required to install competitive transfer prices. Yet, once a "good" system is obtained, executives should be prepared to meet certain objections which critics always raise.

Donald H. and Mahlon R. Straszheim raise questions regarding the extent to which full-cost pricing implies a disregard for short-run market conditions. They explain how current-period measures of market conditions may be useful as predictors of pricing decisions.

On the surface, a kilowatt-hour of electricity may be considered no different than another kilowatt-hour of electricity. But 100 hours of electricity may not have the same value to apartment dwellers on Fifth Avenue in Manhattan at 10 A.M. as 100 hours of electricity would have at 10 P.M. on the same day. Many goods and services, such as electricity, are homogeneous products only if (1) the use to which they are put remains unchanged during the period of time the commodity or service is being used and (2) the value of the product remains unchanged during the same time period. Peak-load pricing recognizes these changes in value.

John T. Wenders explains that traditional theories of peak-load pricing and the regulated firm assume homogeneous production capacity. He demonstrates that when it is optimal to employ capacities with different capital and energy costs, the conclusions of these theories are modified considerably.

13. Surveys of Applied Economics: Price Behaviour of Firms[*]

AUBREY SILBERSTON

INTRODUCTION

The determination of prices has played a central part in economic theory for a hundred years or more. It forms the core of microeconomics, and is often the first topic of economics that students are taught. Its role in the allocation of resources is stressed, and—more recently—its role in the process of inflation. Yet it has been, and remains, a subject of considerable controversy. More recently managerial theories of the firm have been put forward in which the pursuit by managers of goals other than profits has been postulated. During the last few years the theory of the firm has particularly emphasized growth as an objective. This is partly an outcome of the attention given to the role of the manager, but it is also linked with the increasing emphasis on growth in economic theory generally.

As yet, the latest developments in the theory of the firm have not been outstanding in their implications for price theory. This is not necessarily a criticism of them. Pricing decisions are only one of the complex of decisions that a firm must take.

THE MEANING OF PRICE

It is important to realise first that price is not an unambiguous concept. Let us consider, for example, what is meant by the price of a car. Anyone who has ever bought a new car knows that the catalogue price is not the price he will eventually pay. There will be all kinds of optional extras that he can buy. Where he is free to specify these there is no problem—the price now refers to a particular type of car, specified more closely than previously. But there may also be an involuntary ele-

---

[*] *The Economic Journal*, vol. 80, no. 319 (September 1970), pp. 511–75. Cambridge University Press, London, England.

ment in the choice of optional extras. The intending purchaser may find that he can get a deluxe model, but that it may prove very difficult to get a standard model, which is what he really wants. The deluxe model must, in effect, be bought, and the price of the car is therefore higher than appears at first sight.

It has been assumed that prices are fixed by sellers, i.e., that sellers are "price-makers." Where a unique manufactured product is being sold, or a unique service offered, sellers may indeed have great discretion over price. But where a product is standardised and sold in a commodity market the discretion open to sellers is slight: they are effectively "price-takers." This point does not need labouring: every text-book tells the story of how price determination is affected by the structure of the market. It is important to bear in mind, however, that one of the ways in which competition manifests itself in different market situations is in the amount of scope that these give for competition in the various dimensions of price.

The argument of this section can be put another way. It can be said that it is not "price" which has many dimensions: it is "product." There are far more "products" in the car market, for example, than at first appears, and each of these myriad products has its own unambiguous price. This comes to the same thing, of course, but my personal preference is for laying the stress on the dimensions of *price*, since this seems to me the more helpful and natural way of expressing the point.

PRICE BEHAVIOUR IN THEORY

Later in this survey a good deal of attention will be paid to studies of how firms actually determine prices. It is well known, however, that in this field, as in many others, the answers depend a good deal on the questions, and the questions themselves depend on the theoretical approach of the questioner. It will be appropriate therefore to begin our survey with a consideration of the theory of price.

Price theory is usually formulated in terms of the price charged to the ultimate consumer, although little differentiation, if any, is normally made between prices charged by manufacturers and retail prices. For the sake of clarity, it will be best to think, at this stage of the analysis, in terms of the prices facing the ultimate consumer. Other types of price will be considered later. We will also think at this stage of each firm making a single product, although this is notoriously untrue in manufacturing industry.

It is assumed that the reader is familiar with the theory of price as it is normally expounded. Under conditions of perfect competition, it is argued, firms will push output to the point where their marginal cost equals price, and this price is determined by the market. In the long run price is equal to the average cost of production at the (relatively small) scale of output where long-run average cost is at its minimum. This is not because firms want this: they want maximum profits, but competition ensures that they earn "normal" profits only. Under conditions of imperfect competition the demand curve is not horizontal. The firm is a "price maker," and it maximises profits by choosing that combination of price and output at which marginal revenue equals marginal cost. In the long run firms may earn more than normal profits, but the extent to which they can do this depends on the market situation. In conditions of monopoly there will be no tendency for supernormal profits to be competed away, but where there are many firms in an industry supernormal profits may be eliminated altogether: the firms will, however, typically be below the scale at which long-run average cost is a minimum. The picture is less clear under conditions of oligopoly: with firms selling a homogeneous product (the usual assumption in the simplest case) price may end up anywhere between the competitive and the monopoly price, depending on the assumptions made.

The Full-Cost Attack on Imperfect Competition

Joan Robinson was concerned with what she called "imperfect competition," a state of affairs where one of the many conditions needed for perfect competition to exist was absent. In practice, she was particularly concerned with monopoly and with the "large group" case, and said little about nonprice competition and the small group. Chamberlin, on the other hand, was primarily concerned with what he called "monopolistic competition"—the middle ground between pure competition and monopoly, which was especially characterised by product differentiation. Chamberlin's treatment was more comprehensive, though less intensive, than that of Joan Robinson, and it stimulated much work, by authors such as Bain, on the relationship between the structure of an industry and the conduct and performance of the firms within it. Chamberlin attempted, inter alia, to deal with the small group case, but it is generally agreed that his treatment of his case was one of the least satisfactory parts of his work. The analysis of oligopoly, therefore, was left in a weak state. Apart from this, a well-defined price theory emerged from the work of these two authors, although any detailed consideration of Chamberlin's book made clear the yawning cracks opened up in the theory by the introduction of product differentiation.

Triffin's criticism of Joan Robinson and Chamberlin, apart from its technical aspects, was particularly effective in its attack on the notion of group equilibrium. The essence of the attack was that product differentiation, when taken to its logical conclusion, made nonsense of the idea of an "industry" equilibrium. One had to consider the firm (and its immediate competitors) and then the economy as a whole. Perhaps Triffin was too enamoured of the logic of his argument to give sufficient credit to those instances in the real world where industries or subindustries contain firms in more active competition with each other than with firms outside the "industry." Be that as it may, one of the results of Triffin's book was to reemphasise the gap in the theory of the firm left by the unsatisfactory nature of the theory of the small group. Apart from this, Triffin's analysis was essentially in the imperfect competition tradition. He did not doubt that the object of the firm was to maximize its profits and that marginal analysis was an appropriate tool for attaining this objective.

Hall and Hitch, on the other hand, appeared to many to have mounted a root-and-branch attack on the notion of profit maximisation itself. They argued, on the basis of an empirical study of pricing, that firms do not attempt to maximise profits. Instead they base prices on "full" costs, i.e., average direct costs (assumed to be constant over a wide range of output), plus average overhead costs, plus a margin for profit. At the root of this behaviour is the moral principle that there is a price that *ought* to be charged—the "right" price—and this ought to be charged in periods of both good and bad business. To this way of thinking, profit maximisation was the wrong way to approach the question of pricing. As has been pointed out by many critics, including Austin Robinson and Kahn, important elements of profit maximisation, or loss minimisation, entered into the pricing decisions of many of the businessmen investigated by Hall and Hitch. Moreover, Hall and Hitch themselves laid a good deal of stress on the kinked demand curve in cases of oligopoly, with its emphasis on sticky prices in the short run. As they themselves point out, the kink in the subjective demand curve makes the price at this point the profit-maximising price for a wide range of marginal costs, on account of the discontinuity in the marginal revenue curve at this particular price and output.

Of greater interest is the discussion by Hall and Hitch of how price came to be what it is, and how it comes to be changed. They argue, it will be recalled, that a price change is likely to come about as a result of a general change in costs. This is where full costs come back into the picture, but as Kahn has pointed out, the interesting question is—*whose* full costs? Clearly, if an industry is competitive in some sense firms will not each be able to base their prices on their own full costs, regardless of the costs of others. The possibility of price leadership must then be considered, but this subject was not dealt with satisfactorily by Hall and Hitch.

At first sight the work of Andrews appears to follow similar lines to that of Hall and Hitch. On further analysis it contains significant differences, which make it at the same time both more realistic and less satisfactory theoretically. The major difference is inherent in Andrews' use of the concept of the "costing margin." This margin is conceived as an addition to (constant) average direct costs, and "will normally tend to cover the costs of the indirect factors of production and provide a normal level of net profit." In its basic form, therefore, the costing margin gives a similar answer to that suggested by Hall and Hitch, and appears equally, at first sight, to be at variance with profit-maximising ideas. There is a good deal of discussion in Andrews, however, of the circumstances in which there might be some flexibility in the costing margin, in response to competitive and market forces, which brings his theory much closer to a theory of profit maximisation. The characteristics of the type of market with which Andrews is principally concerned—a mature oligopolistic industry, with potential competition limiting the scope for short-run profit-taking—would suggest, even for a firm intent on profit maximisation, a price policy similar to that postulated by him. However, Andrews lays much stress on the costing margin that one *has* to add, and hence on a defensive type of price policy which, it could be argued, is a policy more appropriate to a price *follower* than a price *leader*. "Conventional" maximising theory, on the other hand, is concerned with a firm which, at least in conditions of imperfect competition, has a certain amount of freedom to choose among various policies, including price policies. In this sense conventional theory deals with a price leader, although this is not usually made explicit.

The full-cost, normal-cost debate, and the parallel controversy in the United States, was perhaps more a source of good questions than of useful answers. However, it threw grave doubt on the extent to which businessmen think in the same terms as economists. It also raised the question whether, in many types of market, a policy of maximising profits in a succession of short periods was the best way of maximising profits in the long period. It drew attention to the prevalence in manufacturing industry of price stability, and described the process of price formation more realistically than hitherto. It also raised fundamental questions about the nature of business ethics and motivation generally, questions which are still the subject of vigorous debate.

The Development of the Theory of Oligopoly

While these attacks on the conventional theory of the firm were in progress the theory of oligopoly was being developed by those more in the mainstream of economic thought. Even these writers, however, were led by the nature of the problem to discuss topics far outside those usually treated in orthodox analysis. The fundamental problem of oligopoly is that competition among the few inevitably gives rise to problems of interdependence: no firm can act on the assumption that what it does will not provoke a reaction from its competitors. This reaction cannot be forecast with certainty, although relative costs of production, existing market shares and past history, all help firms to anticipate their rivals' reactions. But other factors, such as the view taken by the entrepreneur of his competitors, his strength of nerve and attitude to risk, have also to be considered before price behaviour can be determined in any particular oligopolistic situation. In the light of this one can appreciate Rothschild's view that to understand oligopoly one needs to understand the rules of war.

The classic approach to oligopoly is via the theory of duopoly. Here formalised models have been constructed in which standard reactions have been assumed by competitors. Cournot's model assumed that each firm would set its own output in the belief that the other firm's output would remain unchanged. Bertrand postulated that a firm would set prices in the belief that the other firm's price would remain unchanged. Stackelberg developed a more realistic model of leadership–followership: the follower behaved as in the Cournot model, while the leader took advantage of the assumed behaviour of the follower. In this model the interesting possibility is raised of both firms wishing to act as leaders, thus giving rise to an aggressive situation, with no determinate outcome.

We return to the more interesting question of the principles on which the price leader, whether one firm or a succession of different firms, fixes price. In general, the models of duopoly together with oligopoly models such as those of Fellner, lead to the conclusion that price will be above that ruling in perfect competition. The greater the number of firms in the group, and the more easily firms can enter it, the nearer the price will be to the competitive level. When the analysis is moved to a more realistic plane it has to be recognised that the perfectly competitive level of price (or costs) may have little meaning in an industry which consists of a few large firms, each enjoying considerable economies of scale. There may still be justification for talking of a departure from competitive price levels, however, in the sense that the price ruling in the industry may yield profits above "normal" to some or all of the firms in the group (i.e., above the level of profits ruling in industry as a whole). This situation may, of course, be compatible with a price level below that which would rule in an industry consisting of small firms in keen competition with each other, because economies of scale may be enjoyed by large firms.

The possibility of entry into a group is clearly very relevant to the level of profits that can be achieved, and hence to the ruling level of price.

Bain formulated his "limit price" theory of entry as early as 1949, some years before his important empirical work on barriers to entry appeared. The "limit price" set by a group of sellers, acting in collusion, is the highest common price which the established sellers believe they can charge without inducing entry into the industry. This price may well be lower than the profit-maximising price in any short period of time, and will depend, inter alia, on the relative costs of "inside" and "outside" firms, and on the conditions of demand in the industry. It may be that, given these relationships, the actual price has to be set above the limit price, thus enabling entry to occur. Or established firms, in order to maximise long-run profits, may choose to set price high enough to induce a limited amount of entry. In other cases it may be possible to maximise profits while setting price below the limit price. The number of possibilities is large, especially when competitive as well as collusive behaviour among established firms, and differences of efficiency between firms, are allowed for. In general, however, opportunities for earning monopoly profits in oligopolistic industries are likely to be closely related to the height of barriers to entry in these industries.

Bain did not set out primarily to formulate a general theory of price equilibrium under conditions of oligopoly. He was concerned with establishing, in a series of notable empirical studies, what factors created barriers to new competition in an industry. His main empirical work was on economics of large-scale production, and he concluded that where such economies were important (and they turned out—in the United States economy, be it conceded—to be a good deal less important than is often thought) they constituted an important barrier to entry. The other main barriers to entry, Bain argued, were product differentiation and absolute cost advantages for existing firms. His view was that the main culprit was product differentiation, and that industries where this was a prominent factor were likely to have high selling costs. He also found that industries with very high barriers to entry tended to have higher profits, and more monopolistic output restrictions, than others. Industries with somewhat lower barriers to entry tended to have lower profits and to be more "workably competitive." Seller concentration alone did not appear to be an adequate criterion of the workability of competition, since it had different effects, depending on the height of the barriers to entry.

Sylos-Labini assumed that if new firms entered the market existing firms would continue to produce as much as before. This would discourage the entry of new firms, since their additional output would depress prices and make the whole market less profitable. New firms could be deterred from entering the market if a large firm in the group set an "entry-preventing" price. The height of this price would depend on the size of the potential entrant, since this would determine his costs (another assumption was that all firms of a given size had the same costs). If price were not changed initially, new entrants would, by increasing the scale of the industry's output, bring down the level of price. They would anticipate such an outcome, because they would realise that existing firms would not reduce their own output. Whether they entered the industry in these circumstances would depend on whether the price level expected to rule after their entry would cover their costs, including their minimum level of required profit. The possibility of entry thus depended on several factors, among these being the relative costs of firms of different sizes, price elasticity of demand in the market and the attitude of the large firms already in the market. These large firms might simply sit there and allow entry; they might fix an entry-preventing price; or they might even adopt an aggressive policy and try to drive out small firms already in the industry. Sylos-Labini considered all these cases and showed how, on his assumptions, determinate solutions could be reached and an equilibrium price arrived at. He also showed that the absolute size of the market was an important consideration which might affect the nature of the final equilibrium. In particular, a large market increased the likelihood of an aggressive price policy on the part of large firms, especially if they acted in agreement with one another. There is no unique solution in the Sylos-Labini model, but the general price tendency is that "the price tends to settle at a level immediately above the entry-preventing price of the least efficient firms which it is to the advantage of the largest and most efficient firms to let live."

Almost the most interesting thing about any model, especially one of price determination, is how it deals with changes in the parameters. In this case changes of costs are obviously of great importance. Sylos-Labini examined this question in the context of the full-cost principle, and argued that, where cost variations are relatively small, the full-cost principle acted as a guide and enabled a new equilibrium to be reached quickly and easily. With large changes in costs, on the other hand, or with changes in the size of the market, in technology, or the quality of products, the upshot was less predictable. He also argued that in the boom the costing margin would tend to fall, partly to discourage entry, while in the slump the margin would tend to rise. But it would fall less and rise more in industries with high entry barriers than in those with low barriers. A fall in the costing margin in the boom was compatible with a rise in the rate of profit on capital because of the rise in output, with contrary results in the slump.

Sylos-Labini's basic thesis, that price tends to settle at the highest entry-preventing price, that this price will be fixed by the large firm and that the full-cost principle will be a useful rule of thumb when costs change, does give a good deal of body to the full-cost story. It also helps to explain how a price may be (honestly) represented by businessmen as having been arrived at by full-cost methods, when the truth is that a whole complex of relevant considerations have actually been taken into account, many of them implicitly only.

Is Bain right, to emphasise the importance of barriers to entry in a world of multiproduct firms, where existing large firms can, as Andrews has argued, probably enter a new "industry" a good deal more easily than completely new firms can be expected to do? Are Bain and Sylos-Labini right to assume that the aim of the large firm will be to maximise its profits in the long run? The meaning and validity of this assumption, and its implications for the behaviour of firms, have occupied a good deal of attention in recent years.

Some Aspects of Monopoly Pricing

Once one has discussed oligopoly, there is in a sense little point in discussing monopoly, since this is equally well treated when considering collusive types of group behaviour. There are, however, one or two topics in this area that are worth referring to briefly. The first is "vintage" pricing, as it is sometimes called, the second is price discrimination, and the third is countervailing power.

Vintage pricing means crudely that higher prices are charged in the early years of the life of a plant because uncertainty about the future makes distant profits too speculative to count on. A similar situation may arise in the early years of the life of a new product. Kaldor has argued, for example, that (except for a minority of exceptional firms) differences in labour and material costs per unit of output mainly reflect the age of equipment. The lowest-cost firms are those with the most recent equipment, while the marginal firms are operating the oldest surviving equipment. The profits earned on new plant will correspond to the required rate of profit on new investment, and the corresponding output price will determine the rate of profit on old equipment. The required rate of profit is very high, Kaldor argues, because "in a world of continual technical progress and obsolescence . . . business firms expect the profits derived from today's equipment to be much smaller and more uncertain in the more distant years." Accordingly, they adopt a short "pay-off period" and an appropriate level of price to reflect this. The more dynamic the industry, the shorter the pay-off period and the higher the price.

This analysis is in effect a monopoly analysis, since it envisages a situation where a firm has a monopoly of the latest equipment, even though this monopoly is short-lived. A more obvious example of the same sort of behaviour applies to the introduction of a new product. Here again, there is a likelihood that the monopoly will be limited in time, and there is a consequential need to charge high prices in the early years. The new product may be protected by a patent, and it has frequently been suggested that the price of a patented product falls, sometimes steeply, towards the end of the life of the patent. This inter-temporal price discrimination is not necessarily a simple question of making hay while the sun shines. It may be that heavy research and development costs have been involved, as well as heavy investment, and there is therefore a drive to recoup these while the monopoly lasts. The opportunity to do so may well be there, since demand for a new product is likely to be inelastic in its early years. This is especially likely to be the case if the level of production takes time to build up. In later years output will be greater, newer products will jostle for attention and demand is therefore likely to be a good deal more elastic. This strategy has the added advantage of enabling the firm to make sharp price reductions in later years in response to the challenge of new competitors.

The possibility of price discrimination under conditions of monopoly is, of course, widely known. The argument here, of course, is that a monopolist will take advantage of less elastic demand in markets which can be kept distinct from those in which demand is more elastic. Obvious examples are that of a doctor charging rich patients more than poor patients, or a firm selling abroad at prices lower than on the home market. An important, but perhaps less well-known case, is that of a firm selling part of its production to a manufacturer, for incorporation in his output, and part direct to consumers. This type of behaviour may be found in the motor industry, for example, where prices charged for articles sold to manufacturers as "original equipment" may be very much lower than those charged to wholesalers and retailers for sale to consumers as replacement parts. In so far as price discrimination of this or other types occurs it means, of course, that full-cost policies are certainly not being followed in every market, since the essence of price discrimination is charging on the basis of what the market will bear, subject to the necessity of covering overall costs.

Price discrimination may also in effect occur with uniform prices. For example, two services may sell at the same price, although the cost of supplying them may be different. Price discrimination in this or other forms, however, need not necessarily lead to high profits. It may be that costs could not be covered at all if price discrimination were not practised.

The problem of pricing in a multiproduct firm has analogies with the case just described. Here there are obvious possibilities for setting prices to yield high profit margins on some products and low profit margins on others. The strength of competition in the markets for the products concerned is obviously likely to be an important consideration. The existence of common costs in a multiproduct firm may also encourage a pricing policy which pays particular attention to the market situation of individual products, since the full costs attributable to the production of any particular product may not easily be ascertainable. Even when common costs are not an important factor, however, a multiproduct firm may find it possible to earn high profits in one part of its business with safety, since the firm's financial results, as shown in its published accounts, will not normally reveal the profits earned on different products. The fact that prices are set well above (or below) any plausible "full-cost" level may therefore escape undetected for some considerable time. In the long run the threat (or the fact) of entry from alternative producers may well squeeze profit margins on old products. Products may also be abandoned if they do not cover the full costs attributable to them: from this point of view, as Robertson has pointed out, it is the average cost of producing them which is relevant in the long run. In the long run, however, there will still be opportunities for high profit margins if the firm succeeds in putting new products on the market from time to time.

It has to be remembered, in all these discussions of price discrimination and behaviour similar to it, that "perfect" price discrimination is rarely possible. Incomplete information, and the difficulty of adjusting prices frequently, limit the extent to which "perfect" price discrimination can be practised. Here there are similarities with problems of "satisficing."

It might be appropriate to add a word here about Galbraith's notion of countervailing power. This envisages restraint being placed on the freedom of action of monopolists or oligopolists by the existence of power in the purchasing market, or in the labour market. This is essentially a monopolist versus monopsonist problem. As such it has no determinate solution, although the solution must lie within a range. Countervailing power is undoubtedly an important phenomenon, although it may not always eliminate the danger of monopolistic exploitation of the consumer. Monopoly profits may be shared by the firms on opposite sides of the market, or by a firm and its labour force. Lower prices to the consumer may, however, result from its existence. For example, firms selling to the large vehicle manufacturers have to reckon with the threat that the vehicle manufacturers themselves may make the products concerned, and this exerts pressure on their prices. Similarly, the buying power of retail firms almost certainly limits monopoly pricing on the part of their suppliers. In cases such as this the benefit of lower buying prices is likely to be felt by the final consumer.

Prices, Products, and Selling Costs

Reference has already briefly been made to the problems raised by the introduction of the possibility of competition in product and selling costs. From a theoretical point of view these problems are considerable, but they can be handled analytically without great difficulty. From an empirical point of view their importance is clearly very great. For the moment, however, we confine ourselves to the theoretical aspects.

Chamberlin introduced product variation and selling costs into his price–output model by the simple device of holding two variables (for

example, price and selling costs) constant, while altering the other variable in such a way as to obtain maximum profits. He repeated the exercise
notionally for all possible values of the other two variables, and thus
arrived at a *maximum maximorum*. This was made to appear straightforward in the case of product variation, but with selling expenses the
problem arose more explicitly that these elements of cost were incurred
to adapt the demand to the product, i.e., to change preferences, rather
than the product to the demand. Chamberlin therefore emphasised the
shifts in the demand curve of the firm that took place as the amount
of selling expenses altered. Having taken account of this effect, however,
he was able to arrive at the maximum profit combination without
difficulty.

How far firms making similar products are able to get away with dis-
similar prices will, of course, depend on whether consumers think that
these products are similar or not. Hence the emphasis, by such writers as
Bishop, on the importance of cross-elasticities of demand under conditions of differentiated oligopoly. But the measurement, notionally or
otherwise, of cross-elasticities of demand does not dispose of the problem.
Cross-elasticities can be altered by advertising, or by the introduction
of new or modified products. Any firm worth its salt is well aware of
this and takes advantage of it. But the scope for product differentiation
is greater in some situations than others; and price behaviour is likely
to be affected by this. Where the scope for product differentiation appears to be small, one would expect prices to be closer together than
otherwise, and the industry concerned to be more "workably" competitive. But it is not always easy to say a priori whether the scope for
product differentiation is small or not in any particular case—an able
entrepreneur can perform miracles of differentiation if he thinks his firm
will benefit thereby.

Considerations of this sort lead one in the direction of arguing, as
several authors *have* argued, that it is very difficult to generalise about
price behaviour, and that a particular industry or group needs to be
studied in some detail before useful predictions can be made. There is
obviously much truth in this, but it can also be maintained that generalisations which are not entirely vacuous can be made about price behaviour, even in a world of differentiated products.

Profit Maximisation

One of the features of the full-cost theory of price is its stress on
"fair" profits and on the influence of this principle on price fixing. What
is by no means clear in the literature, however, is whether the full-cost
principle is thought to be adhered to—on account of the fair-profits
principle—when it is known to reduce profits below the level that could

be attained, or whether it is adhered to because it *is* in fact thought to be the most profitable long-run policy. This question becomes involved with that of the length of the price-maker's time horizon. When this is assumed to be a long one it becomes difficult to say exactly what is implied by the notion of profit maximisation, especially when uncertainty about the future is brought into the picture. Arguments also arise, of the type that arose between Robinson and Farrell, about whether maximising profits in a succession of short periods is the same as maximising profits in the long period. An empirical question is involved here—whether consumers react favourably or not to a flexible pricing policy—but the argument involves also a consideration of what is meant by the long period over which profits are assumed to be maximised.

In some sense "long-run" profits will be preferred to "short-run" profits, but what do "long-run" profits mean? Presumably a time-horizon of several years is implied. Five years might be regarded as short, while over 20 years might be regarded as long. But suppose one compromises on 15 years: this still gives an ambiguous guide-line unless one adds something about the relative importance of different future years. In other words, one must specify the rate at which future profits should be discounted. The firm anxious to survive, assuming it has no short-run crises over liquidity, might well think of applying a very low discount rate, i.e., it would be almost equally happy with a given sum in profits whether it were earned next year or in 15 years time. At the other extreme the barrow-boy might apply a discount rate which approached infinity, both because he would be likely to need money today and because he would probably be in a different "industry" tomorrow. Most firms are likely to apply some positive rate of discount, its height varying with the extent to which they are concerned about future survival. If the rate of discount is high this will imply a short time-horizon, since profits many years hence will have a negligible present value. A long time-horizon will imply a low rate of discount on future profits. The difference between the barrow-boy and the large industrial or commercial enterprise can perhaps best be put, therefore, not in terms of the length of their time-horizon but in terms of the rate at which they discount future profits in their particular "industries."

When new investment is being considered the minimum rate of discount that can be applied to future profits, by a profit maximising firm, is the opportunity cost of capital to that firm, i.e., the market rate, or some rate close to it. Any lower rate would imply that new investment was expected to yield a rate of profit below the market rate. Even a firm not intent on long-run profit maximisation would be likely to run into difficulties, with its shareholders, for example, if it discounted future profits at a lower rate than this.

One can differentiate between a profit-maximising and a non-profit-maximising firm from two points of view. From the short-run point of view a profit-maximising firm will aim to maximise the present value of its discounted stream of profits, given its existing assets. It has to choose a subjective rate of discount at which to do this. If its time-horizon is long it will choose a low subjective rate. The lower the subjective rate of discount it chooses, the lower its prices are likely to be, since a low price policy is probably the best policy to adopt if it is desired to safeguard profits many years ahead. A firm will not be a profit maximiser if, at its chosen subjective discount rate, it makes no attempt to maximise the present value of its profits. If, for example, it has a high subjective rate it will not maximise its profits if it follows a policy which safeguards its markets many years ahead, for example, by charging a low price. A profit maximising policy would in these circumstances imply a relatively high price, yielding high profits in the years immediately ahead.

From the long-run point of view all firms need a rate of return on new investment of at least the market rate. A profit-maximising firm will push its rate of investment to the point where the rate of return on the marginal investment equals the market rate. If the supply curve of funds is rising the firm will maximise its profits at the point where the marginal rate of return on new investment equals the marginal cost of borrowing. A firm will not act as a profit maximiser if it invests beyond this point. Nor will it act as a profit maximiser if it stops short of it, possibly because it is more interested in the maximum rate of return on any given investment project than in maximum total profits.

How does all this connect with the full-cost argument that, in manufacturing industry, firms do not aim to maximise their profits, but aim at "fair" profits only? From the short-run point of view this might simply be taken to imply the choice of a low subjective rate of time discount, with a concomitant low price policy. But this could be a profit-maximising policy, subject to the chosen discount rate. It would not be a profit-maximising policy only if the price policy chosen were not compatible with this discount rate, or if the subjective discount rate itself were set below what would be possible if the stock market were working more perfectly. From the long-run point of view a fair profit policy might imply investing beyond the point where the marginal rate of return on new investment equalled the marginal cost of borrowing. It would be difficult to reconcile a fair profit policy with a low investment policy, calculated to yield a high return at the margin.

It follows from this that it is not at all clear what there is distinctive about a fair profit policy. In so far as high short-run prices are avoided, for example, this may be a profit-maximising policy, subject to a low subjective rate of time discount. Similarly, a firm aiming at fair profits on its new investment may simply be a profit-maximising firm, pushing its investment to the point where the rate of return at the margin just covered the marginal cost of funds. When long-run profit maximisation is correctly interpreted, therefore, it may not differ in any essential respect from a "fair" profit policy. The essential point is not the difference between profit maximisation and nonprofit maximisation but the choice of a long time-horizon—and the low subjective time rate of discount which reflects this.

It is worth referring here to another of the ideas thrown up by the full-cost argument. This is the view, which I was myself guilty of propagating, that firms aim not only at maximising their money profits but also bring into the equation other considerations, e.g., their prestige with the government, with other firms and with their workpeople. On this view, profit maximisation has to be interpreted sufficiently broadly to take these factors into account as well as money profits. The trouble with this line of argument is not that it may not be true—indeed, there is clearly much truth in it—but that it is of no analytical value in this form. As Robertson pointed out, the concept of profit maximisation must not be stretched so far "as to cover all the possible motives that may animate businessmen, thereby robbing the proposition that businessmen normally pursue profit of all empirical content, since profit has now become whatever the businessman pursues." This kind of implicit theorising has generally been avoided by those writers who argue that managers aim to maximise their own utility rather than money profits, in that they specify closely the particular variables that enter into the utility function, and thus give their theories some operational validity.

Behavioural and Managerial Theories of the Firm

Three other theories of the firm need to be considered here. They are the "managerial" theories of Baumol, Williamson, and Marris. They all emphasise the role of the manager and his motivations. Since he is assumed to be motivated by many other considerations than maximising the profits of his firm, the decisions taken are likely to be different in many instances from those to be expected from more conventional theory.

Baumol argues that oligopolistic firms aim to maximise their sales revenue in the long run, subject to a minimum profits level. His reason for adopting this (somewhat unconvincing) model is that, in his experience, managers always emphasise sales rather than profits, and that the prestige of the manager is associated with his firm's sales. Clearly he cannot ignore profits although, since if the firm wishes to continue in existence it must pay acceptable dividends to its shareholders and promise acceptable dividends to those subscribing new capital. Because of this, Baumol argues, each company's minimum rate of profits is set competitively in terms of the current market value of its securities.

One of the implications of Baumol's model is, of course, that profits will be sacrificed for the sake of greater sales. This is likely to lead, *ceteris paribus,* to lower prices than would be charged by a profit-maximising firm, since revenue is maximised when marginal revenue is zero. Another implication is that advertising expenditure would be undertaken if it were thought likely to lead to increased revenue, subject to the minimum profit constraint. Advertising might make it possible to charge a higher price for any given output than would otherwise be the case, and a rise in price is positively desirable, other things equal, since revenue is quantity of sales multiplied by price. But other things might not be equal, since sales may be sensitive to price. In these circumstances the elasticity of sales revenue with regard to advertising expenditure may be such that it is best not to increase price at all. A further implication of Baumol's model is that there may be a conflict between pricing in the long and the short run. In a short-run situation, where output is limited, revenue would often increase if price were raised; but in the long run it might pay to keep price low in order to compete more effectively for a large share of the market. The price policy to be followed in the short run would then depend on the expected repercussions of short-run decisions on long-run revenue.

Williamson's model of "rational managerial behaviour" is based on the assumption that managers conduct the affairs of the firm so as to attend to their own best interests. They will only have real scope to do this when competition is not vigorous: once again therefore an oligopolistic type of market structure is assumed. Williamson argues that managers will operate the firm so as to maximise their utility function. This has as its chief components staff (since the larger his staff, the higher the manager's salary, prestige, etc.), discretionary spending for investments, and management slack absorbed as cost. This last item increases managerial utility by expenditure on luxurious offices and other comparable benefits. Discretionary spending for investment is defined by Williamson as the difference between reported profits and the minimum profits required by shareholders. It reflects investment decisions made by the firm less on the basis of economic necessity (minimum profits include what is needed to raise finance for these investments) than on the success of managers in diverting resources to their own part of the firm, and thus augmenting their prestige. Williamson recognises clearly that the special advantages that insulate a firm from the pressures of competition are often eroded with time, and he argues therefore that this particular model is best restricted to short- and medium-term analysis.

Williamson's model preserves the results of the normal profit-maximising model in conditions of pure or perfect competition. Where competition is weak and demand strong, however, the model predicts that the expansion of staff will exceed that suggested by the normal hypothesis. In addition, expenditure on advertising, managerial luxuries, etc., will grow, and more management slack will be absorbed as cost. When demand weakens these sources of high costs will diminish in size, i.e., they will vary with the business cycle.

It is interesting to contrast the predictions of Baumol's and Williamson's models in the face of an increase in taxation on the firm, and to compare these with the prediction for a profit-maximising firm. If a lump-sum tax is imposed on the firm both Baumol and Williamson predict a reduction in expenditure, since there has in effect been an increase in the minimum profit constraint. In Williamson's case the reduction will be particularly directed towards expenditure on staff. If, however, the increase in taxation is in the rate of profits tax Williamson and Baumol may predict different results. In Williamson's model the firm may increase expenditure on staff, etc., in an effort to reduce "reported" profits, which are less attractive than previously, since they now carry a higher rate of tax. In Baumol's case the firm would reduce these expenditures, since once again the minimum profit constraint has been increased. For a profit-maximising firm, on the other hand, it makes no difference whether a lump-sum tax is levied or the rate of profits tax increased—in both cases output and expenditure will be unaffected, and the firm will take no action.

In spite of their differences from each other and from more conventional models, the models of Baumol and Williamson both resemble the traditional model in that, given their assumptions, a solution can be found analytically.

This is perhaps an appropriate point at which to leave the theoretical analysis of price behaviour and turn to the empirical evidence, such as it is. Only when this has been surveyed will it be possible to draw the threads of the previous analysis together, in an attempt to assess the present state of price theory, and to place price theory in its context as part of the theory of the firm as a whole. At that point it will be appropriate to consider further the quotation from Williamson that has just been given.

PRICE BEHAVIOUR IN PRACTICE

In discussing price theory, empirical studies have from time to time been referred to. There was no avoiding this, especially when dealing with the full-cost school, as exemplified by Hall and Hitch, since the full-cost theory was specifically constructed to explain the findings of the Oxford economists' study of pricing. The empirical findings of Hall and Hitch have been only briefly described, however, and it would be appropriate to start this account of pricing in practice with a further account of them.

Micro Studies of Pricing

Very briefly, since their work is so well known, Hall and Hitch analysed the answers to questionnaires of 38 businessmen, 33 of whom were manufacturers, and the results of the questionnaires were discussed with the businessmen concerned. An overwhelming majority of those questioned thought that a price based on full average costs (including an allowance for profit) was the "right" price to charge. But of the 30 firms adhering to this full-cost principle only 12 adhered "rigidly" to it. Even these 12 firms differed in the way they estimated output for the purpose of calculating the addition to prime costs to be added for overheads: some took "full" output, while most took "actual" or forecast output. The other 18 firms adhered to full-cost "normally" or "in principle," but they would cut prices below the full-cost level if business were very depressed. However, only 2 of the 30 full-cost firms said that they would charge more than full cost in exceptionally prosperous times.

If one takes into account the element of discretion in the treatment of overheads, even in those firms adhering "rigidly" to full cost, it is clear that, taking the 38 firms as a whole, the full-cost principle was interpreted pretty loosely. In particular, the state of the market seems to have played an important part in the prices actually charged. Hall and Hitch's findings threw grave doubts, as was said earlier, on what had appeared to be the previously received doctrine, but the doubts expressed about the validity of the Hall and Hitch findings, by Kahn and others, show how tricky it was (and is) to use empirical work to confirm or deny any particular theory of price.

In spite of the attention focused on the pricing behaviour of firms by Hall and Hitch in Britain, by Machlup and Lester in the United States, and by numerous later writers, there is a paucity of published work of an empirical kind on pricing. Some light has been thrown on the question by what might be called "macro" studies (i.e., statistical or econometric studies: these will be considered later), but studies concentrating on the pricing behaviour of individual firms are rare.

Although many industry studies include a discussion of prices, it is comparatively rare for the *process* of pricing to be investigated in any detail. This is partly because prices are only one of a large number of subjects studied, and partly because many, if not most, industry studies undertaken by economists have deliberately been carried out from the "outside in," so to speak, i.e., they have concentrated on objective data rather than on material derived from interviews, etc. My own work with Maxcy on the British motor industry, for example, discussed prices and price leadership at some length, but it did not investigate the process of pricing, except in a brief reference to General Motors' practice in the early 1920s. Our study did bring out the fact that different firms have to take very different profit margins, even though their cars sell at comparable prices, and to this extent threw doubts on any rigid adherence to the full-cost principle. It also stressed the importance of competition in product in this industry rather than in price. The motor industry may, of course, be held to be so competitive that the market makes it imperative for prices to be similar, but if this can be said of an oligopolistic industry, with pronounced product differentiation, it casts doubt on how extensive the scope can be for full-cost pricing in industry generally.

Joe S. Bain has summarised the pre-war, and immediate post-war, literature in the United States on price and production policies in his chapter on this subject in *A Survey of Contemporary Economics*, published in 1948. He referred there to empirical studies of demand and costs for a number of industries, including automobiles and steel, and then considered "industry" studies for aluminum, steel, newsprint, butter and margarine, motion pictures, cigarettes, oranges, and automobiles, among others. Distinct differences apparently emerged between price behaviour in highly competitive industries with many firms and price behaviour in highly concentrated industries. Barriers to entry, product differentiation, and the number of buyers all affected selling and production costs and, through these, prices. Potential indeterminacy under conditions of oligopoly was often found to be solved in practice by collusive behaviour. Bain pointed out that one of the main achievements of these industry studies was to go behind demand and supply curves to the basic institutional, technological, and other conditions underlying them, and he stressed the complexity of competitive behaviour in actual situations and the need to study the effect of changes through time. He admitted that price theory tended to be "overly general," but he gave a warning (badly needed, if I may say so) that theorising based on empirical studies can easily become "overly specific." One interesting point made by Bain was that businessmen had been reluctant to tell economists how they calculated prices, and to discuss their relations with rival firms. He suggested that the antitrust laws might have been a major barrier here.

Since Bain wrote his survey, a number of other studies of pricing have been published in the United States. The most massive were those carried out by the Subcommittee on Antitrust and Monopoly of the United States Senate Committee on the Judiciary. Hearings on "administered prices" took place over the period 1957–63, and were published in 26 volumes. In addition, reports were published on administered prices in steel, automobiles, bread, and drugs. To attempt to summarise this material other than very briefly would be a labour of Hercules—although admittedly a lesser labour than the original achievement itself. The committee found, in all four of the industries it studied, a pattern of price leadership. Companies in these industries tended to change their prices only after the leader had changed his, even though they might be more efficient then he, with lower costs and higher profit margins. In the drug industry an additional feature was observed. This was that firms, on introducing a new drug, put it on the market at or very near the price charged for an existing drug used to treat the same general type of ailment. This was said by the firms concerned to be "meeting the competition," but it tended to occur even when the new drug might be a good deal cheaper to produce than the existing competitive drug. The result was often high profit margins, which were able to persist because of the "live and let live" attitude of the major firms in the industry, and the patent protection afforded to new drugs. Whether or not margins on new drugs are excessive, in view of the high expenditure of drug companies on research, and the high proportion of failures, is of course still very much a matter of controversy in Britain and other countries, as well as in the United States. It was discussed by the Sainsbury Committee in Britain, and was brought prominently to the fore by the use by the Ministry of Health of the Crown User provisions of the Patent Act to import drugs from abroad more cheaply than they could be obtained from the patent holder. This is not the place to enter into this extensive controversy. All that it is necessary to note here is that the American drug industry undoubtedly displays marked oligopolistic behaviour in its pricing policy, allied with elements of monopolistic behaviour, and that many other drug industries display the same characteristics.

An American study of the A&P company (a grocery chain) by Adelman is of interest because it tells the story of a United States government antitrust suit in which an alleged monopolist was criticised, not for prices which were too high, but for prices which were too low. A&P was accused of lowering the gross margins it aimed for on its products in order to expand its business. In this way it was selling "below cost" and thus indulging in unfair competition. The A&P answer to this was that the greater volume for which it was aiming would bring about lower costs, and hence justify its low prices. So it appeared to have turned out in the event, but apparently the government would have preferred more orthodox costing, i.e., prices based on actual and not on prospective costs. Unfortunately for A&P's own policy many of its local managers were apparently as orthodox in their approach as the government, and the company had the greatest difficulty in persuading its managers to adhere to its policy of low gross margins.

At the other extreme from these studies of oligopolistic industries is a study by Mead of the Douglas-fir lumber industry. Here, in spite of the fact that prices are generally negotiated between buyer and seller, Mead found that conditions prevailed which approximated to those of a perfect market. Prices changed from day to day as market conditions changed. Producers apparently believed that they faced a horizontal demand curve, and had no option but to sell at the market price. There were elements of oligopsony, especially in local purchases by large firms of federal timber, but, by and large, competition prevailed.

Other United States studies have been made of the Midwestern coal industry, copper, food manufacturing, agricultural processing, oil, carpets, electrical machinery, automotive parts, and public utilities such as railroads. One of the major recent studies of pricing in private industry was that carried out by the Brookings Institution and published in 1958 under the authorship of Kaplan, Dirlam and Lanzillotti. Their material was derived from case studies, based on a series of interviews with top management in 1948–51 originally, but subsequently brought up to date. The firms studied were all large ones, and covered a wide variety of industries, including primary production and distribution, as well as manufacturing. General points to emerge were that it was difficult for those interviewed to analyse pricing as a separate process distinct from other policy decisions. It was also found that most of the top executives interviewed did not concern themselves with pricing details: these were delegated to lower levels of management. Large multiproduct companies did not necessarily pursue similar policies in all parts of their business, since circumstances differed from product to product; thus a general policy covering the business as a whole might have to be interpreted differently in different branches of it.

In analysing company pricing policy the authors differentiated between five main types of price policy, giving examples of each. These were pricing to achieve a target return on investment (e.g., General Motors), stabilisation of price and margin (e.g., United States Steel), pricing to maintain or improve market position (e.g., A&P), pricing to meet or follow competition (e.g., Goodyear Tire and Rubber), and pricing related to product differentiation, i.e., different policies for different products (e.g., American Can). These categories were not seen as necessarily being mutually exclusive: they were devised in an attempt to characterise very broadly the predominant policies pursued by firms studied.

In summarising the major influences on the pricing policies of big businesses, Kaplan, Dirlam and Lanzillotti stressed the importance of the character of the product, and the place that a particular product occupied in the product mix. They also emphasised the different pricing objectives of companies, many of which had become traditional. Price and nonprice competition were found to be closely linked, especially in firms relying on service for their products or on product styling. Advertising or style changes were not, however, looked upon as alternatives to price change but as part of the whole competitive "package." Some new products were found to be priced high to begin with, and then lowered in price, while others were found to maintain their initial price (which might be set lower than the initial price under the other policy). In some companies the anti-trust laws were found to be an important influence on price, especially if the company had already been involved in antitrust proceedings. Alcoa, American Can and A&P had all been affected this way. The Robinson–Patman Act had tended to reduce discounts for quantity, and the cement antitrust decision had thrown doubts on basing-point systems of pricing. There was even a suggestion that product differentiation had been encouraged as an alternative to policies of price collusion, on the one hand, or "unfair" prices, on the other, both of which could have been vulnerable on antitrust grounds.

Leadership was another factor found to enter into price policy: its responsibilities as well as its market-dominating aspects. "Administered prices" tended to be adopted by large firms to ensure stability in their industry, to avoid price wars in depression and to prevent price rises in booms. Standard-cost systems provide a rationalisation for such pricing policies, although they were only one of the factors involved. However, not all firms, it was found, could always achieve their pricing objectives in difficult times, while others, such as Swift, considered themselves to a considerable extent at the mercy of market forces. What finally emerges from this study of big business, according to its authors,

is an inability to fit their price policies into a common category . . . in pricing as in other aspects of big business operation, the stable solution is far from having been attained. There is no apparent slackening in the rate of presentation to management of new situations . . . to compel periodic re-thinking and read-justment of company policy and of pricing as an inescapable part thereof.

Finally, mention must be made of a study by Earley, published in 1956, which came to some interesting conclusions. Earley confined his attention to "excellently managed companies," as listed by the American Institute of Management. He got 110 of these companies to complete questionnaires designed to throw light on the extent to which they followed marginalist policies. Marginal accounting and costing principles were found to have a strong hold among these companies, and the bulk followed pricing, marketing, and new product policies that were in essential respects marginalist: as one example, higher profits were normally aimed for in the early years of the life of a new product. Earley reported a widespread distrust of full-cost principles among these firms, and the pursuit of marginalist policies in both the long and the short term. "Marginalism-on-the-wing" is how Earley described their general attitude. The suspicion must arise that Earley simply found what he was looking for, but his study carries conviction, especially as it is widely recognised that sophisticated costing systems are a feature of many large and successful firms—and not only in the United States.

Monopoly and Price Control

This survey has concentrated on the pricing behaviour of private firms in normal market situations. It is not the intention to try to deal here with the very wide area of public control or setting of prices. But it seems desirable to say something briefly on this subject, partly because the official bodies concerned have provided a mass of evidence on pricing, and partly because price behaviour itself may well be affected by public policy in these areas.

Monopoly, or antitrust, policy has, it is generally thought, had an appreciable influence on the nature of competition in many sectors of United States industry. The basic situation is that, following the Sherman, Clayton and other Acts, price collusion is per se illegal, price discrimination is suspect and the collective enforcement of resale price maintenance is forbidden. It is a misdemeanour to attempt to monopolise. Price behaviour has figured prominently in numerous cases brought by the anti-trust division of the Department of Justice and by the Federal Trade Commission. These cases comprise a voluminous literature, and cover every conceivable variety of pricing behaviour. In Britain, on the other hand, monopoly policy is of much more recent origin, at least in its present form. Even so, the reports of the Monopolies Commission, and of cases in the Restrictive Practices Court, cover a wide field. The legal situation is different from that in the United States, in that price agreements are not in themselves illegal.

Be that as it may, these monopoly investigations undoubtedly reveal a considerable variety of pricing practices. They also give some insight into what those responsible for carrying out monopoly policy consider to be a justifiable price policy. Put crudely, it is a policy which aims to give no more than a reasonable (i.e., average) return on capital, with a higher target rate being justified for special risk, for special merit in innovation or for some other desirable aspect of performance. In a sense, the impression is given that what is thought desirable is that prices should be based on the full-cost principle, interpreted as including a "fair" profit margin only. The marginal principle is not necessarily objected to—indeed, it may explicitly be commended—for individual pricing decisions, but the end-result should be fair profits only.

The same type of consideration seems to apply to bodies concerned with price control. War-time price controls were almost all based on the notion of price reflecting costs, plus a fair profit margin. The same principle, in broad outline, was espoused in Britain by the National Board for Prices and Incomes, although in a more sophisticated form. However, we are concerned today with a state of affairs where costs and prices are continually moving upwards. Bodies such as the National Board for Price and Incomes were concerned primarily, in their pricing work, with whether price increases were justified in the light of cost increases. This led them (especially in view of their terms of reference) to study how far costs could be brought down as an alternative to prices being raised, and this was considered in all their reports on proposed increases in price.

Where it is suggested that prices should be based on long-run marginal costs, some appropriate rate of return on capital has to be assumed. This is because long-run marginal cost includes the cost of new investment needed in the long-run, and this must earn some minimum rate of return on the capital to be employed. This rate of return must clearly be a "reasonable" one if it is to be approved. The difference between this and the full-cost approach lies in the particular costs to be chosen on which prices are to be based, not on the level of profits assumed. The results may be very different in practice. Where marginal costs are below previous average costs, a price based on marginal costs may imply a very low profit on past capital, and it may even imply a loss.

Public Utility Pricing

In the United States, among many other countries, there has also been a long history of regulation of public utility pricing through the agency of such bodies as the Federal Communications Commission. This whole question is an extensive one, with a large body of literature in North America, France, and elsewhere. This must be regarded as largely "another subject" from the point of view of the present survey, and it cannot be pursued adequately here. It is, however, probably worth mentioning the current orthodoxy in Britain, as laid down by the government in a White Paper published in 1967. The first principle is that nationalised industries should normally set prices so as to cover their accounting costs in full. But cross-subsidisation is not generally desirable, and the consumer should pay the "true costs" of providing the goods and services that he consumes. Where there is spare capacity, however, prices may be set so as to cover escapable costs only. Similarly, in industries with peak-load problems prices should be low off-peak and high on-peak, where this is administratively feasible: two-part tariffs are commended in such cases. Another principle is that prices should be related to costs at the margin, in the long-run as well as the short-run. Long-run marginal costs include provision for the replacement of fixed assets, together with a "satisfactory" rate of return on the new capital employed. This rate of return is expressed as a minimum test of discount on new low-risk projects: the original rate of 8 percent was raised to 10 percent in August 1969. A final principle is that prices may be set below costs for social reasons, but the government would consider granting subsidies in such cases.

These principles are the outcome of the long post-war discussions among economists on the correct pricing principles for publicly owned enterprises. They are not often suggested for private firms, partly perhaps because these are less likely to be natural monopolies, but mainly because it would be difficult to advocate pricing policies which might involve private firms in heavy book losses. Even the principles advocated for public enterprises reflect the debate among economists only crudely. In particular, they ignore almost completely the problem of the second best, although it is obvious that the economy in general is not working in first-best conditions. In advocating first-best solutions, the Government is not, of course, unaware of the second-best problem, but it presumably takes the view that it is better to aim at the first best, and make allowance for exceptions, than to formulate much more complicated principles, or even to admit that in the present state of economic knowledge no clear principles can be formulated at all.

Marginal-cost pricing was not unknown to British public utilities long before the latest set of principles was formulated. The electricity industry in particular has long had a two-part or multi-part tariff, even though extreme types of marginal pricing—for example, the time-of-day tariff advocated by Little—have not generally been adopted. The coal industry, on the other hand, has pursued a policy much closer to average-cost pricing, with high-cost pits subsidising low-cost pits. At the same time, however, it has attempted to lower costs at the margin by its extensive programme of closures of high-cost pits.

The obvious lesson derived from it is that micro studies of pricing must always be treated with the greatest reserve.

Wholesale and Retail Pricing

This is another subject which can be discussed only briefly. It cannot, however, be ignored, since wholesale and retail margins play a large part in the makeup of the prices paid by consumers.

A distinguishing feature of the wholesale and retail trades is that typically the cost of the goods they buy represents a high proportion of their total costs. The common method of pricing is to add a gross margin to the purchase price to arrive at the selling price. This gross margin is usually similar on similar classes of goods, but, as writers like Jefferys have shown, it may vary greatly between classes of goods. The gross-margin method of pricing is used partly because the cost of handling any particular commodity cannot be calculated separately, since distribution is one of the classic cases of joint costs. Margins differ between different classes of goods for several reasons: their price level; the service they require; the length of time they remain in stock; their perishability; and so on. It can be shown that there is a close relationship between these factors, which determine the level of distributive costs on different goods, and the gross margins commonly added.

Much of the empirical work on retail prices and margins has been carried out in the context of the debate on resale price maintenance, but it has proved difficult to arrive at convincing answers in a field where one is principally attempting to come to conclusions about the prevalence of excess capacity. Other empirical work has been carried out in the context of antitrust policy, as was seen in the discussion of the A&P company earlier. The A&P policy, of setting low prices in an attempt to expand volume and to lower costs, has been characteristic of many participants in the supermarket revolution in Britain in recent years. Here again, however, pricing cannot be separated from other competitive strategies, for example, the policy of standardised "own-brand" commodities in firms such as Marks and Spencer and Sainsbury, in clothing and food respectively.

Taxation and Pricing

Another way of investigating the setting of retail prices is to consider the impact on these prices of taxes on commodities. Nearly every textbook contains a discussion on this subject, illustrated usually with the help of demand and supply curves. It is shown that the less elastic the demand and the more elastic the supply, the more likely it is that such a tax will be passed on in full. In a world where the demand and supply curves of retailers are not widely known, even to the retailers themselves, it is far from easy to discover exactly what the effects on prices of particular commodity taxes are. Superficially it would appear that taxes are passed on in full: for example, when the purchase tax is raised prices seem normally to be raised by the full amount of the increase. What is not so evident is how far the increase is fully passed on in the long run. Where it is difficult to sell adequate quantities at the new price, action may be taken to reduce costs and eventually to make some reduction in price. Or a new type of product may be put on the market which costs less to produce, and which retails, including tax, at a lower price than the previous product. Although it seems rare for tax increases not to be passed on in full at the time they are made, this may occur in difficult market situations. Devices may also be adopted to delay the increase, for example, by selling quantities of the commodity in question on which the old lower tax has allegedly been paid.

In the long run, costs may be raised by a tax, in comparison to what they would have been, because economies of scale have not proved possible to achieve. It has even been argued (especially by manufacturers) that the increase in average short-run costs, because taxation has reduced volume, leads to prices being raised in the short run by *more* than the increase in tax, but there is little evidence for this extreme type of full-cost behaviour. In general, it is probable that commodity taxation is less likely to affect prices through costs in the short run than in the long run.

The empirical evidence on this question is neither extensive nor conclusive. The Richardson committee conducted an inquiry among a number of large businesses. Almost all those questioned in manufacturing and distribution denied that they took profits tax into account in pricing, at least in any direct way. One witness thought that an increase in the tax might lead to a hardening of attitude to prices, but that a reduction would not have a symmetrical effect in lowering prices. There was more support for the view that profits tax affected investment policy, and that higher taxes might lead to higher target prices at the planning stage. American studies by Krzyaniak and Musgrave give some support to the suggestion that the reaction to a change in profits tax may not be symmetrical, and that a reduction might not cause a fall in prices in the short run. Gordon, on the other hand, found no effect on prices in either direction in the short run, i.e., he found no shifting. Taking all the arguments and evidence together, the case for concluding that prices are significantly affected by profits tax changes in the short run is not strong, but the long-run effects on pricing, via investment, may be important. A rise in taxation may raise prices in the long run, while a fall may lower them. This effect will not be due to full-cost methods of pricing, but to a parallel effect on the side of investment—taking prospective profits *after* tax as the objective, and raising pretax target rates of profit when taxes go up.

Macro Studies of Pricing

By "macro" studies I mean in this context studies which do not rely on questionnaires and interviews with businessmen but which rely on the analysis of data, usually published data. Essentially these are statistical and econometric studies. In so far as they nearly always have to rely on inadequate data, and in so far as such studies are both difficult to carry out and open to economic and technical criticism, the conclusions drawn from them must be treated with reserve. Indeed, studies of the same problem quite often come to conflicting conclusions. Nevertheless, studies of this sort have an enormous advantage over the interview type, in that they are far more objective. They also make use of the wealth of data that exists on pricing and related subjects, and provide a most valuable check on other types of research.

These macro studies may be crudely divided into three groups. The first group, while it may use time series, is essentially concerned with the general relationship between market structure, profits, and prices. The second is concerned with how different types of market structure may affect changes over time in the behaviour of prices and profits. The third is not concerned with market structure at all but with movements over time in industrial prices, etc., particularly in periods of inflation. All three groups of studies are of interest in throwing light on the price behaviour of firms, but a problem connected with all of them is that the connection between costs and prices is so close that it is difficult to sort out specific price implications. It is easier to draw conclusions about profits, but these, although of course affected by prices, are also sensitive to movements in output and other variables.

The principal American study is that of Bain. He was concerned especially with barriers to entry, and his findings were briefly referred to above. Bain found that industries with very high entry barriers tended more towards high excess profits and monopolistic output restrictions than others. If product differentiation was an important entry barrier there was a tendency towards high sales promotion expenditure. Industries with somewhat lower entry barriers tended to be more workably competitive, but Bain found little difference between this group, which had "substantial" (but not "very high") barriers, and the group where entry barriers were "moderate to low." Seller concentration was found to be of some importance in explaining "good" or "bad" performance with groups with a given height of barrier to entry, but high seller concentration was particularly significant in its effect on performance when associated with high entry barriers. These findings of Bain, which are, of course, consistent with marginalist behaviour, were confirmed by Mann, using later data for 30 industries. Mann found a big difference in the average rate of profit between those industries where the eight largest firms accounted for over 70 percent of output and those where they accounted for less than 70 percent. He confirmed Bain's findings about the importance of barriers to entry, and found that industries with high barriers to entry and high seller concentration earned distinctly more than highly concentrated industries in other categories. High barriers to entry and high concentration tend, however, to be associated, and George, in examining Mann's results, has suggested that the degree of concentration *as such* may not contribute materially to the explanations of high profitability. The main factors, in his view, are barriers to entry and growth.

The importance of seller concentration on profits has also been investigated in the United States by Schwartzman, Weiss, Levinson, Fuchs, Stigler, and Collins and Preston, among others, although some of these studies were primarily concerned with changes over time. Not all the studies confirmed the finding that high seller concentration and high profits were correlated, but it is interesting that Stigler, after throwing some doubt on the connection in one study, found a positive association in a later study. Collins and Preston, in a survey of 32 food-manufacturing industries, found a curvilinear relationship which in their view strongly supported the hypothesis that there was a positive relationship between concentration and price-cost margins (i.e., the average gross margin as a percentage of average price). No systematic increases in margins accompanied increases in concentration at the lower levels of concentration, but beyond a point increasing concentration was associated with successively larger increases in price-cost margins. High capital-output ratios accounted for only part of the differences, and their conclusion—in contrast to studies such as that of George—was that concentration alone accounted for 50 percent of the variations found.

Comanor and Wilson tackled a somewhat different problem: the relationship between advertising, market structure and performance. They found that advertising appeared to be a highly profitable form of investment. Much of the difference found in profit rates between industries appeared to be explainable by high entry barriers, which were closely linked with high concentration. These entry barriers might have been created by advertising itself, but other entry barriers, such as high capital requirements and substantial economies of scale, also seemed to be important. The authors did not think it plausible to argue that high profits led to high advertising, rather than the reverse, and expenditure on advertising was found to be only weakly correlated with aspects of structure other than barriers to entry.

It is worth referring to a description by Bain of pricing behaviour in a number of oligopolistic industries during the 1930s. Bain was principally concerned with how far collusive conduct in these industries indicated the presence or otherwise of monopoly profits, and on this point he concluded that a study of conduct without a study of performance revealed very little. Of interest here, however, is his description of price "shading" (i.e., of selling below published prices) in the slump in such industries as petroleum and steel. This brings out the point that apparent price rigidities in oligopolistic industries over the trade cycle may conceal the truth, since published prices may be more stable than the actual prices charged. What really occurs is perhaps more likely to be brought out in statistical studies of the type we have been describing than in industry studies of the more conventional type.

The third and final group of studies to be considered are those concerned not primarily with market structure but with movements over time in prices, costs, and profits. This is a field less dominated than the last by work done in the United States. There is, however, a substantial National Bureau volume on the subject, written by Hultgren. He found that prices did not regularly rise and fall with sales, although before the Second World War price variations were more common. Profits fluctuated much more than prices, since they were affected not only by price changes but by changes in output, which affected unit costs as well as the volume of sales. Hultgren found that prices continued to rise as long as sales rose, and declined, if at all, towards the end of the contraction in sales. But price movements were less sharp than movements in costs. When price indices rose they did so much more often in the neighborhood of peaks of activity than of troughs. This suggests that demand influences may have played some direct part in influencing price movements.

Taken together, the studies cited in this section give strong support to the view that high barriers to entry and higher than average profitability go together, and that high seller concentration may also play a part. The evidence for differences of price behaviour over the trade cycle between industries with different degrees of seller concentration appears to be weak. Price behaviour over the cycle in manufacturing industry seems to be much more a function of the nature of the product sold and of changes in the level of costs. In the long run there is a strong negative association between movements in prices and in output per head. Any direct connection between prices and demand in a period of general inflation seems to be a weak one, although here there is rather more controversy among different authors. All agree that cost influences are the most important factor, and it is, of course, well recognised that demand factors may influence costs, both of raw materials and of wages. A rise in costs might, however, be used as an excuse for a rise in profit margins, and some evidence does exist to suggest a direct influence of demand on price in manufacturing industry, although the effect is not a strong one. It has been found that price rises and falls do not occur frequently, and that, even at times of rising costs, the interval between price changes for any one product may be two years or more. The interval may be shorter, however, when costs are rising very steeply. There is no evidence for the general existence of extreme forms of administered pricing, such as the alleged practice of raising prices when costs rise but not reducing them when costs fall.

SUMMING-UP

An attempt must now be made to draw together the theoretical and empirical work on pricing that has been discussed, and to see whether some sort of coherent story emerges. Essentially, this means discussing price behaviour in manufacturing industry, but a little needs to be said about price behaviour in the distributive trades and in publicly owned undertakings.

It might be worth saying first that virtually no doubt has been cast on the fact that several sectors of the economy exist where firms have no real discretion over price. These sectors are not in manufacturing or the distributive trades but in the primary sector. We have seen an example of this in Mead's study of the Douglas-fir lumber industry. In markets such as these sellers have little or no influence over price in the short run. In the long run they influence price through their decisions about whether to remain in the industry or not, i.e., essentially through their investment decisions.

The prices of many primary products are, of course, now influenced by agreements between primary producing countries, for example, in tin and wheat, and also by national governments, so that monopoly elements enter into the pricing process. Also, some prices for primary products, for example, nickel and copper, are greatly influenced by large producing firms. The area in which prices are freely determined by market forces is therefore less wide than might be thought. But when there are a large number of small producers in a market they still have to act as price takers, even when the ruling price may have been influenced by an international commodity agreement. In many ways, also, *exports* of manufactured goods exhibit the same price characteristics as primary products, their prices varying with the state of world demand and supply.

Price behaviour becomes interesting when there is scope for discretion to be exercised by sellers, and this occurs par excellence in manufacturing industry and in public utilities, especially in sales to the home market. In such industries the classic preconditions for perfect competition are never fully satisfied. There are too few firms, products are differentiated, or market is broken up by transport and selling costs. Another problem is caused by the virtual absence of one-product firms, so that an individual firm may operate in several "industries." This makes the notion of some sort of industry equilibrium more difficult to accept than perhaps it once was. Up to a point, these departures from the idea of a perfectly competitive world have occurred because the world has indeed changed—for example, with the growth of large firms, both nationally and internationally. But the main factor is that it has become more and more evident, as analysis and empirical work have developed, that the world was never as simple as it was once represented to be. This last point applies also to some of the early ideas about imperfect competition. It can now be seen that not only is perfectly competitive pricing not widely applicable in manufacturing industry but also that notions of the pricing process derived from the original analysis of imperfect competition leave a great deal to be desired. Few, if any, writers now believe that the pricing behaviour described in Joan Robinson's *Economics of Imperfect Competition,* for example, is a literal description of what occurs in the real world: certainly Joan Robinson herself does not. In the course of time ideas on this whole subject have become more sophisticated, and controversy is now concerned not so much with black and white as with different shades of grey.

Nearly all the evidence supports the view that the home market prices of manufactured products tend to be stable for months or even years at a time. Exceptions occur when a raw material which fluctuates widely in price forms a high proportion of costs, and in such cases the price of the final product may change when that of the raw material changes appreciably. Apart from cases such as this, short-run price stability is the rule, and short-run demand changes do not normally affect price. When demand increases, output tends to be raised and stocks reduced, and if this still does not satisfy demand queues are formed or waiting lists drawn up. Profits rise, not primarily because profit margins are increased but because a given gross margin (i.e., the margin between price and prime costs) yields more and more surplus over prime costs as the quantity sold goes up, while overheads rise relatively little. Even those who argue that some increase in the gross margin is likely to occur at times of high demand would not, I think, deny that it is the increase in the volume of sales which is the prime cause of higher profits.

The evidence also supports the view that the main influence leading to price changes is a change in the level of costs, especially when this is general in its effects. One reason for a change in the level of costs is that the level of demand may change, and in this way demand may indirectly affect price. One of the questions raised in the literature is whether, when an increase in costs is passed on, this leads to an increase in price by the same proportion as the increase in costs or by its absolute amount. If the former occurred this would lead to a larger absolute gross margin than previously, and this would give higher profits (unless overhead costs had risen sufficiently to offset this effect). It has been suggested by Yordon that when wages increase, prices may be raised by the same proportion, but that when raw-material prices increase, prices may be raised by the same absolute amount. In retailing and wholesaling, where percentage gross margins are usual, it would seem to be common for prices to rise in the same proportion as costs. When purchase prices vary greatly over the seasons, or when excise duties are heavy, an absolute rather than a percentage margin may, however, be adopted.

It is at this point that one has to stop recording agreement and enter disputed territory. Indeed, a certain amount of what was said in the last paragraph is in dispute, since some would argue that cost changes are passed on to different degrees at different stages of the trade cycle by changes in percentage gross margins rather by the addition of a constant percentage gross margin to prime costs. The evidence does not support any flamboyant general use of this type of policy, but authors such as Hultgren have found some signs of its existence.

Before exploring such questions further, it is desirable to make some general remarks which are germane to the controversies that remain. It has become increasingly recognised, partly as a result of the work of the managerial and behavioural school of writers, that pricing decisions in manufacturing industry have to be looked at as only one of a set of interlinked policy decisions. Many other aspects of policy have to be considered, including policy towards the introduction of new products, towards advertising, towards actual and potential competitors, towards diversification and mergers, and towards investment and growth. Those making decisions within the firm must do so in the light of all these considerations, explicitly or implicitly, as well as in the right of the market situation of the firm and the state of trade generally. The less pressing the external competitive situation, and the less the threat of takeover, the greater the degree of freedom open to the firm in coming to decisions on these policy matters, including price policy.

One of the questions that arises in this context is that of the identification of those responsible for policy. Much recent work has emphasised the importance of the manager, and has explored the possibility of his attempting to maximise his utility in a way that may not maximise the utility of his shareholders. Cyert and March have stressed that conflicts may arise within what they call the "organisational coalition," so that the outcome of any particular change in external circumstances may not be easily predictable. To predict what may occur, it may be necessary to know a great deal about the individuals and the circumstances involved. Other recent writers of the managerial school, such as Baumol, Williamson, and Marris, have been more inclined to make generalisations about managerial behaviour which have enabled them to make predictions, but they have all thrown doubt on any simple acceptance of static profit maximisation as an objective. They have stressed the importance of not allowing shareholders to become discontented on account of low profits and dividends, and have recognised that there must be some minimum profit constraint if takeovers, etc., are to be avoided. These and other authors have also emphasised the importance placed on the survival of the firm as an objective, and thus the importance of concentrating on long-run rather than short-run profits. Marris, indeed, has framed his theory in terms of the rate of growth of the firm, and has argued that the objective of managers will be to maximise this rate of growth, subject to a minimum profit constraint.

Several authors, notably Simon, have concentrated attention on uncertainty, and on the costs of obtaining information. Simon has suggested that "satisficing" rather than maximising is the best that one can hope to achieve. Indeed, the very notion of profit maximisation has become an ambiguous one when uncertainty and growth have been brought into the picture. Another consideration stressed by the behavioural and managerial schools has been the extent to which a firm's costs may be discretionary, and can thus be reduced if the need to do so is sufficiently great. The concept of "organisational slack" has been introduced to focus attention on this point.

As Williamson has admitted, the analysis of the behavioural and managerial writers has not produced many detailed implications for price behaviour as opposed to other aspects of the behaviour of the firm. It has, however, drawn attention to the process by which pricing and other decisions are taken, and has stressed the need for decisions which reconcile multiple objectives, including those of the managers of the firm as well as of its shareholders, its labour force and others affected by it.

In the light of the work of these writers, the psychological assumptions of the full-cost school now look almost as naïve as those of the marginalist school. It is also clear that both schools omit many important considerations from their analysis. But, even so, the broad controversy between the full-cost and the marginalist writers has not been rendered irrelevant by the modern theorists of the firm. Whatever one says about internal pressures in the firm, the motivation of those making decisions in it, and the composition and ownership of its assets, the external situation of a firm still appears to be of great importance.

The evidence certainly suggests that many of the predictions of the marginalist school (supplemented by the work on barriers to entry) are borne out in practice. There is in the first place ample proof (especially arising from antitrust proceedings) of a wide variety of monopolistic pricing practices and of high profit margins in protected situations. Price discrimination is widespread, as is the practice with firms of taking very different margins on different products. A number of writers have also pointed to the prevalence of "vintage" pricing, i.e., the charging of higher prices in the early years of the life of a product than in its later years. Earley has found evidence for marginal influences on the pricing and other policies of his "excellently managed" companies. The studies of Bain and others have strongly suggested higher profit margins when entry barriers and (less certainly) seller concentration are high. Some empirical studies have suggested a widening of profit margins at times of high demand, although this seems to be done with discretion when it is done at all.

As against this, writers such as Barback have argued for the existence of full-cost behaviour, although I think it is true to say that there is now much less support than formerly for full-cost views, except in rather sophisticated forms. But behaviour such as that suggested by Weiss, who found more profit taking in competitive markets than in concentrated markets in the period immediately after the Second World War, is certainly not implausible.

These and other findings suggest that it may be desirable, in any discussion of price behaviour, to make certain important distinctions in addition to those that are usually made. Three in particular suggest themselves. The first is a distinction between different classes of firms, based on the sophistication of their costing systems and of their management generally. This is not necessarily the same as the distinction between large and small firms, though it may approximate very roughly to it. The point of making this distinction is to suggest that the prevalence of otherwise "marginalist" pricing behaviour may depend to a considerable extent on how good a costing system is employed. As Earley's "excellently managed" firms spread their empires, as they seem likely to do, the sectors where firms think in terms of full costs may become smaller and smaller.

The second distinction concerns the different stages of the life of an industry and the firms within it. In the early days of an industry the competitive situation is likely to be fluid, with high rewards for many firms but considerable instability. As time goes on, the market may well become less buoyant, and the possibility of various types of warfare, including price warfare, more likely. Once the number of firms in the industry has become more or less settled, each will have learned a good deal about the others, and tacit collusion may be practised. It is in this situation of "mature oligopoly" that full-cost behaviour would seem most likely to exist. The situation may not remain stable, however. An existing firm may develop a new product, or may acquire an aggressive manager, or a powerful firm outside the "industry" may enter it. If the situation changes in this fashion price instability may be one of the ways in which the general instability in the industry manifests itself.

The third distinction is that between different historical periods. The studies cited in the present survey have related to three periods of time: the relatively depressed period before the Second World War; the boom that followed the war and lasted until the mid-1950s; and the period of less steady growth, with occasional set-backs, since then. The circumstances and opportunities of these periods have differed widely, and there is some evidence to suggest differences in price behaviour as a result of this.

The prevalence of "marginalist" behaviour may depend therefore on a wide variety of factors, including those just discussed. But the evidence does not give general support to extreme forms of short-run marginalist behaviour in pricing on the home market. There are a number of reasons why this should be so, and why the often superficial impression is given that full-cost methods of pricing are prevalent in manufacturing industry. In part the explanation is administrative: it takes a long time to change a complicated price list, and to make the change known. In part it is the result of uncertainty about the future or the reaction of competitors; of the ambition of managers to keep prices down so that their firms may grow; of the adoption of safer forms of competitive behaviour than price competition, and of a fear of antitrust or other government regulatory activities.

It is important, however, not to forget that competitive forces may sometimes be strong, especially in the long run. A concentration on monopoly or oligopoly situations tends to draw attention away from the many possible sources of competition in western economies. Even under oligopoly, there are many instances of similar prices being charged by firms with very different costs. There is also the possibility of firms entering "industries" other than their traditional ones, either because of the attraction of high profits or because of a desire to diversify in order to grow. Given this threat of entry, many apparently monopolistic firms, or firms which dominate oligopolistic markets, may be restrained in their pricing and profit behaviour. Here Bain's findings that once one departs from industries with high barriers to entry, there is little difference in profitability between groups with "substantial" barriers to entry and groups with "moderate to low" entry barriers, may be of significance. The idea of industry equilibrium in the Chamberlinian sense may now be suspect, but there may still be justification, on the evidence before us, for regarding many sectors of manufacturing industry as "workably" competitive in the long-run.

There is not much that needs to be said here about wholesale and retail pricing. Apart from the fact that the use of gross margins for arriving at selling prices is more prevalent than in manufacturing, the same type of considerations apply. In this sector monopoly is conferred partly by location, but competition between large concerns in town centres and between them and suburban stores sets limits on the extent to which monopoly pricing is practicable. The prevalence of taxes on commodities, with frequent changes in their rates, gives many opportunities for observing price behaviour in response to these changes, but even so, there is much uncertainty about the effect of commodity and other related taxes on retail prices. The study carried out in the Department of Applied Economics at Cambridge on the effects of the selective employment tax has provided useful evidence on this.

Pricing by publicly owned bodies has been mentioned only briefly in this survey as being somewhat outside its scope. The subject of interest in the present context, with the pricing rules laid down by governments and other agencies, expresses some sort of pricing ideal as seen by these authorities. These rules, in Britain at least, are a mixture of average and marginal-cost considerations. Much importance is placed on basing prices as far as possible on long-run marginal costs, i.e., on costs of production in a new plant using the most modern techniques. But the rules also say that investment in new plant should be undertaken only if a test rate of discount can be achieved; since this test rate must be earned, it enters into the calculation of long-run marginal cost. Thus pricing policy and investment policy are intimately connected. This is a point of more general application. Joan Robinson has argued that "to behave monopolistically in the long period sense, means to pursue a cautious investment policy, restraining the growth of capacity relatively to demand." As several antitrust cases have shown, such a policy is not unknown, although it is unlikely to be favoured by Marris-type managers.

Among sectors omitted altogether from this survey have been construction, road transport, services other than distribution, and nonproduced goods, such as second-hand cars, existing houses, and land. Nor has much been said about the pricing of "one-of" products, or products made in small quantities to special order. My excuse for these omissions is partly a lack of published evidence and partly the need to keep the survey to a manageable length.

Other gaps in the present survey are due to the fact that future work needs to be done on pricing, of both an empirical and theoretical nature. It will be evident from what has been said earlier that I am no great believer in what I have called "micro" studies of pricing: studies of the Hall and Hitch or the Barback type, for example. My own experience in the steel industry is only one reason why I hold this view. On the other hand, there is, I think, more to be said for inquiries of the type suggested by Baumol and Quant, into "rules of thumb" laid down by firms for arriving at prices, or into other specific instructions, if such can be found, which are used to determine actual rather than "desired" prices. Computer simulations of market behaviour may also yield interesting insights into the forces making for stability or instability in different types of market situation. Most useful would, in my view, be further studies of a "macro" nature, i.e., investigations of a statistical or econometric type into the relationships that can be deduced from movements in costs, prices, profits, and so on. A number of studies of this kind have been quoted, but many have been concerned primarily with the effect of concentration and monopoly on price, and few with the behaviour of prices in conditions of inflation, or in response to changes in taxes on commodities. More work of this latter type would, I think, be very useful. It would also be of considerable interest if it were possible for such work to be carried out at the level of the firm, and of particular products made by the firm. Such studies would not be easy to devise, and could only be undertaken with the help of data produced by firms, whereas "macro" studies of the type normally carried out have referred to large numbers of firms and have relied mainly on published data. These studies have the advantage of objectivity, but too often give a misleading appearance of uniformity to what is in fact a complex reality.

More needs to be done also in the field of price theory and the theory of the firm generally. To a considerable extent the main ingredients are already to hand, but they have not been welded into a coherent whole, even by such authors as Marris and Williamson. The theory of the firm as depicted in the textbooks is not, in my view, as inadequate as it is often alleged to be, but it is nevertheless both incomplete and relatively unsophisticated. This applies particularly to the theory of imperfect competition. The theory of perfect competition can be said to be an intellectual whole, even though it is static and its practical application is disputable. The theory of imperfect competition, on the other hand, is either so schematic as to be of relatively little practical interest or so piecemeal and detailed that no clear picture emerges. Perhaps the task is impossible—as has been seen, the number of variables to be considered is extremely large—but one cannot help feeling that some further progress could be made. Theories of monopolistic competition and oligopoly, of barriers to entry, of multiple-product output, of managerial motivation and behaviour, of asset holding and stock-market constraints, of technical progress and growth: all these need to be brought into the picture, and their implications for pricing and other aspects of behaviour made clear.

Perhaps it would be appropriate to conclude by considering again the quotation from Williamson given earlier. He said, it may be remembered, that perhaps it was not too great a criticism of managerial models that they could not produce detailed implications for price behaviour, "since price making is surely of subordinate importance to such matters as economic efficiency and equity, on which managerial models yield important . . . implications." Leaving aside the point about managerial models, is Williamson correct in playing down the importance of price making? It may scarcely behoove the author of a survey of price behaviour to say so, but there is much in what Williamson says. As has been frequently stressed here, price policy is one aspect only of the competitive behaviour of the firm, and looked at alone gives a partial picture. It is, of course, of considerable interest and importance in its own right, but since it is only part of the story, it perhaps merits rather less attention than has traditionally been devoted to it. What is most important is to concentrate attention on attempts to study and evaluate the overall performance of firms, and to discover under what conditions, and with the help of which stimuli, their overall economic efficiency is likely to be fostered.

14. Oil Industry Profitability: An Interindustry Comparison of Returns to Equity*

THOMAS J. COYNE

The allegation that American oil companies made windfall profits in 1973 and are doing it again in 1979 is gaining widespread support throughout the United States and abroad. Apparently, a large percentage of the total population considers the word *price* to be synonymous with profit. Oil industry critics have proposed various methods of reducing profits ranging from control of prices to nationalization of the industry; if profits cannot be reduced, perhaps an excess profits tax is in order, some observers argue. If high oil prices and high profits are almost perfectly correlated, this relationship should be revealed in higher financial returns obtained by oil firms on equity invested. This paper analyzes financial returns to equity and comments upon the need for and the likelihood of an excess profits tax being applied to the oil industry.

A principal pricing goal of many major oil companies is maintenance of market share. This goal is achieved by pricing in a manner that allows the firm to match, meet or follow the price established by the most important marketer in each area served. Oil companies seek with this policy a "fair return" (profit) on their investment but, generally speaking, do not define this return with specific figures. Oil industry critics also fail to define what they consider to be a "fair" profit. In the absence of a defined fair profit level, it may be ludicrous to claim the level has been exceeded.

Over the years, the pricing goals of most large oil companies have appeared similar in another way: each firm has wanted to maintain its market share while simultaneously pursuing a position of price stabilization. This approach allowed companies to enjoy satisfactory profits over a prolonged period of time.

This paper studies profits received by each of the seven largest firms in the oil industry in the United States and compares the results with

* *Business Economics,* Spring 1980, pp. 59–64.

returns obtained by leading commercial banks (16), savings and loan associations (2), aerospace (8), and office/business machine manufacturing companies (8). Each firm and each industry of which that firm is a member is analyzed via application of a return to equity model to determine if average returns over time for the oil industry have been equal to, less than, or greater than returns on equity for all or any segment of selected financial or nonfinancial industries. Results for each firm and each industry classification consider profit margin, asset turnover and leverage.

RETURN ON EQUITY (ROE)

Net income, total revenue minus total expense, is a simplified and somewhat traditional way of viewing corporate profitability. It may not, however, be an adequate measure. Even if one could agree with respect to the precise entries to be included in the revenue and expense categories, the resultant "profit" figure would represent only a before-tax entry. Such an entry may or may not result in any reported profitability for a company in the short run because depletion allowances, depreciation schedules and "write-downs" for unprofitable and discontinued facilities are used to shield (reduce) a firm's nominal profit from tax; therefore, a firm's reported short-term profitability figure can be manipulated if net income is assumed to present a valid picture of a firm's profit. A different and better measurement of profit could and perhaps should be used. This measure of profitability compares net equity with total dollar profits generated and is the one presented here.

Equity represents the difference between what a firm owns and what it owes. It is a balance sheet entry revealing the stockholders' ownership and financial position in the company. Generally speaking, the larger the equity for a given number of common shares of stock outstanding, the better the financial condition of the stockholder group. Financial returns to stockholders' equity are calculated by dividing the firm's profit after tax but before dividends by the equity figure. Once calculated, this return allows comparison of stockholder profits to stockholder investment. The return on equity figure is an adequate measure of overall corporate profitability; therefore, throughout this paper, profitability, by definition, is synonymous with return on equity.

FINANCIAL RATIOS

In considering the price and output behavior of a firm and its resultant profitability, if any, it is important to remember that no single variable provides an adequate indication of what is required to influence profitability. As all principles of economics students throughout the country should know by now, an increase in price is not associated automatically with an increase in profitability; in addition, an increase in one or more of a firm's operating costs need not decrease profitability. To the extent that an excess profits tax would represent an increased cost to the firm in the short run, one would be naïve to believe the firm's profitability would have to decrease because of such a tax.

If an excess profits tax is imposed at a time when all other assets are relatively constant or, perhaps, increasing slightly, it is conceivable the firm's profit margin will decline. For oil firms, these profit margins have declined over the past ten years. A declining profit margin could cause return on investment to decline unless asset turnover increases by an amount great enough to offset the decrease in profit margin. Turnover for oil firms has almost doubled while net operating margins declined in the last ten years; return on investment declined also.

The asset turnover to which one refers here is the ratio of sales to total assets (sales ÷ total assets). This ratio reveals the relative efficiency with which resources are used within and by the firm. For oil companies, the higher this ratio, the more efficiently the firm is using its previously acquired refineries, equipment, and/or inventories. Increased asset turnover associated with decreased profit margins, caused, perhaps, by too low a price or too high a cost (tax), could result in higher return on investment.

The oil industry has been characterized in recent years by the existence of declining ROIs and profit margins but by an approximate 100 percent increase in efficiency of resource utilization. In the oil industry, assuming inelasticity of demand for the final product in the short run, it is conceivable that overall corporate profitability could continue to increase even if turnover, profit margin and return on investment decreased, one period to the next.

Return on equity (ROE) may be calculated by application of a firm's (1) asset turnover; (2) profit margin; (3) return on investment (ROI); and, (4) equity multiplier figures. ROE is ROI multiplied by the equity multiplier. Assuming constant or increased profit margins, the higher the asset turnover figure, the greater the firm's ROI. If the equity multiplier remains unchanged, this ROI is directly related to a firm's return on equity. It has been possible for the oil industry to increase its profitability slightly from 1968 through 1977, despite decreased profit margins and decreased ROIs.

A decrease in the asset turnover statistic associated with a constant or decreasing profit margin results in decreasing ROIs and may result in decreased returns to equity unless the equity multiplier is increased; also, decreased profit margins and constant or increased asset turnover figures may be associated with decreased ROIs and decreased returns to equity unless the equity multiplier is increased. Obviously, increases or decreases in ROI are based upon interrelationships between changes in asset turnover and/or profit margins. Changes in returns to equity (profitability) are affected also by these factors but more importantly, perhaps, by the equity multiplier.

Profitability to the firm is the product of its return on investment and its equity multiplier. By definition, this equity multiplier is the ratio of the firm's assets to its net equity. The higher this ratio, the larger the firm's short- and/or long-term liabilities. These liabilities are debts owed by the firm and in the jargon of financial managers may be expressed as "financial leverage."

Firms using financial leverage obviously believe the name of the game is to make money with the use of someone else's money and have all parties to the transaction happy with the arrangement. Positive or favorable financial leverage for the firm exists when it earns more with borrowed money than it pays for it. Generally speaking, a long-term corporate bond costing 9 percent in interest expense should yield something greater than 9 percent, on average, for use of the bonded indebtedness to be beneficial to the firm. Most major American corporations use leverage to the greatest extent feasible. Oil companies are no exception to this rule.

If profitability is defined for the moment in the traditional sense as being equal to net income and assumed to be "too high," it is probable an excess profits tax would cause (a) a decrease in oil company net operating margins, (b) an increase, decrease or no change in their turnover statistic, and (c) an increase, decrease, or no movement in ROI; however, with relative inelasticity of demand for the final product existing in the short run, (d) the equity multiplier might be increased. Such an increase could cause oil company returns on equity to rise, not fall.

If oil company profits (ROE) increased after imposition of a special excess profits tax, the impact of that tax might be to transfer funds indirectly from the consumer to the government. Should the mechanism behave in the manner suggested here, an excess profits tax would have driven corporate profitability higher (ROE) than it otherwise might have been. (Under such a set of circumstances, one might expect oil industry critics to claim, wrongly, of course, that without governmental intervention oil industry profitability would have been even higher.)

The point is this: if profitability for finanacial or nonfinancial firms, including oil companies, is "high" or "low," it is that way because of a number of factors, only one of which might be price. To the extent that an excess profits tax is being considered because oil companies have imposed a succession of price increases on the public, the probability may be quite low that control of these prices and/or imposition of an excess profits tax will result in reduced oil company profitability (ROE). Let's take a closer look.

CRUDE OIL WINDFALL PROFIT TAX

Leverage (equity multipliers) can be used to enhance a company's profits; however, at times, some highly visible firms run the risk of having special attention called to their profits when leverage is used successfully. Such is the case with the oil industry in general, Sohio in particular.

In June 1979, the House of Representatives passed a windfall profits tax. Passage of this House version of the bill assumes that "excess" or "windfall" profits have been, are being, or will be made by oil companies; moreover, these profits should be subjected to a special 50 percent tax rate. Comparison of oil industry profits to selected financial and nonfinancial corporations allows one to test HR 3919's basic assumption and to measure the degree by which oil company profits exceed the profits of other firms and industries with which oil can be compared.

In this study, the banking industry is separated into New York City and non-New York City banks in acknowledgement of the unique position and structure of commercial banks located there. Except for banks located in New York City, every industry tested had higher profitability than the oil industry for the year ended 1977. In each year tested except 1973 and 1974, the office/business equipment industry had significantly greater profitability than the oil industry. Overall, profitability of selected industries often exceeded and always compared very favorably with oil industry profits. This latter statement is particularly pronounced for the three-year period, 1975 through 1977. Oil industry profits were not greater than profits of other industries tested.

If oil industry profits are not excessive relative to industries with which oil firms are compared, is special legislation needed to transfer profits from private to public hands? If oil industry profits are excessive, what is the magnitude of the excess?

For most calendar quarters studied, profitability for each oil firm approximates nicely the return generated by every other firm with which it competes, with one noticeable exception, Sohio. Sohio enjoyed greater profits in 1978 and 1979 than any of its competitors. Overall, annualized oil industry returns compared favorably with profits generated by selected industries. The closeness and similiarity of these unadjusted-for-risk profitability figures cause an unbiased observer to believe oil profits are not excessive.

In 1969, Sohio's quarterly profitability was 1.06 percent; in 1979.2, it

earned 9.94 percent. The earlier figure was the lowest profit earned in
the industry; the latter, the highest. The 1979.2 profit was significantly
higher than any profit generated by any other company over the time
frame studied. Was Sohio's 1979.2 profit excessive, and if so, was that
profit high enough to justify passage of an excess profits tax? Probably
not may be the most correct answer to each part of this question.

Sohio's profitability was significantly lower, on average, from 1968
through 1977 than (a) any oil company studied and (b) any selected
industry with which the oil industry was compared. Even in the oil
embargo-influenced year of 1974, Sohio's profitability was lower on
average than the oil, aerospace, banking, and business equipment industries profits.

In 28 of the 40 quarters of data studied, Sohio had the lowest profitability of any company. It was tied for the bottom position in profitability or was very close to the bottom in almost all of the remaining
quarters. The only exceptions to this statement were the years 1978 and
1979. Sohio acquired the highest profit figure among oil firms only with
its second quarter 1978 results. It managed to record significantly
greater profits than any of its competitors for the year ended 1978; in
fact, it has continued that performance in each of the five quarters since
1978.1. Why?

The oil industry has concentrated during the past ten years on improving asset turnover. In that time, the industry was doubling the
efficiency with which it utilized its assets, Sohio had a turnover decline
from .69 in 1969 to .62 in 1978. Profit margins for the oil industry
declined sharply during this time period, but Sohio's margin jumped
from 4.28 to 8.67 percent. However, even with these higher profit margins, Sohio generated much lower ROIs than the other firms studied.
Sohio's ROIs were increasing, on average, but in no year tested did they
match the oil industry average. With Sohio's ROI being at lower levels
than found elsewhere in the industry, how does one account for Sohio's
significantly higher profitability? The equity multiplier!

Sohio's equity multiplier at the end of 1978 was 253 percent of what
it was at the end of 1969. No firm analyzed came anywhere close to
approximating such an increase. Major movement in Sohio's multiplier
came in 1976. Quite clearly, had this equity multiplier not changed as
dramatically as it did, the favorable results obtained by Sohio in the
last six calendar quarters would not have been possible. Movement of
this magnitude in the multiplier requires a firm to undertake substantial
increases in financial risk.

Traditionally, in a capitalistic economy, the greater the risk, the
greater the potential reward. Profitability is that reward. To the extent
that HR 3919 attempts to transfer some of that profit to governmental
coffers, the firm and industry are being penalized for utilizing their

assets and leveraging their debt structure in a successful manner. If the government is successful in this endeavor, will other successful industries be taxed more heavily in the future?

SUMMARY AND CONCLUSIONS

Financial returns to equity are studied for major firms in the oil industry, yearly 1968 through 1977 and quarterly 1969.3 through 1979.2. These returns are compared with returns generated within selected financial and nonfinancial industries.

Profitability is defined as being synonymous with return on equity. In calculating return on equity, careful consideration is given to asset turnover, net operating margin, return on investment, and the equity multiplier. Attention is directed to the following points:

1. Neither the oil firms nor their critics define fair profit levels. Consequently, excess profits, per se, cannot and have not been defined; yet, with the passage of HR 3919, the government has assumed that excesses exist. The government should be required to prove its "windfall profits" charges or withdraw potentially damaging legislation.

2. Turnover of assets is an important measure of a firm's earning power. For the seven major oil firms, turnover figures doubled during the last ten years. For selected financial and nonfinancial firms, turnovers remained relatively constant or declined slightly. Increases in turnover reveal improved utilization of a firm's assets and contribute positively to a firm's profitability. Oil firms have revealed greater operating efficiency and contribution to profits in this category than have non-oil firms.

3. Profit margin measures a firm's profit after tax as a percentage of sales. It, too, is an important indicator of profitability. Oil firms have experienced declining profit margins over the time frame studied. If prices had been rising at a rate more rapid than cost, these margins might have increased.

4. Return on investment (ROI) is the product of turnover and net operating margin. It is another indicator of corporate profit. ROI declined on average for the oil industry, 1968 through 1977. With the exception of commercial banks, ROI increased or remained relatively constant for selected industries with which oil is compared over the same period of time.

5. The equity multiplier is the ratio of the firm's assets to its net equity. The higher this ratio, the larger the share of the firm's assets financed with debt; also, the higher this ratio, the greater the firm's potential profitability once the break-even point is reached. When

this ratio is multiplied by ROI, the firm's profitability is determined.

6. The equity multiplier times ROI produces a figure known as return
on equity, ROE. ROE is synonymous with profitability.

7. Profitability for the oil industry, even when not adjusted to reflect
higher risks implicit in its operation, was lower than profitability
for the office/business equipment industry for each year tested; in
addition, oil industry profits in 1977 were lower than profits reported by any industry tested.

8. When quarterly returns are presented, no major oil firm appeared
to be making greater profits than other large firms with which it
competed, except for Sohio.

9. Sohio recorded relatively high profits in each of the last six calendar
quarters; however, it recorded the lowest profits of any oil firm
studied in 28 of the 40 quarters tested. As reflected by its equity
multiplier, Sohio accepted unusually high financial risks prior to
realization of its 1978 and 1979 profits.

10. If oil industry profits were too high or too low, they were that way
because of a number of factors only one of which is price.

11. The probability appears low that (a) price controls and/or (b) an
excess profits tax will reduce oil company profitability; instead,
such a tax might cause prices of petroleum products and profits of
oil companies to rise further and overall quantities of products
available in the U.S. markets to fall.

12. Increases or decreases in any one of the following variables will
not cause oil company or industry profitability to rise or fall: (a)
price, (b) cost (tax), (c) asset turnover, (d) net operating margin,
(e) return on investment, or (f) equity multiplier. Government
control(s) of any one or more of these variables could serve primarily to interfere with efficient market mechanisms.

13. It might be premature to call oil industry profits excessive for, as
indicated herein, these profits compared favorably with profits generated by selected industries. If one were to quantify the higher
political, economic, and other risks associated with oil industry
activity vis-à-vis other industries with which oil was compared, oil
profits may be lower than profits earned by other firms and industries.

14. Assuming oil industry profits as reported herein were not excessive
by comparison with other firms and industries, the oil industry
may have been selected for an excess profits tax in a somewhat
arbitrary and capricious manner. One wonders why. If this industry is to be taxed in the manner suggested by HR 3919, other
successful industries might be taxed in a like manner. Increased
taxation via an "excess profits" approach, if applied across indus-

try lines, could change and be detrimental to the price and output behavior of all firms located in the aggregate American economy.

Evidence presented in this paper does not confirm the existence of excess profits in the oil industry; moreover, no published research appears to exist that proves price gouging and profiteering by oil firms. In the absence of such proof, one is hard pressed to support the notion that a windfall profits tax is warranted. If excess profits have been or are being made in any industry, these profits should be clearly defined and identified as such before punitive legislation is drafted, much less passed.

To the extent that HR 3919 represents loose, unfounded charges regarding profitability, its passage into federal law runs the risk of contributing to the destruction of a free economic system and democratic society. It does so by (a) expanding governmental influence at the expense of private property owners and (b) encouraging resistance to somewhat more useful governmental influence at all levels through passage of Proposition 13-type legislation.

Data presented in this paper suggests an excess profits tax as applied to the oil industry in HR 3919 is theoretically unsound; its basic assumptions are incapable of gaining and retaining objective support. However, such a tax might be capable of passage if (a) it is presented in an emotional manner by its proponents and (b) its basic assumptions go unchallenged by the public in general and professional economists in particular.

15. Decentralization and Intracompany Pricing*

JOEL DEAN

A fist fight determined the intracompany transfer price policy that is in effect today in a major oil company. The issue was the price at which gasoline would be transferred from the company's refinery to its marketing division.

The present heads of the marketing and refining divisions had witnessed, as loyal but appalled lieutenants, the contentious negotiations that culminated in the fight. When these two men came to power, they vowed that their interdivisional bliss would not be marred by any arguments over intracompany pricing as had their predecessors'.

They finally found a way to abolish all disagreements about transfer prices. They simply abolished transfer prices, thereby neatly tossing out the baby with the bath.

This story—now a legend in the company—is probably exaggerated, and other events certainly contributed to the outcome. It does show, however, that the subject of this article is as disturbing as it is important: how and where to set prices for products that are transferred between divisions (or between different stages of processing and distribution) inside the company.

Our industrial system today is made up of many large, multiple-product, multiple-process companies. As these companies have expanded, it has become generally recognized that the best pattern for their managerial organization is one of decentralization, i.e., the setting up of more or less autonomous operating divisions within a company. But as more and more large companies have adopted divisional management, they are finding that splitting up the enterprise and exhorting the divisional managers to go out and set new records for sales or production does not always accomplish the hoped-for profit results.

For an autonomous division to be an economically effective operation it has to follow the same basic rules of behavior as any independent firm competing with other independent firms, and this implies the same

* Harvard Business Review, vol. 33, no. 4 (July–August 1955), pp. 65–74. (Copyright © by the President and Fellows of Harvard College; all rights reserved.)

standards of economic performance—profits. But how can it be held to such competitive standards if there is no sound way to price the products transferred to it or from it in dealings with other divisions of the same company? In that question lies the reason for this article.

In the course of the discussion I shall set forth these propositions:

1. Transfer prices are necessary for almost all large companies. Trying to do without them sacrifices so much that it is no solution at all.

2. Intracompany 'price discrimination is not good business, either for the individual firm or for private enterprise in general.

3. There is need of a new system of transfer prices featuring: (a) profit centers with operational independence, access to sources and markets, separable costs and revenues, and profit intent; and (b) competitive pricing among these centers.

4. Such a system has many advantages. It brings the division manager's interests closer to those of top management, provides a more accurate basis for evaluating his performance, bulwarks his independence, and gives him sound guides in purchasing and marketing decisions.

5. Most present systems for setting transfer prices, by contrast, are inadequate. They employ economically indefensible methods, keep many losses hidden, and have a negative value in the making of management decisions.

6. It takes time and patience to install competitive transfer prices. Top management will find it easier to make the change-over if it follows eight rules drawn from experience. Executives should also be prepared to meet certain objections which critics are likely to raise.

Here are the key terms which will be used in this article:

1. *Transfers* mean movement of product between operating units within the largest policy-making unit, regardless of corporate entities; for example, transfers within the family of companies represented by the Cities Service Oil Company or among the divisions of E. I. du Pont de Nemours & Company.

2. *Product* should be broadly interpreted to include raw materials, components, and intermediate products and services as well as finished products in the ordinary sense of the word.

3. *Transfer price* refers to the net value per unit that records the transaction for the purposes of operating statements.

NEED FOR SOUND PRICING

Why not do the same as the oil company referred to at the start of this article and dispose of the problem altogether by doing without transfer prices?

For most large firms this solution sacrifices too much. Our peace-loving oil company, for example, now has no knowledge of the cost and value of gasoline, heating oil, and other petroleum products at various stages of refining and distribution. Abolition of transfer prices prevents meaningful measurement of the profits of individual operating units, such as refineries, bulk stations, and service stations. It also prevents accurate estimates of the earnings on proposed capital projects. Basic decisions about market penetration, pricing, and capital expenditures are cut adrift from cost or profit moorings. And there is no way to assure that the product will be directed where it will produce the highest dollar return, either as among alternative processes or as among alternative channels and levels of distribution. The river of crude oil suddenly goes underground, disappearing from cost and profit sight, and comes up again at the consumers' doors, millions of processing dollars away.

So abolition is not the right answer. In fact, it is no solution at all. For most large companies the problem remains one of learning how to live with and use some system of internal transfer pricing. Sound transfer prices give division managers both the economic basis and the incentives for correct decisions. They also provide top management with profit and loss information indispensable for evaluation of the results of complex combinations of managerial skills and diverse facilities. Thus correct transfer prices are the basis for attaining the managerial decentralization sought by virtually every large American enterprise today.

One reason this has been such a problem for executives is that no systematic analysis of transfer pricing principles and policies has, so far as I can learn, heretofore been available.

Transfer prices have significance for public policy as well as for private policy. Criticism of vertical integration has focused on pricing of intracompany transfers. It is alleged that discrimination within the company hurts competition. For example, oil refineries are supposed to gain an advantage by charging their marketing affiliates lower prices than their independent customers, and aluminum and copper producers are supposed to benefit similarly in favoring their fabricating affiliates. Actually, shoving the profits around inside the company and into safe corners serves no useful purpose and succeeds only in confusing both operating managers and top management. But the fact that intracompany price discrimination is not the good business that many companies think it is hardly makes public criticism less damaging.

Fortunately, the correct economic solution for the company's managerial problem—transfer prices determined competitively—also solves this public policy problem.

NEW CONCEPT

How can the hodgepodge of intracompany pricing methods that is found in many large companies today be avoided? What is an economi-

cally realistic basis for intracompany pricing applied uniformly throughout the whole company? The answer lies in a new system of executive
control which has the two intermeshed features of profit centers and
competitive transfer prices.

Profit Centers

Before responsibility for profits or losses can be assigned, it is necessary that the management of the particular operation be in fact made
primarily responsible for its economic performance. Four characteristics
distinguish this type of autonomous unit from service functions.

1. *Operational Independence.* Each profit center must be an independent operating unit, and its manager must have a large measure
of control over most if not all operational decisions that affect his profits.
This means that he must have considerable discretion in determining
the volume of production, methods of operation, product mix, and so
forth, subject only to broad policy discretion from top management.
The areas of the company where this independence of action cannot
exist should properly be considered as service centers. For them, the
volume and character of services rendered are to a large extent determined by decisions originating outside their divisions; an example is
the public relations department.

2. *Access to Sources and Markets.* The profit-center manager must
have control over all decisions relating to sources and markets. He must
be genuinely free to buy and sell in alternative markets both outside
the company and inside. For example, the manager of the canned meat
division of an integrated meat packer must know that it is just as respectable to buy uncured hams outside the company as to buy from
the company's own pork division.

Freedom to trade is essential to the new concept because it dissolves
alibis. Brother buyer and seller have ample incentive to reach agreement
on prices if neither is restricted to a particular source or market. They
have almost no incentive, and everybody feels cheated, if these channels
are predetermined.

The required access to sources and markets cannot be created by
edict; outside sources or markets must either be there or be capable
of creation. To illustrate, crank shaft and other major components of
an automobile engine require highly specialized machine tools already
in the possession of the supplying division. It is impracticable to get
a sound figure on what it would cost to supplant the intracompany
manufacturing source, since an outside supplier will not make a realistic
bid unless the company signifies its willingness to make a long-run commitment sufficient to cover his installation of major facilities. Without
this commitment, freedom to trade in such cases is meaningless.

3. Separable Costs and Revenues. A profit center must be able to split off its costs and find an economically realistic price of the end products; otherwise measurement of its profit performance is impossible. This requirement eliminates service-type staff activities from consideration.

4. Management Intent. A distinction between a profit center and a service center can also be drawn in terms of management's intention. Only if the basic goal is profits should the operation be treated as a profit center.

A service activity may contribute as much or more *in fact* to the company's profitability as an operating division, but still not qualify because top management does not and should not judge its performance solely on the basis of profitability. For example, the legal department could be run as a captive law firm and be judged by its performance in producing profits by chasing ambulances inside the company. But despite its ability to meet the requirements of operational independence, access to outside customers and talent, and separable costs and revenues, the legal department should not be made a profit center because individual decisions cannot be controlled by the profit motive.

In surveying operations within the company to determine which should be profit centers, management may want to restudy the fundamental objectives of each operation. The proclivity to view many activities as service center lean-tos for major divisions or the company as a whole should not lead top executives to ignore the advantages of conducting every possible operation as a profit center. Particular care should be taken in marginal cases like this one—

A captive steel mill that produces a substantial part of the requirements of a large manufacturer of equipment turns in a poor profit performance. This is due in part to the fact that it is not judged by profits alone; management's intent is to meet the requirements and specifications of the fabricating divisions at the expense of efficient scheduling and profitable product mix. Under these circumstances, the mill is viewed as a service function. It could, however, be operated as a profit center. While the difficulties of negotiating price premiums for special steels and special scheduling would be great, a price on the mill's unique services to the fabricating divisions would lead to correct allocation and remove the wasteful illusion that these special services are free.

To summarize, the modern integrated, multiple-product firm functions best if it is made into a sort of miniature of the competitive, free-enterprise economic system. The firm should be comprised of independent operating units that act like economic entities, free to trade outside the company as well as inside. Each such entity or profit center will, in seeking to maximize its own profits, do what will also maximize the profits of the entire company, just as individual firms in a private-enterprise society, by seeking their selfish advancement, generate the high productivity and well-being of a competitive economy.

Competitive Pricing

The underlying requisite for profit-center controls is competitive prices negotiated in arm's length bargaining by division managers who are free to go outside the company if unhappy with prices paid by or to brother division managers.

Small differences in the unit price of transferred products can make big differences in the division's profits and executive bonuses. Intracompany pricing must preserve the profit-making autonomy of the division manager so that his selfish interests will be identical with the interests of the company as a whole. This can be accomplished by following three simple principles:

1. Prices of all transfers in and out of a profit center should be determined by negotiation between buyers and sellers.

2. Negotiators should have access to full data on alternative sources and markets and to public and private information about market prices.

3. Buyers and sellers should be completely free to deal outside the company.

The practical benefits of sound transfer pricing for profit-center control are not always obvious. Many companies—especially if they are decentralized—seem to get along fine without it, never knowing what they are missing. This is because decentralization "digs gold with a pickax." In the flush of gratification for this great improvement over old authoritarian ways management may neglect the tools to get the most out of it.

In a big company there is danger that interest in making profits will be diluted as a result of managerial specialization and the separation of operation from ownership. The parochial ambitions of operating managers need to be held in check; performance should be judged in terms of alibi-proof, objectively measured profits. When transfer prices are economically correct and profit centers are properly established, top management can delegate and still have peace of mind, because the division manager's targets and incentives will be so set up that his interests are identical to those of top management.

How to protect the independence of operating divisions against the insidious encroachment of staff advice, the restrictions of policy rules, and the fettering effect of top-level supervision is an ever present problem. The fact that top management finds it necessary to protest so much about the independence of its division managers often shows how limited this independence is in reality. Competitively negotiated transfer prices bulwark the independence of operating divisions by making possible meaningful measurement of economic performance.

The harm that can be done by arbitrary and authoritative pricing of intracompany transfers is hidden. Such prices lead to sins of omission as well as sins of commission. They fail to give definitive indication of the profitability of added volume. They rob management of an economically correct basis for evaluating various profit figures. They provide a distorted and incorrect measure of the economic desirability of different channels of distribution. Bad transfer prices can also misdirect capital investment and cause friction and dissension among executives.

But negotiated competitive transfer prices can prevent these losses. They can make the division's procurement, processing, pricing, and distribution sensitive to market requirements and responsive to competitive alternatives. They provide sound guidance in making purchasing decisions, indicate the extent to which additional processing will be profitable, and direct the flow of products so as to make the greatest net profit for the company. Furthermore, the very process of negotiation avoids arbitrariness and tends to create agreement. This eliminates the cause of much friction and ill feeling.

OTHER PRICING SYSTEMS

What about existing systems of setting transfer prices? How adequate or inadequate are they? Various bases are now in use, such as:

1. *Published market prices.* Example: uncured hams priced to the canning division at prices reported in the *National Provisioner*.

2. *Marginal cost.* Example: electric motors transferred to the refrigerator division at cost of materials plus direct labor.

3. *Full Cost Plus.* Example: gasoline transferred to the transportation division at the refineries' full costs plus a "fair" profit markup.

4. *Sales Minus.* Example: transfers of gasoline from the refinery at the retail price minus an allowance for the marketing department's services in getting it from the refinery to the customer.

5. *Traditional Prices.* Example: the transfer price of financing service, a customary 6 percent.

The choice among the different transfer pricing systems depends both on the kinds of information that are available and on the objectives that the management hopes to accomplish through the system.

If no measurement of the competitive market price exists for the intermediate product, some type of cost basis may have to be used, unless a negotiated price can be based on indirect alternatives of buying and selling units. But choice among cost bases may be narrowed by the kind of cost records used.

In the event that available information does permit a free choice, then what management wishes to accomplish by intracompany pricing should determine the system to be followed. For example, if a company wishes to use intracompany pricing as the primary means for controlling costs and profits, for measuring operational results, and for directing the product flow in the most profitable ways, some sort of market price system is clearly indicated.

Now let us examine the relative advantages and disadvantages of the different systems used today for setting transfer prices, so that we can see how they compare with the competitive pricing method advocated here.

Published Market Prices

Basing intracompany transfers on published statistical reports of market price has much merit. It often approximates the ideal of a competitive transfer pricing system. But practical difficulties arise from three sources:

1. *Conditions may make published statistics an inaccurate statement of the market price for the size, quality, timing, and location of the intracompany transaction.* Market price statistics often have systematic time lags which make them an inaccurate picture of the true market at near turning points. Also, they may represent a different quantity, grade, type of package, or duration from the intracompany transaction.

For example, published prices of intermediate products and services usually pertain to the spot price, whereas the intracompany transfer calls for a long-term contract price, which is usually lower and more stable. Thus, rates for chartered oil tankers, which fluctuate wildly, are not an adequate basis for pricing stable intracompany water transport.

Some of these deficiencies in the published market price can be partly remedied by market-determined price spreads for term contracts as opposed to spot prices, carload lots as opposed to small lots, and bulk as opposed to packaged products. But if these spreads are large, it is likely that they cannot be established objectively in a manner that will be satisfactory to buyer and seller without negotiation.

2. *The market place may not offer a real alternative for the intracompany buyer or seller.* The volume traded on the market may be so small compared with intracompany transactions that an attempt to get supplies there would drive up the price. Or the quality standards of its market plan may be lower than those of the company or fail to meet the peculiarities of design and appeal of the company's own brand, so that price comparisons are futile.

3. *It may be difficult to distinguish between nominal price quotations and real ones.* No matter how honestly and carefully prices are reported,

there are times when a very few strategically placed transactions can make a big difference in the published price. When these published prices affect the divisional manager's promotion and pay, he cannot be expected to be blind to opportunities to "make" the market. Cunning maneuvers of this sort are hardly in the company's interest.

Marginal Cost

Next to negotiated transfer pricing, marginal-cost pricing is most defensible economically. Under this plan transfer prices are based on the additional cost caused by the production of an additional unit of the product. Moderately close approximation to marginal cost can be made by confining costs to those that vary with volume and are traceable—i.e., direct costs. This is the best of the authoritarian pricing schemes for these reasons: (1) it determines cost of underlying processes in terms that are relevant for short-run operating decisions on pricing, promotion, and product policy; (2) the buying division has a guide as to when it is in the company's interest to acquire a product or material from outside sources so long as it knows the short-run marginal cost of producing the product inside the company; and (3) troublesome and contentious problems of assigning overhead costs to joint product operations and changing overhead loadings as a result of variations in operating rates are avoided.

Marginal-cost pricing has, however, several distinct disadvantages:

(1) Divisional profit and loss statements are made meaningless as a measure of economic performance. All contributions to profits are passed along to the final operation, and therefore no profits appear for earlier divisions. This gives the last division, frequently the sales division, a big cushion for maneuvering. No wonder sales divisions like marginal-cost transfer pricing!

(2) Where many divisions handle products in succession, operating management may overlook profitable changes in methods or product flows because the inefficiencies of one division are covered up by the low costs of more efficient divisions that worked on the product in earlier stages.

(3) Commercial abilities that are so desirable in a well-rounded division manager are stunted under marginal-cost transfer pricing. He is isolated from the pitfalls and opportunities of the market and is confined to the role of a service division manager.

Full Cost Plus

Cost-plus pricing sets intracompany prices on the basis of the complete costs of the producing unit plus some allowance for profit. Many variations of the system, both as to the cost base and the add-on, are possible.

The commonest cost base is orthodox accounting costs for the latest period. Normal cost and standard cost are sometimes used. The add-on or profit ranges from a niggardly coverage of overheads to a markup on sales which produces a handsome return on investment. The standard for the amount of profit takes two principal forms: (a) a margin on sales and (b) a rate of return on investment. In practice, partly because of the difficulty of determining profit margins on reasonably similar operations, the margin is usually set arbitrarily.

Bare costs with no add-on were more common in the past than now. They are frequently justified on moral grounds: that it is wrong to take profit out of the hide of a brother division. Today, full cost plus a "reasonable" rate of return on the investment of the selling division appears to be gaining wider acceptance.

Supporters of full cost-plus pricing of transfers claim these conflicting virtues of the system:

(1) That the company is assured of an adequate profit on the entire process if transfer prices at each stage force the addition of a profit.

(2) That no company can make money by selling things to itself and allowing divisions to exploit each other; therefore prices limited to costs plus a fair margin should be used to prevent conflict and promote cooperation.

(3) That cost-plus pricing assures that the economic benefits of integration will be achieved and will be passed on to the company's customers.

(4) That cost-plus pricing makes the producing and supplying units attend to the business of producing cheaply without being diverted by concern about commercial problems of pricing sharply.

None of these virtues, however, minimize the fact that cost-plus pricing is arbitrary and authoritarian. As such, it provides a poor basis for evaluating division performance, it beclouds profits, and it inevitably diverts production into uneconomic channels.

Sales Minus

Basing intracompany transfer prices on what the customers pay has considerable vogue, particularly in organizations which are strongly market oriented. Transfer prices are geared to final selling prices by subtracting allowances that more or less completely provide for the costs and profits of intervening operations. For example, retail price lines of sheets and pillow cases once governed transfer prices for the textile mill subsidiary of a merchandising organization. Similarly, in the case of an integrated wholesale distribution unit, $4 was subtracted from the price paid by the retailer on a certain kind of canned food to get the transfer price from the canning factory to the distribution department. The factory allowed $2 a case for direct costs (transportation, promotion, etc.) and another $2 a case for overhead and profits.

This system has the virtue of being oriented toward the market value of the final product. However, it shifts the full impact of fluctuations in final price to the basic production units of an integrated firm, with the intermediate processing and marketing operations sheltered by an assured margin. In a buyer's market like that recently experienced in textiles, sales-minus pricing for gray goods would come close to what outside textile mills, hungry for business, could be forced to sell at. Under these supply and demand conditions, transfer prices that would approximate competitive market prices and realistically negotiated prices would result from sales-minus pricing. In a seller's market, by contrast, sales-minus pricing will undershoot the market; a division will not be able to get from intracompany transfers what it could get from outsiders or what it could negotiate at arm's length with brother divisions.

Traditional Prices

A weird throwback to medieval times when the concept of "just" price prevailed is occasionally encountered in modern business. The use of traditional prices in transfer pricing belongs in this category. An example is the costing of financial services at 6% in intracompany charges; such a rate has borne no relationship to the market place within the memory of today's executives.

It is hard to see any advantages in this method, beyond the fact that it is as convenient and consistent as most of the concepts of feudalism. But the other methods now in vogue are not much more useful. All have serious shortcomings; none can be relied on to produce profit-oriented decisions by division managers.

INSTALLATION AND OPERATION

We turn now to the more mundane problems of what needs to be done to install and operate competitive transfer pricing.

Comprehensive Study

A practical starting point is a systematic, impartial study of the intracompany pricing methods the company is now using, and the facts that can be marshaled concerning market prices and market price relationships. The next thing to do is to lay the foundation of understanding of the economic and management philosophy, the benefits, and the problems of this new concept of competitively negotiated intracompany dealings.

Managers of profit centers and of service centers need a new orientation—one that is pointed toward the economics of their operation rather than exclusively toward the technology of the operation. When they become managers of profit centers rather than merely managers of factories, they need a new set of ideas, values, and facts, with dimensions broad enough to embrace marketplace choices and competitive return on capital expenditures. All this takes time as well as education. Overnight installation by a presidential decree of the new transfer-price and profit-center policy is not likely to succeed or last.

Gradual Progress

After the research and educational foundation has been laid, a program of gradual installation can be tailored to the company's needs. The following rules should prove helpful:

1. *Widen the coverage gradually.* Start with areas where competitively negotiated pricing is easiest and take on the tougher ones as know-how improves.

2. *Apply first to basic volume.* Start with negotiated prices on the minimum basic quantities needed for planned future production. Negotiate term contracts for the distant future, so that both buyer and seller will have maximum fluidity and alternatives. Then gradually move toward arrangements for the fluctuating sector of volume for which real alternative outside sources get quite restricted. For these negotiations the trading experience and regard for long-term interests gained in previous dealings will help to steady the bargaining by curbing temptations toward exploitation in the short run.

3. *Establish pricing guides through research.* For products and components where the producing division has had no occasion to study market prices and outside trading opportunities, a foundation of knowledge must be laid so that neither brother division will be handicapped by ignorance in negotiating a competitive price. It takes time to dig this information up and to familiarize operating executives with its use.

4. *Set pricing limits temporarily.* These initial limits on the range of prices over which bargaining can take place will become as vestigial as the hip bone of a whale when the system gets into operation. But they provide assurance and prevent undue exploitation of ignorance at the outset. For example, a lower limit on price might be set by an estimate of the marginal cost, and the upper limit might be the commercial price charged outsiders plus 5 percent.

5. *Limit the volume of outside trading initially.* The freedom to trade outside can be temporarily restricted by setting volume limits as, for instance, 75 percent inside the company, 25 percent outside the company. Those who fear that the advantages of integration will be dissipated are reassured by this expedient.

Price Mediator

One executive is needed to (a) pull together the transfer-price and profit-center investigations, (b) organize the conferences and training sessions, and (c) supervise the gradual installation of the new system of economic controls. To ease the transition, both emotionally and economically, this executive also can temporarily undertake to mediate the negotiation of some transfer prices.

Note that the price mediator should not attempt to arbitrate. The experience with price arbitration is almost universally bad. It is expensive and time consuming, and the results do not satisfy either party. Everyone feels cheated, and everyone has an alibi for his profit and volume results. Instead the mediator should aim at securing agreement by keeping the negotiations going, by supplying information, and by exercising business judgment on issues of fact as well as on commercial alternatives. For example, one transfer-price mediator in a meat packing firm reviewed and substantially deflated cost information which was burdened with fictitious charges for packaging and shipping sausage material at successive stages of processing. Up to this time the selling division had been using these costs in good faith for internal decisions as well as in transfer-price bargaining with other divisions. The delusion that these were rock-bottom incremental costs led the selling division to set its refusal price at a level which was above the market. Such a price would have led to idle facilities and would have sacrificed incremental profits if the buying division had been forced to go outside to get the supplies.

One of the functions of the mediator, particularly in the early stages of installation, is to distill the truth from conflicting, misguided, exaggerated, and prejudiced pricing facts which the negotiating parties often bring to a mediation conference. To illustrate again—in negotiating transfer prices for a pharmaceutical firm, the participants faced two major common problems: (a) the outside market was very thin, with a wide spread resulting between highest and lowest prices at which sales were made; and (b) the transactions covered by this range differed from the intracompany transactions in volume, packaging, location, and so on. Quite naturally, each party came to the negotiations with a highly biased sample of market transactions to support its point of view. The triumph of the transfer-price mediator was to demonstrate to both parties that extreme prices, ranging from $.50 a pound to $1.50 a pound, were inapplicable; he managed to narrow the range within which both parties agreed that the real market lay for the transactions in question.

As profit-center managers gain experience in using the competitive pricing system and grow to appreciate its value, the effective mediator will work himself out of a job.

Term Contracts

The period over which the transfer prices are to be negotiated should be at least as long as the planning period required to design and schedule production, or to dig up satisfactory alternative outside sources, whichever time period is longer. For example, the planning and design period for automobiles is so long that in the short run, say over the next quarter, the divisions which make basic engine components have no real alternative market for their product. Similarly, the vehicle divisions could not on short notice dig up alternative outside sources for properly designed engine parts. Many operations are characterized by short-run inflexibility of alternatives especially where design, quality, and packaging must conform to rigid and publicized specifications. A product made to such specifications has passed the point of no return.

In such cases, *short*-run negotiations (less than three or four months for the automobile manufacturer) concerning transfer prices have the. hallmark of. bilateral monopoly; they are similar to wage-rate negotiations. They generate heat, bad temper, and rarely produce economic transfer prices that are gauged and policed by outside alternatives and freedom to use them.

But over a long period even a branded product like an automobile can properly be subject to transfer prices that have the virtues and characteristics of a free-enterprise system. If long-term specifications contracts are negotiated, the buying unit will generally be able to get outsiders to bid on products made to its requirements, and a producing unit will have a real choice—either to adapt its output to other uses or to again assume the commitments on design, volume, and productive facilities which are tied to the branded product.

Good Businessmen

Successful operation of a profit center under a miniature free-enterprise system within the corporate fold calls for talents and experience often summed up by the tag, "He is a good businessman."

These abilities need to be systematically cultivated because they are not likely to have survived in a big corporate bureaucracy where transfer prices have been authoritarian. Executives of highly centralized companies are likely to have been reared as if they were in one big happy family, in which each child has an assigned set of chores and emphasis is on cooperation and the subordination of individual desires to group interests. Some executives may have forgotten how to make independent decisions. They will need help in taking responsibility for decisions in a profit-center controlled company where anything that affects their profit is their business, where performance is judged by how much profit they can make, and where right, independent opinions quickly improve the executives' profit and loss statements.

ANSWERING OBJECTIONS

Any new system of transfer prices will be criticized, and this one particularly because it removes needed alibis and may blemish careers by exposing executives' inadequacies. In addition, it may appear to be fundamentally opposed to the reason for existence of a large multi-product corporation. Therefore anyone who is considering this new system of intracompany pricing and profit control needs to give some thought to the objections that are likely to be viewed as most telling by those who doubt. The following questions are ones which I have encountered constantly in work in the field.

"Why can't our company get along without transfer prices?" Some companies can. There is no need for management coordination through an apparatus of economic transfer prices and profit achievement measures if all complicated managerial functions can be competently exercised by one small, closely knit group of men. This was found to be true of a regional grocery chain. But very few large companies have such an administrative setup.

In some situations it may be possible to devise mathematical models which can solve empirically all the problems of allocating facilities, materials, and intermediate and finished products without continued exercise of managerial judgment and know-how. In these cases transfer prices are not essential, either. In using the new computers that are here and on the horizon management is handicapped, however, by the shortage of analytical ability and judgment needed to set up models which will adequately reflect fluid and changing alternatives at every stage.

"Why worry, since we already have that kind of transfer price?" Many companies think they have competitive transfer prices, but most of them do not. The consequences of noncompetitive transfer prices are present, but they seem to spring from such other causes as selfishness and lack of team spirit. There are two clear symptoms of noncompetitive pricing which cannot be explained away: (a) a continuous awareness of a conflict between the interest of the operating unit and what appears to its managers to be the interest of the company as a whole, reflected in self-congratulation for putting the company's interest before that of the division; and (b) the prevalence of exhortations not to let transfer prices prevent the company from making money.

"Will the benefits of integration be lost?" Integration which is actually economically justified has such great and clear benefits to both buying and selling divisions that competitive transfer pricing is not a threat. Only integration which does not produce economies—which does not

profit both the buying and the selling division—will be eliminated by virtue of division buyers and sellers going outside the company. This assumes that the division managers are alert to the possible conflict between their short-run and long-run interests, both in maintaining customer relations and in having a stable and sure source of supply.

"Will cooperation be undermined?" Measuring profit-center performance on a competitive economic basis motivates each unit to do what is in its own best profit interest. These interests, if the transfer prices are determined economically and the profit centers properly defined, are identical with the interests of the company. Rivalry to make the best profit showing will certainly encourage shrewd, hard-headed negotiations, but the promotion of mutual economic interests will, as always, stimulate cooperation.

"Does perishability of a product rule out negotiable transfer pricing?" Physical perishability does not create a new kind of problem. Physical perishability causes price sacrifices, and it is this economic perishability alone that matters. Negotiated prices have proved practical for perishable products; indeed, they have been used for them in the market place for thousands of years.

"Will the system work if there is no true market price?" This does not matter. Sometimes the negotiated price will be above the general market average, sometimes below. So long as buyers and sellers are free to know and to choose competitive alternatives, the price will be mutually agreeable and will be determined by supply and demand forces for that particular kind of transaction.

Published data on market prices are likely to be too fragmentary and too unreliable to determine transfer prices; they should be used as a guide only. Sometimes negotiation leads to agreement to use the particular published price as a bench mark. However, this is not because the figure is published but because the negotiating parties agree to its economic validity.

"Will profit centers be shortsighted in their quest for gain?" No system of transfer prices and performance measurement makes judgment unnecessary in appraising the value of hanging on to a customer and in balancing long-run and short-run interests. Shortsightedness is no more likely with good transfer prices than with bad. Profit-center managers have a big stake in their long-run future, and good supervision can clarify this stake and induce a long view when short-run profits conflict.

"Will the sales organization sell too cheaply?" The rather general mistrust of the business acumen of the marketing organization is a peculiarity of the big bureaucracy. From it stem the practices of kidding the sales organization about costs, pushing products down its throat, and rigging transfer prices to make marketing operations look like losers. The result is that atrophy of commercial instincts sometimes associated with sales specialization.

Under the proposed system the sales organization will control factors that determine its profits, will be held responsible for the profits, and will have its profit performance measured. Given this encouragement, there is no reason to expect that salesmen should be any less capable of acting like businessmen than are engineers or accountants.

The company's interests require, not simply top price or top volume, but top profit. Sometimes a larger profit contribution comes from a bigger volume at lower price; sometimes it is the other way around. With this method, sales units will have the knowledge, the authority, and the incentive to sell the product at prices that will produce the greatest profits for themselves and therefore for the company. These advantages in turn will put the units in a better position to develop and attract men who are competent merchandisers.

CONCLUSION

Difficulties of installation and operation *can* be overcome; questions of criticism and skepticism *can* be met. Management will do well to make the necessary effort in view of the deficiencies of existing transfer pricing systems:

1. Economically indefensible methods of intracompany pricing are widely used in American industry.

2. Losses sustained from bad transfer prices do not show up on any set of books, because what would have happened under economically correct transfer prices will never be known. Anyone who has tried to restate in terms of correct transfer prices what has been reported in terms of wrong ones will testify to the practical impossibility of measuring the foregone profits. In other words, whatever losses result from noneconomic transfer prices are well and forever hidden.

3. Bad transfer prices do not necessarily lead to losses; but if they do not, it is because no attention is paid to them in making decisions. In some companies the critical decisions concerning flow of product, degree of processing, and channels and geography of distribution can be made without reference to any internal costs or prices. In such companies bad transfer prices may do no harm—they also do no good. And if the operations of these companies do not require an economically correct system of transfer prices, they probably require no intracompany pricing at all.

As a practical matter the chances are strong that an unsound system of transfer pricing *will* cause harm. For a large integrated organization with a diversified product line which is sold to a variety of industrial, commercial, and consumer market levels, the only system which will accomplish the needs of management is one based on negotiated competitive prices.

16. An Econometric Analysis of the Determination of Prices in Manufacturing Industries*

DONALD H. STRASZHEIM and
MAHLON R. STRASZHEIM

INTRODUCTION

The theory of price determination in manufacturing industries has focused primarily on the role of market structure, especially market power, in explaining variation across industries in pricing behavior. Whether prices tend to be affected by short-run demand and supply conditions or whether prices change only occasionally in response to changes in "full costs" is generally traced to the extent to which markets are competitive or oligopolistic.

The best and most up-to-date test of the role of concentration is by Eckstein and Wyss, who estimated price equations for 16 two- and three-digit manufacturing sectors using quarterly data through 1971. Differences in the equations across industries could be traced to industry concentration. Demand and cost variables provided a good fit in the more competitive sectors, whereas in the more concentrated industries, variables that represented a full cost pricing model provided a statistically superior fit. Capacity utilization, which Eckstein and Wyss suggest is a proxy for short-run market disequilibrium arising from pricing inflexibility, proved significant only in oligopolistic industries with medium concentration ratios. For the most highly concentrated industries, the rate of return on equity and/or long bond rates were virtually the only important explanatory variables of statistical significance, suggesting a long-run target rate of return approach to pricing in these sectors.

This paper extends the Eckstein-Wyss analysis, estimating price equations for 24 two- and three-digit manufacturing sectors using quarterly data. Our equations include orders data for those sectors where data are available and newly derived unit labor cost data, variables which Eck-

* *Review of Economics and Statistics,* vol. 58, no. 2 (May 1976), pp. 191–201.

stein-Wyss did not use, and we are generally able to improve on their fits. While specification of the effects of the several short-run influences on prices is restricted by multicollinearity between output, orders, utilization rates, and unit labor costs, we observe both competitive and oligopolistic sectors exhibiting price responsiveness to short-run market variables. Our results suggest a different interpretation of the role of industry concentration in industry pricing than Eckstein-Wyss.

I. THEORY OF INDUSTRY PRICING AND EQUATION SPECIFICATION

Eckstein and Fromm's classic paper on industry pricing outlines two predominant models of industry pricing: (1) a competitive model in which prices respond to changes in short-run demand and marginal cost functions; and (2) an oligopolistic, full cost pricing model in which prices do not respond to short-run changes in market conditions but rather adapt slowly to changes in the long run-level of unit costs. The latter is defined to be that level of costs associated with some standard or projected rate of output, one which presumably averages out any short-run, random fluctuations in demand.

The principal issues in specifying equations to test these alternative formulations involve how short-run versus long-run factors are to be represented. To test the applicability of the competitive market model, changes in demand and short-run marginal costs must be included in the price equation. Unit labor and materials costs are the most important elements in short-run marginal costs. Variations in capactiy utilization may be a useful proxy for short-run cost changes. Because many inputs are fixed in the short run, changes in utilization rates will be directly related to productivity and hence inversely related to short-run marginal costs. However, periods in which utilization rates rise to very high levels may be ones in which short-run marginal costs are rising as capacity is strained. Sharply rising utilization rates may also be a proxy for demand conditions, or lengthening delivery schedules and order backlogs.

There are no observable measures of ex ante shifts in the short-run demand curve. However, orders, output, and utilization rates all may be useful describers of demand shifts. Changes in these variables reflect both ex ante demand shifts and pricing behavior. Variation in unfilled orders, inventories, or utilization rates—which Eckstein and Fromm label "disequilibrium phenomena"—would imply that price changes have not been as large as would be required to maintain stable inventories, a constant backlog of unfilled orders, or a constant utilization rate. All other things equal, larger swings in these variables will be observed in industries with less flexible prices. Even in competitive industries with quite flexible prices, utilization rates, shipments, and order backlogs are not constant at every point in time. Both changes in order backlogs or delivery rates and price changes are part of the short-run market clearing process. At the level of aggregation typically used in "industry" studies, these variables are, therefore, all potentially useful proxies for shifts in ex ante demand.

Eckstein-Wyss suggest these variables will be useful in explaining prices in less competitive sectors, where prices are less flexible. We postulate the reverse—as a proxy for short-run market conditions these "disequilibrium factors" may prove insignificant in industries with a long-run, full cost approach to pricing but should be significant in competitive industries as measures of short-run changes in market conditions.

The customary formulation of the full cost pricing model assumes that most firms establish prices based on some concept of unit costs at a "standard" level of output, but neglect short-run variations in demand or productivity. An implicit consensus on "full costs" can substantially reduce uncertainty in oligopoly markets. Generally, the literature has focused on the distinction between the long and the short run as the key characteristic used by an industry in defining standard costs. One means of representing long-run influences in price equations is to select cost measures which are invariant to cyclical variations in output. With regard to labor costs, for example, average hourly earnings are likely the best indicator of "full costs" since this series is little affected by cyclical variations in output. Alternatively, cost measures with cyclical variations may be smoothed. A moving average eliminates short-run variations and hence may be a useful description of "long-run" cost influences.

However, anticipating our results, there may be circumstances in which current-period measures of market conditions may be a useful predictor of pricing decisions. In some instances a large increase in demand or costs in the current quarter indicates a change which will not be reversed. A change in negotiated wage rates or a price change of a key material input are obvious examples on the cost side. Just what type of demand change can be construed as signaling a "permanent" shift is less obvious. In a period of large increases in demands or costs, which would allow the industry to raise its price without substantially affecting output, all firms may tacitly agree that a formula based on a weighted average of past period prices or costs is no longer relevant. During such periods, short-run market conditions as reflected in current-quarter data on order backlogs, utilization rates, or input prices, are highly visible to all, and may prove relatively easy to use as a basis for tacit agreement on prices. The inclusion of such variables in current quarter form may prove significant for oligopolistic and competitive industries alike.

Following Eckstein-Wyss, we use the ratio of current quarter prices to a four-quarter weighted average of past prices as our dependent variable, as follows:

$$PAV_t = \frac{P_t}{+ .4P_{t-1} + .3P_{t-2} + .2P_{t-3} + .1P_{t-4}}.$$

As Eckstein-Wyss note, the average lag of two quarters in the denominator results in PAV_t exhibiting significant autocorrelation even if the underlying price series P_t does not. In addition to facilitating comparison of our results with theirs, their arguments for this form are persuasive. Using the absolute level of prices as the dependent variable in price equations is unsatisfactory since prices and costs will necessarily be closely related over time. Use of first differences of prices introduces substantial noise into the dependent variable.

We use the same form, the ratio of the current quarter value to a weighted average of past period values for several of the independent variables—output, unit labor costs, average hourly earnings, input prices, capacity utilization, new orders, unfilled orders, and long bond rates—and use the same set of declining weights in the denominator as for the price variable. The objective is to average out short-run or random changes which are reflected in current-quarter data. There is no basis on a priori grounds or in the data for specifying any particular form of this averaging function. We reject the use of a very long averaging period of several years; a long period would likely aggregate over periods of both rising and falling demand since most of the post-war cyclical downturns have been about one year long. By including a variable in both current-quarter and weighted average form in the equation, "short-run" versus "long-run" influences can be investigated.

We postulate an adaptive process governing price changes, which we represent by including the lagged dependent variable in the equation and by assuming first order autocorrelation may be present:

$$y_t = \alpha + \gamma y_{t-1} + \beta X_t + u_t$$
$$u_t = \rho u_{t-1} + \epsilon_t$$

X_t is a vector, ϵ_t is a random error term with zero mean, and $\rho < 1$. Such a specification could arise from Nerlove's adaptive expectations model, or a more general adaptive process in which the lagged dependent variable is included in firms' decisions regarding prices. In either case, autocorrelation in the error is likely. In industries in which current market conditions are dominant in the determination of prices, the lagged term may be insignificant since past period observations may no longer be relevant in firms' formation of price expectations. The lagged dependent variable proves highly significant for most industries to illustrate its role in the equation, we note briefly the results when the lagged dependent variable is excluded. Consistent, asymptotically efficient estimates of ρ and the parameters in the price equation can be obtained by least squares, non-linear regression. Estimates were made using programs available from Data Resources, Inc., Lexington, Massachusetts. Where the estimate of ρ proved insignificant (t less than one) we revert to ordinary least squares estimation.

Multicollinearity among our independent variables constrains the equation specification. Substantial intercorrelation exists between output, costs, and capacity utilization expressed in current quarter form. For most industries, output and utilization rates are highly correlated and quarterly data on unit labor costs and output are correlated in some industries. Intercorrelations among these variables when each is expressed as a ratio of the current quarter value to a weighted average over the previous four quarters are relatively modest. Our criterion for equation specification given these collinearity constraints was to include all variables with the expected sign and if the estimated coefficient had a t-ratio greater than one. In the event that two variables were highly intercorrelated and a choice needed to be made between two specifications, each of which included only one of the two variables of interest with the appropriate sign, we chose the best fit.

II. INDUSTRY ESTIMATES

The nature of available data at the two-digit and lesser levels of aggregation is a major constraint on econometric analysis of industry pricing. The Bureau of Labor Statistics wholesale price data are available at a very disaggregated level. However, there is little systematic quarterly data on labor costs, shipments, and other important explanatory variables beyond the two-digit level, and hence it is necessary to do the analysis at this level of aggregation.

Employment, wages, and overtime hours data are available for most sectors. (Data for All Manufacturing were used for the remaining industries.) We used average hourly earnings, excluding payment for overtime hours. The evidence indicates that firms largely neglect short-run variations in labor productivity in their pricing decisions. It is, therefore, appropriate to exclude differentials in wages associated with overtime hours in measuring wage costs.

Input price data are not generally available at the two-digit level. Eckstein-Wyss developed input price series for 12 industries by aggregating the prices of their inputs by SIC category, based on input requirements from the 1958 input-output table. We use these input price series below. Orders data are available from the Department of Commerce only for certain industries in the durables goods sector. We tried the level of new orders, order backlogs, and the ratio of order backlogs to shipments

262 Readings in Managerial Economics

in attempting to measure the effect of changing orders on prices. The rate of return on equity for two-digit manufacturing industries has been derived from the Federal Trade Commission's *Quarterly Financial Reports*. A four-quarter weighted average of profit rates by industry was calculated to account for seasonal variation. Capacity utilization rate series by industry are available from the Wharton School of Finance for industries approximating the two-digit SIC classification and from the Federal Reserve Board for certain industries. Both sets of data were used in the estimation.

The following are the independent variables used, and their sources:

AHE = index of average hourly earnings, excluding overtime (Bureau of Labor Statistics).

PIN = index of input prices (Eckstein-Wyss, 1972).

FRB = index of industrial production (Federal Reserve Board).

ULC = index of unit labor costs, derived from total wage costs, average hourly earnings times average weekly hours times average employment (Bureau of Labor Statistics), divided by total output (Federal Reserve Board).

RIB = rate of interest on composite of AA rated corporate long-term bonds (Moody's).

RREQ = percentage rate of return on equity, four-quarter moving average (FTC *Quarterly Financial Reports for Manufacturing Corporations*).

UTIL = percentage capacity utilization rate (Wharton School of Finance and Federal Reserve Board).

ORDERS = index of new orders received (Department of Commerce).

A suffix of AV to these variables indicates the variable is expressed as the ratio of the value in the current quarter to a four-quarter past period weighted average.

Before examining the variation in the estimated price equations for industries of different concentration levels, it is useful to test for differences in the variability in demand. As noted, the extent of demand variability can affect short-run market conditions. For example, in industries with very stable demand curves, there might be little short-run variation in output or utilization rates and hence these variables would prove insignificant in price equations, even though demand shifts did induce price changes. Ex post quarterly variations (as measured by the ratio of the standard deviation of quarterly changes to the mean quarterly change) in output or utilization rates do differ by industries, but the differences are unrelated to industry concentration. Nor is concentration correlated with price variability. Sectors exhibiting the most quarterly variability in prices include both very concentrated and non-concentrated sectors.

The estimated price equations are presented in Table 1, with the industries arranged by their concentration ratio as of 1963. Elasticities evaluated at the mean appear in Table 2. The lagged dependent variable proves significant in all industries except ferrous metals. For about half the industries, the autocorrelation coefficient is also significant. There is no relationship between industry concentration and the goodness of fit. The equations with the lowest $\bar{R}^2$ are tobacco (0.484), petroleum (0.489), rubber (0.494), and instruments (0.590). Equations for all other sectors exhibit $\bar{R}^2$ greater than 0.60, with 13 of the industries having $\bar{R}^2$ greater than 0.75.

The equations include four measures of "long-run" costs—average hourly earnings, input prices, unit labor costs, and long bond rates—each expressed as a ratio of the current quarter to a weighted average of the previous four quarters. Except in a few industries, these variables expressed in this form are not highly intercorrelated. These cost variables dominate the results. Average hourly earnings as a measure of labor costs proved significant in eleven of the equations, and in four other instances the average hourly earnings variable was omitted from equations because it was correlated with either orders or output variables which provided a better fit. Straight-time earnings proved a far better predictor of prices than unit labor costs. In only four industries were unit labor costs significant, although, in two cases this variable was correlated with average hourly earnings and hence rejected because the latter provided a better fit. Apparently even the most competitive industries largely neglect quarterly or cyclical fluctuations in unit labor costs in their pricing. Even averaging unit labor costs over several quarters seldom defines a useful variable in explaining prices. Also, the estimated price elasticities for average hourly earnings were several times greater than for unit labor costs when the latter were statistically significant.

Input prices proved statistically significant in four of the thirteen industries for which data were available—food, petroleum, ferrous metals, and fabricated metals. In the cases of food and petroleum one factor accounts for a large share of costs. Unfortunately, no data were available for several other sectors with important single material inputs —tobacco, leather and lumber. Eckstein-Wyss also found input prices to be significant in chemicals, machinery, paper, apparel, and furniture. We have no explanation for this discrepancy with our results.

The other "long-run" cost measures included in the equations were capital costs. Long bond rates are not significantly correlated with any other included variables, and had a t-ratio in excess of one in fourteen

TABLE 1
Industry Price Equations

SIC Industry	Concentration Ratio (percent)	Constant	Lagged Dependent Variable	Variables in Past Period Weighted			
				AHEAV	PINAV	FRBAV	ULCAV
371 Motor Vehicles	77.0	.3408 (4.0)	.6397 (7.6)	—	—	—	—
21 Tobacco manufacturing	66.8	.5064 (4.4)	.4350 (3.9)	—	n.a.	—	—
333 Nonferrous metals	65.3	.3211 (1.4)	.4849 (2.2)	—	—	—	—
281 Basic chemicals	56.2	.1715 (2.0)	.7379 (8.0)	.0698 (1.0)	—	—	—
36 Electrical equipment	55.9	.2797 (4.4)	.6448 (8.9)	—	—	—	—
30 Rubber/plastics	51.2	.4739 (4.3)	.4854 (4.1)	—	—	—	—
28 Chemicals/allied	49.1	.0680 (1.0)	.7379 (9.6)	.1135 (1.6)	—	—	.0319 (1.4)
38 Instruments	45.4	.2849 (2.0)	.4520 (4.4)	.2571[h] (2.1)	n.a.	−.0517 (2.6)	—
32 Stone/clay/glass	43.7	−.0736 (1.0)	.7970 (8.0)	.2626 (2.1)	—	.0184 (1.1)	—
33 Primary metals	42.9	.5576 (1.9)	.3186 (1.0)	—	n.a.	—	—
283 Drugs	42.0	.1309 (1.5)	.6107 (6.0)	.1584 (1.7)	n.a.	.0386 (1.8)	.0562 (1.9)
20 Food/kindred	41.7	.2374 (4.0)	.4245 (6.5)	—	.3408 (9.3)	—	—
208 Beverages	41.3	.4044 (1.4)	.5561 (1.9)	—	n.a.	—	—
29 Petroleum products	40.4	−.3424 (1.0)	.2533 (1.0)	—	.6198 (3.3)	.4608 (2.5)	—
331 Ferrous metals	39.4	−.1175 (0.9)	.0488 (0.5)	.4522 (5.0)	.5440 (8.0)	—	.0688 (4.8)
22 Textile products	36.8	.0409 (0.3)	.6151 (4.5)	.1746 (2.6)	—	.0941 (6.2)	—
35 Nonelectrical machinery	36.7	.1009 (1.5)	.4982 (7.6)	.3273 (5.3)	—	—	—
26 Paper/allied	36.5	.2088 (0.8)	.4684 (1.5)	.2370 (0.9)	n.a.	—	—
39 Miscellaneous manufacturing	34.3	.5672 (4.5)	.4283 (3.8)	—	n.a.	−.0712 (2.8)	n.a.
34 Fabricated metals	28.5	.3411 (1.5)	.5863 (2.5)	—	.0500 (1.0)	—	—
31 Leather/products	26.2	−.2268 (0.9)	.5461 (2.8)	—	n.a.	−.3691 (3.5)	.2991 (1.6)
24 Lumber/wood	23.4	−.0064 (0.6)	.4621 (1.9)	—	n.a.	.3955 (3.1)	—
25 Furniture/fixtures	21.9	.1604 (2.6)	.7085 (12.3)	.1049 (1.5)	n.a.	—	—
23 Apparel	19.5	.1440 (1.9)	.7353 (9.1)	.0756 (2.9)	n.a.	.0267 (2.4)	—

n.a. signifies not available, p is autocorrelation parameter, t-statistics are in parentheses. Concentration ratio is per
[a] Index, new orders received.
[b] Ratio, backlog of unfilled orders/output.
[c] Index, backlog of unfilled orders.
[d] AV form of [b].

Average (AV) Form

RIBAV	ORDERAV	RREQ	FRB	ULC	UTIL	ORDERS	ρ	$\bar{R}^2$	S.E.E.
.0213 (1.3)	—	−.00075 (2.6)	—	.0110 (1.3)	—	n.a.	—	.738	.00577
.0938 (2.9)	—	−.00679 (2.5)	—	.0638 (2.6)	—	n.a.	—	.484	.01111
.1673 (1.9)	—	−.00501 (2.1)	—	—	.00041 (1.0)	.0462[a] (1.5)	.515 (1.9)	.764	.01035
—	—	—	—	—	.00023 (2.2)	n.a.	−.223 (1.4)	.614	.00437
.0230 (1.3)	.0310[d] (1.9)	—	—	—	.00012 (1.5)	.0129[b] (1.4)	—	.819	.00510
.0310 (1.1)	—	—	.0121 (2.4)	—	—	n.a.	—	.494	.00894
—	—	—	—	.0112 (1.7)	.00040 (2.5)	n.a.	—	.798	.00291
.0669 (3.7)	—	—	.0134 (3.1)	—	—	n.a.	—	.590	.00520
—	—	−.00080 (1.9)	—	—	—	n.a.	—	.850	.00486
.0802 (2.4)	.0050[e] (0.3)	—	—	.0199 (1.1)	—	.0260[a] (1.7)	.372 (1.1)	.779	.00762
—	—	—	—	—	n.a.	n.a.	—	.645	.00383
—	—	—	—	—	—	n.a.	—	.801	.00672
.0377 (1.5)	—	−.00320 (1.3)	.0349 (1.7)	—	n.a.	n.a.	.402 (1.1)	.775	.00630
—	—	—	—	—	—	n.a.	.374 (1.4)	.489	.02028
—	—	—	—	—	—	—	.622 (5.6)	.867	.00529
—	.0325[f] (1.7)	−.00019 (0.3)	—	.0395 (2.2)	—	n.a.	.390 (1.9)	.885	.00290
.0102 (1.1)	—	—	—	—	.03664[g] (2.5)	.0267[b] (3.7)	—	.934	.00248
.0570 (2.2)	—	—	—	—	.02515[g] (0.5)	n.a.	.365 (1.1)	.611	.00629
.0440 (3.3)	—	−.00052 (1.2)	—	n.a.	.00047 (2.9)	n.a.	—	.715	.00404
.0179 (1.4)	—	−.00041 (1.2)	—	—	—	.0117[c] (1.5)	.313 (1.1)	.916	.00283
—	—	—	—	.0157 (0.6)	—	n.a.	.339 (1.4)	.645	.01797
—	—	—	.0576 (1.1)	.0933 (0.8)	—	n.a.	.408 (1.5)	.653	.02595
.0212 (2.5)	—	−.00021 (1.0)	.0066 (1.5)	—	—	n.a.	—	.879	.00240
.0094 (1.5)	—	—	—	.0095 (2.1)	—	n.a.	—	.910	.00200

cent of total industry output produced by four largest firms. *1963 Census of Manufactures.*

[e] AV form of [a].
[f] FRBAV, lagged two additional quarters.
[g] AV form.
[h] Wage series used was for All manufacturing.

TABLE 2
Industry Elasticities Evaluated at the Mean, and Median Current Quarter and Stationary State Elasticities

SIC	Industry	Variables in Past Period Weighted Average (AV) Form										
		AHEAV	PINAV	FRBAV	ULCAV	RIBAV	ORDERAV	RREQ	FRB	ULC	UTIL	ORDERS
371	Motor vehicles	—	—	—	—	.0217	—	-.0103	—	.0105	—	—
21	Tobacco manufacturing	—	—	—	—	.0953	—	-.0924	—	.0615	—	—
333	Nonferrous metals	.0712	—	—	—	.1706	—	-.0477	—	—	.0338	.0405[a]
281-	Basic chemicals	—	—	—	—	—	—	—	—	—	.0193	—
36	Electrical equipment	—	—	—	—	.0235	.0308[d]	—	—	—	.0103	.0121[b]
30	Rubber/plastics	—	—	—	.0316	.0318	—	—	.0097	—	—	—
28	Chemicals/allied	.1157	—	—	—	.0682	—	—	—	.0125	.0345	—
38	Instruments	.2602	—	—	—	—	—	—	-.0104	—	—	—
32	Stone/clay/glass	.2654	—	.0185	—	—	—	-.0077	—	—	—	—
33	Primary metals	.1618	—	—	—	.0816	.0050[e]	—	—	.0196	—	.0227[a]
283	Drugs	—	—	.0408	—	—	—	-.0277	—	—	—	—
20	Food/kindred	—	.3403	—	.0558	—	—	—	—	—	—	—
208	Beverages	—	—	—	—	.0385	—	—	.0308	—	—	—
29	Petroleum products	—	.6217	.0467	—	—	—	—	—	—	—	—
331	Ferrous metals	.4562	.5418	—	.0688	—	—	—	—	—	—	—
22	Textile products	.1772	—	.0953	—	—	.0325[f]	-.0013	—	.0401	—	—
35	Nonelectrical machinery	.3303	—	—	—	.0104	—	—	—	—	.0362[g]	.0248[b]
26	Paper/allied	.2408	—	—	—	.0583	—	—	—	—	.0251[g]	—
39	Miscellaneous manufacturing	—	—	.0720	—	.0448	—	-.0054	—	—	.0417	—
34	Fabricated metals	—	.0501	—	—	.0182	—	-.0039	—	—	—	.0087[c]
31	Leather/products	—	—	.3636	.3004	—	—	—	.0512	.0142	—	—
24	Lumber/wood	—	—	.3976	—	—	—	—	.0057	.0970	—	—
25	Furniture/fixtures	.1603	—	—	—	.0216	—	-.0020	—	—	—	—
23	Apparel	.0764	—	.0268	—	.0094	—	—	—	.0089	—	—
	Median value of current quarter elasticities	.1772	.4411	.0467[h]	.0023	.0357	i	-.0072	.0202[h]	.0223	.0338	i
	Median value of stationary state elasticities	.2882	1.6280	.1549[h]	.3206	.0674	i	-.0125	.0377[h]	.0438	.0467	i

[a] Index, new orders received.
[b] Ratio, backlog of unfilled orders/output.
[c] Index, backlog of unfilled orders.
[d] AV form of [b].
[e] AV form of [a].
[f] FRBAV, lagged two additional quarters.
[g] AV form.
[h] Negative values excluded from calculation of median elasticities.
[i] Medians not calculated.

industries. The evidence for a target-rate-of return approach to pricing was represented by including the rate of return on equity. Just as in the Eckstein-Wyss study, this variable had a t-ratio exceeding two for the three most concentrated sectors—motor vehicles, tobacco, and nonferrous metals. The rate of return on equity also proved significant in six additional industries.

Unlike the Eckstein-Wyss results, long bond rates and the rate of return on equity proved significant for both competitive and concentrated sectors alike. Even in some of the least concentrated sectors, e.g., furniture, fabricated metals, and textiles, industry pricing decisions appear sensitive to long-run rates of return on equity or capital.

Inclusion of output in the equations is a simple test of whether demand side factors influence prices independent of costs. Output expressed as the ratio of the current quarter to a four-quarter past period weighted average is significant in the price equations for seven sectors. For two highly competitive sectors, leather and lumber, the elasticities on the output variables exceed 0.25 and are far greater than the elasticities for other included variables in the equations. These two industries exhibit average variability in output and utilization when compared to other industries, but above average variability in prices. These are the only two sectors where the evidence suggests demand factors are a principal determinant of prices. In stone/clay/glass, drugs, petroleum, textiles, and apparel, the output variable is also significant in the price equation, but the elasticities for output in these industries' equations are well above the elasticities for the included cost variables.

Inclusion of output, unit labor costs, orders, or utilization rates in current quarter form is a test for the relevance of short-run market conditions. One or more of these variables prove statistically significant in all but six industries. The elasticities for the included variables expressed in current quarter form are well below the elasticities for the weighted average form of these variables. Because of the high collinearity among these variables, no general inferences can be drawn about the relative importance of short-run cost versus demand influences. There is no evidence from the results that one of these several measures of short-run market conditions or costs is a better predictor of price changes than another. On a criterion of best fit, the basis for our specification, no one of these several measures is included in the equations more often than any other. Nor is there any evident pattern among industries of different concentration rates. Unlike Eckstein-Wyss, we find either the capacity utilization rate or output, which are highly correlated, significant in both competitive and oligopoly sectors.

Orders data were available for six industries, and proved statistically significant in each case except one, ferrous metals. None of the measures of short-run market conditions proved significant for ferrous metals,

TABLE 3
Goodness of Fit with and without Lagged Dependent Variable

	Sic Industry	With Lagged Dependent Variable			Without Lagged Dependent Variable		
		R^2	S.E.E.	ρ	R^2	S.E.E.	ρ
371	Motor vehicles	.737	.00578	.156 (0.7)[a]	.720	.00596	.690 (6.6)
21	Tobacco manufacturing	.477	.01118	.112 (0.4)[a]	.459	.01137	.403 (3.3)
333	Nonferrous metals	.764	.02035	.515 (1.9)	.723	.02202	.768 (7.8)
281	Basic chemicals	.614	.00436	−.233 (1.4)	.585	.00452	.657 (6.3)
36	Electrical equipment	.819	.00509	.213 (0.9)[a]	.742	.00545	.658 (7.1)
30	Rubber/plastics	.508	.00882	.283 (0.4)[a]	.477	.00910	.489 (3.9)
28	Chemicals/allied	.786	.00296	.041 (0.2)[a]	.759	.00314	.810 (9.7)
38	Instruments	.584	.00523	.091 (0.4)[a]	.533	.00555	.441 (3.6)
32	Stone/clay/glass	.848	.00490	.071 (0.4)[a]	.840	.00502	.706 (7.8)
33	Primary metals	.779	.00761	.372 (1.1)	.741	.00723	.609 (5.5)
283	Drugs	.651	.00374	.122 (0.5)[a]	.628	.00386	.604 (5.7)
20	Food/kindred	.798	.00677	.064 (0.4)[a]	.749	.00760	.543 (4.4)
208	Beverages	.775	.00630	.402 (1.1)	.738	.00679	.764 (9.3)
29	Petroleum products	.489	.02028	.374 (1.4)	.495	.02017	.574 (5.2)
331	Ferrous metals	.867	.00529	.622 (5.6)	.868	.00529	.662 (6.9)
22	Textile products	.885	.00290	.390 (1.9)	.811	.00373	.722 (6.8)
35	Nonelectrical machinery	.920	.00249	.060 (0.3)[a]	.902	.00277	.465 (4.1)
26	Paper/allied	.611	.00629	.365 (1.1)	.556	.00672	.603 (5.3)
39	Miscellaneous manufacturing .	.710	.00407	−.398 (0.2)[a]	.704	.00414	.264 (1.9)
34	Fabricated metals	.916	.00282	.313 (1.1)	.903	.00304	.708 (7.0)
31	Leather/products	.645	.01797	.339 (1.4)	.544	.02039	.664 (6.2)
24	Lumber/wood	.653	.02595	.408 (1.5)	.597	.02802	.677 (6.2)
25	Furniture fixtures	.869	.00244	.818 (0.5)[a]	.849	.00262	.712 (8.9)
23	Apparel	.910	.00200	−.342 (0.2)[a]	.895	.00216	.695 (6.9)

ρ is the autocorrelation parameter. t-statistics are in parentheses.
[a] Where $t < 1.0$, ordinary least squares estimates are shown in table 1.

supporting the thesis of a full cost approach to pricing for this sector. While the orders variables are generally highly correlated with output and capacity utilization rate variables, it was possible to include the utilization rate in the equations for three of the five sectors. In two of the most concentrated of these sectors, nonferrous metals and electrical equipment, the elasticities on the orders variables are as high as the elasticities for other included cost variables. In the other industries with lesser concentration rates, the elasticities on orders are much below the elasticities of included cost variables.

Two comments regarding the nature of the distributed lag structure are worth noting. First, inclusion of lagged values of the dependent variable in the equation implies that a change in an exogenous variable affects prices in all succeeding periods by decreasing amounts. The new steady state solution to prices will be β_i/γ times the change in X_i, where β_i is the coefficient on X_i. The elasticity for the steady state solution is therefore $1/\gamma$ times the one period elasticity. Median values of these estimated elasticities evaluated at the mean of the independent variable are presented in Table 2. Virtually all the steady state elasticities are well below unity. The elasticities for average hourly earnings and input prices dominate the results.

We have also estimated the equations omitting the lagged dependent variable but retaining the assumption of first order autocorrelation. The qualitative conclusions regarding the significance of long-run versus short-run market influences discussed above are essentially unchanged. The fits are only marginally worse. Table 3 compares the results with and without the lagged dependent variable. As expected, the autocorrelation no longer picked up by the lagged dependent variable is now captured in the estimated ρ.

III. CONCLUDING OBSERVATIONS: MARKET STRUCTURE

Our results suggest a very different interpretation of the role of industry concentration than Eckstein-Wyss. In brief, it is difficult to distinguish between the equations for the more concentrated versus the less concentrated sectors. The interest rate and the rate of return on equity, proxies for capital costs especially relevant to oligopolistic sectors, prove significant just as often in the equations for less concentrated industries. We have reviewed alternative classifications of these industries in search of some pattern in the estimates. Neither industry growth rates nor rates of return on equity over the sample period proved useful as an industry classification scheme. If oligopolistic sectors do price differently, it is not evident in these data at the two-digit level of aggregation.

Our results also raise questions regarding the extent to which full cost pricing implies a disregard for short-run market conditions. Orders, output, capacity utilization, and other cost data in current quarter form often prove significant for the more concentrated industries, though the elasticities are well below those for the variables expressed as past period weighted averages. While these results are not inconsistent with a "full cost" pricing theory, they suggest that the "short run" may be important to firms' pricing decisions in oligopoly markets.

17. Peak-Load Pricing in the Electric Utility Industry*

JOHN T. WENDERS

1. INTRODUCTION

   The traditional theory of peak-load pricing argues that peak period users should bear marginal operating costs and all of the marginal capital costs, and off-peak users should be charged prices which cover only marginal operating costs. These results appear prominently in the Berlin, Cicchetti, and Gillen report to the Energy Policy Project of the Ford Foundation and have recently been emphasized by the well-known economist-regulator, Alfred E. Kahn. In addition, economists have extended peak-load pricing theory to include the effect of a regulatory constraint, with the conclusion that the regulated utility will set off-peak prices at the same level as an unconstrained monopolist and set peak prices below the level that would be set by an unconstrained monopolist. The implication of this analysis is that the regulated firm will, therefore, expand productive capacity beyond the level that would be set by the unconstrained monopolist, possibly even beyond the level that would maximize social welfare. This is a logical variant of the well-known A-J-W theory of overcapitalization.

   The purpose of this paper is to urge caution in the application of peak-load pricing theory to the electric utility industries. Cost minimization in this industry requires that heterogeneous electric generation technologies be used to produce demands of different duration, and this modifies the usual conclusions of peak-load pricing theory. In particular, I shall show that off-peak marginal cost prices almost always should include some marginal capacity costs and that the profit maximizing regulated electric utility may set price *above* marginal cost at the peak and *below* marginal cost during the off-peak in order to encourage the expansion of capital-intensive base load generating capacity.

   The analysis presented below is concerned with only the fixed peak pricing problem—the possibility that marginal cost pricing may shift the peak is explicitly excluded. In addition, it is assumed that the objective

* *Bell Journal of Economics*, vol. 7, no. 1 (Spring 1976), pp. 232–41.

is to maximize economic welfare in the market for electricity, and this assumption is implemented formally by maximizing the sum of consumer and producer surpluses.

2. LONG-RUN CAPACITY ADJUSTMENTS

Since electricity can be produced by using different technology or capacity mixes, it is important that the electric utility adopt that combination of capacities which will meet its pattern of demand at minimum cost. Assume that three-generation technologies are available to the utility—base, intermediate, and peak load—all of which have different annual capacity and energy costs per KW. For notation the subscript 1 will be used for peak-load capacity, 2 for intermediate load capacity, and 3 for base load capacity. The symbol B_i will be used to designate the annual marginal and average capital cost for each technology, and it is assumed that $B_3 > B_2 > B_1$. The symbol b_i will be used to designate the marginal and average energy cost of producing a KW of electricity *for one year*, and it is assumed that $b_1 > b_2 > b_3$. Thus, base load capacity has high capital costs and low energy costs, while peak capacity has low capacity costs and high energy costs. Intermediate capacity lies somewhere in between these extremes. In addition, it is assumed that $b_1 + B_1 > b_2 + B_2 > b_3 + B_3$. Table 1 gives a rough estimate of the magnitudes involved from data supplied by Tucson Gas and Electric Company.

TABLE 1
Annualized Capital and Energy Costs by Plant Type

Type of Load	Type of Plant	B_i	b_i
Base	Coal steam	$100.00	$ 20.81
Intermediate	Oil steam	40.00	175.20
Peak	Internal combustion	20.00	240.90

Source: Tucson Gas & Electric Company.

The optimal mix of these three capacities depends on the pattern of load demand experienced by the utility. Figure 1 shows a load duration curve. This curve is a descending arrangement of the hourly demand for electricity during a year. Thus, at least KW_3 amount of capacity is needed for t_2 hours the year, while at least KW_2 is needed for only t_1 hours. t^* represents the number of hours in a year = 8,760. t_1 and t_2 divide the year into three periods, each of which make up a fraction of the year defined by $w_1 = t_1/t^*$, $w_2 = (t_2 - t_1)/t^*$, $w_3 = (t^* - t_2)/t^*$.

Suppose this utility has built KW_3 units of base load capacity, and is contemplating increasing this capacity by one KW. As an alternative, it must consider the cost of one additional unit of intermediate capacity.

FIGURE 1
Annual Load Duration Curve

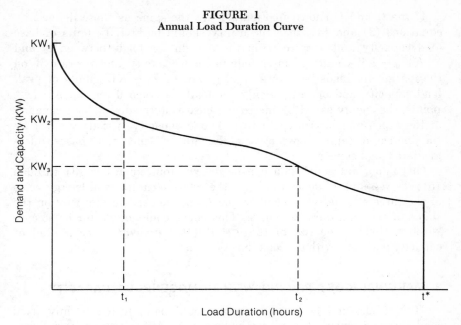

Thus, the marginal cost of an additional unit of base load capacity (MC_3) must be weighed against the marginal cost of an additional unit of intermediate load capacity (MC_2), where the energy cost of t_2 kilowatt hours is included in these marginal costs. The relevant marginal costs are

$$MC_3 = B_3 + (t_2/t^*)b_3 \qquad (1)$$

$$MC_2 = B_2 + (t_2/t^*)b_2. \qquad (2)$$

Clearly, if $MC_3 < MC_2$, base load rather than intermediate load capacity should be added, and this should continue up to the point where $MC_3 = MC_2$, or

$$t_2/t^* = w_1 + w_2 = \frac{B_3 - B_2}{b_2 - b_3}. \qquad (3)$$

A similar argument shows that intermediate load capacity should then be added up to the point where $MC_2 = MC_1$, or,

$$t_1/t^* = w_1 = \frac{B_2 - B_1}{b_1 - b_2}. \qquad (4)$$

And, since $w_1 + w_2 + w_3 = 1$,

$$w_3 = 1 - \frac{B_3 - B_2}{b_2 - b_3}. \qquad (5)$$

If the t_1 and t_2 shown in Figure 1 are the same as those defined by equations (3) and (4), then the utility should build KW_3 units of base load capacity and operate it on the margin for loads between t_2 and t^*, $KW_2 - KW_3$ units of intermediate load capacity and operate it on the margin for loads between t_1 and t_2, and $KW_1 - KW_2$ units of peak load capacity and operate it only for loads between 0 and t_1. At these points, the energy saved by increasing base (intermediate) load capacity at the expense of intermediate (peak) load capacity is exactly offset by the increased capital cost associated with the increased base (intermediate) load capacity.

One important conclusion can be drawn from equations (3) through (5): w_1, w_2, and w_3 depend only on the relative capital and energy costs of the three alternative capacities and do not depend in any way on the shape of the load duration curve. This curve could be flatter or steeper without altering the size of the w's. But the *amount* of each kind of capacity will vary with the load duration curve.

3. MARGINAL COST PRICING WITH HOMOGENEOUS CAPACITY

Having shown how capacity mix should be adjusted to any fixed load duration curve, the next problem is to define the optimal prices which should be charged. The usual theory of peak load pricing assumes that all capacity is homogeneous. While this is at variance with the analysis of the previous section, it is useful for purposes of comparison to expose the pricing problem by using this assumption.

Assume that the load duration curve is divided into three pricing periods. During the first period, which lasts for z_1 fraction of the year, demand is at an annual rate of Q_1; during the second period, which lasts z_2 fraction of the year, demand is at the annual rate of Q_2; and so on for the third period. By definition, $Q_1 > Q_2 > Q_3$. Since output is quoted as annual rates, there is a one-to-one relationship between the KW_i needed to produce Q_i units of output. It is assumed that the markets in these three periods are separable and independent and that the same capacity (with annual capital cost B) serves all three periods.

The welfare optimum will be reached by maximizing the sum of producer and consumer surpluses, given by the integrals of demand curves less costs. The objective function is

$$W = \sum_1^3 z_i \int_0^{Q_i} P_i dQ_i - \sum_1^3 z_i b_i Q_i - BQ_1, \qquad (6)$$

where the P's refer to annualized prices in each of the three pricing periods. The differing subscripts on the b's indicate that the marginal energy cost of serving each of these periods may be different even when there is only one kind of generating capacity. The above maximization yields the following set of optimal prices in the three pricing periods:

$$P_1 = b_1 + B/z_1 \tag{7}$$

$$P_2 = b_2 \tag{8}$$

$$P_3 = b_3. \tag{9}$$

These results show that only peak users bear any marginal capital costs, and the off-peak users bear only the marginal energy costs of their usage. The result is explained by the fact that only peak usage presses against capacity, and, therefore, only these users should bear the incremental capital costs of the system. This is the familiar result demonstrated by Boiteux, Steiner, and Williamson, among others.

4. MARGINAL COST PRICING WITH MIXED CAPACITY

Let us now pull together the analysis of the last two sections. In Figure 2, the load duration curve is represented as a simple step function; the dashed vertical lines indicate the break points in load duration among the three supply periods and correspond to the optimal t_1 and t_2 derived in the first part of this paper. The peak pricing period, when

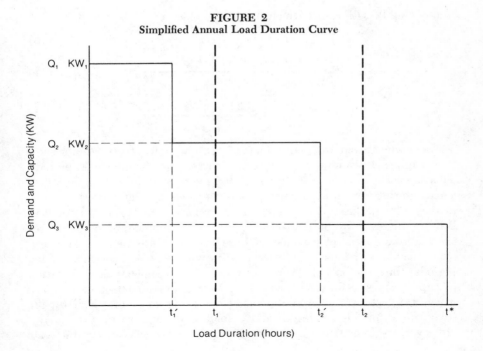

FIGURE 2
Simplified Annual Load Duration Curve

quantity Q_1 is demanded, lies wholly within the peak supply period and will be served by peak load capacity on the margin; the second pricing period is assumed to be served by intermediate load capacity on the margin; and the third pricing period is served by base load capacity on the margin. Peak capacity operates only during the first or peak pricing period, intermediate load capacity operates during both the first and second pricing periods, and base load capacity operates during all three pricing periods. Thus, $z_1 = t'_1/t^*$, $z_1 + z_2 = t'_2/t^*$, $z_1 < w_1$ and $z_1 + z_2 < w_1 + w_2$. These assumptions make up only one of the many cases that can be enumerated. The present case is used for illustrative purposes only, and it is not intended that this case be considered as typical.

What prices should be charged during these three pricing periods? Total energy costs are given by

$$C_o = b_3 Q_3 + (z_1 + z_2)(Q_2 - Q_3)b_2 + z_1(Q_1 - Q_2)b_1$$

and total capital costs are

$$C_k = B_3 Q_3 + B_2(Q_2 - Q_3) + B_1(Q_1 - Q_2).$$

The equation for total welfare then becomes

$$W = \sum_1^3 z_i \int_0^{Qi} P_i dQi - C_o - C_t.$$

Maxmizing W with respect to output then yields:

$$P_1 = b_1 + B_1/z_1 \tag{10}$$

$$P_2 = \frac{(z_1 + z_2)b_2 - z_1 b_1 + B_2 - B_1}{z_2} \tag{11}$$

$$P_3 = \frac{b_3 - (z_1 + z_2)b_2 + B_3 - B_2}{z_3}. \tag{12}$$

When contrasted with equations (7) through (9), these results show that capital costs now appear in the prices for the off-peak periods. This is easily explained in terms of marginal cost. For example, when a user during the third pricing period, denoted by the subscript three, increases his usage, this requires that more base load capacity be added. But an increase in base load capacity to accommodate period three users allows for a substitution of base load for intermediate capacity, which can also be used by users during the first and second pricing periods; thus, the only difference is that $B_3 - B_2$ appears as an addition to capacity costs. Further, there is at least a partial offset to this rise in capital costs, since lower base load operating costs $(z_1 - z_2)b_3$, are substituted for higher intermediate load operating costs $(z_1 + z_2)b_2$. However, we know from equation (3) that the increase in capital costs

$(B_3 - B_2)$ will be exactly offset by the reduction in energy costs $(z_1 + z_2)(b_2 - b_3)$ only if $z_1 + z_2 = w_1 + w_2$. Since $z_1 + z_2 < w_1 + w_2$, then the offset is not complete and P_3 will exceed b_3. The offset will be complete for both off-peak pricing periods if $z_1 = w_1$ and $z_2 = w_2$. In this case, equations (3), (4), and (5) can be appropriately substituted for the z's in equations (11) and (12) to yield $P_2 = b_2$ and $P_3 = b_3$.

The example analyzed above, and shown in Figure 2, is only one of the possible alternative relationships between three supply and pricing periods. However, the following generalizations can be drawn.

1. An off-peak price will have no marginal capital cost component only when the supply and pricing periods are such that: (a) only one kind of generating capacity should be built, e.g., when $z_1 > w_2$, (b) the supply and pricing periods exactly coincide, as in the above case when $z_1 = w_1$, or $z_1 + z_2 = w_1 + w_2$, or (c) an off-peak pricing period is wholly contained within one of the supply periods (e.g., when $z_1 > w_1$ and $z_1 + z_2 < w_1 + w_2$).

2. In all other cases, off-peak prices will contain a marginal capital cost component. In these cases the size of the off-peak price varies inversely with the size of the next highest pricing period(s)—the partial derivatives of P_2 with respect to z_1 and P_3 with respect to $(z_1 + z_2)$ are both negative. This is due to the fact that the energy saving off-set to marginal capital costs varies directly with z_1 (for pricing period two) and $z_1 + z_2$ (for pricing period three) in the example analyzed above.

5. PEAK LOAD PRICING AND THE REGULATED FIRM

Extension of the above analysis to the theory of the regulated firm is reasonably straightforward. I assume that the objective of the regulated firm is to maximize profits (π) subject to a regulatory constraint governing its rate of return on total capital. Formally, the objective is to

$$\text{Maximize: } \pi = TR - C_o - C_k$$
$$\text{subject to: } TR - C_o - C_R = 0,$$

where

$$TR = z_1 P_1 Q_1 + z_2 P_2 Q_2 + z_3 P_3 Q_3$$
$$C_o = b_3 Q_3 + (z_1 + z_2)(Q_2 - Q_3) b_2 + z_1 (Q_1 - Q_2) b_1$$
$$C_k = rk_3(Q_3 + X_3) + rk_2(Q_2 + X_2 - Q_3 - X_3) + rk_1(Q_1 + X_1 - Q_2 - X_2)$$
$$C_R = sk_3(Q_3 + X_3) + sk_2(Q_2 + X_2 - Q_3 - X_3) + sk_1(Q_1 + X_1 - Q_2 - X_2)$$

and

$TR = $ total revenue
$r = $ cost of capital
$X_i = $ excess capacity in units of output, Q_i

TABLE 2

Summary of Peak and Off-Peak Prices for Welfare Maximum, Uncontrained and Regulated Monopoly

	P_1	P_2	P_3
Welfare maximum	$b_1 + B_1/z_1 = MC_1/z_1$	$\dfrac{(z_1 + z_2)b_2 - z_1b_1 + B_2 - B_1}{z_2}$ $= MC_2/z_2$	$\dfrac{b_3 - (z_1 + z_2)b_2 + B_3 - B_2}{z_3}$ $= MC_3/z_3$
Unconstrained monopoly	$\dfrac{MC_1}{z_1(1 + 1/E_1)}$	$\dfrac{MC_2}{z_2(1 + 1/E_2)}$	$\dfrac{MC_3}{z_3(1 + 1/E_3)}$
Regulated monopoly (independent demand)	$\dfrac{MC_1 - B_1}{z_1(1 + 1/E_1)}$	$\dfrac{MC_2 + B_1 - B_2}{z_2(1 + 1/E_2)}$	$\dfrac{MC_3 + B_2 - B_3}{z_3(1 + 1/E_3)}$
Regulated monopoly (interdependent demand)	$\dfrac{MC_1 B_1 - I_1}{z_1(1 + 1/E_1)}$	$\dfrac{MC_2 + B_1 - B_2 - I_2}{z_2(1 + 1/E_2)}$	$\dfrac{MC_3 + B_2 - B_3 - I_3}{z_3(1 + 1/E_3)}$
Where	$I_1 = z_2Q_2\dfrac{\partial P_2}{\partial Q_1} + z_3Q_3\dfrac{\partial P_3}{\partial Q_1}$	$I_2 = z_1Q_1\dfrac{\partial P_1}{\partial Q_2} + z_3Q_3\dfrac{\partial P_3}{\partial Q_2}$	$I_3 = z_1Q_1\dfrac{\partial P_1}{\partial Q_3} + z_2Q_2\dfrac{\partial P_2}{\partial Q_3}$

$s =$ regulated rate of return $(s > r)$

$k_i =$ capital-output ratio for each kind of generating capacity $(B_i = rk_i)$.

This analysis assumes that $z_1 < w_1$, and $z_1 + z_2 < w_1 + w_2$, and is thus comparable to the case analyzed in detail in the previous section. It is also assumed that the firm is able to operate off the production frontier and carry excess generating capacity of each kind (X_i).

Table 2 shows the prices which will be charged during each of the three pricing periods. Here, MC_i is the unannualized marginal cost and E_i is the elasticity of demand in the ith pricing period. The first row repeats the welfare maximizing prices derived in the previous section. The second row shows the prices which would be charged by an unconstrained monopolist. The third row gives the profit maximizing prices which should be charged by the regulated monopoly under the assumption that demand in each pricing period is independent of the demand in the other two periods. The fourth row shows what prices should be charged when these demands are interdependent.

It is useful to contrast these results with those of Bailey and White (BW) who assume that a single capacity serves all users.

1. When demands are independent, BW find that off-peak prices are the same as for an unconstrained monopolist. The results of row three in Table 3 show that both off-peak prices are reduced below those of the unconstrained monopolist. Since constrained profits increase with capacity—whether peak or off-peak—a lowering of off-peak prices allows for an increase in base and/or intermediate load capacity unlike BW's model, which assumes that all capacity is determined only by peak demand. In addition, it can be shown that these off-peak prices will be reduced below the welfare maximizing prices (Table 3, row one) when

$$-E_2 > \frac{MC_2}{B_2 - B_1}$$

and/or

$$-E_3 > \frac{MC_3}{B_3 - B_2}.$$

With the values for capital and energy costs presented in Table 1, these critical values for the elasticity of demand are 0.74 and 0.21, respectively. This would indicate that off-peak prices which are below the welfare maximizing prices are not improbable. This conclusion is modified somewhat when interdependent demands are allowed (Table 2, row four), and where strong substitution relationships among the three pricing periods serve to raise the regulated monopoly's off-peak prices.

2. BW emphasizes that the regulatory constraint results in a lowering of peak price below the unconstrained monopoly level and that peak price might even be lowered below the welfare maximizing level. The result in Table 2 show that BW's results may be obtained in our model. However, since off-peak prices will be lower in our model—and quite possibly below the welfare maximizing level—the necessity for the lowering of peak prices is reduced. It can be shown that, with independent demands, the peak price will be kept above the welfare maximizing level when

$$-E_1 < \frac{b_1 z_1}{B_1} + 1$$

Again, with the capital and energy costs found in Table 1, this critical value for the elasticity of demand is 4.7. In addition, allowing for interdependent demands, strong substitution relationships among the three demand periods serve to further modify the necessity of reducing peak prices by raising the peak price above what it would be with independent demands.

3. Finally, BW emphasizes the possibility of a reversal between peak and off-peak prices. Since our model has shown that off-peak prices will be lower, and peak prices higher, than those obtained with BW's model, the possibility of peak/off-peak price reversals is similarly reduced.

6. CONCLUSION

The traditional theories of peak-load pricing and the regulated firm both assume homogeneous production capacity. The above analysis has demonstrated that when it is optimal to employ capacities with different capital and energy costs, the conclusions of both these theories are modified considerably, and these modifications are particularly relevant to the application of these theories to the electric power industry.

part FIVE
Capital Budgeting

INTRODUCTION

Capital budgeting is a major topic in many managerial economics texts. Capital budgeting procedures and techniques are utilized by companies planning long-term investment projects. It is a process which requires an understanding of the time value of money and, simultaneously, the cost of capital; also, its use assumes one's ability to predict net cash inflows and outflows from a specific investment.

Known also as investment decision making, equipment replacement analysis, and the analysis of capital expenditures, it is concerned with choices among the investment alternatives available to the firm, with the goal of accepting the most profitable alternatives and rejecting the others.

Main parts of capital budgeting include (1) the cost of capital, (2) replacement policy and the estimation of useful life, (3) ranking criteria, and (4) uncertainty. Work on the cost of capital has grown so technical in recent years as to be largely inaccessible on the introductory level. Until the results and controversies associated with the names of Modigliani and Miller are synthesized, they must be ignored here.

In economics, it is not uncommon for wide disparities to exist between theory and practice. Capital budgeting does not differ in this regard. The theory of capital budgeting assumes the existence and application of sophisticated analytical techniques; in practice, executives may ignore results of the analysis. James C. T. Mao surveys this condition and suggests ways in which current theory may be modified to make it more operationally useful.

Often an organization goes into debt to finance its needs. In doing so, it uses someone else's money to make money. There is nothing wrong with this practice provided the borrower and the lender agree with the terms of the loan. However, as a firm acquires debt, its capacity to assume new debt changes, as does its cost of capital. In a classic presentation of corporate debt policy, Gordon Donaldson explains how to make better debt-equity decisions.

Joel Dean's article is concerned with the extension of capital budgeting into the field of advertising. It argues that so long as responses to advertising occur with a delay, advertising expenditures are a form of capital investment and should be treated as such.

Federal guarantees to the Chrysler Corporation are newsworthy currently. Debate centers on whether to bail out the ailing automobile company or let it fail. Critics argue the corporation will fail even if it receives federal financial aid. A somewhat similar problem arose in 1971. At that time, Lockheed sought federal loans which were to be based on the economic merit of the firm's L-1011 Tri-Star program. U. E. Reinhardt reveals a method of analysis by which the U.S. Congress could have determined the merits of Lockheed's request. The same methodology could be used to analyze the break-even point of all major investments being considered by private or public sector organizations.

18. Survey of Capital Budgeting: Theory and Practice*

JAMES C. T. MAO

I. INTRODUCTION

There exists a wide disparity between the theory and practice of capital budgeting. During the past 15 years, the theory of capital budgeting has been characterized by the increased application of such analytical techniques as utility analysis, mathematical programming, probability, and statistical theory. The practice of capital budgeting has no doubt changed at the same time, but business executives do not appear to have adopted many of the new techniques. The purpose of this paper is to compare current theory with practice: (1) to discuss the nature of the gap and the reason for its existence, and (2) to try to lessen this disparity by suggesting ways of modifying theory to make it more operationally meaningful. To aid discussion, this paper is divided into four sections: objective of financial management, risk analysis in investment decisions, profitability criteria for investment selection, and conclusions.

It is difficult, if not impossible, to characterize the current theory of capital budgeting in a few words. By current theory, I shall mean the type of work on capital budgeting that appears in journals such as *Management Science, Journal of Finance, Journal of Financial and Quantitative Analysis,* and *Engineering Economist.* These theories generally make use of modern quantitative tools. By current practice, I shall present the findings of case studies I conducted during the summer of 1969. In all, I interviewed eight medium and large companies in the following industries: electronics, aerospace, petroleum, household equipment, and office equipment. I held full-day discussions in each company interviewed. Because of the small sample I do not wish to put forward any statistical generalizations about current practice. However, since the companies studied were chosen for the efficiency of their management, they do give a preliminary view of current capital budgeting practices in firms with progressive management.

_____
*_Journal of Finance,_ vol. 25, no. 2 (May 1970) pp. 349–60.

II. OBJECTIVE OF FINANCIAL MANAGEMENT

Theory

Any theory of optimal investment decisions is premised on the existence of an objective function which the firm maximizes. Current financial theory generally assumes that the firm should maximize the market value of its common shares. There is a growing body of literature that explains how share values are determined under conditions of uncertainty. For example, according to John Lintner, a perfect capital market with homogeneous investor expectations, the risk of a security in a portfolio is measured by the weighted average of the variance of its return and the covariances between its return and other returns. The price of a share, then, is a function of its expected earnings, the pure rate of interest, the price of risk, and risk measured in this way.

Before discussing what financial executives regard as their objective, let us examine the objective of maximizing share value from an operational viewpoint. In order to implement this objective, the financial executive needs criteria for choosing between alternative time patterns of share prices within his planning horizon. Current theory does not provide this. Of course, this issue will not arise under conditions of certainty and perfect capital market, since the action which maximizes share value at the end of the firm's horizon also maximizes share prices throughout the horizon. (See figure 1A.) Since curve I dominates curve II,

FIGURE 1

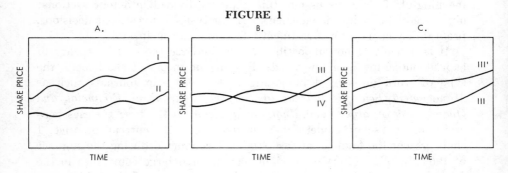

it is clearly preferable. However, under conditions of uncertainty and imperfect capital market, the relative share prices at the end of the horizon do not necessarily determine the relationship between the prices during the time span. Two possible courses of action could thus easily result in time patterns of share prices with multiple crossings. (See figure 1B). In the latter case, the objective of maximizing share value has no operational meaning until there are criteria for choosing between crisscrossing price patterns. To make this choice, we may wish to consider the duration for which one pattern exceeds the other, as well as the timing and size of the difference. One formula which incorporates these considerations is the following:

$$\phi = \int_0^T (P_t - P_t')e^{-rt}\, dt \tag{1}$$

where P_t and P_t' stand for share prices as depicted by curves III and IV respectively, r stands for the rate of discount, and T stands for the time horizon. A simple rule would be to choose time pattern III if $\phi \geq 0$, and to select time pattern IV otherwise. It should be noted that this problem is quite similar to choosing between criss-crossing loss functions in decision theory, and perhaps some of its criteria could be used to choose alternatives here.

Let us suppose that time pattern III is preferred. How is it possible to improve curve III further so that the share price will be raised at every point along the time pattern? (See figure 1C.) To put it differently, if there is an earnings per share (eps) series that corresponds to price pattern III, how should the eps series be modified to raise share prices from curve III to curve III'? B. G. Malkiel has shown that under conditions of certainty the price-earnings ratio of any stock is equal to the price-earnings ratio of a standard reference stock, adjusted for the difference in growth rates and the duration of this difference. Although he applied his model to conditions of uncertainty, the complexities involved prevented him from constructing a full uncertainty model. Here, we shall make a simple extension of Malkiel's certainty model by introducing the risk factor. Risk is to be measured by the standard deviation to the eps series, calculated with regard to its trend. An eps series with a higher trend and less risk would result in a uniformly higher price.

To illustrate how this risk measure can be implemented, let us say that eps at any time t, denoted as $x(t)$, is the sum of three components:

$$x(t) = a + bt + c \sum_{h \in H} \sin \frac{t}{h} + u \tag{2}$$

where a, b, c are constants, h is an element of a set of incommensurate real numbers and t stands for time. Component $a + bt$ is the trend, component $\sum_{h \in H} \sin \dfrac{t}{h}$ is the sum of a set of sine functions with incommensurate periods, which results in nonperiodic oscillations; and component u is the source of random fluctuations. If we denote $x^*(t)$ as the trend value of $x(t)$, then our risk measure, the standard deviation about the trend, is given by the formula:

$$\sigma = \left\{ \frac{1}{N} \sum [x(t) - x^*(t)]^2 \right\}^{1/2} \tag{3}$$

where N stands for the number of observations. It should be noted that the concept of risk presented here is the risk of a security considered by itself. This risk concept needs to be modified if investors have sufficient resources to diversify their portfolios. In that case, the distinction made by some financial writers between diversifiable and nondiversifiable risks is relevant. It is the nondiversifiable component that determines the risk of a security in a portfolio context.

Practice

The executives interviewed were asked what they regarded as the objective of financial management. More specifically, they were asked whether they chose between alternative courses of action so as to maximize the value of the firm. Here is a sample of the answers given:

Our objective is to finance the high growth rate of this company. Since we do not use debt, we have to make sure that we earn enough profit to finance the growth. It may be that share value is maximized as well, but we don't think about that.

We have a goal of earnings per share which we manage astutely every quarter. Because this is a young, growing company, it is important in terms of future financing that we do not disappoint the investing public.

The thing that means the most to the stockholder is the value of their stock. In determining the value of stock, the most critical factor is probably the earnings per share, but it also involves the fact that you are not static but moving forward and increasing your earnings per share. To increase earnings, you have to have sales growth which is the life blood of any business.

The goal of the financial manager is to have his company produce a record that will enable it to raise capital at the lowest possible cost. To accomplish this goal, he needs a proper concept of stability and a proper concept of growth. In this company, we try to achieve a growth rate of 15 to 18 percent, compounded annually, in both sales and earnings.

Although most of the comments are self-explanatory, three points should be noted. First, while some executives did not explicitly state that the maximization of the value of the firm was their goal, this reason was implicit in all their answers. Since the management is operationally oriented, the goal of maximizing share value is translated into operating targets of growth and stability in the earnings stream. Second, the executives tend to view the value of their company independently of the effect of diversification by the investing public. From a practical standpoint, this approach has the advantage of being simple. Theoretically, this approach to valuation is adequate if the nondiversifiable risk represents a substantially large proportion of the total risk. Third, if the maximization of share value depends upon consistent growth, then it becomes vital for executives to have a constant flow of new ideas.

Although the executives may search continually for new ideas, financial theorists have not contributed much to understanding how new ideas can be generated.

III. RISK ANALYSIS IN INVESTMENT DECISIONS

Concept of Risk

Theory. A central aspect of any theory of capital budgeting is the concept of risk. Most financial writers argue that firms should choose portfolios rather than projects, and they measure the risk of a portfolio by the variance of its return.[1] This approach to the analysis of risk is a straightforward adaptation of Markowitz's quadratic programming model of portfolio selection. Although the variance is easy to manipulate mathematically, financial writers have not been completely satisfied with the concept of risk. In fact, Markowitz himself had reservations about choosing variance as a measure of risk. Beside variance, he considered five other alternative measures of risk: the expected value of loss; the probability of loss; the expected absolute deviation; the maximum expected loss; and the semi-variance. The first four measures were rejected for one reason or another as unsuitable. For the remaining two measures, variance and semi-variance, Markowitz preferred the latter for theoretical reasons, but chose the former because of its familiarity and ease of computation.

Why is semi-variance a better measure of risk than ordinary variance? Consider investment return, R, as a random variable with known probability distribution. If h stands for a critical value against which the actual values of R are compared, and $(R - h)^-$ if $(R - h) \leq 0$ and for zero if $(R - h) > 0$, then S_h (semi-variance with h as the reference point) is given by the formula:

$$S_h = E[(R - h)^-]^2 \tag{4}$$

where E is the expectation operator. In words, semi-variance is the expected value of the squared negative deviations of the possible outcomes from an arbitrarily chosen point of reference. In contrast, variance is the expected value of the squared deviations (whether positive or negative) of the possible outcomes from the mean of the random variable. This means that semi-variance evaluates the risks associated with different distributions by reference to a fixed point which is designated by the investor. The variance measure introduces no such refinement, but uses the means of the distributions, which may vary widely, to make the

---

[1] Return could refer to either internal rate of return, net present value, payback period, or some other measure. We are purposefully leaving the term "return" undefined, so that we can proceed with the discussion of risk.

judgments. Also, in computing semi-variance, positive and negative deviations contribute differently to risk, whereas in computing variance, a positive and a negative deviation of the same magnitude contribute equally to risk. In essence, then, since capital has an opportunity cost, the risk of an investment decision is measured primarily by the prospect of failure to earn the return foregone. Semi-variance is more consistent with this concept of investment risk than ordinary variance.

Practice.   The business executives interviewed were asked what they understood by the term "investment risk":

Risk is the prospect of not meeting the target rate of return. That is the risk, isn't it? If you are one hundred percent sure of making the target return, then it is a zero risk proposition.

Risk is financial in nature. It is primarily concerned with downside deviations from the target rate of return. However, if there is a good chance of coming out better than you forecast, that is negative risk (a sweetener) which is taken into account in determining the security of an investment.

There are three things that concern me in evaluating the risk of an investment: the chances of losses exceeding a certain percent of my total equity, the chances of earning the required rate of return, and the chances of breaking even on a cash flow basis. Cash break-even is kind of a survival point. [The investment decisions in this company are few, but large in size.]

There are some projects in the company which I don't think are going to pay off, and I disagree with the fellows who are running the show. These projects are the risky investments. Also, I never worry about the project return going above the target return. Risk is what might happen when the return is going to be less.

These statements give rise to two observations. First, when the investment decision involves only a small portion of the resources of the company, risk is primarily considered to be the prospect of not meeting some target rate of return. However, when the investment concerns a large proportion of the company's resources, risk also involves the danger of insolvency. Second, the executives' emphasis on downside risk indicates that their concept of risk is better described by semi-variance than by ordinary variance.

To verify further the empirical relevance of semi-variance as a risk measure, a test was designed in which the business executives were asked to choose between two hypothetical distributions of investment returns. Each investment is assumed to cost x dollars now, and after one year to return the cost of x dollars plus the profit (or loss) as given by the probability distributions in figure 2. In this figure, each asterisk represents one possible investment outcome, and hence distribution A has a mean of 3, variance of 4 and a semivariance of 1, whereas distribution B has a mean of 3, variance of 4, and a semi-variance of zero.[2] For this test, it

---

[2] For this example, the critical value h in the definition of semi-variance is taken to be zero.

FIGURE 2

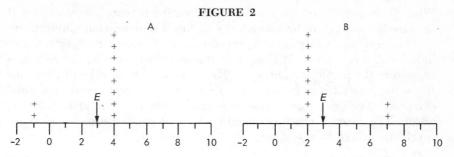

is necessary to use a cost figure that the executive is familiar with, and which produces a rate of return that is reasonably close to his target rate of return as to call for considerable deliberation before arriving at a decision. Although both the target rate of return and the assumed cost of investment varied from company to company, for the sake of discussion we shall assume this cost to be $100,000 and the target rate of return 20 percent. The executives were asked to assume a position of capital rationing in which they had to choose either A or B. About one third of the executives chose A, another third chose B, and the remaining third indicated that their choice would depend on circumstances.

The reasons given for the decisions vary from company to company, but the following quotes summarize the major viewpoints:

Why do I pick A? Well, I am going to earn a profit of 4 in eight out of ten times and suffer a loss of 1 in the other times. Sure, the investment is risky, but that is part of the game. I would be very much surprised that anyone in our industry wouldn't pick A because we face this kind of risk all the time.

Because of the current tight money situation, I am worried about capital replacement in the event of loss. If we were in a period when capital could be easily replaced at a reasonable cost, then I would have an enhanced willingness to take on risky investments. In any case, I would never pick A unless I could get a reasonable repetition of the projects to enable the averages to come home.

Our present portfolio has a sufficient number of high risk-high return projects in it, so I would probably select B. But at another point in time I might look at those projects in terms of the portfolio aspect and pick A.

Project B has an 80 percent chance of returning 20 percent on my investment. Since my target return is 20 percent, I would probably play safe and accept B. Also, I prefer B because I have seen more heads roll as a result of negative returns.

Executives seemed more likely to choose A if their businesses accustomed them to that degree of risk, if they personally preferred risky ventures, and if they could control the loss possibility in A through diversification.

When these conditions are absent, the executive is more likely to pick B because the absence of loss possibility makes it a more secure investment.

The previous analysis was concerned with a choice between two individual investments. It is equally important to examine the risk concept from the portfolio viewpoint. The executives were asked to imagine the same alternatives on a larger scale, where x represented the total company investment, and questioned as to which portfolio they would select. The answer was unanimously B, and their reasons were most succinctly voiced by the statement of one executive:

> The key is survival. We will take a chance on evaluating individual projects rather optimistically, but we will not take a chance on the main company. One of our obligations is to sustain this company in life and every time we put it in a minus position, it dies a little bit if not in total.

This evidence is consistent with semi-variance as a concept of risk. If semi-variance is used by the business executives, there is a possibility that it may also be the risk concept used by security investors. If so, the definition of the risk of individual securities within a portfolio needs to be adjusted, with corresponding alterations to the existing theory of share valuation under uncertainty.

Method of Incorporating Risk

Theory. For the present, let us accept variance as a measure of risk. How does current theory incorporate risk into investment analysis such that, given two investments with different returns and different risks, the factors can be adjusted to reach a single figure with which to compare the investments? Two methods can be distinguished: the certainty equivalent approach and the risk-adjusted discount rate approach. When the method of certainty equivalent is used, the value of an investment is calculated by discounting the random cash flows at the pure rate of interest. The resulting expected value and variance are converted into their certainty equivalent with the risk eliminated. This certainty equivalent figure determines the profitability of the investment. Under the method of risk-adjusted discount rate, the value of an investment is calculated by discounting the expected cash flow at a rate that allows for the time value of money and also for the risk present in the cash flow. The investment is profitable if the resulting value is positive.

Whichever approach is used, the investor must also decide between the single project or the portfolio framework of investment selection. This distinction can be illustrated most easily by using the certainty equivalent approach to risk analysis. In current theory, the single project approach is justified if the firm contemplates only one investment during its planning horizon. A good example of this analysis is the work of Frederick

S. Hillier who derived formulas for calculating the expected value and variance of NPV from the cash flow distributions associated with an investment. However, when more than one investment may be taken, the firm's optimal selection of investments must be based on an examination of all possible combinations of investments, rather than the examination of single investments. When the portfolio approach is used, the model is generally an adaptation of the Markowitz portfolio selection model with 0–1 conditions imposed on the decision variables to reflect project indivisibility. A different model which also employs the portfolio approach is the chance-constrained model of R. Byrne, A. Charnes, W. W. Cooper, and K. Kortanek in which they imposed a probabilistic payback constraint over all investments simultaneously. The objective is to pick those projects which satisfy the constraints while maximizing expected net present value.

Practice. The executives' method of incorporating risk is primarily the risk-adjusted discount rate approach. In all companies interviewed, although the executives talked about the concept of probability, none used an explicit probabilistic framework for investment analysis. The operating division proposing a project has the responsibility of forecasting the incremental cash flows associated with the investment. In some companies, three sets of figures are forecast: optimistic, pessimistic, and most likely. The optimistic and pessimistic figures denote the range of possibilities. The "most likely" figure does not mean the mode: it is a conservative estimate which the executives consider as having a probability of about .75 of being attained or exceeded. In fact, one executive requires a minimum probability of .80 from his staff.

In most instances, the chief financial executive will receive the analysis of an investment based upon the most likely figure, and containing all the underlying assumptions. The executives were questioned as to what particular aspects of a report were most instrumental in their decisions:

The project justification may run into volumes, but I am still going to ask my project manager one question: Why do you believe we can get a 5, or 10, or 15 percent share of the market against our competition. If he sells me on this and on the accuracy of his cost estimate, then it is a worthwhile risk venture.

Before committing myself, I ask what else can we use the investments for, if things should go wrong. A project may have a fast payout, but it is not a good investment if we can't hedge our risk of failure.

Sometimes I make a decision truly on the basis that I have enthusiastic support from the people that are going to implement it. I also look at their track record.

In essence, the executive is trying to check the accuracy of the most likely figure. He is modifying the projected outcome by considering the human factor and by introducing a contingency plan. His dilemma is the uncertain nature of his forecasts. The real difficulty is the search for a reliable probability distribution of cash flows to base the decision upon. Thus, if a theorist begins his analysis with an assumed probability distribution, he has assumed away one critical aspect of the problem involved.

Next, although the firms do use the portfolio approach to investment, the method of implementation and the reasons for its use differ from current theory. Current theory visualizes the investor in a portfolio framework as follows. He obtains the cash flows for the set of investments, and derives from them the means, variances, and covariances of the returns. He then chooses that portfolio of investments which gives the best combination of risk and return. But in reality, since these project analyses are submitted independently by separate divisions, no allowance is made in the risk assessment for the covariances between projects. In other words, the proposals top management receive do not contain the figures necessary for evaluating project risks on a portfolio basis in the manner presented by current theory.

The executives were asked how they introduced the portfolio approach in their investment decisions, and more specifically what was the objective and method of diversification. Diversification is thought of in terms of major activities, not with regard to every piece of capital expenditure. In practice, this involves a long-range plan (usually five years) which sets out broad guidelines for the operating divisions. The plan may call for changing, or adhering to the emphasis placed on existing activities, or for incorporating brand new ideas or products. This is where critical decisions regarding diversification are made. In formulating this plan, the executives group the many activities of the company into larger, global areas of concern, not into particular, isolated investments. Details of variances and covariances are generally left in the background. Theoretically, diversification is concerned with stabilizing the earnings stream; but, in practice, the executive is often more concerned with growth.

IV. CRITERIA FOR INVESTMENT SELECTION

Theory. In the above discussion of return and risk, we purposefully used the term "return" in its generic sense, without defining it as internal rate of return (IRR), net present value (NPV), payback period, or accounting profit, so that we could focus on the concept of risk. Current theory generally regards IRR, or its equivalent NPV, as a better measure of return than either the payback period or the accounting profit. The reason for this preference is that under conditions of certainty, of two investments of equal size, the one which has a higher IRR results in higher value for the firm. This preference has been carried over to conditions of uncertainty without sufficient critical analysis. Both the payback period and accounting profit have been regarded as inferior, because at best they can only be used to approximate the IRR. However, since the payback period is usually justified as a method of incorporating risk, a much more pertinent criticism is the limited applicability of the payback period as a method of risk analysis. Also, since reported earnings do affect share prices, investment decisions must consider the effect on accounting profit, if the goal is to maximize share values.

Although theorists have advocated IRR and NPV for measuring return, they are aware that the majority of business still use the payback period and/or the accounting profit criterion. Two reasons have been advanced to explain the relatively slow acceptance of the IRR and NPV criteria. One explanation focuses on the failure of IRR and NPV criteria to consider the effect of an investment on reported earnings. Thus, in choosing between two investments, the application of the IRR (or NPV) criterion may result in the acceptance of those investments which have a higher level of earnings, but which also produce an erratic eps pattern. Since the price-earnings ratio tends to vary inversely with the stability of earnings, the strict application of IRR criterion does not guarantee the maximum value for the firm. The other approach shows how the payback period can incorporate factors which the IRR does not pay full attention to. In their paper, Byrne, Charnes, Cooper, and Kortanek attempted to explain the common use of the payback period as a way of minimizing the risk of lost opportunities. More recently, H. Martin Weingartner tries to explain the payback method as a measure of the "liquidity" of an asset and as a simple device for "the resolution of uncertainty." In the next subsection, we shall look at the practice to determine which measure is actually used and why.

Practice. Of the eight companies questioned about investment criterion, two make primary use of the IRR, four use IRR together with accounting profit and payback, and two use accounting profit, payback, and an "exposure index," which measures the probability that the maximum investment loss will exceed a specified percentage of the firm's total equity. The two companies using primarily IRR are growth companies with closely held stock which finance growth through internal generation of funds, and whose typical investments are small in relation to the total resources of the firm. The four companies which use IRR together with accounting profit and payback are publicly held companies which rely heavily on external sources to finance growth, and whose businesses are fairly risky and competitive. The remaining two companies are similar to the above four in terms of stock ownership and in their reliance on outside capital. However, they differ in one major aspect. Their investments are more risky because of strong industry competition and because of their few, but large, investments.

These findings suggest that the payback period is primarily a risk measure. Accounting profit, since this is what the financial community focuses on, is especially important if the company is widely held and relies on external sources of financing. IRR is most likely to be the major criterion in closely held firms which are less worried by erratic patterns in their per share earnings, which finance themselves, and which make many small investments so that the risk in any one investment is not critical.

V. CONCLUSIONS

In making these case studies, I have focused on the essential points of disparity between the theory and practice of capital budgeting. The evidence suggests that there are at least six ways in which current theory can be modified to make it more operationally meaningful:

1.   If we accept the objective of investment decisions to be maximizing the value of the firm, then we must provide the financial executive with a criterion for choosing between criss-crossing time patterns of share prices. The choice criteria in decision theory may be relevant to this analysis.

2.   Current theory generally explains the equilibrium value of a firm in a static model. However, the financial executives need a dynamic model which explains how investors appraise eps series which exhibit different patterns over time.

3.   Variance is the generally accepted measure of investment risk in current capital budgeting theory. There are theoretical reasons for preferring semi-variance and the evidence is more consistent with semi-variance than variance.

4.   Accurate estimates of cash flows are crucial to the investment decision process. To date, theorists have emphasized the analysis of investments with assumed cash flow distributions. Theorists can contribute even more by developing concepts and techniques which will enable the executives to make more reliable cash flow forecasts.

5.   Current theory views diversification as a means to stabilize earnings. In fact, the executive may be more concerned with the objective of stable growth. More emphasis by theorists on ways to search for new and profitable growth opportunities seem appropriate.

6.   While theorists recommened the IRR (or NPV) criterion of investment appraisal, this study confirms the prevalence of the payback period and the accounting profit criteria in practice. The theorists must identify the reason why financial executives prefer these alternative criteria and modify the IRR (or NPV) method to make it more generally applicable.

19. New Framework for Corporate Debt Policy[*]

GORDON DONALDSON

Why are many common rules of thumb for evaluating a company's debt capacity misleading and even dangerous?

Why is outside experience and advice of limited value as a guide to top management's thinking about debt capacity?

What approach will enable management to make an independent and realistic appraisal of risk on the basis of data with which it is already familiar and in terms of judgments to which it has long been accustomed?

The problem of deciding whether it is wise and proper for a business corporation to finance long-term capital needs through debt, and, if so, how far it is safe to go, is one which most boards of directors have wrestled with at one time or another. For many companies the debt-capacity decision is of critical importance because of its potential impact on margins of profitability and on solvency. For *all* companies, however large and financially sound they may be, the decision is one to be approached with great care. Yet, in spite of its importance, the subject of corporate debt policy has received surprisingly little attention in the literature of business management in recent years. One might infer from this either that business has already developed a reliable means of resolving the question or that progress toward a more adequate solution has been slow.

In my opinion, the latter inference is closer to the truth. The debt-equity choice is still a relatively crude art as practiced by a great many corporate borrowers. It follows that there is a real opportunity for useful refinement in the decision-making process. However, there is little evidence, at present, of serious dissatisfaction with conventional decision rules on the part of those responsible for making this decision. Over the past three years I have been engaged in sampling executive opinions on debt policy, and I have found little indication of the same kind of ferment as is going on with regard to capital budgeting decisions.

The primary purpose of this article, therefore, is to stimulate dissatis-

[*] *Harvard Business Review,* vol. 56, no. 5 (September–October 1978), pp. 149–64.

faction with present-day conventions regarding debt capacity and to suggest the direction in which the opportunity for improvement lies. I intend to show that the widely used rules of thumb which evaluate debt capacity in terms of some percentage of balance sheet values or in terms of income statement ratios can be seriously misleading and even dangerous to corporate solvency. I also intend to develop the argument that debt policy in general and debt capacity in particular cannot be prescribed for the individual company by outsiders or by generalized standards; rather, they can and should be determined by management in terms of individual corporate circumstances and objectives and on the basis of the observed behavior of patterns of cash flow.

The question of corporate debt capacity may be looked at from several points of view—for example, the management of the business concerned, its shareholders or potential shareholders, and, of course, the lender of the debt capital. Because each of these groups may, quite properly, have a different concept of the wise and proper limit on debt, let me clarify the point of view taken in this article. I intend to discuss the subject from the standpoint of the management of the borrowing corporation, assuming that the board of directors which will make the final decision has the customary mandate from the stockholders to act on all matters concerning the safety and profitability of their investment.

For the reader who ordinarily looks at this problem as a lender, potential stockholder, or investment adviser, the analysis described in this article may appear at first sight to have limited application. It is hoped, however, that the underlying concepts will be recognized as valid regardless of how one looks at the problem, and they may suggest directions for improvement in the external as well as the internal analysis of the risk of debt.

NATURE OF THE RISKS

In order to set a background for discussing possible improvements, I will first describe briefly certain aspects of conventional practice concerning present-day decision rules on long-term debt. These observations were recorded as a part of a research study which sampled practice and opinion in a group of relatively large and mature manufacturing corporations. The nature of this sample must be kept in mind when interpreting the practices described.

Hazards of Too Much Debt

The nature of the incentive to borrow as an alternative to financing through a new issue of stock is common knowledge. Debt capital in the amounts normally approved by established financial institutions is a comparatively cheap source of funds. Whether it is considered the cheapest source depends on whether retained earnings are regarded as "cost free" or not. In any case, for most companies it is easy to demonstrate that, assuming normal profitability, the combination of moderate interest rates and high levels of corporate income tax enable debt capital to produce significantly better earnings per share than would a comparable amount of capital provided by an issue of either common or preferred stock. In fact, the advantage is so obvious that few companies bother to make the calculation when considering these alternatives.

Under these circumstances it is apparent that there must be a powerful deterrent which keeps businesses from using this source to the limits of availability. The primary deterrent is, of course, the risks which are inevitably associated with long-term debt servicing. While it is something of an oversimplification to say that the debt decision is a balancing of higher prospective income to the shareholders against greater chance of loss, it is certainly true that this is the heart of the problem.

When the word *risk* is applied to debt, it may refer to a variety of potential penalties; the precise meaning is not always clear when this subject is discussed. To most people, however, risk—so far as debt is concerned—is the chance of running out of cash. This risk is inevitably increased by a legal contract requiring the business to pay fixed sums of cash at predetermined dates in the future regardless of the financial condition at that time. There are, of course, a great many needs for cash —dividends, capital expenditures, research projects, and so on—with respect to which cash balances may prove inadequate at some future point.

Too Little Cash

The ultimate hazard of running out of cash, however, and the one which lurks in the background of every debt decision, is the situation where cash is so reduced that legal contracts are defaulted, bankruptcy occurs, and normal operations cease. Since no private enterprise has a guaranteed cash inflow, there must always be *some* risk, however remote, that this event could occur. Consequently, any addition to mandatory cash outflows resulting from new debt or any other act or event must increase that risk. I have chosen to use the term *cash inadequacy* to refer to a whole family of problems involving the inability to make cash payments for any purpose important to the long-term financial health of the business; cash insolvency is the extreme case of cash inadequacy. It should be emphasized that although debt necessarily increases the chances of cash inadequacy, this risk exists whether the company has any debt or not, so that the debt-equity choice is not between some risk and no risk, but between more and less.

CONVENTIONAL APPROACHES

Observation of present-day business practice suggests that business-men commonly draw their concepts of debt capacity from one or more of several sources. Thus, they sometimes—

1. *Seek the counsel of institutional lenders or financial intermediaries* (*such as investment bankers*): Most corporate borrowers negotiate long-term debt contracts at infrequent intervals, while the lender and the investment banker are constantly involved in loan decisions and so, presumably, have a great deal more experience and better judgment. Further, it is apparent that unless the lender is satisfied on the question of risk, there will be no loan. Finally, banks and insurance companies have a well-established reputation for being conservative, and conservative borrowers will take comfort from the fact that if the lender errs, it will likely be on the safe side.

2. *See what comparable companies are doing in this area of financial management:* Every business has an idea of those other companies in or out of the industry which are most like themselves so far as factors affecting risk are concerned. Since this is an aspect of corporate policy which is public information, it is natural that the debt-equity ratios of competitors will be carefully considered, and, lacking more objective guides, there will be a tendency to follow the mode and reject the extremes. This approach has an added practical appeal; group norms are important in the capital market's appraisal of a company's financial strength. If a company is out of line, it may be penalized—even though the deviation from the average may be perfectly appropriate for this company.

3. *Follow the practices of the past:* There is a very natural tendency to respect the corporation's financial traditions, and this is often apparent with regard to debt policy. Many businesses take considerable pride in "a clean balance sheet," an *Aa* rating, or a history of borrowing at the prime rate. It would border on sacrilege to propose a departure which would jeopardize these cherished symbols of financial achievement and respectability! The fact that these standards have apparently preserved corporate solvency in the past is a powerful argument for continuing them, particularly if the implications of a change cannot be precisely defined.

4. *Refer to that very elusive authority called "general practice," "industry practice," "common knowledge," or, less respectfully, "financial folklore":* Remarkable as it seems in view of the great diversity among companies classified as industrials, there is widespread acceptance of the belief that an appropriate limit to the long-term borrowing of industrial companies is 30 percent of capitalization (or, alternatively, one third).

The origin of, or rationale for, this particular decision rule has been obscured by the passage of time, but there is no doubt that it has become a widely honored rule of thumb in the decisions of both borrowers and lenders.

Fallacy of Double Standard

Without denying the practical significance of some of the considerations which have led businessmen to follow these guides in formulating debt policy, it must be recognized that there are serious limitations inherent in using them (separately or as a group) as the *only* guides to appropriate debt capacity.

First, consider the practice of accepting advice from the lender. As the lender views the individual loan contract, it is one of a large number of investments which make up a constantly changing portfolio. When negotiated it is only one of a stream of loan proposals which must be acted on promptly and appraised in terms of the limited information to which generalized standards are applied. The nature of the risk to the lender is necessarily influenced by the fact that this loan is only a small fraction of the total sum invested and that intelligent diversification goes a long way to softening the impact of individual default. Further, even when default occurs, all may not be lost; in time the loan may be "worked out" through reorganization or liquidation.

All this is small comfort to the borrower. The individual loan which goes sour—if it happens to be *his* loan—is a catastrophe. There are few businessmen who can take a lighthearted attitude toward the prospect of default on a legal contract with the associated threat of bankruptcy. To most, this is viewed as the end of the road. Also, it is important to recognize that while the lender need only be concerned about servicing his own (high priority) claims, the borrower must also consider the needs which go unsatisfied during the period prior to the time of actual default when debt servicing drains off precious cash reserves.

This is not to imply that the lender is insensitive to individual losses and their effect on the business concerned; but it does mean that risk to the lender is not the same thing as risk to the borrower, and, consequently, the standards of one are not necessarily appropriate for the other. The lender's standards can at times be too liberal—as well as too conservative —from the borrower's point of view.

Some will argue that, as a practical matter, the borrower must accept the debt-capacity standards of the lender, else there will be no contract. However, this implies that there is no bargaining over the upper limit of the amount that will be supplied, no differences among lenders, and/or no shopping around by borrowers. While all institutional lenders do have absolute limits on the risks they will take (even at a premium interest rate), there is often some room for negotiation if the borrower is so disposed. Under some circumstances there may be valid reasons for probing the upper limits of the lender's willingness to lend.

Lessons of Experience

The second source of guidance mentioned is the observed practices of comparable businesses. This, too, has its obvious limitations. Even assuming strict comparability—which is hard to establish—there is no proof that the companies concerned have arrived at their current debt proportions in a deliberate and rational manner. In view of the wide variations in debt policy within any industry group, there can be little real meaning in an industry average. And what happens if every member of the group looks to the other for guidance? The most that can be said for this approach to debt policy is that the company concerned can avoid the appearance of being atypical in the investment market so far as its capital structure is concerned. But, as in most areas of business, there is a *range* of acceptable behavior, and the skill of management comes in identifying and taking advantage of the limits to which it can go without raising too many eyebrows.

Even a company's own direct experience with debt financing has its limitations as a guide to debt capacity. At best, the evidence that a particular debt policy has not been a cause of financial embarrassment in the past may only prove that the policy was on the conservative side. However, if assurance of adequate conservatism is the primary goal, the only really satisfactory policy is a no-debt policy.

For companies with some debt the experience of past periods of business recession is only partial evidence of the protection a particular policy affords. In most industries, the period of the past 20 years has produced a maximum of four or five periods of decline in sales and earnings. This limited recession experience with the behavior of cash flows—the critical consideration where debt servicing is involved—can be misleading since cash flows are affected by a variety of factors and the actual experience in any single recession is a somewhat unique combination of events which may not recur in the future. Thus, the so-called test of experience cannot be taken at face value.

Inescapable Responsibility

In summing up a criticism of the sources from which management commonly derives its debt-capacity standard, there are two aspects which must be emphasized. Both of these relate to the practice of relying on the judgment of others in a situation where management alone is best able to appraise the full implications of the problem. The points I have in mind are as follows:

1. In assessing the risks of running out of cash because of excessive fixed cash obligations, the special circumstances of the individual firm are the primary data that the analyst has to work with. Management has obvious advantages over outsiders in using this data because it has free and full access to it, the time and incentive to examine it thoroughly, and a personal stake in making sensible judgments about what it observes. Even the judgments of predecessors in office are judgments made on information which is inadequate when compared to what management now has in its possession—if only because the predecessor's information is now 10 to 20 years old. (Subsequently, we will consider how management may approach an independent appraisal of risk for the individual business.)

2. The measurement of risk is only one dimension of the debt-capacity decision. In a free enterprise society, the assumption of risk is a voluntary activity, and no one can properly define the level of risk which another should be willing to bear. The decision to limit debt to 10 percent, 30 percent, or any other percentage of the capital structure reflects (or should reflect) both the magnitude of the risk involved in servicing that amount of debt *and* the willingness of those who bear this risk—the owners or their duly authorized representatives—to accept the hazards involved.

In the last analysis, this is a subjective decision which management alone can make. Indeed, it may be said that corporation has defined its debt policy long before a particular financing decision comes to a vote; it has done this in its choice of the men who are to make the decision. The ensuing decisions involving financial risk will reflect their basic attitudes —whether they see a situation as an opportunity to be exploited or a threat to be minimized.

A most interesting and fundamental question comes up here—one that underlies the whole relationship between management and the shareholder; namely, does management determine the attitude toward risk bearing which the stockholders must then adopt, or vice versa? This is part of the broader question of whether management should choose those financial policies which it prefers and attract a like-minded stockholder group (taking the "if they don't like it, they can sell out" approach) or by some means or other determine the attitudes and objectives of its present stockholder group and attempt to translate these into the appropriate action.

I do not propose to pass judgment on this difficult problem in the context of this article. The fact is, by taking one approach or the other—or some blend—management *does* make these decisions. With respect to risk bearing, however, one point is clear: responsible management should not be dealing with the problem in terms of purely personal risk preferences. I suspect that many top executives have not given this aspect the attention it deserves.

Reasons for Current Practice

Having considered the case for a debt policy which is internally rather than externally generated, we may well ask why so many companies, in deciding how far to go in using OPM (other people's money), lean so heavily on OPA (other people's advice). The answer appears to be three-fold:

1. A misunderstanding of the nature of the problem and, in particular, a failure to separate the subjective from the objective elements.
2. The inherent complexity of the objective side—the measurement of risk.
3. The serious inadequacy of conventional debt-capacity decision rules as a framework for independent appraisal.

It is obvious that if a business does not have a useful way of assessing the general magnitude of the risks of too much debt in terms of its individual company and industry circumstances, then it will do one of two things. Either it will fall back on generalized (external) concepts of risk for "comparable" companies, or it will make the decision on purely subjective grounds—on how the management "feels" about debt.

Thus, in practice, an internally generated debt-capacity decision is often based almost entirely on the management's general attitude toward this kind of problem without regard for how much risk is actually involved and what the potential rewards and penalties from risk bearing happen to be in the specific situation. The most obvious examples are to be found in companies at the extremes of debt policy that follow such rules as "no debt under any circumstances" or "borrow the maximum available." (We must be careful, however, not to assume that if a company has one or another of these policies, it is acting irrationally or emotionally.)

One of the subjects about which we know very little at present is how individual and group attitudes toward risk bearing are formed in practice. It is apparent, however, that there are important differences in this respect among members of any given management team and even for an individual executive with regard to different dimensions of risk within the business. The risk of excessive debt often appears to have a special significance; a man who is a "plunger" on sales policy or research might also be an arch-conservative with regard to debt. The risk of default on debt is more directly associated with financial ruin, regardless of the fundamental cause of failure, simply because it is generally the last act in a chain of events which follows from a deteriorating cash position.

There are other bits of evidence which are possible explanations for a Jekyll-and-Hyde behavior on risk bearing in business:

Debt policy is always decided at the very top of the executive structure whereas other policies on sales or production involving other dimensions of risk are shaped to some degree at all executive levels. The seniority of the typical board of directors doubtless has some bearing on the comparative conservatism of financial policy, including debt policy.

There is also some truth in the generalization that financial officers tend to be more conservative than other executives at the same level in other phases of the business, and to the extent that they influence debt policy they may tend to prefer to minimize risk per se, regardless of the potential rewards from risk bearing.

What Is a Sensible Approach?

The foregoing is, however, only speculation in an area where real research is necessary. The point of importance here is that, whatever the reason may be, it is illogical to base an internal decision on debt policy on attitudes toward risk *alone,* just as it is illogical to believe that corporate debt policy can be properly formulated without taking these individual attitudes into account.

For the purposes of a sensible approach to corporate debt policy we need not expect management to have a logical explanation for its feelings toward debt, even though this might be theoretically desirable. It is sufficient that managers know how they feel and are able to react to specific risk alternatives. The problem has been that in many cases they have not known in any objective sense what it was that they were reacting to; they have not had a meaningful measure of the specific risk of running out of cash (with or without any given amount of long-term debt).

It is therefore in the formulation of an approach to the measurement of risk in the individual corporation that the hope for an independent appraisal of debt capacity lies.

INADEQUACY OF CURRENT RULES

Unfortunately, the conventional form for expressing debt-capacity rules is of little or no help in providing the kind of formulation I am urging. Debt capacity is most commonly expressed in terms of the balance sheet relationship between long-term debt and the total of all long-term sources, viz, as some percent of capitalization. A variation of this ratio is often found in debt contracts which limit new long-term borrowing to some percentage of net tangible assets.

The alternative form in which to express the limits of long-term borrowing is in terms of income statement data. This is the *earnings coverage* ratio—the ratio of net income available for debt servicing to the total amount of annual interest plus sinking-fund charges. Under such a rule, no new long-term debt would be contemplated unless the net income available for debt servicing is equal to or in excess of some multiple of the debt servicing charges—say, three to one—so that the company can survive a period of decline in sales and earnings and still have enough earnings to cover the fixed charges of debt. As we will see shortly, this ratio is more meaningful for internal formation of policy but also has its limitations.

Now, let us go on to examine each type of expression more closely.

Capitalization Standard

Consider a company which wishes to formulate its own debt standard as a percent of capitalization. It is apparent that in order to do so the standard must be expressed in terms of data which can be related to the magnitude of the risk in such a way that changes in the ratio can be translated into changes in the risk of cash inadequacy, and vice versa. But how many executives concerned with this problem today have any real idea of how much the risk of cash inadequacy is increased when the long-term debt of their company is increased from 10 percent to 20 percent or from 20 percent to 30 percent of capitalization? Not very many, if my sample of management information in this area has any validity. This is not surprising, however, since the balance sheet data on which the standard is based provided little direct evidence on the question of cash adequacy and may, in fact, be highly unreliable and misleading.

While we do not need to go into a full discussion here of the inadequacies of relating the principal amount of long-term debt to historical asset values as a way of looking at the changes of running out of cash, we should keep in mind the more obvious weaknesses:

1. There is a wide variation in the relation between the principal of the debt and the annual obligation for cash payments under the debt contract. In industrial companies the principal of the debt may be repaid serially over the life of the debt contract, which may vary from 10 years or less to 30 years or more. Thus the annual cash outflow associated with $10 million on the balance sheet may, for example, vary from $500,000 (interest only at 5 percent) to $833,000 (interest plus principal repayable over 30 years) to $1.5 million (interest plus principal repayable over 10 years).

2. As loans are repaid by partial annual payments, as is customary under industrial term loans, the principal amount declines and the percent

of capitalization ratio improves, but the annual cash drain for repayment *remains the same* until maturity is reached.

3. There may be substantial changes in asset values, particularly in connection with inventory valuation and depreciation policies, and as a consequence, changes in the percent of capitalization ratio which have no bearing on the capacity to meet fixed cash drains.

4. Certain off-the-balance-sheet factors have an important bearing on cash flows which the conventional ratio takes no cognizance of. One factor of this sort which has been receiving publicity in recent years is the payments under leasing arrangements.

(While various authorities have been urging that lease payments be given formal recognition as a liability on balance sheets and in debt-capacity calculations, there is no general agreement as to how this should be done. For one thing, there is no obvious answer as to what the capitalization rate should be in order to translate lease payments into balance sheet values. In my opinion this debate is bound to be an artificial and frustrating experience—and unnecessary for the internal analyst—since, as will be discussed later, it is much more meaningful to deal with leases, as with debt, in terms of the dollars of annual cash outflow rather than in terms of principal amounts. Thus a footnoting of the annual payments under the lease is entirely adequate.)

Earnings-Coverage Standard

The earnings-coverage standard affords, on the surface at least, a better prospect of measuring risk in the individual company in terms of the factors which bear directly on cash adequacy. By relating the total annual cash outflow under all long-term debt contracts to the net earnings available for servicing the debt, it is intended to assure that earnings will be adequate to meet charges at all times. This approach implies that the greater the prospective fluctuation in earnings, the higher is the required ratio (or the larger the "cushion" between normal earnings and debt-servicing charges).

This standard also has limitations as a basis for internal determination of debt capacity:

1. The net earnings figure found in the income statement and derived under normal accounting procedures is *not* the same thing as net cash inflow—an assumption which is implicit in the earnings-coverage standard. Even when adjustments are made for the noncash items on the income statement (depreciation charges), as is commonly done in the more sophisticated applications, this equivalence cannot safely be assumed. The time when it may be roughly true is the time when we are least concerned about the hazards of debt, i.e., when sales are approximately the

same from period to period. It is in times of rapid change (including recessions) that we are most concerned about debt burden, and then there *are* likely to be sharp differences between net income and net cash flow.

2. The question of what the *proper* ratio is between earnings and debt servicing is problematical. In a given case should the ratio be 2 to 1 or 20 to 1? If we exclude externally derived standards or rules of thumb and insist that a company generate its own ratio in terms of its own circumstances, how does it go about doing it? Perhaps the best that could be done would be to work backward from the data of past recessions, which would indicate the low points of net earnings, toward a ratio between this experience and some measure of "normal" earnings with the intention of assuring a one-to-one relationship between net earnings and debt servicing at all times. However, if this is the way it is to be done, the estimate of minimum net earnings would itself provide the measure of debt capacity, and it would be unnecessary to translate it into a ratio. Further, as already noted, there are hazards in a literal translation of past history as a guide for the future. And what of the case where the company has experienced net losses in the past? Does this mean that it has no long-term debt capacity? If a net loss is possible, *no* ratio between normal net earnings and debt servicing, however large, will assure the desired equality in future recessions.

The earnings-coverage standard does not appear to be widely used by industrial corporate borrowers as a basis for formulating debt policy. Where it is used, it appears either to derive from the advice of institutional lenders or investment bankers or merely to reflect the borrower's attitude toward risk bearing. Its use does not seem to indicate an attempt to measure individual risk by some objective means.

A MORE USEFUL APPROACH

Granted the apparent inadequacies of conventional debt-capacity decision rules for purposes of internal debt policy, is there a practical alternative? I believe there is, but it must be recognized immediately that it rests on data which are substantially more complex than what the conventional rules require, and involve a considerably larger expenditure of time and effort to obtain and interpret. However, in view of the unquestioned importance of the debt-equity decision to the future of individual businesses, and in view of the fact that, as will be shown later, the data have a usefulness which goes well beyond the debt-capacity decision, there is reason to give this alternative serious consideration.

The basic questions in the appraisal of the magnitude of risk associated with long-term debt can be stated with deceptive simplicity: What are the chances of the business running out of cash in the foreseeable future? How are these chances changed by the addition of X thousands of dollars of annual interest and sinking fund payments?

First, it is necessary to specify whether our concern is with "running out of cash" in an absolute sense (cash insolvency) or merely with the risk of cash inadequacy, that is, running out of cash for certain purposes considered essential to management (for example, a minimum dividend on common stock). We can consider both of these possibilities, but let us focus for the moment on the ultimate hazard, the one commonly associated with excessive debt—the chance of complete depletion of cash reserves resulting in default on the bond contract and bankruptcy.

There are, of course, a variety of possible circumstances under which a company might have its cash reserves drained off. However, considering the problem from the point of view of mature, normally profitable, and reasonably well-managed companies, it is fair to say that the primary concern with debt is with what might happen during a general or industry recession when sales and profits are depressed by factors beyond the immediate control of management. Thus, when the experienced business executive wishes to instill the proper respect for the hazards of too much debt in the minds of aggressive young men eager for leverage, he will recount harrowing tales of disaster and near-disaster in the early 1930s.

Refocusing on Problem

The data we seek are information on the behavior of cash flows during the recession periods. An internal analysis of risk must therefore concern itself not with balance sheet or income statement ratios but directly with the factors which make for changes in cash inflow and outflow. Further, since we are dealing with the common denominator of all transactions, analysis must inevitably take into account *all* major influences on cash flow behavior. In short, the problem is a company-wide problem. All decisions involving cash should be included, and where cash solvency is at stake, there can be no meaningful boundaries on risk except those imposed by the corporate entity itself.

Therefore, it is somewhat artificial to think in terms of "the cash available for debt servicing," as the earnings-coverage standard does, as if it were an identifiable hoard when a number of needs equally as urgent are competing for a limited cash reserve. Consequently, the problem to which this article was originally addressed—determining the capacity to bear the incremental fixed charges of long-term debt—is in reality a much more general one: viz, the problem of *determining the capacity to bear incremental fixed cash outflows for any purpose whatever.*

Assessing Key Factors

The analysis which is proposed in this article as a way of resolving this problem can only be briefly summarized here. It includes:

1. *Identification:* At the outset, it is important to identify the primary factors which produce major changes in cash flow with particular reference to contractions in cash flow. The most significant factor will be sales volume; many of the other factors will be related in greater or lesser degree to sales. However, to cite the example of another major factor, cash expenditures for raw materials, the relationship to sales volume in a downswing is not at all an automatic one since it also depends on:

The volume of finished-goods inventory on hand at the onset of the recession.

The working relationship between finished goods on hand, work scheduled into production, and raw-materials ordering.

The level of raw-materials inventory.

The responses of management at all levels to the observed change in sales.

For most factors affecting cash flow there will be a degree of interdependence and also a range of independent variation, both of which must be identified for the purpose of the analysis.

2. *Extent of refinement desired:* Obviously the list of factors affecting cash flow which are to be given separate consideration could be lengthy depending on the degree of refinement desired; and the longer the list, the greater the complexity of the analysis. It is therefore essential to form a judgment in advance as to how far refinement in the analysis can or should be carried in view of the objectives of the analysis. It is possible for this cash flow analysis to range all the way from simple and relatively crude approximations to the other extreme of involved mathematical and statistical formulas and even to the programming of recession cash flows on a computer.

In their simplest form, cash flows can be considered in terms of accounting approximations derived from balance sheet and income statement data. Thus, for example, sales revenues might be adjusted for changes in accounts receivable to derive current cash inflow, and cost of goods sold could be converted into expenditures for goods actually produced by adjusting for changes in inventory levels. However, the hazard of simplification is that important changes may be obscured by combining factors that at one time may "net each other out" and at some other time may reinforce each other. For instance, changes in dollar sales are produced by changes in product mix, physical volume, and price.

Here is where the internal analyst has a major advantage. Experience tells him what factors should be given separate treatment, and he has access to the data behind the financial statements so he can carry refine-ment as far as he wishes. Ideally, the analysis should be in terms of cash and not accrual accounting information; that is, it should be in terms of cash receipts (not dollar sales) and cash expenditures for raw materials received (not an accounting allocation for raw materials according to the number of units sold).

3. *Analysis of behavior:* Given a list of all major factors affecting cash flow, the next step is to observe their *individual* behavior over time and in particular during recessions. The objection raised earlier to using historical evidence as a guide to debt capacity was that, as usually em-ployed, it is an observation of the *net* effect of change in all these factors on particular occasions—an effect which can be seriously misleading. But if management takes the individual behavoir of these factors into ac-count, the problem is minimized to a point where it can be disregarded.

Past experience in a company with an established position in its in-dustry commonly leads its management to the sensible conclusion that, while it is theoretically possible for the physical volume of sales, for ex-ample, to contract to zero in a recession period, in practice there are rea-sons why this is highly unlikely to occur. These reasons relate to funda-mental and enduring forces in the economy, the industry, the competitive position of the company, consumer buying habits, and so on. Thus past experience will suggest a range of recession behavior which describes the outside limits of what recession can be expected to do in the future.

These limits I wish to refer to as the *maximum favorable limit* and the *maximum adverse limit* (referring to the effect on cash flows and the cash position). By combining the evidence contained in historical records and the judgment of management directly involved in the making of this history, we can describe these limits of expected behavior for all factors affecting cash flow. It will be part of our analysis to do so, taking careful account of interdependent variation for reasons given earlier.

4. *Expected range of recession behavior:* On the basis of such in-formed observation it may be concluded, for example, that the recession contraction in physical volume of sales is not expected to be less than 5 percent nor more than 25 percent of the sales of the period immediately preceding the recession. These are the maximum favorable and maximum adverse limits of sales for the company in question. It may also be con-cluded that the recession is not expected to last less than one year nor more than three years and that no more than 40 percent of the contraction will be concentrated in the first year of the recession. Naturally, our in-terest focuses on the maximum *adverse* limit, since we are attempting to assess the chances of running out of cash. By setting such boundaries on the adverse recession behavior of a major factor influencing cash flows we are beginning to set similar boundaries on the recession behavior of the cash flows themselves.

At this point a question presents itself which has major implications for the subsequent character of the analysis: Is it possible to say anything meaningful about the behavior of sales volume or any other factor *within* the limits that have just been described?

PROBABILITY ANALYSIS

It is possible that there may be some historical evidence in the company on the comparative chances or probabilities of occurrence of sales contractions of, say, 5–11 percent, 12–18 percent, 19–25 percent (or any other breakdown of the range), but the statistical data are likely to be sketchy. It is perhaps more likely that management might, on the basis of experience, make some judgments such as, for example, that the contraction is most likely—say, five chances out of ten—to fall in the 12–18 percent range; that the chances of its falling in the 5–11 percent range are three chances out of ten; and that the chances of falling in the 19–25 percent range are two chances out of a possible ten.

If this kind of information can be generated for all factors affecting cash flow, then it is possible to come up with a range of estimates of the cash flow in future recession periods based on all possible combinations of the several factors, and for each estimate a numerical measure of its probability of occurrence. The whole set collectively will describe all anticipated possibilities. By totaling the separate probabilities of those combinations of events exhausting the initial cash balance, we can describe in quantitative terms the overall chances of cash insolvency. Ideally we want to know that the chances of cash insolvency, as described by this process of analysis of cash flows, are, say, 1 in 20 or 1 in 50.

Problems to Surmount

However, in order to measure precisely the risk of cash insolvency, we need estimates of probability that are within the expected range of behavior and not just the limits of behavior. There are important practical problems that stand in the way of obtaining this type of information and conducting this type of analysis:

Although the analysis suggested above appears relatively simple, in practice it could be quite complex, requiring the guidance of someone experienced in probability theory as well as in financial analysis to steer the study of cash flows around potential pitfalls. The problems center mainly on (1) accurately describing patterns of adjustment over time and (2) assessing the varying degrees of interdependence among the variables. These difficulties are not insurmountable, however, since statisticians have resolved similar ones in the case of other types of business problems.

Past recession periods may not have provided enough experience with respect to the behavior of sales, collections, inventory levels, and so forth, on which to base firm estimates of probabilities over the entire range of possible behavior. Some companies have had only two or three recessions in the past 20 years, and even then sometimes statistics are lacking (although presumably management will have some impressions about the events). But *some* experience with varying recession circumstances is essential even to make a guess. Speaking generally, this limitation on a comprehensive appraisal of the risk magnitude is far more serious than the one of technical competence mentioned first.

Top management will not base critical decisions, such as debt policy, on data which it does not understand and/or in which it does not have confidence. This, I believe, is the primary obstacle which stands in the way of widespread use of a comprehensive cash flow analysis as a basis for risk measurement and the determination of debt capacity at the present time.

Because the method is complex (particularly in contrast to the customary rules of thumb) and because the judgments on probabilities and other aspects of the analysis may appear—and may in fact be—tenuous, management may well be unwilling to use the results, particularly when corporate solvency is at stake.

However, when all this is said, the fact remains that much of present-day practice is seriously inadequate, and there is an urgent need for a more meaningful approach to the problem, particularly as far as the borrower is concerned. Thus there is a strong incentive to explore the opportunities for partial or approximate measures of the risk of cash insolvency within the general framework suggested by the comprehensive analysis. One such approach is that to be described. Its aim is to produce an indicator of risk magnitude which can be derived from more conventional and less complex data in which management has confidence.

Analysis of Adverse Limits

The new approach focuses on the expected *limits* of recession behavior and in particular on the maximum adverse limit. It is based on the assumption that while management may be unable to assess with confidence the probabilities within the range, it usually has strong opinions as to the expected limits and would be prepared to base decisions on such expectations. Thus, to return to the example of the sales contraction, management may be unwilling to assign the "betting odds" to the three intervals between a 5 percent and a 25 percent contraction, but it probably does have strong feelings that 25 percent is the "absolute" limit of adversity within the foreseeable future. This feeling is based not merely on past statistics but on an expert appraisal of all the facts surrounding the customer's buying habits and circumstances, the competitive situation, and so on.

Following this procedure leads to a set of estimates of the maximum adverse limit of recession behavior covering each factor affecting cash flow, and it is a comparatively simple matter then to come up with an estimate of the maximum adverse behavior in any future recession of net cash flow itself—in terms of the minimum dollars of net inflow—(or maximum dollars of net outflow), period by period. Making similar judgments as to the maximum adverse conditions immediately preceding the recession —including prerecession cash balances—it is next possible to determine whether, under such maximum assumptions, the company would become insolvent and, if so, how soon and by how much.

This calculation in itself will give management some "feel" for the nearness or remoteness of the event of cash insolvency. It may demonstrate, as I have done in the case of certain companies, that even under these maximum adverse assumptions the company still has a positive cash balance. If this is so, the amount of this minimum balance is an objective judgment of the total amount of incremental fixed cash charges which the company could assume without *any* threat of insolvency. Making some assumptions about the nature and the terms of the debt contract, this figure could be converted into the principal amount of additional debt which could be assumed with the expectation of complete safety.

Suppose, on the other hand, that the maximum adverse assumptions produce a negative cash balance, indicating the possibility of insolvency under certain adverse conditions. This does not mean that the long-term debt is excluded (except for those managements for whom any action which creates or increases the risk of insolvency, no matter how small it may be, is intolerable). The more likely response will be that, provided the chances are "sufficiently remote," the company is fully prepared to run the risk.

Thus we are back to the problem of assessing the magnitude of the risk and the extent to which it would be increased by any given amount of debt. As a means of gaining a more precise impression of the chances of insolvency at the adverse end of the range of recession behavior, without going through the formal process of assigning probability values, I suggest that a second adverse limit be defined for each of the factors affecting cash flow. This will be called the *most probable adverse limit*. It reflects management's judgment as to the limit of *normal* recession behavior, as opposed to the maximum adverse limit, which includes all possibilities, however remote.

Modes and Ranges

A visual representation of these two adverse limits of behavior is shown in Exhibit 1. Assuming experience and expected behavior are somewhat normally distributed about a mode (i.e., the value of most frequent occurrence), there will be:

1. A range of values clustered around this point, where most of past experience has been concentrated and where "bets" as to what the future is likely to bring will also be concentrated.

2. Extremes at either end of the range representing events that have a relatively small chance of happening.

It will be seen that the most probable limit cuts off the extreme "tail" of the frequency distribution in a somewhat imprecise and yet meaningful way. In setting the limits of expected sales contractions, for example, management would be saying that while sales *could*, in its judgment, contract as much as 25 percent, a contraction is *not likely* to exceed, say, 20 percent. This 20 percent is then the most probable adverse limit. While my terms may be new to businessmen, the distinction described is one which is commonly made and one on which judgments as to risk are often based.

From the data on the most probable adverse limits of the various factors affecting cash flow, the most probable adverse limit of recession *net* cash flows would be calculated and, from this, the most probable minimum recession cash *balance*. This last figure reflects management's best judgment as to the adverse limit of what is "likely to happen" as opposed to what "could happen" to net cash flows.

Guidelines for Policy

At this point it should be noted that, when considering cash flows from the point of view of solvency, the list of possible expenditures would be stripped down to those which are absolutely essential for continuity of corporate existence and for the generation of current income. (We will presently bring into consideration other less mandatory expenditures such as dividends and capital expenditures.) Thinking in these terms, suppose the recession cash flow analysis indicates that under the maximum adverse assumptions the minimum cash balance would be negative, say, a deficit of $1.5 million. Suppose further that under the most probable adverse assumptions the minimum recession cash balance is a surplus of $3 million. How are these estimates to be interpreted as a guide to corporate debt capacity?

First, it is obvious in this example that management's expectations

EXHIBIT 1
Example of Maximum and Most Probable Limits of Recession Behavior

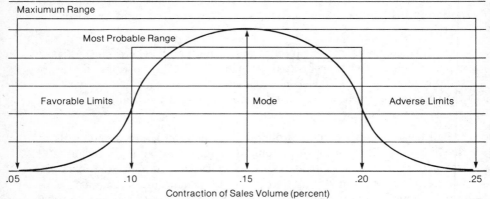

Probability of Occurrence
(number or weight of estimates in arbitrary units)

Maxiumum Range

Most Probable Range

Favorable Limits   Mode   Adverse Limits

.05   .10   .15   .20   .25

Contraction of Sales Volume (percent)

about the factors governing cash flow include the possibility that the company could become insolvent without any additional debt. However, this possibility is considered to have a relatively remote chance of occurrence since when the analysis is restricted to the most probable limit of recession behavior, the company is left with a positive minimum cash balance. The amount of this balance is a rough measure of the *total amount of additional fixed cash outflows (e.g., debt charges) which could be incurred without creating the threat of insolvency* in the event of normal recession conditions. Thus:

If the likely limit of the recession is expected to be two years, the company could stand additional debt servicing of $1.5 million per year of recession. This sum can be readily converted into an equivalent principal amount. Assuming a 20-year-term loan repayable in equal annual installments and bearing 5 percent interest, an additional debt of approximately $15 million could be considered safe under ordinary recession conditions.

Let me emphasize that the cash balance would not be taken as a guide to debt capacity unless management were prepared to live with some chance of insolvency—a chance which would obviously be increased by the new debt. If management were not so inclined, it would reject debt or alternatively adopt a debt limit somewhere between zero and $15 million. In any case, management would not increase debt *beyond* $15 million unless it were prepared to accept the chance of insolvency within the most probable range of recession experience. Because of the way the most probable limit has been defined, the chances of insolvency would be expected to increase rapidly and substantially if debt were to exceed $15 million by any significant amount.

There is, of course, nothing sacred about the $15 million limit set by management's judgment on the limits of normal recession experience. There is no reason why some managements would not increase debt capital substantially above this figure, assuming the funds were available. Such a step depends entirely on the willingness to bear the financial risks and on the potential rewards for such risk bearing. The foregoing type of analysis does, however, perform the essential function of alerting management to the range of debt beyond which risks may be expected to increase substantially.

Practical Advantages

It is now apparent that the analytical approach proposed here produces a criterion stated in terms of *the number of dollars of debt servicing* that are acceptable within management's concepts of risk bearing at a given point in time. The criterion is derived entirely from within and is completely independent of external judgments or rules of thumb. While it is admittedly crude and approximate when compared with the theoretical ideal of risk management, I believe it to be meaningful and useful in practice and, in this as in other respects, superior to the conventional forms for expressing debt limits.

It must be added, however, that because the recommended analysis is partial and approximate, those who adopt it must use it as they use current decision rules. That is, they must use it as a general guide and not as a precision instrument. For most managements this will be entirely adequate.

BETTER DECISION MAKING

One of the real advantages of this approach to debt capacity is that it raises—and answers—a much broader question. As previously indicated, the analysis is actually concerned with the capacity to assume additional fixed cash outflows of any kind, and whatever capacity is demonstrated is not confined to debt servicing. Thus, if it is concluded from the example just given that the company in question can stand an additional outflow in recessions totaling $3 million, the first decision to be made by management is *how to use this capacity.*

There are a variety of ways in which the capacity may be used: to cover payments under a lease contract, to maintain a continuous research program, to stabilize employment, to pay a regular dividend in good times and bad, and so on. These are all competing uses for whatever capacity exists. With the information that the cash flow analysis provides, management now can begin to assign priorities and have some idea of how far it can hope to go in realizing its objectives. If debt servicing is given top priority, then the data have been a means of defining debt capacity.

It is because the proposed analysis has much broader significance than the question of debt (important as that question may be) that I believe the expenditure of time, effort, and money required to generate the data needed is well justified for the individual corporation. The analysis provides information which lies at the base of a whole range of financial and other decisions and has continuing significance. Moreover, most corporate treasurers have the staff and the basic data to undertake a careful and detailed study of the behavior of factors affecting cash flow.

Testing for Cash Adequacy

Up to this point the analysis of cash flow has been discussed in terms of cash solvency. As indicated earlier, this means that attention is confined to outflows which are vital to survival. It was also indicated, however, that the risk of insolvency was part of a broader family of risks, described as the risk of cash inadequacy.

In discussing the question of solvency with management we often find that while there are certain expenditures which *could* be slashed to zero in an emergency, there is a reluctance to take action which would put management in a position of having to do so. These are expenditures which must be treated as mandatory for policy reasons, because management believes that to interrupt them would be detrimental to the long-term interests of the corporation. Among the best examples of such expenditures are certain minimum payments for research, for capital assets, and for preferred and common dividends.

This situation can readily be incorporated into the type of analysis outlined earlier. I refer to the method for doing this as the *test for cash adequacy* as opposed to the test for cash solvency. As soon as management has defined the "irreducible minimum" for these expenditures under recession conditions, they are merely added to the outflows of the previous analysis; then the figure generated for the maximum adverse or most probable adverse recession cash balance is the balance which remains over and above such payments. To return to the example previously used:

The effect would be to wipe out all or some portion of the most probable minimum balance ($3 million) or to add to the maximum adverse deficit ($1.5 million). Thus, if the irreducible minimum is considered to be two years of common dividends at $500,000 a year plus $1 million of minimum capital expenditures, the result would be to cut the most probable balance back to $1 million. The capacity to assume additional fixed cash outflows is thereby substantially reduced. Obviously management in this case is giving priority to the dividend and capital expenditures over debt leverage—or over any other use for the funds on hand.

One of the benefits of such an analysis is to make management's priorities explicit, to recognize their competing character, and to make possible a reevaluation of their relative importance to the company.

Making separate tests for cash solvency and cash adequacy serves another important purpose. Most discussions of the hazards of debt imply that the danger is the risk of insolvency, and this danger is usually treated with proper respect. However, our analysis may demonstrate that within the range of management's expectations there is little or no risk of insolvency but a substantial risk of cash inadequacy, particularly if large amounts of long-term debt are added.

If, in the past, management has been setting limits on debt in terms of an assumed risk of insolvency and now finds that the only significant risk is that of inability to meet certain minimum dividend payments and the like, it may well be disposed to assume a greater magnitude of risk and take on more debt. A management which would reject the risk of insolvency if it exceeded a chance of 1 in 50 might be prepared to accept a risk of abandoning cash dividends for a year or two if the chance did not exceed, say, 1 in 20.

In short, once management knows the *kind* of risk it is taking, it may begin to draw distinctions between one form of contingency and another and not operate on the general assumption that the only concern is that of possible insolvency. Better information is thus a prerequisite for better decisions.

Reappraising Present Rules

Assuming management can, by the means described, come up with an independent appraisal of its long-term debt capacity, what does this imply for existing decision rules obtained from external sources or inherited from the past? Does it mean that they will be ignored completely? The answer is likely to be no. Debt policy cannot be made in a vacuum. It must take account of the lenders' willingness to lend and also of the reactions of equity investors who make judgments on the risks inherent in the corporation.

One of the first results of the analysis, therefore, is to reappraise existing debt-capacity decision rules. To illustrate:

Suppose a company has been assuming, as many do, that it can safely incur long-term debt up to a maximum of 30 percent of capitalization. This rule can be translated into its equivalent of dollars of annual debt-servicing charges and directly compared with the results of the recession cash flow analysis. In view of the fact that the rule probably has been derived from external sources, it is likely that the annual debt servicing which it permits either exceeds or falls short of the amount of cash flow indicated by the internal analysis.

In view of the approximate nature of the analysis, however, this is not likely to cause a change in debt policy unless the amount of the variation is substantial. It is also possible, of course, that the existing decision rule and the cash flow analysis will produce the same result—in which case the existing rule will appear verified. But this cannot be known in advance of the analysis, and in any case the data have been converted into a form which is much more meaningful for the purposes involved.

Such a comparison gives a measure of management's attitude toward the risk that is implicit in the existing decision rule (although management probably had no clear idea of what the risk magnitude was at the time the rule was established).

The results of the cash flow analysis can also be compared with the lender's concept of debt capacity—if different from that of the corporation. While lenders are often reluctant to make statements on the outside limits of what they will lend, they will, from time to time, give indications of what they consider an appropriate capital structure for a given industry and company. If the borrower's appraisal of his capacity exceeds that of the lender, he may well decide to push the latter to the limit of his willingness to lend. Without good cash flow data, many borrowers appear reluctant to argue their case aggressively, probably because of uncertainty about where the safe limit lies.

The results can also be related to other aspects of the debt-capacity question, such as the requirements for an A bond rating or the risk expectations of equity investors which appear to be implicit in some price-earnings ratio (assuming this can be determined). Once again, the comparison is between whatever unused debt capacity is indicated by the internal analysis and the standards imposed by external considerations with the aim of probing the acceptable and useful upper limits of long-term debt.

I have carried out this type of analysis for a sample of companies in different industries and made comparisons with existing debt-capacity standards of both the corporations themselves and their lending institutions. The data strongly indicate that there are, in fact, major inconsistencies between managements' explicit expectations regarding recession cash flows and the expectations which are implicit in accepted ratios of debt capacity. The evidence is by no means adequate to make any safe or meaningful generalization about the overall character of industrial debt policy. Nevertheless, among the large and mature corporations which are the basis of the study the evidence seems to suggest:

Either the risks of debt have been significantly overrated by a substantial number of firms.

Or some managements tend to be unusually conservative toward this aspect of corporate risk.

FUTURE TRENDS

The trend of economic events in the past 20 years suggests that there is both a need and an opportunity for a more refined approach to the debt-equity choice in corporate structures. As the specter of the depression of the 1930s has faded into the past and confidence in our capacity to avoid a repetition of extreme economic stagnation has grown, a new generation of corporate executives has shown increasing willingness to use long-term debt financing as a source of funds for consolidation and expansion.

As long as long-term debt is avoided or kept to minor proportions, crude decision rules providing wide margins of safety are quite adequate. As the proportions of debt increase, however, the need for a sharper pencil and a more careful analysis grows. This need is further reinforced by the increase in other kinds of fixed cash commitments such as lease payments and the noncontractual but nonetheless vital steady flows required for research, dividends, and the like. Greater stability in the economy over an extended period is likely to encourage a variety of rigidities in cash outflows, and simple rules of thumb are inadequate to cope with the problems these present.

Along with the increasing need for improved analysis has come a greater capacity to carry out this analysis. This improvement derives both from better data and from improved techniques of processing and analyzing data. Financial executives today have access to far more data on cash flows and the factors behind cash flows than they did 20 years ago—far more, in fact, than many are actually putting to use. They also have access to more sophisticated approaches to the analysis of complex data and to machines which can reduce it to manageable proportions. As times goes on and financial management becomes increasingly familiar with these tools of analysis and more aware of the opportunities they afford, the current reluctance to adopt a more complex analytical framework is bound to diminish.

But there is one hitch. However sophisticated the financial officer may be in the newer techniques, there is little merit in serving up a diet of financial data to the board of directors, as a basis for the financial decision, which is too rich for their current digestive capacity. It is for this reason that I have not attempted in this article to convert the reader to a full-scale internal analysis of risk and its components. Rather, I have taken on the more modest objective of alerting top management to four key points bearing on the debt-capacity decision:

1. While external sources of advice can and should be consulted as an

aid to decision making, the question of debt capacity is essentially an internal one to be settled by management with reference to its individual circumstances and individual preferences.

2. Current rules of thumb regarding debt capacity are seriously inadequate as a framework for this decision.

3. The answer lies in a knowledge of the behavior of cash flows and in having a useful measure of the capacity to assume incremental fixed cash outflows.

4. Management needs approaches that will enable it to approximate debt capacity within the context of data with which it is already familiar and in terms of judgments to which it has long been accustomed. The approach described in this article meets these criteria.

By accepting and acting on these points, management would take an important step forward toward debt-equity decisions in which borrowers and lenders alike could have greater confidence.

20. Measuring the Productivity of Investment in Persuasion*

JOEL DEAN

I. PROLOGUE

My starting point in this article is ten propositions, which are debatable, at least as boldly stated here:

1.   Much advertising (and other corporate persuasion) is in economic reality partly an investment. The investment mix varies over a wide spectrum.

2.   Investments in promotion are different from conventional capital expenditures, but their peculiar traits do not disqualify promotion from investment treatment.

3.   Profitability must be the basic measurement of the productivity of capital invested in promotion. Despite the multiplicity of conflicting corporate goals, the overriding objective for decisions on investment of corporate capital should be to make money.

4.   The main determinants of profitability of an advertising investment that need to be estimated are the amount and timing of added investment and of added earnings, the duration of advertising effects, and risks.

5.   The measurement concepts of capital productivity that must be estimated are future, time-spotted, incremental, after-tax cash flows of investment outlays and of added profits from added sales.

6.   Discounted cash-flow analysis (DCF) supplies the yardstick of investment worth which is most appropriate for promotional investments. By comparison, payback period, though widely used, has no merit.

7.   Advertising belongs in the capital budget. Promotional investments should be made to compete for funds on the basis of profitability, i.e., DCF rate of return.

8.   The criterion for rationing scarce capital among competing investment proposals should be the DCF rate of return. The minimum acceptable return should be the corporation's cost of capital—outside market cost or internal opportunity cost, whichever is higher.

*Journal of Industrial Economics, vol. 15, no. 2 (April 1967), pp. 81–108.

9. Plopping advertising into the corporation's capital budget will not perform a miracle. The most that it can do is to open the way for a research approach which is oriented to the kind of estimates that are relevant and that will permit investment in promotion to fight for funds on the basis of financial merit rather than on the basis of personal persuasiveness of its sponsor. Judgment cannot be displaced by DCF analysis and computers. But judgment can be economized and improved.

10. To make this investment approach produce practical benefits will require an open mind, fresh concepts, substantial research spending, and great patience.

Readers who find these propositions unacceptable as a point of departure should stop here. Right-thinking readers who persist are warned that the analysis is necessarily technical, studded with charts and culminated by mathematics.

My paper has two interrelated parts: theory and measurement. It is primarily concerned with the conceptual framework for deciding how much to invest in promotion. Measurement problems are examined only incidentally and mechanics of application not at all. The analysis is presented in terms of advertising; but is equally applicable to all forms of promotion. Advertising is used because it is the purest and most indisputable form of persuasion cost and for many firms also the largest. For clarity, the analysis is narrowed to one product and one medium. In principle, however, it is extensible to all forms of corporate persuasion. Allocation of the advertising budget among media and among products is not formally tackled but the decision-making apparatus could be logically extended to these problems. The interplay of promotion with other ways of getting business such as product improvement and pricing is, for simplicity, bypassed.

My approach, blushingly labeled "profitometrics," can be previewed thus: because most advertising is in economic essence a capital expenditure, the question of how much to invest in advertising (and other forms of persuasion) is a problem of investment economics. A new approach is therefore required: economic and financial analysis of futurities. This approach focuses on future aftertax cash flows, centers on the profit productivity of capital and relies on quantitative estimates.

II. THEORY OF OPTIMUM PROMOTIONAL OUTLAY

A. Two Time Horizons

Strictly and elegantly, all promotion can be viewed as investment, since there is some time lag in its benefits, even though short. Nevertheless, the problem of determining optimum persuasion outlay can, in principle, be solved in two separate time-horizon settings: (1) immediate-impact promotion, where most of the benefits come soon; and (2) delayed-impact promotion, where benefits are deferred and often cumulative.

Pure forms of either are rare or nonexistent. Most promotion brings about some benefits quickly and others spread out into the future. The proportion accounted for by either kind depends on the product, the nature of the promotional benefit, and perhaps the character of the media. The controlling determinant is the anatomy of the purchasing decision, which differs greatly among products.

Pure types are nevertheless notoriously appealing for developing principles. As a first approximation, therefore, we shall examine each category separately. The immediate-impact case will be studied first.

B. Two Decision Increments

Two kinds of decision increments in promotional investment need to be distinguished: (1) intensity increments and (2) project increments.

The first kind, intensity increments, are small increments of additional depth of investment in a single advertising submedium. The intensity increment of investment is pertinent (a) when outlays can be varied by small additions, and (b) when the decision is to select, by examining this growing edge, that amount of advertising outlay which would maximize the rate of return from this investment project.

The second kind, project increments, are pertinent when the incremental unit of decision is the entire advertising project. The choice (because of indivisibility or other restraints) is to take it or leave it. Under these circumstances, we do not have the choice of a panorama of outlay amounts. Consequently, optimization of the advertising amount is not the problem. Instead, what is at issue is acceptance versus rejection of the entire project. The total advertising outlay of the project is, therefore, in this case, the pertinent increment of investment. And the question is whether the added profits from resultant sales as they spread through time will or will not produce a rate of return greater than the cost of capital.

In both situations the basic concept is incremental. In the intensity-increment case, we use profitometrics analysis at the margin to select, from a gradation of alternative outlays, that investment amount which is optimum. Hence, small increments are the vehicle of decision for optimizing the size of this investment project. In the project-increment case, lacking this fluidity of choice, we use the profitometrics method to stack the entire project against alternative uses of capital, so as to make it fight for funds in rate-of-return rationing of the corporation's scarce capital.

Both kinds of increments are normally needed. Optimization of some sort (within the restraints) may be presumed to have taken place before a project of the all-or-none sort comes for capital-rationing decision. The intensity-increment analysis leads us to an optimum depth of advertising investment. But the entire project might nevertheless fall short of the minimum profitability requirement, e.g. cost of capital. To find this out we need to estimate the capital productivity of the project increment.

The two kinds of decision increments are, for illustrative purposes, examined separately for the two kinds of time horizons in the analysis which follows. For the first time-horizon, namely immediate-impact advertising, intensity increments are alone used. For the second time-horizon, namely delayed-impact promotion (investments), both kinds of decision increments are needed. For one-shot investments, intensity increments are examined for one treatment and project increments for another. For spread-out investments, both are needed, but the analysis is in terms of project increments only.

C. Immediate Impact Promotion

The basic tenet of the profitometrics approach to decisions on immediate-impact advertising outlay is simple common sense: advertising expenditures are justified to the extent that they cause increases in sales which add enough to corporate profits to warrant the outlay. To determine if this is the case, we must measure two things: (1) the effect of advertising on sales, (2) the effect of sales on profits.

To illustrate these ideas in simple terms, I have a series of charts and tables relating to direct-mail promotion of a book. In our example, we have assumed that the price will remain the same at all rates of sale considered, and, further, that the added cost of production and physical distribution per copy—which we call the incremental production cost—will also not change. These assumptions are realistic for a surprisingly wide range of commodities.

Exhibit 1 shows the kind of relationship we can reasonably believe exists between advertising and sales and which in fact has been found to exist when measurements have actually been made. You will observe that the increase in sales attributable to advertising becomes less and less as more and more advertising is used. That is, the increase in sales resulting from spending $9000 on advertising rather than $8000 is less than the increase in sales attributed to the expenditure of $2000 rather than $1000. This conforms to common sense: initial advertising attracts the most susceptible customers and subsequent advertising must be more and more intense to induce the less susceptible to become customers. As an example, consider the response to successive mailings of adver-

EXHIBIT 1
Effect of Advertising on Sales

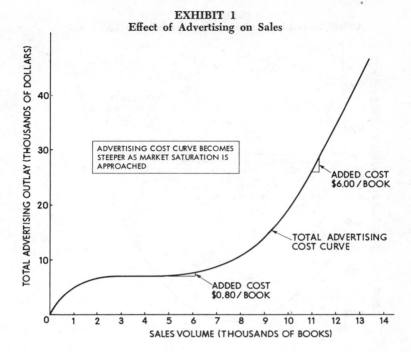

tisements for the book. The initial mailing will bring in the customers while subsequent and more intense persuasion may be required to induce recipients of other mailings to become customers. As a result, the added advertising outlays required to sell one more copy increases from $.80 to $6.00 in our example. (The curve in Exhibit 1 traces total costs. The slope of this curve, that is the rate of climb, indicates added cost of selling one more book.) The same form of relationship is found when single mailings are made to lists that differ in susceptibility.

Exhibit 2 shows the same basic relationship restated in terms of the added advertising outlay required to produce added units of sale—a relationship that might be called the incremental advertising cost curve.

The second measurement that this approach requires is the relationship between sales and profits. Exhibit 3 shows the relationship following from our assumptions that the price is independent of promotional outlays and that incremental production costs remain the same over the range of variation in sales that it seems relevant to consider. Because price stays the same and incremental production cost is constant, the incremental prepromotional profit remains constant. That is, leaving advertising costs aside for the moment, each additional book that is sold results in a constant increase in profits—$6.00 in our example.

EXHIBIT 2
Added Advertising Cost Necessary to Make An Added Sale

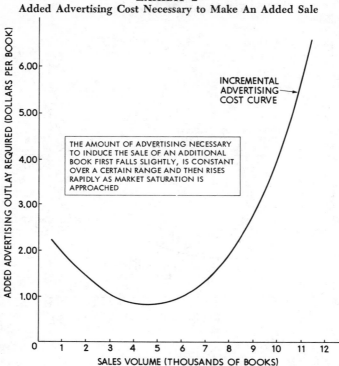

We can now combine the two measurements to see how large the advertising outlay should be. In Exhibit 4 we superimpose the curve representing the relationship between advertising and sales of Exhibit 2 on the chart representing the relationship between sales and profit. We can see that advertising beyond the intersection of these two lines results in an absolute reduction in profits. That is, beyond the point of intersection it costs more than $6.00 to increase sales by one book whereas the increase in sales by one book adds only $6.00 to our profits.

Exhibit 5 summarizes in a table the analysis of immediate-impact one-shot advertising outlays charted in Exhibits 1, 2, 3, and 4.

D. Delayed Impact Advertising

Most advertising is an investment, in essence, since it has delayed as well as immediate impacts. This kind of advertising requires a different kind of economic analysis from that described above. The appropriate analysis is directed at the productivity of the capital tied up in a promotional investment measured in terms of rate of return.

EXHIBIT 3
Effect of Sales on Profit

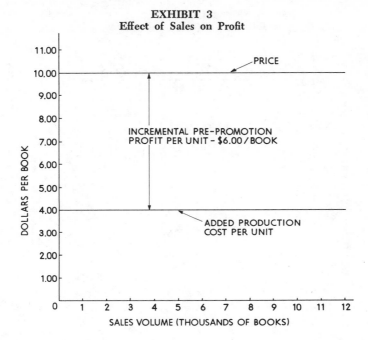

In measuring capital productivity it is convenient to classify promotional investments into two categories: (1) one-shot promotions, where all or most of the outlay is made all at once; and (2) spread-out investments, where outlays are sprinkled over a period of years.

1. *One-Shot Investments.* For one-shot investments in advertising there are two alternative attacks. One is a simple extension of the preceding analysis of immediate-impact advertising. The second is a pure-investment approach which, though compatible with the first, gets at the problem in a different way, namely through DCF measurements of capital productivity. Incidentally, this second attack is alone suitable for spread-out investments.

(a) *Patch-on Analysis.* Exhibit 6 illustrates how the analysis of immediate-impact advertising which is summarized in Exhibits 1, 2, 3, and 4 can be patched up to account for the follow-on effects of a one-shot advertising investment. Essentially the process is: (1) estimate the incremental per-unit profits (or other benefits) from follow-on sales in each follow-on year; (2) find the present value at the corporation's cost of capital of each year's profits; (3) sum them as a single figure of present worth of incremental profit from follow-on sales; and (4) add this sum to the incremental prepromotion profit from immediate sales. This present-value sum in our illustration is $14.24 a unit. The

EXHIBIT 4
Effect of Advertising on Profits

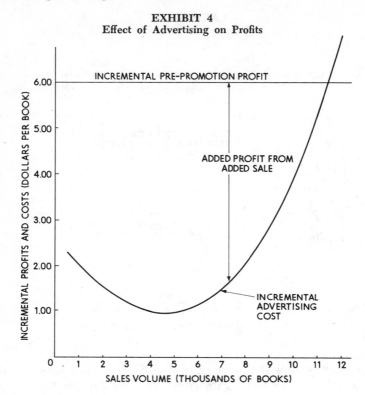

resulting aggregate of incremental profit from immediate plus follow-on sales supplies a cutoff criterion identical in concept to that illustrated in Exhibit 4.

Exhibit 6 indicates quite plausibly that the amount that it is economic to spend on a one-shot advertising outlay is greater when it has follow-on effects than when it does not.

This simplified solution presumes that the corporation's overall cost of capital has been measured, that it is used as a cutoff for rate-of-return rationing of funds for other capital expenditure, and that the corporation's internal opportunity cost of funds is not significantly higher than this market cost.

How the add-on for follow-on sales that is diagrammed in Exhibit 6 is computed is shown in Exhibits 7 and 8. Exhibit 7, like Exhibit 5, examines six alternative levels of advertising outlay. It goes further by also considering the effects upon sales and profits in the second year. Exhibit 8 is derived by extending Exhibit 7 in that it shows several follow-on years. Exhibit 8a shows how we calculate the present value of immediate and follow-on effects of the sale of one additional book.

EXHIBIT 5

One-Shot Advertising Outlay with no Follow-on Effect

	Advertising Outlays ($1000)		Effect on Sales (1000 units)		Effect on Prepromotion Profits ($1000)		Effect on Net Profit per Unit of Added Sales ($ per unit)		
	Altern. Total Advt'g Outlays	Differential Advt'g Outlays	Total Sales	Differential Sales	Total Profits	Differential Profits	Increm. Pre-prom. Profits	Increm. Advt'g Cost	Added Net Profit from Added Sales
A	5	5	1.7	1.7	10.2	10.2	6.00	2.94	3.06
B	10	5	7.8	6.1	46.8	36.6	6.00	.82	5.18
C	15	5	9.0	1.2	54.0	7.2	6.00	4.17	1.83
D	20	5	10.0	1.0	60.0	6.0	6.00	5.00	1.00
E	25	5	10.9	.9	65.4	5.4	6.00	5.56	.44
F	30	5	11.6	.7	69.6	4.2	6.00	7.14	−1.14

EXHIBIT 6
Effect of Advertising on Profits: One Shot
with Follow-on Effects

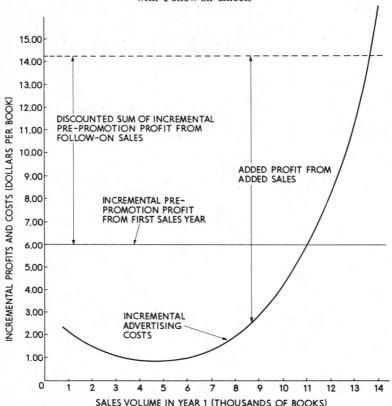

Follow-on profits are discounted to a present value at 10 percent and then added to the immediate profit to give a total present value of $14.24. Exhibit 8b shows this present value stacked up against incremental advertising costs to provide a net incremental profit figure.

(b) *New-Cloth Analysis.* There is an alternative but intellectually compatible attack on the problem of a one-shot advertising outlay with follow-on effects. It is to treat the entire outlay as an investment by starting anew and measuring directly the capital productivity of the immediate, together with the follow-on, benefits. The investment profile of a one-shot advertising outlay which has follow-on effects is diagrammed in Exhibit 9. The outlay is portrayed in the negative section of the chart as a down-bar. The whole-life incremental prepromotion profits are depicted for each year in the positive section of the diagram as bars of diminishing length. This illustrates the kind of timetable used for DCF calculation of the rate of return for such an investment.

EXHIBIT 7

One-Shot Advertising Outlay with Follow-on Effects

	Alternative Advertising Outlays ($1000)		Sales (1000 units)				Profits ($1000)				Face Value of Differential Profit Sum
			First Year		Second Year		First Year		Second Year		
	Total	Differential	Total	Differential	Total	Differential	Total	Differential	Total	Differential	
A...........	5	5	1.7	1.7	1.1	1.1	10.2	10.2	6.6	6.6	16.8
B...........	10	5	7.8	6.1	5.2	4.1	46.8	36.6	31.2	24.6	61.2
C...........	15	5	9.0	1.2	6.0	.8	54.0	7.2	36.0	4.8	12.0
D...........	20	5	10.0	1.0	6.7	.7	60.0	6.0	40.2	4.2	10.2
E...........	25	5	10.9	.9	7.3	.6	65.4	5.4	43.8	3.6	9.0
F...........	30	5	11.6	.7	7.7	.4	69.6	4.2	46.2	2.4	6.6

EXHIBIT 8A
Follow-on Effects Due to One-Shot Advertising Outlay

Year	Incremental Prepromotion Profit*	Present Value at 10 percent
1	6.00	5.71
2	3.99	3.44
3	2.65	2.06
4	1.76	1.24
5	1.17	.75
6–10	2.02	1.04
		Total 14.24

* Assumes that quantity sold during year n due to promotional outlay at time o is Q $(.665)^{n-1}$ where Q is quantity sold during year 1.

EXHIBIT 8B
Added Net Profit Per Book from Added Sale Due to One-Shot Advertising Outlay with Follow-on Effects

Total ($1000)	Incremental per Book	Present Value of Incremental Prepromotion Profit per Book from 8a ($)	Added Net Profit per Book from Added Sale ($)
5	2.94	14.24	11.30
10	.82	14.24	13.42
15	4.17	14.24	10.07
20	5.00	14.24	9.24
25	5.56	14.24	8.68
30	7.14	14.24	7.10
35	10.00	14.24	4.24

The calculation format is illustrated in Exhibit 10. The investment amount ($200,000) is shown as a negative value. For convenience it is put in the column entitled *Incremental Prepromotion Profits,* where the incremental prepromotion profits estimated for each year are shown as positive amounts. In the next four columns these face-value amounts are translated into present value by discounting each at four trial rates of return: 30, 20, 18, and 17 percent.

The mechanics of the DCF method of measuring the productivity of capital consists essentially of finding that interest rate which discounts the future earnings of an advertising investment to a present value precisely equal to the investment outlay. This rate (roughly 18 percent

EXHIBIT 9
Investment Profile of One-Shot Advertising
Outlay with Follow-on Effects

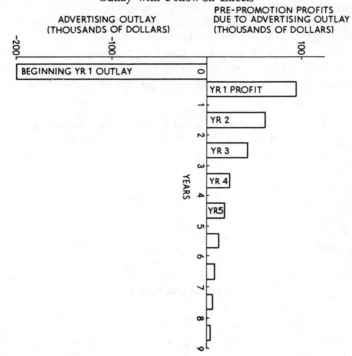

EXHIBIT 10
Discounted Cash-Flow Method of Computing Rate of Return from One-Shot
Advertising Investment with Follow-on Effects

Year	Added Pre-promotion Profits (face value) ($1000)	Present Value Discounted at			
		30 percent	20 percent	17 percent	18 percent
0.	(200)	(200)	(200)	(200)	(200)
1.	96	83	87	88	88
2.	64	41	47	50	49
3.	43	20	26	28	27
4.	29	10	15	16	15
5.	19	5	8	9	8
6.	13	2	4	5	5
7.	9	1	2	3	3
8.	6	1	1	2	2
9.	4	—	1	1	1
10.	3	—	—	—	—
	Net present value	(37)	(9)	3	(1)

in our illustration) is the true rate of return on that investment. It is the highest rate of interest that could be paid to an outsider to whom you turn over all the earnings of the project to pay back the loan and still come out with a zero balance at the end of the project's economic life (i.e. its stream of incremental earnings).

The source of the typical time shape of follow-on incremental profits is shown in Exhibit 11, which charts profiles of follow-on incremental sales obtained by an added dollar of advertising. Plausible profiles of

EXHIBIT 11
Profiles of Follow-on Incremental Sales from an Added Dollar of Advertising Outlay at Beginning of Year 1

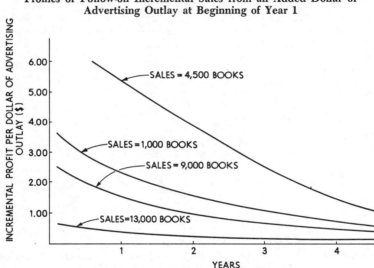

follow-on incremental sales from an added dollar of advertising indicate that the impact of a one-shot promotional outlay does not die—it just fades away. If, as we have assumed, marginal production costs are constant with output rate and if prices are independent of promotion, then incremental prepromotion profits would follow the same pattern. Exhibit 7 shows how these would be derived, and Exhibit 8 shows their time shape.

The present-value variant of DCF analysis provides an alternative route to measurement of investment profitability. Instead of computing the individual rate of return for the promotional project it applies a "go, no-go" gauge to promotional investments. It does so by merely computing the present value of time-spotted incremental profits discounted at the corporation's cost of capital. If this present value is greater than the face value of the one-shot advertising outlay, then the promotional investment should be made (assuming an adequate allowance in the estimates for any above-average risk this particular project may entail). Unless the corporation's opportunity cost of capital is significantly higher than its market cost, the promotion investment should be made, since the productivity of capital exceeds its price.

This DCF variant is illustrated in Exhibit 8, where the present value of incremental prepromotion profits is stacked up against the incremental advertising outlay to produce a net present increment profit per book. This net present value decreases as the level of output increases and will eventually become zero at the maximum-profit advertising outlay.

To summarize, in measuring the productivity of one-shot promotional investments (i.e. outlays which have follow-on effects), we can use three kinds of economic techniques:

1.   Patch-on analysis: graft a summary figure of the present value of follow-on benefits on to the value of first-year incremental profits, which is the criterion of optimum outlay for immediate-impact advertising.

2.   New-cloth analysis of the DCF rate of return: treat the initial year of benefits as earnings of the advertising investment as well as all the follow-on years. Compute DCF project rate of return, after allowing for any unusual risks of the advertising investment as compared with rival corporate investments. If its DCF return is higher than the

EXHIBIT 12
Investment Profile of Spread-out Advertising with Follow-on Effects

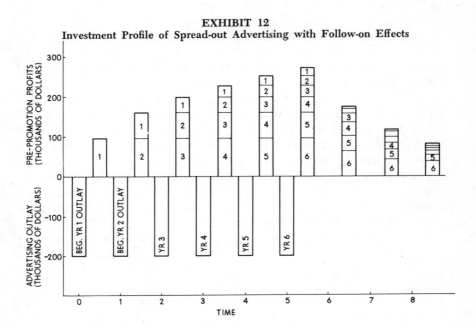

corporation's market or opportunity cost of capital, the project should be accepted.

3. Present-value version of DCF analysis: simply find the present worth of the entire stream of incremental prepromotion profits (adjusted for risk) using a single discount rate, namely, the corporation's cost of capital. If this is bigger than the outlay, accept the project.

2. *Spread-Out Investments.* So much for one-shot outlays. Now we turn to the second and more common category of promotional investments, namely those spread out over a number of years. For spread-out investments, several analytical treatments are possible; modern investment-economics practice has, however, narrowed them to the two variants of DCF analysis: (1) individual project return, and (2) present value at cost of capital.

The investment profile of a spread-out advertising investment is shown in Exhibit 12. Diagrammed by down-bars in the negative section is the advertising investment of $200,000 each year for six years and then none for four years. The incremental prepromotion profits caused by each year's advertising trail off over a six-year period following the pattern suggested in Exhibit 9. For each year they are identified with numbers corresponding to the year of advertising outlay which caused them.[1] Profit bars are slightly offset, primarily for clarity, but also to indicate some time lag.

The net balance of cash flows from spread-out advertising investment with follow-on effects is illustrated in Exhibit 13. It is derived from Exhibit 12 in a manner diagrammed for the first year where the down-column is the net balance of an advertising outlay of $200,000 and an incremental profit of $96,000. This balance each year is shown in black and traced by a solid line. It is this net balance which is fed into the DCF computation to save arithmetic.

Exhibit 13 also shows the cumulative balance of outlay and inflow for each year. This cumulative balance is shown by crosshatched columns. The dotted line which hooks up these columns indicates that after the fifth year, in terms of face (not discounted) value cash flows, the advertiser has got his bait back in incremental profits. But he has not yet any return on his investment, and the only thing that matters for such a return is what happens after he gets his bait back. Productivity of capital is *not* measured or even indicated by how *soon* he gets back his advertising investment (payback period).

The mechanics of applying both variants of the DCF measurement

---

[1] The cumulative impact of this time pattern can be seen most clearly by tracing the effects of year 1, diagrammed at the pinnacle of the profit bar for successive years. By year 7 the effects of the first year's advertising have disappeared; by year 8 the effects of the second year's advertising have, too, and so on. After advertising ceases at the end of year 6, the follow-on benefits of this and previous years continue for several years but trail off in aggregate.

EXHIBIT 13
Profile of Net Balance of Cash Flows from Advertising Outlays
Spread Over Six Years

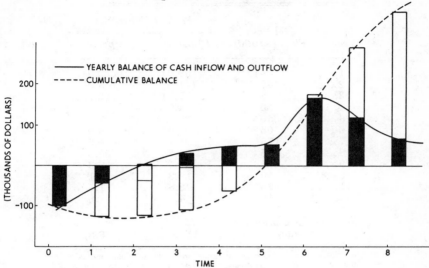

of the productivity of a promotional investment are illustrated in Exhibit 14. For each year the advertising outlay and the prepromotion incremental profits of Exhibit 12 are shown and are netted as in Exhibit 13. The DCF project rate of return is computed from continuous discount tables; it is found to be 18 percent. The present-value variant of DCF is also applied, with cost of capital assumed to be 10 percent. With this value of money the advertising investment promises plus values, since discounted incremental profits when summed are bigger than the present value of the advertising outlays by $1140.

Hence we see that for promotional investments of the spread-out type, DCF measurement of the productivity of the capital that is tied up gives management an engine of analysis which can cope with a stream of future investment outlays forecasted to produce a fluctuating, delayed, and cumulative stream of prepromotional incremental profits. This analysis makes it possible for promotional investments to compete for corporate funds on an objective rate-of-return basis of economic merit, and for investments in persuasion to become an integral part of the firm's planning and rationing of capital.

Thus, there are at least two decision edges for each medium. For example, in direct-mail advertising of a book one decision is where to cut off in working down candidate mail lists which have been laddered as to productiveness. The other decision is where to stop in progressively more intensive promotions of each mail list thus selected.

For immediate-impact advertising the criterion is the same for deci-

EXHIBIT 14
Discounted Cash Flow Method of Computing Return for Spread-out Investment

Year	Net Cash Flow ($1000)	Present Values* at	
		10 percent	18 percent
1.	(104)	(109.0)	(112.0)
2.	(40)	(41.0)	(45.0)
3.	5	(7.7)	(12.0)
4.	30	4.0	6.2
5.	50	25.0	17.7
6.	65	32.0	18.0
7.	175	91.4	54.0
8.	115	54.3	30.0
9.	75	32.1	16.3
10.	50	19.3	9.1
11.	25	8.8	1.3
12.	15	4.8	.6
	Net present value	114.0	(6.0)

* Since continuous discount tables are used, each year's net cash flow must be separated into beginning year outlay and "through year" inflow before being discounted.

sion edges. It is the point where incremental costs of advertising equal incremental profits.

For delayed-impact advertising, the investment decision can be all or none, in which case the cutoff criterion is where the rate of return equals the cost of capital.

The concept that a corporation's investments in promotion should be made to compete with traditional capital expenditure proposals for scarce investable funds is illustrated in Exhibit 15, where the rate-of-return ladder for capital rationing is portrayed.

The idea is simple and plausible. Investment proposals should be ranked on the basis of productivity of capital. In rationing capital, the corporation should work down the rate-of-return ladder until its investable funds are exhausted, if it is unwilling to go to market for additional capital and if the rate of return on the least profitable project thereby accepted is higher than the corporation's market cost of capital. If, on the other hand, the corporation is willing to secure additional capital which can be profitably invested then it should work down the rate-of-return ladder to its market cost of capital (e.g. 10 percent,) accepting all projects above that cutoff and rejecting all below it.

DCF analysis has three variants. The project rate-of-return variant is that illustrated in Exhibit 15. The present-worth variant has also been discussed and used in the preceding analysis. By computing the

EXHIBIT 15
Rate-of-Return Ladder for Capital Rationing

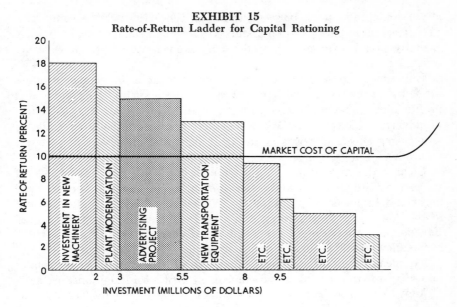

present worth of the benefits of a project at the corporation's cost of capital, all projects on the rate-of-return ladder whose profitability is greater than cost of capital are implicitly accepted by this "go, no-go" gauge and all below it rejected. The third variant, labeled "profitability index," is simply the ratio of the present-worth variant to the amount of capital tied up. If this profitability ratio is greater than 1, the project has a DCF return which beats cost of capital and is implicitly accepted. The profitability-index variant differs from the present-worth variant only in expressing results as a ratio rather than in terms of subtraction.

III. MEASURING THE EFFECTIVENESS OF PROMOTION

Measuring effectiveness of advertising is a big subject, contentious and technical. It would go beyond the scope and space limitations of this paper to do more than touch on a few aspects of it which relate most closely to measuring the productivity of investments in persuasion.

Measurement of the effects of advertising has two dimensions: kinds of effects, and techniques of measurement.

A. Kinds of Advertising Effects

There are basically four kinds of advertising effects that can be measured: (1) effects on behavior (sales), (2) effects on attitudes (usually brand preferences, but sometimes attitudes toward the company), (3) effects on intentions to buy, and (4) effects on the level of knowledge (usually brand awareness, but sometimes knowledge of product characteristics or uses).

Sometimes the explicit purpose of advertising is to change people's attitudes quite apart from the effect of those attitudes on sales and profits. This paper is, however, restricted to a consideration of the effect of advertising on profits. We shall therefore judge the four kinds of advertising effects in terms of the light they cast on advertising's effect on profits.

Clearly the most direct relationship is between profits and sales. If we can measure advertising's effect on sales, we have all the material necessary to measure profitability. We must, of course, take account of the effect of advertising not only on present but also on future sales. For example, the value of a new customer depends on his "loyalty-life" expectancy as well as on his emulation value.

To measure all *other* kinds of effects of advertising, it is usually necessary to translate observed changes in attitudes, intentions, or levels of knowledge into changes in sales. This is usually difficult. The translation can be avoided only when the findings are negative. Sales could not have been favorably affected by advertising if there was no improvement in brand preferences, intentions to buy, brand awareness, etc.

To interpret positive findings, however, it is necessary to know how much sales will increase because of a given improvement in consumer attitudes, intentions, or knowledge. Although the relationship between changes in these indirect effects and changes in sales can sometimes be estimated at given points in time by making both direct and indirect measurements, there is no assurance that the relationship will be stable through time. This basic fact limits the usefulness of measurements of these indirect effects in determining the optimum size of the advertising budget. Therefore, direct measurement of the effect of advertising on sales is usually the only firm basis for the application of the profito-metrics approach.

B. Measurement Techniques

Just as there are different kinds of effects that can be measured so there are different techniques for measuring them. Techniques can be put in two groups: (1) controlled experiments, and (2) nonexperimental techniques.

1. *Controlled Experiments.* By far the most powerful technique available for measuring the effect of anything—be it chemical compounds or advertising—is the designed experiment. No other technique provides such precise information with so little ambiguity. Controlled experiments

deserve to be better understood. There is ample evidence that business-men have failed to appreciate and utilize fully this very powerful tech-nique for providing useful information.

These are three basic principles to designed experiments: (1) The factor being investigated—whether it be advertising or penicillin—must be administered to identifiable subgroups of the entire group in which you are interested. If you are interested in all consumers in the United States, you must administer your advertising to only a portion of these consumers. (2) The subgroup exposed to the facts being investigated must be representative of the entire group which is of interest. (This means that the subgroup must be selected by some random process, defined in its technical, statistical sense.) (3) The difference between changes in the subgroup and the rest of the group (or some portion of it) must be measured before and after the factor being investigated is administered. (This means that controlled experiments on the effects of advertising would involve measuring the rates of sale before and after the advertising in groups which had been exposed to the advertising and groups which had not.)

Many businessmen fail to realize that experimentation, which has been so productive in the natural sciences, can be used with equal valid-ity in business and advertising research even though the subject investi-gated is the uncontrollable behavior of people. The designing and in-terpretation of experiments is a technical process to be performed by trained statisticians, but businessmen should understand the potential value of such experiments to all executives responsible for the control of substantial discretionary expenditures.

It is much easier to carry out controlled experiments of this sort in some advertising media than in others. For example, it is very hard to conduct a controlled experiment for a promotion that uses mass media like television or radio, since we cannot isolate randomly selected groups only one of which was exposed to the promotion. Radio and TV promo-tions have an impact on all households in a specifiable geographic area that own receiving equipment. Thus, it is necessary to match up groups of geographic areas rather than groups of individual households, and random selection is not usually feasible.

In contrast, a promotional campaign conducted by mail is ideally suited for a carefully controlled scientific experiment aimed at gauging the effectiveness of the promotion quickly and accurately. A process of selecting every *nth* household or of sampling candidate mailing lists presumably produces a random group within the mailing-list population. And two such groups constitute a matched pair of random samples with all the characteristics required for comparison. Thus, the main problem with measuring the effectiveness of a mail promotion is obtaining data on sales to individual households in each of the matched groups.

Even for mass media, where matched random-sampled groups cannot in general be obtained, there are statistical procedures capable, in principle, of producing reliable results. Instead of comparing sales in perfectly matched (randomly selected) groups, one can compare sales in areas exposed to the promotion with sales in areas not exposed, adjusting the comparison statistically for whatever differences exist between buyers in the two areas. That is, while the groups are not matched in the sense of being the same in all respects except exposure to the promotion, the effect of the differences between the groups on sales can sometimes be independently estimated, and consequently we can estimate the net effects of the promotion. Whether this procedure will produce reliable results depends on the adequacy of the adjustments for differences.[2]

Painful experience with the practical difficulties of developing controlled experiments in this area make me recognize that competitors can sometimes, without making the outlays, learn much about research findings and even, under some circumstances, distort results. I am aware that the variables that determine a product's sales are numerous and hence that it is impossible to control all variables except the one under study. But this impossibility exists in the physical sciences, too, and it has not prevented the enormous productivity of the controlled experiment here. The variation caused by factors other than the one examined is usually greater in the social sciences. But because we know it is bigger we can sometimes design the experiment so as to show us how much of the variation comes from these irrelevant factors.

2. Nonexperimental Techniques.   When the measurements ideally called for in the profitometrics approach are not feasible, it is sometimes possible to obtain, by inferior means, suggestive indications of the effect of advertising. Information about changes in consumer attitudes, buying intentions, and levels of product and brand knowledge can sometimes provide valuable negative information about advertising effects. However, for positive usefulness it is necessary to measure the relation between sales behavior and these indications of buying conditioners. Bridging this gap metrically is difficult indeed.

An inferior technique of measurement is that involving information gathered in a nonexperimental situation. Data can often be obtained

---

[2] Ideally, if we know that two areas are matched in all critical respects except that household income is higher in one area (the one receiving the promotion) than in the other, and if we know the true relationship between household income and sales, we can obtain an accurate estimate of the promotion's influence on sales by a simple comparison of sales adjusted for the known income difference. But in the real world, groups of people in "matched" areas differ in a variety of subtle ways that we do not fully understand and cannot adequately measure. As a consequence, we can only approximate the true effects of a promotion on sales, and the measurement is subject to a good deal of uncertainty.

with less planning, cost, and technical knowledge than is required for experimentation. The basic and inevitable deficiency of nonexperimental data is that it is never possible to be sure what they mean. There is an inherent ambiguity in all nonexperimental data which makes it impossible to identify and measure causal relationships with certainty and precision. If you are interested in measuring the effect of advertising on sales with the use of historical data relating to advertising and sales, you will always run the research risk that any observed correspondence between increases in sales and advertising is the result of something other than the effect of advertising on sales. For example, when the advertising budget is set as a fixed percentage of sales, the research risk is that sales have determined advertising rather than vice versa. Or conceivably, both advertising and sales increased during periods of rising national income and prosperity and decreased during periods of declining national income, correlation being partly spurious. Under these circumstances, it would be hard to isolate and measure the effect of advertising on sales. The picture gets even more confused when one recognizes the important effects of concurrent changes in competitors' advertising and product policies during the period.

No amount of data can prevent the possibility of several different and perhaps equally plausible interpretations of the results. Under such circumstances the interpretation often chosen is one which conforms to preconceptions or prejudice. This, of course, largely destroys the function of the measurement.

To sum up, profitometrics requires the measurement of the effects of advertising on sales and the effects of sales on profits. These effects ideally should be measured by means of controlled experiments. Delayed and cumulative impacts should be analyzed in terms of the investment return produced by the stream of incremental profits over the loyalty-life expectancy of the customers acquired by the advertising investment.

IV. SOME IMPLICATIONS

There are some interesting implications of this analysis and its underlying postulates:

1. Most promotional outlays are in economic reality (even though not for bookkeeping, for taxpaying, or for conversation) largely investments.

2. Although most companies have multiple objectives the overriding corporate goal for the decisions on investment of corporate capital should be to make money. The basic measurement of the productivity of capital invested in promotion must therefore be profitability.

3. For immediate-impact advertising in principle, profits can be maximized by pushing spending up to the point where the added adver-

tising cost of increasing sales by one unit just equals the incremental prepromotion profit which the additional sale will create. For advertising whose significant effects are "quick and dead," the incremental profit obtained from the sale adequately measures worth.

4. For advertising whose impact is delayed and cumulative and whose results may create a stream of repeat sales, a more complex measure of worth is needed. Because such advertising is really an investment, purchasing customers by promotion is like purchasing annuities. The value of a customer, like the value of an annuity, is the present worth of the stream of future profits he will produce. How long this stream will last has a profound effect on customer worth. It is partly determined by gestation period, partly by the new customer's loyalty life.

5. The investment-profitability yardstick that is realistic and economically appropriate for promotional investments derives from discounted cash-flow analysis (DCF). It has three variants: (a) project rate of return, (b) present worth at cost of capital, and (c) profitability index.

6. Because much promotion is really an investment (happily expensable for tax purposes), it should compete for funds with alternative ways of investing them. This rivalry for capital should be on the basis of profitability. The present worth of the stream of profits which the promotion can yield should be compared with the cost of funds and with the present worth of the stream of profits which could be obtained by the best alternative use of funds.

7. In rationing scarce capital among competing investment proposals, the cutoff or minimum acceptable rate of return should be the corporation's cost of capital—outside market cost or internal opportunity cost, whichever is higher.

8. The estimates necessary for practical application of discounted cash flow analysis *can* be made:

(a) Incremental production cost and prepromotion profit per unit can be predicted cheaply with adequate precision for most mass-produced products.

(b) The effect of advertising on sales is far more difficult to estimate. Yet progress must be and is being made here. Of the various kinds of estimating techniques, the controlled experiment is by far the most precise and powerful means of measuring advertising's effect on sales.

(c) The cost of its equity capital can, with modern techniques, be measured and predicted with sufficient precision so that no corporation is today justified in refusing to use it in sourcing and rationing its capital.

(d) The cost of direct-debt capital is easy to measure with precision. The cost of indirect debt, such as lease debt and oil payments debt, is harder to measure, but workable approximations can be made.

(e) The mix of equity and debt capital that is economic for each corporation can be estimated with adequate accuracy. The mix that is probable for the future (which often differs from the existing mix) is all that is needed to complete the estimate of the corporation's combined cost of capital.

9. There are a number of reasons why the profitometrics approach has not been widely used in determining the advertising appropriation. The basic explanations for this oversight are, I think (1) lack of a determined desire to find the most scientific solution for this intricate management problem, (2) ignorance of the potentialities of modern research techniques for this problem, and (3) quite normal distrust of practically any sort of analysis which is not easily understood by the untrained layman. Economic analysis, even in its most managerial applications, sounds academic, and a DCF investment approach to the advertising budget sounds formidable as well as being unfamiliar.

21. Break-Even Analysis for Lockheed's Tri Star: An Application of Financial Theory[*]

U. E. REINHARDT

One of the more controversial issues during the 1971 Congressional hearings over emergency loan-guarantee legislation was the economic merit of Lockheed's L-1011 Tri Star program. In those hearings, Lockheed sought a federal guarantee for $250 million of additional bank credit required for the completion of that program. The loan guarantee was designed to help Lockheed over the severe liquidity crisis that followed the Defense Department's refusal to absorb all of the cost overruns Lockheed had experienced on a number of military contracts.

Spokesmen for Lockheed insisted that the Tri Star program was basically sound and in jeopardy only because of the independently generated liquidity crisis. The opponents to the guarantee, on the other hand, argued that the program had been economically unsound from the outset and was doomed to financial failure whether or not the loan guarantee was granted.

The debate on this issue proceeded almost entirely on the basis of estimated "break-even" sales. In his testimony before Congress, Lockheed's chief executive asserted that this break-even point would be reached at sales between 195 and 205 aircraft. Although at the time of the hearings Lockheed had placed only 103 firm and 75 optional orders, management was confident that sales would eventually reach or exceed the predicted break-even point and that the project would thereby become a "commercially viable endeavor."

One infers from the context of the debate that Lockheed defined the break-even point as that level of sales at which cumulative revenues just cover the algebraic sum of all development and production costs associated with the Tri Star. Oddly enough, no one during the hearings took Lockheed to task for excluding from this definition one of the more significant costs of producing new aircraft: the opportunity cost of the requisite tech-

* *Journal of Finance*, vol. 28, no. 4 (September 1973), pp. 821–38.

nology and to the construction of appropriate production facilities. There is evidence that, for the Tri Star, these outlays may have amounted to as much as $1 billion, much of which is likely to remain committed to the project for the better part of a decade. To overlook the opportunity cost of such funds is clearly a major error.

In this paper the Tri Star project is reexamined in terms of a capital-budgeting framework. The objective of the analysis is two-fold. First, it serves to illustrate how standard economic and financial theory can be brought to bear on the solution to real-world business problems. Second, it demonstrates the contribution financial theory can make towards rational decision-making in the public sector. From the Congressional hearings one gathers that the loan-guarantee legislation was passed in the belief that the Tri Star program was commercially viable, an impression Lockheed had tried hard to convey with its own break-even projections. Our analysis suggests, however, that the inclusion of the opportunity cost of funds among the total costs of the Tri Star tends to raise the actual break-even sales for the program to a level almost twice as high as the estimates submitted by Lockheed to Congress. It is clear, then, that Congress made its decision in this case on the basis of highly misleading information.

Section II below sets forth the theoretical model underlying our analysis. The section also indicates the various sources from which our revenue and cost estimates have been pieced together. The empirical results from the analysis are presented in Section III. Some necessary *caveats* are offered by way of summary in Section IV.

II. THE BASIC ANALYTIC FRAMEWORK

It is widely agreed among students of corporate finance that, for practical purposes, the most appropriate evaluation criterion for a corporate investment project is the net present value of that project. Assuming continuous cash flows, this criterion is defined as

$$NPV(k) = \int_0^T [R(t) - C(t)] e^{-\rho t} dt, \qquad (1)$$

where $NPV(k)$ denotes the net present value of the project, discounted at the corporation's effective annual cost-of-capital rate, k; $R(t)$ and $C(t)$ denote the stream of cash revenues and cash outlays at time t; T is the investment horizon (the last period for which a cash flow is posited); and the continuously compounded discount rate ρ is equal to $\log_e(1 + k)$. For purposes of this analysis we pretend that $t = 0$ falls somewhere into the spring of 1968 when Lockheed decided to go ahead with the Tri Star program.

For a project consisting of the development, production and sale of a

new commercial aircraft, the revenue stream is composed of down payments made by the airlines upon placing their orders and of payments
upon delivery of the aircraft. The stream of cash outlays consists of three
distinct though over-lapping phases, namely:

1. The outlays associated with the Research, Development, Testing
   and Evaluation (RDTE) phase, covering the range of activities
   from the initial design stage to the evaluation of prototypes;
2. Outlays associated with the Initial Investment and Tooling phase,
   covering the construction of appropriate production facilities and the
   manufacture or procurement of the machine tools, assembly jigs, etc.,
   required during the production phase; and
3. The costs of manufacture (or procurement) of components and their
   assembly into the airframe.

Hereafter, the costs associated with phases 1 and 2 will be referred to as
the *non-recurring* costs. Costs associated with phase 3 will be referred to
as *recurring* or *production* costs.

A. The Non-recurring Costs of the Tri Star Program

In developing the L-1011 Tri Star airbus, Lockheed has not had the
benefit of significant spillovers from a similar military aircraft. The project has therefore required heavy outlays on research and development.
For obvious reasons Lockheed itself has kept a tight lid on its Tri Star
cost data. It is possible, however, to piece together a fairly reliable cost
estimate from bits of information revealed during the Congressional hearings in the financial press or in trade journals. These sources suggest
rather consistently that the total nonrecurring outlays on the Tri Star
program have amounted to at least $800 million and probably to as much
as $1 billion.

An analyst privy to Lockheed's internal records would, of course, be
able to project the exact time path of the nonrecurring cost stream fairly
accurately and construct his evaluation model accordingly. Such details
are not available in the public record. In the absence of better information
it is perhaps not unreasonable to approximate the sum of the phase 1 and
phase 2 costs by a more or less even flow over the period beginning at
time $t = 0$ and ending with the onset of the production phase at time
$t = A$. In other words, we estimate the rate of RDTE and Initial Investment outlays at time t to be

$$C_t = \frac{R + I}{A}, \qquad \text{for} \qquad 0 < t < A, \qquad (2)$$

where R denotes the total RDTE costs associated with the project, I denotes the total initial outlay on production facilities and tooling, and A

denotes the number of months elapsed between the beginning of a serious development effort at $t = 0$ and the onset of the production phase. In the light of the preceding comments, our analysis proceeds on the assumption 800 million $\leqq R + I \leqq 1 billion.

The first delivery of a Tri Star to an airline was made in April 1972. This delivery, however, was about six months behind schedule; it should have been made sometime in the fall of 1971. The slippage was caused primarily by an unforeseeable slippage in the development of the Tri Star's Rolls Royce engines. It is therefore reasonable to suppose that Lockheed based its own calculations in 1968 on an assumed gestation period of not more than 42 months. The present analysis therefore proceeds on the assumption that parameter A in equation (2) is equal to 42.

B. Recurring Production Costs and the Learning Curve

Past studies of aircraft production have led to the remarkable discovery that, for any given type of aircraft, the cumulative average (recurring) production cost per aircraft (excluding any amortization of non-recurring costs) tends to decline by a more or less constant percentage between doubled quantities of production. Thus, if Q denotes any given number of aircraft produced and Y_Q the corresponding cumulative average production cost, then the average cost at an output level of $2Q$ tends to be γY_Q, where γ—the so-called learning coefficient—has a value less than unity and remains virtually constant over all empirically relevant values of Q. The assumption of a constant learning coefficient is almost always incorporated into cost models used by airframe manufacturers. It is therefore most likely that Lockheed's break-even calculations for the Tri Star are based on such an assumption as well.

The learning effect in aircraft assembly may be expressed mathematically by the formula

$$Y_Q = Y_1 Q^{-b} \tag{3}$$

where, in addition to the already familiar symbols, Y_1 denotes the first-unit cost and $b = -\log(\gamma)/\log(2)$. The parameters of this function can be estimated from cost data quoted in an article in *Barron's*. According to the article, presumably knowledgeable industry sources in 1971 estimated the cumulative average production cost per unit after the production of the 150th Tri Star (i.e., Y_{150}) as \$15.5 million. The corresponding figure for a volume of 300 Tri Stars was estimated to be \$12.0 million. If one makes the plausible assumption that these estimates were derived from a conventional learning curve such as equation (3), then the value of b is found to be equal to 0.3619188 and the implied first-unit cost (Y_1) is found to be approximately \$100 million. These parameter estimates are equivalent to a learning coefficient (γ) of 77.4 percent, an estimate that is perfectly consistent with recent research on learning in aircraft production. Such research has indicated that, for complex modern aircraft, learning coefficients between 75 percent and 78 percent are typical.

If $Q(t)$ denotes the total number of Tri Stars that will have been produced by the end of period t, and $Y_{Q(t)}$ the corresponding cumulative average production cost, then, using equation (3), the cumulative total production cost at time t can be written as

$$TC(t) = Y_1[Q(t)]^{(1-b)} \qquad (4)$$

and the rate of production costs experienced at time t is given by

$$C(t) = (1 - b) Y_1[Q(t)]^{-b} \partial Q(t)/\partial t. \qquad (5)$$

According to testimony given before the House Committee on Banking and Currency, Lockheed's original production schedule called for the production of 220 Tri Stars over a period beginning in late 1971 and ending in late 1977. This schedule is equivalent to an average production rate of three aircraft per month. Although the production rates foreseen in the original schedule do fluctuate somewhat from year to year, we shall find it analytically more convenient to posit a constant monthly production rate, N, for the entire program, so that $Q(t)$ can be written as

$$Q(t) = (t - A)N. \qquad (6)$$

For the most part we shall base our calculations on a value of $N = 3$. But we shall experiment also with plausible alternative values for N.

The projected time path of recurring costs for the Tri Star program can now be expressed as

$$C(t) = (1 - b) Y_1(t - A)^{-b} N^{(1-b)}, \qquad (7)$$

for

$$A = 42,$$
$$b = .369188,$$
$$Y_1 = \$100 \text{ million},$$
$$t > A$$

where $t = A$, it will be recalled, denotes the onset of the production phase. As will be indicated shortly, the average price the airlines were expected, in 1968, to pay for the Tri Star (excluding any inflationary escalation) appears to have been somewhere between \$15 and \$16 million. Within that price range, we estimate a positive cash flow from the program after production of about the 50th aircraft. This estimate is virtually identical to that made public by Lockheed, whose chief executive testified before the Senate hearings that "a break-even point in terms of cash flow is reached at approximately the 50th aircraft in 1973. This cash break-even point compares production costs with sales price." Our recurring production cost estimates, therefore, appear to be fairly close to Lockheed's own forecast.

C. Lockheed's Cost of Capital

Much has been written about the problem of estimating the value of the cost-of-capital rate, k, in practical applications. One's approach to the problem depends essentially on the goals the firm is expected to pursue.

In a capitalist society it is normally assumed that, at any point in time, the management of a private corporation should conduct the affairs of the firm so as to maximize the wealth of existing shareholders. If this is the ultimate goal of corporate investment, then the appropriate cost-of-capital rate can be shown to be equal to

$$k = \sum_{j=1}^{j=n} (W_j k_j) \tag{8}$$

where k_j is the effective annual after-tax cost per dollar of the j-th source of funds and W_j is the proportion (measured at the aggregate market value of the underlying security) of the j-th source of funds in the long-run capital structure deemed optimal by the firm.

A review of Lockheed's historical record reveals that, under normal conditions, the firm tends to prefer a capital structure with about 30 percent debt and 70 percent equity. For a company in the rather unstable aerospace sector, this relationship is probably viewed as a prudent limit. At any rate, between the late 1950s and 1967 Lockheed has generally remained within this debt limit. Since 1968 the company's debt-to-equity ratio has, of course, risen enormously, and almost certainly against the company's wishes.

If one assumes that Lockheed's desired long-term capital structure consists of about 30 percent short- or long-term debt and 70 percent common stock and retained earnings (weighted at market values), then equation (8) can be restated as

$$k = .3k_d + .7k_e \tag{9}$$

where k_d denotes the average after-tax cost of debt and k_e the cost of equity capital.

In 1968, Lockheed probably faced an average after-tax cost of debt (k_d) between 4 percent and 5 percent. The effective rate would, of course, be higher if there were insufficient profits that could be shielded by interest expenses. In view of the likelihood of that circumstance, we may assume that k_d was equal to at least 5 percent.

It is more difficult to arrive at an estimate of the cost of equity capital,

k_e. The theory of investors' behavior suggests that, if investors in the stockmarket, on average, believe that a firm's dividends per share will tend to grow at an average annual compound rate g over the long run, the firm's cost of equity capital can be approximated by the expression

$$k_e = \frac{D}{P} + g, \tag{10}$$

where D denotes the dividends per share announced for the current period, and P is either the current market price per share (if k_e refers to the cost of retained earnings) or the net proceeds per share (after flotation costs) of a new commonstock issue (if k_e refers to the cost of new equity capital).

Between 1957–61 and 1964–68, Lockheed's cash earnings per share increased at an average annual compound rate of 19.1 percent. The corresponding growth rate for cash dividends per share was 22 percent. As late as April 1969, the *Value Line Investment Survey* forecast a future average annual growth rate in cash earnings per share of 6.5 percent. One might therefore set the growth rate, g, in equation (10) at 6 percent to 7 percent.

Lockheed's dividend yield (D/P) in 1968 was 4.2 percent. It had been close to 4 percent ever since the mid-1960s. If one takes into account the fact that, because of flotation costs, the ratio D/P for new equity is higher than the current dividend yield, then one is led to conclude that Lockheed's average cost of equity capital in 1968 must have been close to 12 percent.

Upon insertion of the estimated values of k_d and k_e into equation (9), Lockheed's overall cost-of-capital rate, k, prior to the acceptance of the Tri Star project is found to be somewhere between 9 percent and 10 percent. In view of the enormous marginal business risk the Tri Star project added to Lockheed's overall business risk, an argument can be made to apply a cost-of-capital rate of at least 10 percent, or possibly even higher, to the Tri Star program.

It is clear that the cost-of-capital rate calculated above reflects essentially the opportunity costs borne by the suppliers of corporate funds (primarily shareholders). By appealing to something called the "organizational instinct of self preservation," some writers in finance have argued that in many situations the more relevant opportunities are those faced by the corporation itself rather than the almost unlimited opportunities faced by shareholders. If corporate opportunities are limited, it is argued, a much lower discount rate may be acceptable.

In order to accommodate several alternative views on the proper cost-of-capital rate, the Tri Star program will be evaluated here for values of $k = 5$ percent, $k = 10$ percent and $k = 15$ percent. It may be mentioned, however, that this author is not impressed by a financial theory predicated on the "instinct for organizational self preservation" and considers the 10 percent rate as the minimum defensible rate in the present case.

Those who do set store by the *corporate-opportunities* concept, however, will no doubt acknowledge that the range of opportunities to be evaluated by the corporation includes diversification into other lines of business through merger, or, at a minimum, investment of corporate funds in financial securities. In 1968, high-grade, long-term corporate bonds sold at yields between 8 and 9 percent and tax-exempt municipals yielded in excess of 5 percent. The latter rate must surely be viewed as the lowest conceivable opportunity cost of Lockheed's funds.

D. Revenues from the Tri Star Program

The time profile of cash revenues from the Tri Star program depends on the price the airlines pay for the aircraft, the manner in which payment is made, and on the monthly rate, N, at which Lockheed produces and delivers the planes. For present purposes it is assumed that all customers pay the same price, although in fact there may be small price differences depending upon the interior layout ordered by individual airlines.

By mid-1971 Lockheed's customers had advanced about $260 million for future deliveries of the Tri Star. One way of handling these down payments within a capital-budgeting framework would be to treat them as cash revenues received during the RDTE and Initial Investment phases and to deduct them from the nonrecurring costs incurred during those phases. From an analytical standpoint this approach would certainly be sound. But without knowing the precise payment pattern it is difficult to implement that approach here.

An alternative approach, however, suggests itself. It is inconceivable that the airlines would commit funds of this magnitude without promise of a return either in the form of explicit interest charges or in the form of a discount off the price paid by customers who have not made any down payment. One may, therefore, treat the $260 million down payments as ordinary interest-bearing loans. The only distinguishing features of the loans are that they are granted by airlines rather than by banks, that some of the interest is paid in the form of a lower sales price rather than as periodic interest payments, and that the loans are repaid in kind (aircraft) rather than with cash. On this interpretation it is analytically acceptable to lump the down payments in with the rest of the firm's traditional sources of funds and to pretend that all cash revenues are earned as the aircraft are delivered to customers.

The original price of the Tri Star is said to have been $14.7 million including the propulsion system of three engines. Subsequently the price has been adjusted upward via escalator clauses in Lockheed's sales contracts. The average price is currently said to be between $15 and $16 million. Although the price will undoubtedly rise further in step with inflationary increases in production costs, such price increases per se will not affect future cash flows since they have an exact contemporaneous counterpart in costs. It is therefore legitimate to evaluate the Tri Star program in terms of a constant base price envisaged in 1968. In line with that reasoning, the flow of revenues at time t may thus be defined as

$$R(t) = PN, \quad \text{for} \quad t > A. \tag{11}$$

A base value of $P = \$15.5$ million is probably not far off the mark, though perhaps somewhat on the high side. The bulk of our analysis will be based on that value, although we shall evaluate the program also at other assumed values for P.

E. Summary of the Evaluation Model

The basic components of our model can now be combined into the overall net-present value of the Tri Star project:

$$NPV(k) = [1 - tx]\left[NP \int_A^T e^{-\rho t}\, dt - \frac{R+I}{A} \int_0^A e^{-\rho t} dt \right.$$

$$\left. - (1-b)\, Y_1 N^{(1-b)} \int_A^T (t-A)^{-b} e^{-\rho t} dt \right] \tag{12}$$

where, in addition to the already familiar symbols, tx denotes the effective tax rate on corporate profits faced by Lockheed, and T denotes the last period during which production takes place. In equation (12), the first term within the large brackets is the present value of all future revenues from the project, with "present" understood to mean the spring of 1968. The second term in the brackets is the present value of all RDTE and Initial Investment outlays, and the third term is the present value of all future production costs.

In equation (12), the third term within the large brackets on the right-hand side can be restated as the product of a set of constants and the integral of the gamma function. Upon evaluation of the remaining integrals in equation (12), the latter becomes

$$NPV(k) = [1 - tx]\left[NP\left(\frac{1 - e^{-\rho(T-A)}}{\rho e^{\rho A}}\right) - \left(\frac{R+I}{A}\right)\left(\frac{1 - e^{-\rho A}}{\rho}\right) \right.$$

$$\left. - (1-b)\, Y_1 \left(\frac{N}{\rho}\right)^{(1-b)} e^{-\rho A} \sum_{j=0}^{\infty} \left[\frac{(-1)^j [\rho(T-A)]^{j+1-b}}{j![j+1-b]}\right] \right]. \tag{13}$$

The diagrams presented in the next section have been developed from equation (13), and from the parameter estimates indicated in the previous sections.

III. THE APPARENT PROFITABILITY (OR LACK OF IT) OF THE TRI STAR PROGRAM

A. Estimated Net Present Values and Break-Even Sales: The 1968 Perspective

Figure 1 below presents estimated net present values of the Tri Star program at alternative sales levels and discount rates. The curves are drawn on the assumption that the total nonrecurring costs of the program $(R + I)$ are $900 million, that the average price per aircraft (P) is $15.5 million, that an average of three aircraft per month are produced and sold (N), that the Development and Initial Investment phase (A) is 42 months, that Lockheed faces a 50 percent tax rate (tx) and that the Tri Star program costs will always have positive income to shield. These assumptions are indicated in the upper left corner of the diagram.

The curve labeled "$k = 0$ percent" is a plot of net-present values at a zero cost-of-capital rate. At any given level of sales, the vertical distance

FIGURE 1

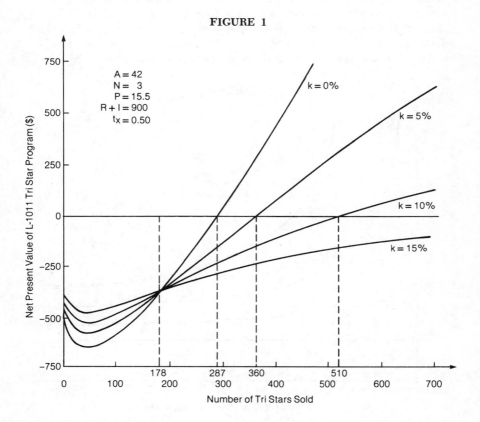

between this line and the horizontal line labeled *BE* represents the projected profit (or loss) *prior to deduction of any capital costs.* Virtually the entire debate before Congress was based on this concept of "profits." According to our cost model, the "naive" break-even level of sales implicit in this concept of "profits" is about 287 aircraft. This estimate is much higher than Lockheed's original forecast, although it is not too far off the company's recently announced, revised break-even estimate of 275 aircraft. Our estimate is also quite close to the break-even estimate of 300 Tri Stars suggested by the industry sources quoted in *Barron's.*

For sales volumes exceeding 287 Tri Stars, "profits" prior to capital costs are projected by our model. It is also seen from Figure 1 that for a sales volume of 178 orders, the model predicts a "loss" prior to capital costs of close to $370 million.

The curves labeled "$k = 5$ percent," "$k = 10$ percent" and "$k = 15$ percent" are similar to that labeled "$k - 0$ percent," but here the cost-of-capital has been explicitly taken into account. At an assumed effective cost-of-capital rate of 5 percent per annum, the estimated break even level is about 360 aircraft; at 10 percent this level rises to about 510 aircraft; at 15 percent the break-even point exceeds 1,000 aircraft.

Figure 1 is based on the assumption that Lockheed will produce and deliver the Tri Stars at an average rate of three aircraft per month. The sensitivity of the break-even volume to the assumed delivery schedule is

FIGURE 2

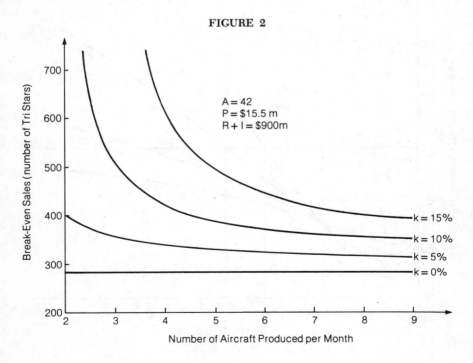

A = 42
P = $15.5 m
R + I = $900m

indicated in Figure 2. At cost-of-capital rates in excess of 5 percent, a speed-up in deliveries becomes increasingly beneficial. These benefits, however, accrue at a diminishing rate. Little appears to be gained by pushing deliveries beyond a rate of about 6 per month.

From the point of view of managerial decision making, Figure 3 is perhaps the most interesting constellation of program variables. The set of curves in that figure represents estimated break-even sales as a function of the sales price per Tri Star. The lower curve of each pair of curves is based on assumed nonrecurring costs $(R + I)$ of $800 million, the upper on $1 billion. The three pairs of curves are drawn on the assumption of a zero, 5 percent and 10 percent cost-of-capital rate, respectively, as is indicated in the graph.

For a given level of nonrecurring costs and a given discount rate, any price-sales combination falling above the corresponding curve in Figure 3 yields a positive net present value fo rthe Tri Star program. Any price-sales combination falling below the curve, on the other hand, is associated with a negative net present value. Each of the curves may therefore be viewed as the break-even frontier corresponding to the assumed values of $R + I$ and k.

The curves in Figure 3 may be superimposed on the demand schedule for Tri Stars Lockheed appears to have faced in 1968. For the program to

FIGURE 3

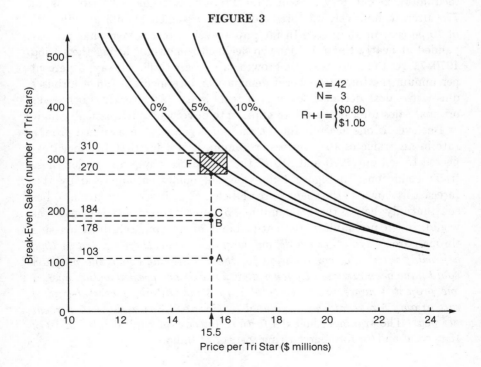

be economically viable, at least one point on that demand curve would have had to fall onto the relevant break-even frontier or, preferably, onto the positive side of that frontier.

Unfortunately even the approximate shape of the demand curve perceived by Lockheed is unknown to outsiders. But we do know at least some points on the perceived and on the actual demand curves for the Tri Star.

As indicated earlier, at the time of the Congressional hearings in mid-1971, Lockheed claimed to have orders for 178 Tri Stars of which 103 were firm orders and 75 were so-called second-buys or options that are subject to cancellation by the customer. These orders were probably negotiated at prices (prior to inflationary escalation) in the neighborhood of $15.5 million. In Figure 3, the sales levels of 103 and 178 are indicated as points A and B. By the end of October 1972 total orders had increased only by 11 aircraft (117 firm and 67 options). The total of 184 aircraft is shown as point C in Figure 3. All three sales levels lie very much below the break-even frontier, even if one posits only $800 million in nonrecurring costs and excludes capital costs from total program costs altogether.

In all fairness it must be acknowledged that, in 1968, Lockheed probably forecast sales in excess of 178 aircraft. From the testimony before Congress one gathers that Lockheed had originally hoped to capture 35 to 40 percent of a total free-world market of 775 wide-bodied airbuses of the medium range category for which the Tri Star is designed. The forecast of 775 aircraft, however, was predicted on an assumed annual growth rate of 10 percent in air travel. In fact, air travel in recent years has not expanded at nearly this rate; it even declined somewhat during the period 1970–71. At the more realistic growth rate in air traffic of, say, 5 percent per annum the total free-world demand for intermediate range airbuses during the next decade is estimated to be only 323 aircraft. Lockheed's original sales forecast therefore appears to have been unrealistically high.

But even if one accepts, for the sake of argument, an assumed growth rate in air traffic of 10 percent per annum, it is clear that Lockheed expected to sell only 270 and 310 of the 775 aircraft required under those traffic conditions. In Figure 3 the range of points encompassed by this forecast is shown as the shaded area labeled F. This set of figures also lies substantially below the $800 million 5 percent break-even frontier as would, in all probability, the entire band of demand schedules passing through area F. *In other words, one may doubt that there existed in 1968 a feasible price-sales combination for the Tri Star at which the program could have been expected to generate a positive net present value, even if one projected nonrecurring costs of only $800 million, a cost-of-capital rate of only 5 percent and an annual traffic growth as high as 10 percent per year!* The argument holds, *a fortiori*, for cost-of-capital rates of 10 or 15 percent and/or for nonrecurring costs of $1 billion.

B. The Economic Value of the Tri Star Program in 1971

Our analysis sheds light also on a proposition that was offered by Lockheed (and by former Treasury Secretary Connally) during the Congressional hearings on the loan guarantee. According to this proposition, a federal guarantee to Lockheed was in the national interest because it would be the height of folly to abandon a project on which close to $1 billion had already been spent. It is clear from the testimony that this proposition was based essentially on the well-known "sunk-cost fallacy" that heavy past expenditures *ipso facto* justify future expenditures. But even a more careful analyst at the time might have accepted Lockheed's proposition on the intuitive belief that future revenues from the Tri Star program would surely justify all expenditures yet to be incurred as of mid-1971. As it turns out, one's intuition in this case may be quite misleading.

In Figure 4, the break-even point for the Tri Star is plotted against various assumed levels of "nonrecurring costs yet to be incurred as of mid-1971." It will be noted that parameter A—the remainder of the development phase—has been set to six months. As is apparent from the diagram, a break-even level of 150 Tri Stars is indicated even if one applies a zero discount rate and posits no further nonrecurring costs past mid-1971. The reason for this rather high break-even point is that during the

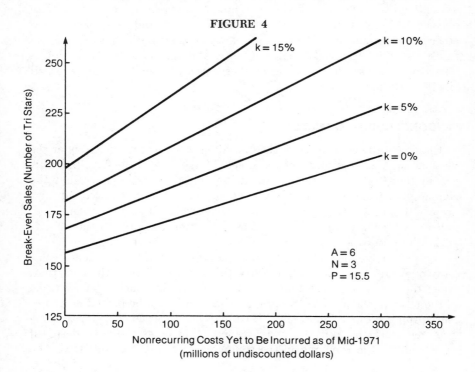

FIGURE 4

early part of the production phase, the recurring costs per aircraft are far in excess of the price paid by the airlines. Indeed, it was noted above that the cash flow on the program becomes positive only after about the 50th Tri Star has been sold.

If one discounts future cash flows at 10 percent—as one should—then the break-even level rises to about 180 aircraft if an average of 3 Tri Stars are produced per month, or to 175 at a monthly production rate of 4 aircraft. Finally, if there were any nonrecurring outlays yet to be incurred as of mid-1971, the relevant break-even level might well have exceeded 200 aircraft. It would appear, then, that from Lockheed's own perspective in mid-1971 the Tri Star program was not a sure winner even if all non-recurring costs incurred prior to that date had been written off. After all, 75 of the 178 orders then in hand were merely options.

From society's point of view, the economic merits of the program were still more dubious. It is reasonable to assume that, had the Tri Star program been abandoned in 1971, most of Lockheed's market share would probably have accrued to McDonnell Douglas's very similar DC-10. And these DC-10s would have been produced on a far lower point of the learning curve than will Lockheed's Tri Stars. At the present time there is a serious question whether either of the two companies will earn a positive return on their airbus projects. Congress in 1971 might therefore have asked itself the question whether two languishing projects are better than one economically sound and one abandoned project, and whether it is necessarily in the national interest to guarantee the production of two virtually identical types of aircraft at high average costs, when the alternative is to make do with one of these aircraft produced, however, at significantly lower costs.

IV. CONCLUDING REMARKS

One is led to conclude from the preceding analysis that even under the most favorable conditions Lockheed could have viewed the Tri Star project, in 1968, as "commercially attractive" only if one assumes that the company was prepared to advance the enormous sums required for that project without asking for any positive return on this investment and, indeed, without even seeking to recover through the project the out-of-pocket interest expenses on the funds borrowed for the project.

It is, of course, not difficult to think of reasons why an aerospace company might follow such a policy. First, there may have been the hope that, under the amorphous cost definitions used in the aerospace business, some of the costs of the Tri Star program could eventually be passed on to defense projects. Furthermore, Lockheed may have viewed the Tri Star program as something akin to a "loss leader," that is, as a project designed to reestablish the company in the commercial aircraft market. If so, the program ought not to be evaluated in isolation but instead as an integral part of a much longer-range investment strategy aimed at developing a more diversified set of business activities. Under such a strategy, the Tri Star program might make economic sense in spite of its own dubious profit potential.

In conclusion it is appropriate to remind the reader also that the present analysis is based on cost data pieced together from a variety of outside sources that may not reflect Lockheed's true cost record accurately. Although our estimates of nonrecurring and recurring costs appear to be consistent with Lockheed's testimony before Congress, one cannot rule out the possibility that the use of Lockheed's internal cost data in our model might have led to somewhat different results.

In this connection, however, it may be mentioned that the pessimistic conclusions reached here find an echo in the prognosis offered by Willard F. Rockwell, chairman and chief executive of North American Rockwell (a prominent aerospace company). As the latter was quoted in the *Los Angeles Times:*

Talk to anyone who has really studied the situation and they'll tell you that the guarantee is really only the first go and that they're going to need more money after that and that they're still going to lose their shirts on the L-1011. . . . The only way that Lockheed could conceivably break even on the project is by getting the entire market for the airbus."

This prognosis does, of course, not sit well with Lockheed. The company's chairman stated before the House Committee on Banking and Currency:

We know that various people outside our company and with no access at all to our data . . . have made varying statements about break-even points, market potential, and ultimate profitability of the L-1011. *Obviously we discount this kind of projection."* (Italics added)

One simply cannot suppress the response: "Wouldst thou hadst discounted thy cash flows instead!"

part SIX
Forecasting

INTRODUCTION

The general subject of forecasting may be divided in two ways: (1) according to the forecast period, whether short run or long, and (2) according to the forecasting method, whether "subjective" (judgmental) or "objective" (based on economic relationships and statistical techniques). The article by John Lewis cuts across this classification, concerning itself with method in short-run forecasts. Lewis argues that many of the short-run methods are complementary, that a good combination of subjective and objective methods can achieve better forecasts than either when used alone.

The "economic-indicators" approach to forecasting is an objective method discussed briefly by Geoffrey H. Moore. Subtle relationships exist between and among specific measures of economic activity such as employment, output, income, capital investment, and so on. If perceived properly, Moore says, these relationships are useful to one attempting to forecast economic developments.

Objective, econometric methods of forecasting may be very useful if they predict short-range changes in, say, a dependent variable. But whether complex econometric methods provide more accurate forecasts than simpler econometric methods is the subject of much debate. J. Scott Armstrong compares and contrasts the folklore and fact of forecasting with econometric methods.

Input-output analysis as a tool in economic forecasting is available to us primarily because of the pioneering effort of Nobel prize-winning laureate, Wassily Leontief. His work relates the production of each industry to its consumption from every other industry. Input-output tables are provided for the entire economy by the U.S. government. These tables differ in a statistical sense from those provided initially by Leontief; yet, they are based on ideas initially revealed by Leontief.

Anthony E. Bopp and John A. Neri compare the results obtained by forecasting the price of gasoline via utilization of three different methodologies. Their results indicate a simple regression equation that relies on the forecast of one exogenous variable often gives satisfactory results.

22. Short-Term General Business Conditions Forecasting: Some Comments on Method*

JOHN P. LEWIS

The assignment that gave rise to this paper stipulated that I should first establish some kind of classification of general short-term forecasting techniques and then evaluate the several techniques on the basis of their showings during the past two or three years. What follows, however, does not really attempt the second of these tasks. One's impulse to construct batting averages is forestalled, for one thing, by the near impossibility of defining the universe from which a sample of representative forecasts might be drawn. Moreover, it is far harder to classify forecasters than forecasting techniques; few of us in practice are willing to stick exclusively to a particular technique, no matter how partisan to it we may be (and in this habit of mixed practice, I shall be saying, we are very wise.) Furthermore, insofar as one *can* associate particular forecasters or forecasting groups or exercises with particular techniques, the variance in recent performance is much greater between the best and worst records within particular categories than it is among the best performances in the several categories. Finally, as one who must sometimes practice the art himself, I feel, in any event, that there is a certain basic indecency about displaying forecasters' comparative batting average publicly. To do so is too much like reading a paper to an open meeting of a county medical society in which one undertakes to spell out which local doctors lost the most patients last year.

Accordingly, my purpose here will be to dwell, rather than upon batting averages, upon the potentialities for complementarity among the several major forecasting approaches. In doing so, I hope largely to avoid contentiousness, of which we have already had altogether too much with respect to short-term forecasting methodology. The central, if pious, thesis of the paper is that all of us who find ourselves engaged in the

* "Short-Term General Business Conditions Forecasting: Some Comments on Methods," by John P. Lewis. Reprinted from *Journal of Business*, vol. 35, no. 4 (October 1962), pp. 343–56, by permission of The University of Chicago Press © Copyright 1962, The University of Chicago Press.

forecasting enterprise rather urgently need every bit of quasi-respectable help we can get from one another.

I. SOME GROUND CLEARING

I propose to focus my discussion on five varieties of forecasting techniques that currently constitute the professional economic core of the activity—(1) leading indicators of the National Bureau of Economic Research (NBER) variety, (2) the leading monetary indicators that have been pioneered by Professor Milton Friedman and his associates, (3) use of those surveys of spenders' intentions and of other compilations of advance plans and commitments that, I believe, Martin Gainsbrugh was the first to label collectively as "foreshadowing indicators," (4) econometric model building, and (5) that looser, less elegant, but more comprehensive variety of model building that has been called many things, which I prefer to label "opportunistic."

These techniques have certain common characteristics. They share a certain professional respectability and orthodoxy; they are not, within the trade, regarded as crackpot approaches (although this, if one looks at the history of the art, is not necessarily a cause for reassurance). They all invite some use of the economists' trained skills; thereby they implicitly assume that a systematic marshalling of such skills can yield insights into the near-term economic future that an intelligent layman would be likely to miss. In this sense they are not diffident techniques. Finally, they all are genuinely professional techniques in that they are regimens for arriving by mainly dispassionate, quasi-objective procedures at technically honest answers to the question of what the unfolding condition of the economy is likely to be. They are not the best techniques, in other words, for telling bosses, Presidents, congressmen, and other decision makers what they want to hear. All of these techniques, to be sure, can be twisted to yield preconceived answers, but at least they create tensions—they set up conflicts of loyalties—in any conscientious professional when he is called upon to abuse them in this fashion.

By concentrating on these five varieties of technique—the two kinds of leading-indicator analysis, the foreshadowing indicators, and the two kinds of model building—we shall be leaving out of account a fair part of the total methodological terrain. We shall pass over, for example, those analytical cults whose basic forecasting hypothesis is that inexorable, rhythmical cycles in activity are so deeply rooted in the laws of the economy that all the forecaster needs to do is, first, identify the relevant cycles by penetrating the cunning veil which nature seems to cast over them; second, locate the present position of the economy in the identified cycle or cycles; and then, third, proceed to read future business conditions right off the calendar. It would be presumptuous to say that the rhythmical cycle hypothesis has no place at all in sensible forecasting practice—it has certain, although limited, uses, for example, in the inventory field—but those who retain it as their principal general forecasting doctrine have, by now, been consigned to the crackpot category, and I think deservedly so.

We also shall be passing over a rather mixed bag of forecasting practices that I have labeled elsewhere as the "agnostic techniques"—meaning by that those more or less self-evidently weak methods for probing the future to which people resort when they doubt their capacity to do anything better. They may, for example, adopt a no-change hypothesis, projecting the latest period's level to the coming period, or, if they want to be a bit more sophisticated, they may extrapolate the recent trend to future periods. In the very best contemporary forecasting, of course, there are a number of points at which practitioners still fall back on precisely this procedure. However, if no-change extrapolations were the craft's universal methodology, it would be professionally bankrupt.

General expectations surveys also belong in the "agnostic" category. I am referring now to surveys, not of respondents' spending intentions or even of their own sales expectations, but of their anticipations of general business conditions. Such general expectations surveys may provide the forecaster with some useful data of a psychological sort, but if they are viewed as producing self-contained forecasts in their own right, their use rests on the hypothesis that the blind can lead the blind—if they do it collectively, that is. Then there is that variety of forecaster whom we might call "the parasitical agnostic"—the fellow who relies, via the Joe Livingston type of survey, upon the consensus of the experts. This, of course, is a fairly sensible, if unambitious, procedure, and, in fact, such surveys are of great utility to the experts themselves. For if there is any quality that ill suits a practicing forecaster it is arrogant indifference to what others in the trade are saying. All the same, the surveying of expert expectations obviously is a derivative forecasting methodology at best; it would cease to exist if the only experts were those who were expert in surveying experts' expectations.

Gerhard Colm has suggested to me one other methodological category that ought to be included in the list, but it too I shall largely pass over here. Colm's suggestion is the "cynical" forecast, and his example is the curious inability of the Council of Economic Advisers late in the Eisenhower Administration to detect the approach or even the start of the recession of 1960–61. I would prefer a slightly less harsh label— say, the "contrived" or "ulterior-motive" forecast—and, to balance things up politically, suggest as another example the present Administration's forecast of a $570 billion GNP for 1962. This last has not entailed any violent wrenching of professional standards, but Administration economists rather plainly have been looking on the bright side for a reason.

Having brought the matter up, I want to make a couple of quick comments on central-government forecasting, particularly that done within the executive office of the president. Two separable problems are involved. One is simply the feedback problem that besets any highly influential forecaster, public or private: Shall he allow himself to be deflected by the fact that his prognostications are likely, themselves, to have some impact upon business conditions in the forecast period? The accepted answer to this question, it seems to me, is "No." An agency like the Council of Economic Advisers should do the most accurate job it can of identifying the prospects likely to emerge under existing policies. But then when, by following this no-nonsense procedure, it finds itself about to release a pessimistic forecast, it also should do what it can to see that there comes, packaged with the forecast, a program of policies whose adoption would tend to make the disappointing forecast become untrue.

The other, and much stickier, problem under which official forecasters labor is that of occasional but stubborn direct political constraints. At least two economic-policy changes presently under discussion in Washington would relax the political inhibitions under which government forecasters lately have been working. One is the proposed delegation of increased standby stabilization powers to the president. This would weaken the presently inhibiting assumption that the tempo of adjustments in fiscal policy directed by business conditions necessarily should match the tempo of our congressional and electoral calendars. The second—and, in this context, the more important—reform may occur in the field of budgeting practice. Moves are under way to deflate further the traditional administrative budget concept and, in particular, to inject some sort of business-style distinction between capital and current outlays into federal accounting. Such a change, which would parallel the standard practice in most West European countries, could, as one of its by-products, greatly ease the constraint that the balanced-budget fetish has been imposing on responsible forecasters.

But I stray too far afield. For the ulterior-motive type, like the agnostic and rhythmical-cycle types, of forecasting lies beyond the boundaries to which I want to confine the burden of this discussion.

II. SOME LIMITATIONS OF THE TECHNIQUES USED SINGLY

As for the central core of professional short-term forecasting techniques, a commentator at this juncture, I think, must deliberately choose what the mood of his commentary is going to be. One could readily take a very bullish view of things, for the state of the art plainly is greatly improved from its condition a generation or even a decade ago. It would be equally legitimate, however, to adopt a thoroughly bearish stance and enlarge on the theme that, when you come right down to it, we are still practicing alchemy, not chemistry. So long as two intelligent persons or groups practicing the "same" techniques can come out with radically different forecasting answers, our scientific pretensions do not become us very well.

As indicated already, however, my own choice of a theme is neither gloom nor buoyancy but, rather, synthesis. I want to emphasize the complementarity of the several techniques we have under inspection, and this can best be done in two stages. First, I want to suggest some of the weaknesses that each of the five conventionally respectable techniques exhibits as a self-sufficient, go-it-alone device. But then, second, I want to underscore the contribution that each of these techniques can make to a properly comprehensive and synthesized forecasting exercise.

A. NBER Leading Indicators

The point has been rather widely made by now that the National Bureau of Economic Research type of leading indicator analysis constitutes a good bit less than a complete set of forecasting tools. This comes as no shock to the more responsible users and proponents of leads-and-lags analysis. However, a brief summary of the limitations of the method may still be in order. They seem to me to be these:

In the first place, the NBER leading indicators are inherently weak devices for detecting the *magnitude* of coming changes in business conditions. Their purpose is the detection of coming turning points, but, despite the improvements that Julius Shiskin lately has attempted in this regard, they have little capacity for disclosing how sharp the turn will be or how high or deep the upswing or downswing will go.

In the second place, the leading indicators as a group are quite short-range devices. Even if there were no problem of garbled signals, they would, as a group, give us no more than six months' advance notice of a coming downturn in the economy—and far less than that in the case of upturns.

In the third place, there *is* a problem of garbled signals. Looked at individually the leading indicators series run jagged courses. When any given wiggle occurs it usually takes two or three months to tell whether the leading indicator really has turned a significant corner or not, and by then, of course, much of its lead has been eaten up. Moreover, the leads of the particular indicators are not consistent from cycle to cycle, making it difficult to guess how soon a signaled change may occur. More important, the several leading indicators almost never all point in the same direction, especially in months just prior to general turns in business conditions. And while the "diffusion indexes" represent a natural and probably necessary attempt to cope with this last problem, they suppress most of the illuminating detail in the series that underlie them; typically they give no weight to the magnitudes of the expansions and contractions in the component series; they weight all of the components together as if they were of equal intrinsic importance; and, despite all of this, the diffusion indexes themselves are highly irregular in their movements.

Finally, as a self-sufficient technique, the leads-and-lags approach has this major limitation: it implicitly assumes a very high degree of structural rigidity in the economy. It has no adequate way of coping, for example, with major changes in the structure of demand. It is in such terms, I think, that one must explain the few past occasions—in 1951, 1956, and in 1959—on which the leading indicators have given concerted and prolonged false signals.

B. The Leading Monetary Indicators

The rest of us are much indebted to Friedman and his colleagues for emphasizing in recent years the degree to which the rate of change in the money supply tends to lead changes in general business activity, and changes in monetary reserves lead the money supply, and changes in central bank policy lead monetary reserves. The efforts to marshal the evidence underlying these assertions, to establish a format for the presentation of pertinent indicators, and to interest some of our reserve banks and other financial institutions in their publication have been all to the good.

Despite my reading of some of Friedman's writings on the subject and several lucid papers by Beryl Sprinkel, however, I confess to some confusion as to how far the proponents of the leading monetary indicators mean to go in claiming self-sufficiency for them as forecast devices. This confusion is rooted, in turn, in my confusion about the theoretical debate from which advocacy of the leading monetary indicators seems to emerge.

I am rather puzzled by the alleged contest between so-called modern quantity theory and the better contemporary versions of what is called income and expenditure theory. It seems to me just as evident that early Keynesian theory went much too far in underrating the role of money as a determinant of general economic activity even as the quantity theorists of the twenties went too far in overrating it. Surely it was a mistake to believe that the frail stem of the money rate of interest could bear the full burden of the impact of finance and financial institutions on investment activity, just as it was a mistake to talk as if monetary and credit conditions had a direct impact only on investment and not also upon such other sectors as consumer buying of durables and state and local government outlays. I should have supposed that today just about any journeyman analyst of the so-called income and expenditure persuasion, and certainly any sensible forecaster working in that tradition, is, therefore, vitally concerned with monetary prospects. That, indeed, is precisely why such analysts are very *much* interested in the current posture of the Federal Reserve and are sometimes critical of it. And that is why they prize the help Friedman et al. are giving us in identifying the time linkages that seem to relate changes in monetary policy to changes in the availability and cost of finance.

But to go beyond this to the opposite extreme and accept the leading monetary indicators as *sufficient* tools for predicting general business conditions would seem to me a most bizarre procedure. It would rest on the hypothesis that, for predictive purposes, the economy could be treated as if central bank decision making were the only significant independent variable in the system. For better or worse, things are more complicated than this. The capacity for influential autonomous decision making is far more widely dispersed. Considerable quantities of it lodge also, for example, in the Congress, in the White House, in the Finance Committee of the United States Steel Corporation, in Detroit, in all the great industrial houses and major labor organizations in the country and, even, in fifty million households. The responsible general forecaster must, somehow or other, directly concern himself with all of this pivotal decision making, not just with a particular slice of it. Academically, it is an interesting exercise to imagine that one had to settle for a single, go-it-alone set of predictive indicators and then debate the question of which would be the more reliable—the monetary set or some other? But this is a good deal like the question with which good book would you most like to be cast on a desert isle? Neither question has much practical relevance. As a practical matter, there seems to be no reason for the general forecaster to confine himself to so spare and oversimplified a predictive hypothesis as sole reliance upon the leading monetary indicators would imply.

I do not mean to accuse Friedman and his associates of actually advocating exclusive reliance upon their wares, but some of their arguments have seemed to me susceptible to such a misinterpretation. The leading monetary indicators also have two more specific limitations.

First, the series on changes in monetary reserves and in the money supply, even after seasonal adjustment, are, like many of the NBER leading indicators, subject to rather violent gyrations. Thus it is much harder to detect, from the current data, a change of direction in the smoothed trends of these series than might first appear when one looks at the dramatic shifts in the ex post multimonth averages that the published charts of these series typically display.

Second, I would make the strange-sounding complaint that the average lead that the rate of change in the money supply is alleged to have over general cyclical downturns—namely, some twenty months since the mid-twenties, is really too *long* to be very useful for forecasting purposes. Recent cyclical fluctuations in the American economy have appeared more or less to have followed a three-phase format. In a recession phase activity falls away from its long-term growth trend. In a second, recovery phase, it moves back up toward the long-term trend. But then, in a third, normal-growth or normal-prosperity phase, it moves *along* the trend. And this is the key point: most of us would say that it is impossible to predict at the time it starts how long this third, along-the-trend phase of the cycle is likely to be. There are certain internal dynamics within the system that may tend roughly to govern the durations of most recession and recovery phases. But the duration of the prosperity phase probably is another matter; it appears to depend upon the particular sequence of demands—first, in autos, for example, then in plant and equipment or national defense, and then perhaps in state and local government—that happens to emerge as a result of the particular combination of decision making that occurs in a particular field.

Thus to tell me—as in effect the monetary change indicator does—that these prosperity, along-the-trend phases of cycles since the 20s have *averaged* about 20 months really does not help very much. It gives me no confidence at all that such will be the case this particular time. Especially it gives me no such confidence if I believe, as I do, that there is nothing inevitable or immutable about cyclical rhythms and that deliberate discretionary changes in federal fiscal and monetary policies often decisively affect the duration of prosperity periods.

C. Foreshadowing Data

If it is jousting with a straw man to disprove the self-sufficiency of the leading indicators as forecast devices, it would be still worse to belabor the point that foreshadowing data—the spenders' intentions surveys, the federal budget, contract construction awards, new orders of durable goods manufacturers, and so on—do not in themselves constitute a full kit of forecasting tools. For I know of no serious developer or advocate of such data who has ever hinted that they can single-handedly generate a forecast. On the contrary, there has from the beginning been an alliance between the assemblers of foreshadowing data and model builders, especially of the less elegant, looser persuasion, with the former, of course, supplying much of the latter's inputs. For the sake of the present record, however, and because one still does occasionally encounter people who seem to think that if we could only finish the job of blanketing the GNP with intentions surveys, we would have the forecasting problem licked, let me venture just a few comments on the limitations of the foreshadowing series.

In the past the approach has been constrained by sheer problems of technique—for one thing, in the area of sampling and survey methods, and for another thing, with respect to the interpretation of the sequences of decreasingly tentative expectations and decreasingly conditional decisions into which the surveys from time to time dip. Franco Modigliani, however, has made sense of this latter matter, and certainly our better sampling and survey technology has become highly sophisticated. It is my layman's impression, therefore, that technical problems no longer are the real roadblocks in the area.

However, the coverage of the foreshadowing series is not yet all that it might be. There are some gaps—notably in the case of state and local government outlays—where spenders do indeed make advance plans, commitments, or conditional spending decisions (in the case of state and local governments they are a matter of public record) but where we simply have no agency yet that has assumed the task of systematically collecting or sampling and collating them.

But there are major segments of the GNP—notably in the area of consumer soft goods and services—that are destined, I should think, to remain effectively immune to intentions surveys, no matter how willing the surveyors may be, for the simple reason that buyers in these fields do not do enough coherent advance planning so that they themselves can recognize and report it.

Finally, there is the familiar but important point that the existence of plans, even strongly intentioned plans, offers no assurance that they will be carried out. The forecaster must convert the finding of an intentions survey into a forecast at his own peril. In particular when he makes such a conversion he must assume that the general economic developments that the expenditure planner does *not* foresee are not going to thwart his spending intentions. Modigliani has supplied us with a very intriguing refinement of this point—namely, that if the survey can canvass a respondent's sales or income expectations at the same time it canvasses his spending intentions and if it can be shown that past discrepancies between intended and actual outlays have been related to the discrepancies between expected and actual sales or incomes, it may be possible systematically to "correct" the intentions figure for forecasting purposes—*if* the forecaster is in a position to second-guess respondents' reported sales or income expectations. This approach seems to me to have considerable promise: perhaps even more in the fields of consumer intentions and of business inventory intentions, than in the plant and equipment sector where Modigliani first experimented with it. But as he emphasizes it must be used within the framework of a general model-building exercise. For only in such a context would the forecaster have any real basis for judging that spenders' expectations of future sales or incomes are unlikely to be realized. Modigliani's point, in other words, only underscores the conclusion that foreshadowing series are not go-it-alone devices.

D. Econometric Models

I shall focus my remarks about the limitations of general short-term econometric forecasting upon the single example of the present version of the original Klein-Goldberger model over which Daniel Suits now presides at the University of Michigan. This is one of the oldest econometric forecasting exercises with a continuous work record. It would appear to be fairly representative of its genus. And, for our purposes, it has the overwhelming advantage of just having been laid out for all of us to see in Suits's lucid article in the March 1962 *American Economic Review*.

Judging from this sample of one, we can draw the happy conclusion that econometric forecasting has been in process recently of getting constructively corrupted. In the course of drafting my book on *Business Conditions Analysis* about five years ago, I was casting about for a sharp distinction to be drawn between econometric model building and the less rigorous varieties that I call "opportunistic." I hit on these propositions. A true econometrician was a man, first, who insisted on cranking his forecast out of his explicit simultaneous-equation model without hedging or judgmental adjustment. He insisted, second, upon selecting all of the independent variables in his equations and deriving all of their parameters from an analysis of historical time series. By this definition, Suits no longer is an econometrician—which is to say, the definition is out of date.

There are two striking concessions that Suits's present methodology makes to the "practical" considerations espoused by opportunistic model builders. First, he now freely plugs in—instead of a rather lame investment function that makes business fixed capital spending wholly dependent on last year's profits and last year's growth in plant-and-equipment stock—an intentions-survey result (in this case, the McGraw-Hill) as his business fixed-investment input. (Incidentally, he has not yet, so far as I can tell, adopted the Modigliani proposal for making a systematic correction in the intentions figure to compensate for the "error" in investors' sales expectations.) Second, the Michigan team now evidently feels free to tinker with the "a" constants in any or all of its linear equations to make allowance for judgmental considerations regarding the particular year at hand that it feels the formal model does not adequately encompass. In short, you might say that the Michigan group has become nothing but a bunch of elegant opportunists—and with good results. Its forecast record since it began corrupting its model in this considered fashion is a good bit better than it was in the early and middle fifties.

As it is represented by the present Michigan exercise, therefore, econometric model building already has gone a long way toward overcoming limitations with which I would have charged it a few years ago. But it is still far short of having surmounted its basic problem of excessive rigidity—that is, in effect, excessive simplification. To attempt to cram the myriad complexity of the economy into even a thirty-two-equation model entails, as Suits is careful to emphasize, an heroic abstraction. This is evident if one considers the model's lack of nimbleness in adjusting to the sort of temporary and significant but unusual development that is forever cropping up and of which the looser model builder routinely takes account. For example, most opportunistic model builders, I should suppose, added a bit extra to their inventory investment estimates for the first quarter of 1962 to allow for some steel stockpiling and then shaved their second and/or third quarter estimates a compensating amount. The Suits model has no explicit, untinkered-with capacity for handling such refinements. Its limitations become most evident if one considers the stark simplicity of the theories of sector-demand determination that underlie some of its expenditure equations.

Indeed, I would urge sector-demand specialists who have not already done so to look carefully in Suits' March 1962 article in the *American Economic Review* at the demand functions for their own particular sectors—at the equations, for example, for automobiles, for other consumer durables, and for housing starts. They are apt to find themselves a bit amazed that a forecasting technique that indulges in such gross oversimplifications with respect to the particular sectors in which they are expert can produce such generally good GNP forecasts as the Michigan model has done in recent years. That it can, of course, is dramatic testimony to the importance in general forecasting of that quality which is econometric model building's particular strength—namely, the quality of internal consistency. Even when many of its sector legs rest on quite mushy foundations, a model of the economy whose income-distribution and receipts, expenditures, and savings relationships all are internally consistent, judged by past experience, has a pretty fair chance of hitting the aggregates. But this does not mean that mushy sector forecasting and an incapacity for encompassing the idiosyncrasies of a particular period are admirable qualities in their own right.

E. Opportunistic Model Building

It is almost a contradiction in terms to imagine the looser forms of model building as being self-sufficient with respect to the other tech-

376 Readings in Managerial Economics

niques. For the very essence of this approach—the reason I call it "opportunistic"—is its scavenging quality. Opportunistic model building is a procedure for gathering data, information, and insights of just about any conceivably relevant kind and for assembling them, in some orderly manner, into a coherent and quantified statement of prospects. I already have mentioned this approach's particularly heavy dependence upon inputs of foreshadowing data; in addition, sensible practitioners have ravenous appetites for help of other kinds.

Nevertheless, as a kind of horrible example, one can conjure up an imaginary forecaster who might take some pleasure in thinking of himself as a model builder and would indeed express his outlook judgments in the form of a GNP breakdown. But his would be strictly a laundry-list style of forecasting. He would simply go down the sector list, making up forward estimates, one by one, by some intuitive process out of whatever mix of past data, current gossip, and recent comments in the business press he happened to have at hand. He would not even bother to avail himself of the foreshadowing data systematically. He would ignore the insights that the NBER leading indicators might give him into the timing of coming changes in general activity and the help that the leading monetary indicators could supply as to prospective money and credit conditions. He would simply put down his sector forecasts, tot them up, and call the sum his forecast. The entire theory of aggregate demand determination underlying his analysis would consist of the national-income accounting identity that the GNP equals the sum of its parts. His analysis would contemplate no intersectoral, no income-expenditure, and no asset-expenditure interactions. The only internal-consistency test to which it would submit would be one to make sure that the GNP components did, indeed, add up to the total. And his mathematical requirements would be limited, not just to arithmetic, but to addition and subtraction.

Although I have called the foregoing an imaginary horrible example, a good bit of the actual short-term forecasting being done today comes uncomfortably close to fitting this description. This serves only to prove that something fairly close to go-it-alone opportunistic model building is, indeed, possible. But it also, it seems to me, is almost self-evidently foolish.

III. THE OPPORTUNITY FOR SYNTHESIS

So much for my argument that none of our five major short-term forecasting techniques is an island—at least not a very successful island when a consolidation of the five is perfectly feasible. The case for consolidation already has been anticipated considerably in the case against separatism. Thus I propose to enlarge on it only briefly, and shall do so in a moment.

A. A Few Substantive Comments on Opportunistic Model Building

First, by way of an aside, I want to get in a few somewhat more explicit licks on the craft of opportunistic model building. These are intended mainly as discussion provokers; I shall put my points very sketchily and, in a couple of cases, vulnerably.

The Usefulness of a Capacity Concept. The most controversial of the points I want to make about model-building practice is that such analysis can be greatly assisted by the incorporation of an explicit capacity concept. One must grant, of course, that capacity is a fuzzy, ambiguous, imprecise, not directly measured variable. But it generalizes about characteristics of the economy that are objective, dated, and vitally important. In one guise or another it is an essential concept for the general forecaster if he is going to discharge his ultimate function, which is to predict the basic healthiness of economic activity in a coming period. For that healthiness will depend most pivotally not on the absolute level of output but on the relationship between output and normal productive capacity. Such is plainly the crucial consideration, for one thing, in the case of general price prospects. For it is quite impossible to formulate any working hypothesis about the price-output relationships that changes in demand will encounter during a forecast period without formulating, at least implicitly, some assumption about the level and growth rate of capacity during the period.

The prospective relationship of capacity to output, adjusted for cyclical variations in output per man-hour, in the labor force, and in average working hours, likewise is the pivotal consideration for unemployment forecasting. Thus, although a model-building group may keep its capacity estimates invisible to the naked eye, as, for example, Suits's group does at Michigan, implicitly they are present in one form or another if the group is attempting to do a comprehensive forecasting job. The best procedure, I think, is to bring the capacity estimates out into the open where they can be seen and be argued about.

The Need for Explicit Sector Income Estimates. A second practice that I would urge upon opportunistic model builders is the construction of a model that forces the analyst to make explicit the breakdown of the gross national income into net receipts of governments, net foreign transfers by government, gross retained earnings of business, and disposable personal income that he is setting over against his final-demand breakdown. For only by this means does one have a framework that facilitates allowance for the impacts of expenditures in one sector upon those in others and that permits very much of the internal-consistency testing that is model building's greatest potential advantage.

If I read him rightly, Friedman may raise an eyebrow at this suggestion on the ground that I am asking for models with built-in multipliers, and that it can be shown that in this economy during the past several decades "investment multipliers," or "autonomous sector" multipliers have in fact been highly unreliable phenomena. With Friedman's findings of fact I heartily agree; indeed, they are what I would expect since I believe that the stability characteristics of the economy have been considerably improved during the past generation, with most of that improvement taking the form of just such a weakening of the intersectoral cumulative mechanisms as Friedman's findings suggest. In particular, we beneficently have managed, partly thanks to the so-called built-in stabilizers, greatly to reduce the sensitivity of disposable personal income (DPI) to declines in the GNP.

However, the inference for forecasting practice that I draw from all this is not that multiplier effects therefore should be banned from outlook models but rather than they require considerably more elaborate treatment than our simplified textbook theories of a few years back seemed to suggest. In a little semiannual forecast exercise that we run at Indiana, for example, we do three things. First, we separate consumer durables from the rest of consumption and treat them as a quasi-autonomous sector of the same sort as housing or plant and equipment. This is on the thesis that the aggregate of consumer soft goods and services is a much more stable function of DPI than is total consumption. Second (and this is the newest wrinkle of the three in our practice) we nevertheless treat the relation between soft goods and services consumption as being cyclically variable within fairly narrow limits. Third, and most important, we explicitly forecast the ratios of DPI to personal income and of personal income to GNP, treating both of these also as being cyclically variable.

Thus, in effect, we systematically incorporate into the model a rather highly variable multiplier that, in particular, takes explicit account of the tax-less-transfers and retained-earnings leakages between GNP and DPI. Rightly or wrongly, we attribute most of the very good luck that we have had with the exercise the last two or three times around to the more careful efforts we have been making along these lines.

Inventories and Net Exports.   My other two substantive comments are far narrower in scope, and I shall no more than mention them. Both concern matters rather urgently in need of further investigation. First, it appears to me that our forecasting doctrines for inventory investment presently are in a state of some theoretical disarray. Having become rather thoroughly disenchanted with the practical usefulness of inventory-sales ratios as guides for inventory forecasting, many of us have become rather excited about the greater utility of new orders and order backlogs as indicators of prospective changes in manufacturers' inventories. In this we have followed the lead, for example, of the Duesenberry-Eckstein-Fromm model of a few years ago. The trouble, however, is that this new doctrine really makes sense only for those industries that produce to order, not to stock, and have little or no finished-goods inventory. Consequently, for improved inventory forecasting I suspect that we need a considerably more disaggregated approach than is now customary; we need to know a good bit more than published data presently reveal of the differing degrees to which different manufacturing sectors rely, on the one hand, upon order backlogs and, on the other, upon finished-goods inventories for cushioning the lags of their output behind their demand; knowing this, we need to forecast changes in manufacturing inventories by fabrication stages; and, I suspect, in the case of manufacturers' finished stocks as well as trade inventories we need to hark back to inventory-sales ratios but with renewed attention to inventory-cycle models.

The other point is simply that net-export forecasting is in a bad way because of the average forecaster's or forecasting group's inability to make any closely reasoned prediction of exports. With the passing of the dollar shortage it no longer is legitimate to assume that the volume of United States exports will be determined simply by the volume of dollars that the United States supplies to the rest of the world through its imports and its transfers abroad of public and private capital. But lacking this short cut, the general forecaster is left with an apparent but impossible need to predict demand developments the world over if he is to make a considered estimate of United States exports. Because of the comparatively narrow limits with which net exports move, the problem is not a particularly serious one for the aggregate domestic forecast. But if anyone can come up with a new legitimate short cut to export prediction, he certainly at least will ease the consciences of many of us.

B. Joining the Techniques Together

By way of conclusion, let me indicate how the five forecasting techniques upon which we have been focusing can sensibly complement one another. Perhaps this can be conveyed most succinctly by describing what I would regard as an ideal short-term forecasting exercise.

In the first place, this would be a group exercise. Outlook analysis is an activity, I think, in which the group has an inherent advantage over the lone wolf, partly because it benefits from a division of labor, partly because it must be considerably judgmental and gains from an effort to achieve a consensus. Second, it would be a continuing exercise.

I frankly would become bored as a member of a staff that gave its uninterrupted attention to the business outlook, and there are comparatively few organizations that could afford a fairly elaborate staff that had this single function. However, we are conjuring up an ideal, and there is no denying the expertise that comes with daily immersion in the outlook problem. Third, it would be a rather highly structured exercise. The free-wheeling virtuosity of gifted seat-of-the-pants analysts always is impressive, but it also is commonly overrated, and it has very little transferability. One quality of an ideal forecasting organization would be a considerable ability to maintain continuity despite changes in personnel. Well-defined tasks, procedures, and analytical doctrines would all contribute to this end.

I would place at the head of such a staff a seasoned opportunistic model-builder with a good measure of forecasting experience, theoretical sophistication, and executive ability. I would associate with him three deputy directors, each of whom would have cognizance of the whole operation. One Friedman would be asked to nominate; one Geoffrey Moore or Arthur F. Burns would nominate; and the third would be a first-class econometrician whose professional sensibilities, however, did not bruise too easily. The balance of the staff would be composed mainly of specialists who were immersed in the lore and data of particular demand and/or industry sectors.

The format of my idealized exercise would be a simultaneous equation model—indeed, a far more elaborate model than that presently employed at Michigan—and all members of the staff would require the limited command of mathematics necessary for translating their views into the terminology of such a model and for comprehending its manipulation. The point here would be for the exercise to avail itself of the maximum internal-consistency insurance, and its feasibility would depend upon ready and continuing access to adequate electronic computer services.

The equations in the model, however, would be subject to constant tending. Variables (and, as necessary, equations) would be added or subtracted and parameters would be altered as fast as, and for whatever reason, the staff judged such changes appropriate. In fact, each equation would constitute a summary statement of the staff's presently operative forecasting doctrine for the particular demand sector or the particular income relationship involved. It would be the responsibility of each sector forecaster to keep his equation(s) in a continuing state of repair so that at any given moment the most accurate forecast of which the staff currently was collectively capable, with the help of a computer, could be cranked out of the model with minimum delay.

Foreshadowing data with built-in adjustments, where appropriate, along the lines that Modigliani suggests would figure very prominently as inputs into the model. Monetary and credit variables would be more explicitly knit into the model than has been customary with econometric models to date, with the leading monetary indicators being incorporated as lead devices for signaling later changes in the money supply and credit availability. Moreover, despite the realistic complexity that would be built into the model, the forecasting staff would not consider its findings to be inexorably bound to the model results. In particular, the NBER leading indicators would be used as an independent aid for timing prospective changes of course in the economy, a feat at which opportunistic model building is notoriously clumsy.

This, perhaps, is enough to convey the gist of what I have in mind. Few of us, probably, ever will work in circumstances that closely parallel the conditions just sketched. But at least we can strive for whatever intertechnique collaboration fits our particular scale of operations. We can recognize that not merely should the several respectable short-term forecasting techniques be able to coexist; they have far more to gain from outright alliance than they do from internecine bickering.

23. The Analysis of Economic Indicators*

GEOFFREY H. MOORE

Business cycles, large and small, appear to be a continuing feature of the economic landscape. A turn up or down in the economy is clearly an event of major social significance. Considerable interest therefore attaches to the means whereby an economic turn can be forecast and its extent can be estimated. That is the role of economic indicators, which rest on the numerous measurements of the pulse of the economy made by government agencies, private organizations and individual economists. The analysis of economic indicators (a subject in which my colleagues and I at the National Bureau of Economic Research have been much interested) is a well-developed technique for ascertaining what the many pulse readings are saying about the state of the economy.

Economic indicators are often likened to a barometer because they register some significant aspect of the performance of the economy, are sensitive to changes in the economic climate and may portend further changes. A barometer, however, measures only one characteristic of the atmosphere. Moreover, the barometer itself does not cause a change in the weather. Hence it is frequently in a disparaging sense that the term barometer is applied to an economic indicator; the implication is that the indicator is only a barometer, having no real causal significance and covering only a small part of what one should know about economic change.

Such characterizations may apply to many individual economic indicators, but they do not apply to indicators as a class. Economic indicators have come to embrace virtually all the quantitative measures of economic change that are continuously available. One can find daily, weekly, monthly and quarterly indicators; they measure production, prices, incomes, employment, investment, inventories, sales, and so on, and they record plans, commitments, and anticipations as well as recent transactions. Some of the indicators, such as the unemployment rate or the consumer price index, are calculated by the federal government on

* *Scientific American,* vol. 232, no. 1 (January 1975), pp. 17–23. Reprinted with permission.

the basis of elaborate sampling surveys conducted each month. Others, such as the indexes of stockmarket prices and the surveys by purchasing agents of prices, orders, and inventories, are constructed by private organizations on the basis of information they collect or obtain as a by-product.

As a result the economist or businessman interested in forecasting change is faced, like the weather forecaster, with a mass of factual information that pours in constantly. He must assess in some systematic way what the information says about the present and the future. The technique of indicator analysis embraces various systematic ways of looking at this information with a view to discerning significant developments in the business cycle.

One of the earliest systems of the kind, which was devised shortly before World War I, came to be known as the Harvard ABC curves. The A curve was an index representing speculation, more specifically stock prices. The B curve represented business activity, measured by the dollar volume of checks drawn on bank deposits. The C curve represented the money market, measured by the rate of interest on short-term commercial loans. Historical studies, particularly those carried out by Warren Persons of Harvard University, showed that these three curves typically moved in sequence: stock prices first, bank debits next, and interest rates last, with the lagging turns in interest rates preceding the opposite turns in stock prices. The economic logic of the sequence was that tight money and high interest rates led to a decline in business prospects and a drop in stock prices, which led to cutbacks in investment and a recession in business. The recession in turn led to easier money and lower interest rates, which eventually improved business prospects, lifted stock prices, and generated a new expansion of economic activity.

The system came to grief in the Great Depression of 1929 because the interpreters of the curves took too optimistic a view and failed to foresee the debacle. Economists generally regard the episode as one of the great forecasting failures of all time. Curiously, however, the timing of the sequence of events on which the system was originally based has in large measure persisted. This is not to say, however, that the ABC curves would still suffice if they were revised; since 1929 much more comprehensive systems of indicators have been developed, and the empirical and theoretical base on which they stand has been far more thoroughly studied, documented, and tested.

The sharp recession of 1937–1938, which occurred before the economy had fully recovered from the Great Depression, helped to spur that development. In the fall of 1937 Henry Morgenthau, Jr., the Secretary of the Treasury, asked the National Bureau of Economic Research (which is a private, nonprofit research agency) to devise a system of indicators that would signal when the recession was nearing an end. At that time the quantitative analysis of economic performance in the U.S. did not approach today's standards. The government's national income and product accounts, which form the foundation of much modern economic analysis, were just being established. Other vital economic statistics, including unemployment rates, were being developed or refined by public agencies trying to provide information that would be useful in fighting the depression. Few statistical series were issued in seasonally adjusted form, as they are now. Comprehensive econometric models (systems of equations expressing quantitative relations among economic variables), which are widely employed now to forecast the economy and to evaluate economic policies, were virtually unknown then.

Under the leadership of Wesley C. Mitchell and Arthur F. Burns the National Bureau of Economic Research had since the 1920s assembled and analyzed a vast amount of monthly, quarterly, and annual data on prices, employment, production, and other factors as part of a major research effort aimed at gaining a better understanding of business cycles. This project enabled Mitchell and Burns to select a number of series that, on the basis of past performance and of relevance in the business cycle, promised to be fairly reliable indicators of business revival. The list was given to the Treasury Department late in 1937 in response to Morgenthau's request and was published in May 1938. Thus originated the system of leading, coincident, and lagging indicators widely employed today in analyzing the economic situation, determining what factors are favorable or unfavorable, and forecasting short-term developments.

Since 1938 the availability, the study, and the use of economic indicators have been greatly expanded under the leadership of the National Bureau of Economic Research, the U.S. Bureau of the Census, and other public and private agencies. The list of indicators assembled in 1937 was revised in 1950, 1960, and 1966 to take account of the availability of new economic series, new research findings, and changes in the structure of the economy. A new evaluation is currently in progress under the auspices of the U.S. Department of Commerce. With each revision the performance of the indicators both before and after the date of their selection has been carefully examined and exposed to public scrutiny.

In 1957 Raymond J. Saulnier, who was then chairman of the President's Council of Economic Advisers, asked the Bureau of the Census to develop methods whereby the appraisal of current business fluctuations could take advantage of the large-scale electronic data processing that was becoming available at the time, with the results to be issued in a monthly report. Experimental work done over the next few years under the leadership of Julius Shiskin, who was the chief economic statistician of the Bureau of the Census, resulted (in 1961) in the publication by the Department of Commerce of *Business Cycle Develop-*

ments. (It is now called *Business Conditions Digest;* under both names economists have referred to it as *BCD,* and those initials appear on its cover in larger type than the full name does.) This monthly publication has greatly increased the accessibility of current indicator data and of various statistical devices that aid in their interpretation. As a result the analysis of the indicators has become a major tool of economic forecasting among the economists whose interest is in the current and future performance of the economy.

As I have noted, the analysis of economic indicators rests on an empirical footing and a theoretical one. Both the selection of particular indicators and the emphasis given to them have been guided by what is understood of the causes of business cycles. Obviously one would wish to examine recent changes in any economic process that is believed to play a significant role in any widely accepted explanation of cyclical fluctuations.

Many different explanations have been advanced for these fluctuations. Some of them lay primary stress on the swings in investment in inventory and fixed capital that both determine and are determined by movements in final demand. Others assign a central role to the supply of money and credit or to government spending and tax policies or to relations among prices, costs, and profits.

All these factors undoubtedly influence the course of business activity. Some of them may be more important at a given time than others. No consensus exists, however, on which is the most important or even on how they all interact. Hence it is prudent to work with a variety of indicators representing a broad range of influences. Ready access to a wide range of indicator data enables one to test competing or complementary hypotheses about current economic fluctuations.

With this principle in mind the National Bureau of Economic Research has classified economic activities into a few broad categories of closely related processes that are significant from the business-cycle point of view. Indicators have been selected from each group. The principal categories now included in *Business Conditions Digest* are employment and unemployment; production, income, consumption, and trade; fixed capital investment; inventories and inventory investment; prices, costs, and profits; money and credit; foreign trade and payments, and federal government activities (table 1).

The reader will note that these categories do not include all aspects of the economy. For example, statistics on agriculture, state and local government, population and wealth are omitted. Nevertheless, the categories do provide a framework of factors that enter into theories of the business cycle and are important in assessing the performance of the economy.

Within each category research on business cycles has uncovered sta-

TABLE 1

Economic Process	Relation to Business Cycle			
	Leading	Roughly Coincident	Lagging	Unclassified
Employment and unemployment	Average workweek and overtime Hiring and layoff rates New unemployment insurance claims	Job vacancies Total employment and unemployment	Long-duration unemployment	
Production, income, consumption, and trade		Total production, income, and sales		
Fixed capital investment	New investment commitments Formation of business enterprises	Backlog of investment commitments	Investment expenditures	
Inventories and inventory investment	Inventory investment and purchasing		Inventories	

TABLE 1
(*continued*)

Prices, costs, and profits	Sensitive commodity prices Stock prices Profits and profit margins Cash flow	Wholesale price index for industrial commodities	Labor costs per unit of output	Consumer price index
Money and credit	Money and credit flows Credit delinquencies and business failures	Bank reserves Interest rates on money market	Outstanding debt Mortgage and bank-loan rates	
Foreign trade and payments				Imports, exports, and export orders Balance of payments
Activities of federal government				Receipts and expenditures Defense orders, contracts, and purchases

Classification of indicators is done in two ways. One is by major economic process, such as employment and unemployment. The other is according to the relation the indicators have to turns in the business cycle. The leading, roughly coincident, and lagging indicators shown in the table represent only a small portion of the many indicators that are normally classified in this way.

tistical series that behave in a systematic way. These findings have provided a basis for selecting particular indicators and classifying them according to their characteristic cyclical behavior (see figure 1). Two of the chief characteristics one looks for are the regularity with which the indicator conforms to business cycles and the consistency with which it leads or lags at turning points in the cycles. Other relevant considerations are the statistical adequacy of the data (since the statistical underpinning of an indicator has a bearing on how well the indicator represents the process it is supposed to reflect), the smoothness of the data (since highly erratic series are difficult to interpret at a given point in time), and the promptness with which the figures are published (since out-of-date figures have a limited bearing on the current situation).

Empirical measures of these characteristics have been drawn up for large numbers of indicators in the categories listed above. Such measures have been employed in the attempt to obtain data capable of conveying an adequate picture of the changes in the economy as it moves through stages of prosperity and recession. In addition the behavior of the indicators after they have been selected has been monitored closely. Many of the indicators have survived several successive evaluations. For example, the indexes of the average workweek, construction contracts, and stock prices were on both the 1937 and 1966 lists of the National Bureau of Economic Research.

The same lists of indicators have also been tested by their performance in other countries, notably Canada, Japan, and the United Kingdom. Every new recession or slowdown provides additional evidence against which the indicators can be assessed, as does every upturn. All this examination and reexamination has accumulated a large amount of empirical evidence that demonstrates both the value of the indicators and their limitations.

A sampling of this evidence is contained in the accompanying illustrations. Let us consider the indicator called the quit rate, which measures the number of people in manufacturing industries (per 100 employed) who voluntarily leave their jobs (see figures 2 and 3). The raw data are statistically decomposed in order to measure and eliminate regular seasonal variations and irregular movements. With factors that are unrelated to the business cycle thus removed, the indicator reveals the tendency for quits to diminish during a recession as new jobs become harder to find and to increase when more prosperous conditions return. The seasonally adjusted quit rate therefore reflects the view that workers have of the labor market and of economic prospects generally.

Most economic indicators today are available in seasonally adjusted form. Some of them are seldom reported in any other way. Examples of indicators that are invariably adjusted for seasonal factors include the gross national product, the unemployment rate, and the index of industrial production.

FIGURE 1

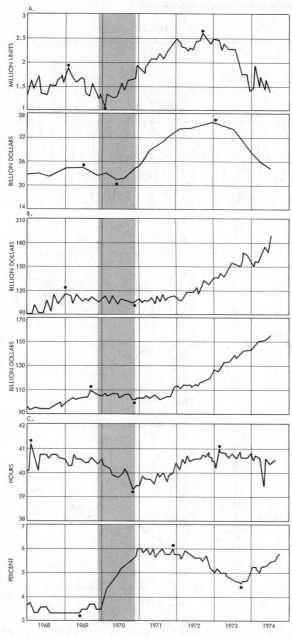

Relations among indicators are traced through the business-cycle contraction of 1969–1970. The three pairs of curves represent leading indicators (top) and the activities they led (bottom), namely housing starts and expenditures on residential structures (a), orders for plant and equipment and corresponding expenditures (b), and average workweek in manufacturing industries against unemployment rate (c). Dots show peaks and troughs.

FIGURE 2

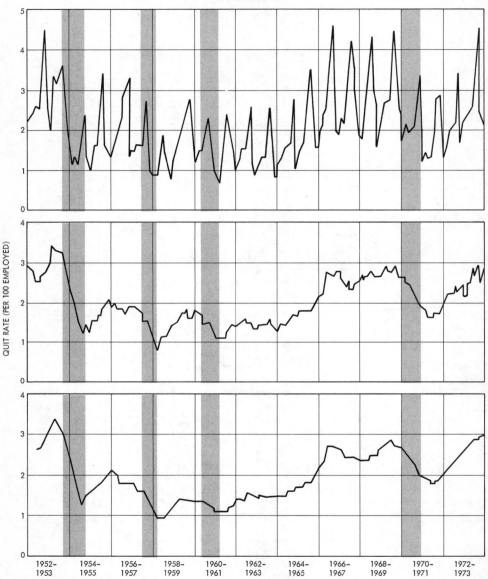

Construction of an indicator involves the removal of factors that are unrelated to the business cycle. Here the indicator is the quit rate, meaning the number of people per 100 employed who voluntarily leave their jobs. At top is the curve reflecting the raw data, with shaded areas showing four periods of recession. Below it is the seasonally adjusted curve. Bottom curve shows the cyclical movement and the long-term trend of the quit rate.

FIGURE 3

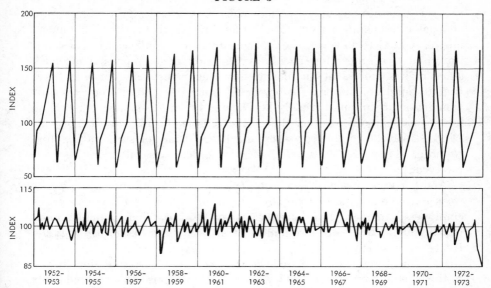

Elements removed from the quit-rate curve are a seasonal component (top) and an irregular component (bottom), which includes such factors as strikes and errors in sampling.

The smoothing of irregular factors is less commonly practiced because the techniques are somewhat less routine. Certain statistical series, however, are subject to much wider irregular movements than others are because of differences in sampling error or in the effects of such factors as the weather and strikes. It is therefore useful in interpreting current changes to have a standard measure of the size of these irregular factors compared with the size of the movements reflecting long-term trends and the events of the business cycle. (In economic discussions these latter factors are often called trendcycle movements.)

Two measures of this kind are provided for all the indicators carried in *Business Conditions Digest*. One shows how large the average monthly change in the irregular component is with respect to the average monthly change in the trend-cycle component. The other shows how many months must elapse on the average before the change in the trend-cycle component, which builds up over a period of time, exceeds the irregular component, which does not. For example, the measures show that monthly changes in housing starts are likely to be dominated by "noise," but that when these changes are measured over spans of four months, the trend-cycle "signal" becomes dominant. On the other hand, the index of industrial production is much less affected by noise, so that monthly movements are more significant.

The most important characteristic of an indicator from the point of view of forecasting is of course the evidence it provides concerning future changes in economic activity. Indicators differ in this respect for numerous reasons. Certain types, such as housing starts, contracts for construction, and new orders for machinery and equipment, represent an early stage in the process of making decisions on investment. Since it takes time to build a house or a factory or a turbine, the actual production (or completion or shipping) usually lags behind the orders and contracts. The lag depends on, among other things, the volume of unfilled orders or contracts still to be completed; where goods are made for stock rather than to order there may be no lag because orders are filled as they are received.

Another kind of lead-lag relation exists between changes in the workweek on the one hand and employment on the other. In many enterprises employers can increase or decrease hours of work more quickly, more cheaply, and with less of a commitment than they can hire or fire workers. Hence in most manufacturing industries the average length of the workweek usually begins to increase or decrease before a corresponding change in the level of employment. The workweek is therefore a leading indicator with respect to the unemployment rate.

Many bilateral relations of this kind have been traced. The matter obviously becomes more complex, however, when the relations are multilateral. Indexes of stock-market prices, for example, have exhibited a longstanding tendency to lead changes in business activity (the Harvard ABC curves relied in part on this tendency), but the explanation seems to require the interaction of movements in profits and in interest rates, and other factors as well. A cyclical decline in profits often starts before a business expansion comes to an end; the proximate cause is usually a rapid rise in the costs of production. Interest rates also are likely to rise sharply. Both factors operate to reduce the attractiveness of common stocks and depress their prices, even though the volume of business activity is still rising. Near the end of a recession the opposite tendencies come into play and lift stock prices before business begins to improve.

One way to cut through such complexities instead of pursuing each bilateral or multilateral relation separately is to measure leads and lags against a common standard. For this purpose a chronology of business cycles has proved useful. The National Bureau of Economic Research has defined business cycles in such a way that peaks and troughs can be dated with reasonable objectivity. (Indeed, much of the dating procedure can now be carried out by computer.) Since the vast majority of indicators that are of interest show cyclical movements conforming to these general business cycles, the peaks and troughs in each indicator can be matched with those of the business cycle to determine characteristic leads and lags.

Following this plan, groups of indicator series that typically lead, coincide with or lag behind turns in the business cycle have been identified (see figure 4). Summary indexes of these groups can be employed (as individual indicators can) to measure the relative severity of an economic downturn as it progresses from month to month. For example, indications

FIGURE 4

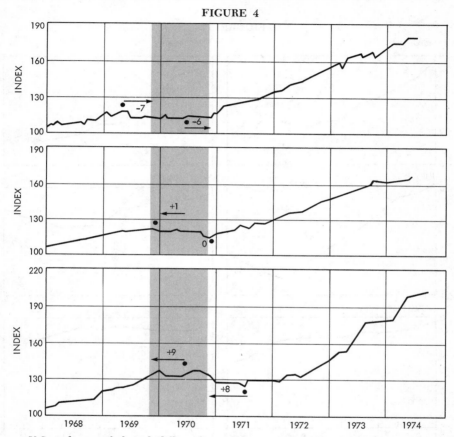

U.S. indicators behaved differently in the recession of 1969–1970 according to whether they were leading (top), coincident (middle) or lagging indicators (bottom). Each curve represents an index of several indicators in its class. Negative numbers with arrows mean the curve was that number of months ahead of the corresponding peak or trough in the business cycle. Positive numbers mean the curve was that number of months behind the cycle.

of a slowdown in the U.S. economy began to accumulate during 1973. Early in 1974 it was possible to conclude that if a recession was under way, a reasonable choice for the date of the business peak from which it started was November 1973. Percentage changes from then to successive months in 1973 and 1974 were calculated for a number of indicators month by month as new data became available and were compared with changes over corresponding intervals in earlier recessions, which had exhibited varying degrees of severity (figure 5).

With such a monitoring scheme one could observe the relative severity of the current decline and draw certain inferences based on the fact ᵗhat

FIGURE 5

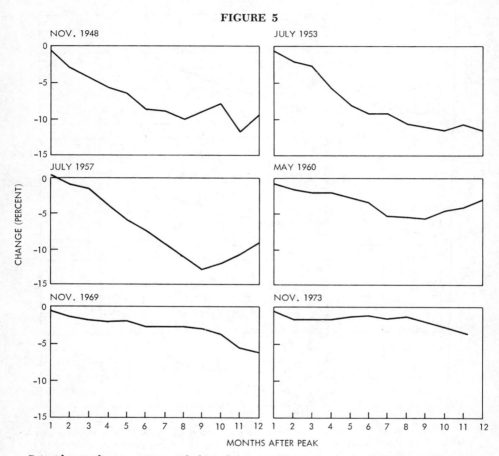

Coincident indicators are traced through six recessions, starting with the data of the business peak preceding the recession. Each curve represents the percentage change in the index of five indicators, namely industrial production, nonfarm employment, unemployment rate, personal income in constant dollars, and total sales in constant dollars. Through October 1974 the current decline most nearly resembled the ones in 1969–1970 and 1960–1961.

the rankings among different recessions have usually not changed a great deal after the first few months. The figures show that the decline of 1974 was relatively sharp early in the year as the effect of the oil crisis began to be felt. According to the latest data available (for October 1974) as of this writing, however, the decline in most indicators appeared moderate compared with the declines in earlier recessions over corresponding intervals. The major exceptions were the sharp declines in housing starts and in prices of common stocks, both of which reflected the sharp rise in interest rates and rapid inflation.

It is of course essential in any appraisal of the economic outlook to take into account actual and prospective policy actions by the government. Such actions include tax reductions or increases, changes in required bank reserves, changes in military expenditures and the establishment of a program of public employment. They often do not fit readily into the framework of indicators, although their effects, together with other influences, may be registered promptly in orders, contracts, housing starts, stock prices, and so on. Still, certain indicators do provide a nearly continuous reading on government activities (figure 6).

Government moves are often countercyclical. In a recession, for example, the government can exert a stimulative effect on the economy by making bank deposits or currency more readily available or by spending more than tax revenues are bringing in. The impact of such measures is a matter of debate. Indeed, it is possible to argue from the figures that policy shifts by the government have sometimes contributed with a lag, to the cyclical movements in the economy that they were designed to offset.

The analysis of economic indicators is one way of assessing the behavior of the economy. Econometric models of the business-cycle process are another. Although the two techniques have developed along independent lines for many years, they have come together at a number of points. The mathematical equations that characterize econometric models can handle elegantly and systematically such matters as multilateral relations among indicators, the distinction between seasonal movement and other types of movement, the influence of changes in government policy, and the plausibility of alternative theoretical explanations of the cycle.

The econometric models focus their explanatory power on such roughly coincident indicators as the gross national product, unemployment, and the rate of inflation. Often they include such cycle-leading indicators as housing starts, the average workweek, stock prices, and changes in business inventories, together with such lagging indicators as mortgage interest rates and investment in plant and equipment. Although the models have so far had a mixed record in representing and forecasting developments in the business cycle, with the result that the competition among alternative models is keen and changes in the specifications of each model are frequent, no user of indicators can afford to ignore the insights that econometric models bring to economic analysis. By the same token, people working with models can benefit from the empirical findings of indicator analysis and from the additional information that indicators often provide from outside the boundaries of a particular econometric model.

FIGURE 6

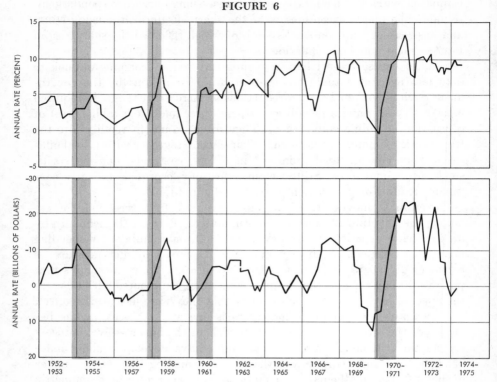

The role of government through four recessions is indicated by curves that portray rates of change in money supply (top) and federal surplus or deficit (bottom). On the bottom curve a rise indicates a shift toward a smaller surplus or larger deficit, a fall the opposite. The behavior of curves in recessions indicates the interaction of government policy with the business cycle.

Economic indicators of all types are followed more widely in the U.S. than in most other countries. The growth of trade, travel, and international finance, however, has increased the demand for promptly available statistics and readily accessible analytical records. In 1974 the National Bureau of Economic Research began a program of assembling and analyzing indicators for a dozen industrial countries.

Fortunately the indicator approach is sufficiently flexible to be adapted readily to situations where, as in many countries since World War II, economic recessions have taken the form of retardations in the growth of aggregate activity rather than absolute declines, and where such retardations may have been deliberately induced by government policies in order to cool off inflation or restore a deteriorating trade balance. Moreover, the approach is flexible enough to accommodate differences among countries in the types of indicator data that are available or are most revealing. For example, in Europe statistics on job vacancies are relied on more than in the U.S. and data on the international migration of workers are more significant because they have larger effects on the size of the work force.

Futhermore, since many economic indicators are available in physical units (such as man-hours of employment or tonnage shipped) or can be expressed in constant prices, a system of indicators can be adapted to conditions where a high rate of inflation dominates the behavior of data that are expressed in current prices. Many countries have recently experienced such conditions. Physical indicators of demand, such as housing starts, hiring rates, and orders for materials, can be expected to throw light not only on subsequent changes in output and employment but also on changes in prices and wages.

FIGURE 7

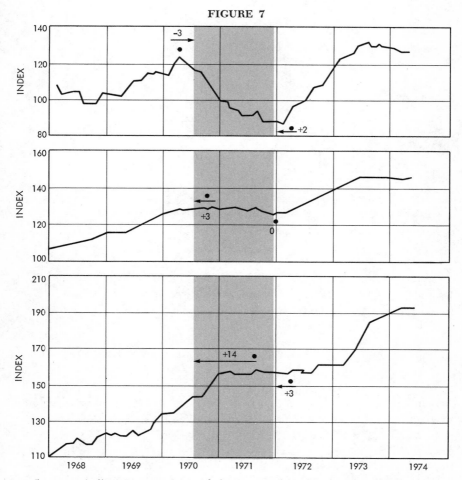

Japanese indicators are portrayed for a recession that ran from July 1970 to December 1971. The method of presentation is the same as for figure 4.

Our study is exploring these paths. Results already in hand for Canada, Japan (figure 7), the United Kingdom, and West Germany demonstrate the feasibility of the approach and its potential value in observing and appraising international fluctuations in economic growth rates and the accompanying trends in price levels, foreign trade, capital investment, and employment. One can envision the evolution of a worldwide system of indicators, built on the plan originally developed for the United States, to support the analysis of economic indicators on a global scale.

24. Forecasting with Econometric Methods: Folklore versus Fact[*]

J. SCOTT ARMSTRONG

INTRODUCTION

This paper is concerned with the use of econometric methods for forecasting in the social sciences. Although this is not the only use of econometric methods, it is one of the ways they are used; it is also the use that can most easily be validated. The paper examines only the predictive validity of econometric models. The importance of predictive validity has long been recognized by econometricians: "The ultimate test of an econometric model . . . comes with checking its predictions."

"Econometric methods" are defined in this paper as quantitative approaches that attempt to use causal relationships in forecasting. In particular, they refer to models based on regression analysis. This definition conforms to common usage of the term *econometric methods*. *Folklore* is used here to reflect what econometricians believe, as judged by what they do. *Fact* is based upon published empirical studies.

The first part of this paper draws upon evidence from social psychology to explain why folklore persists. Most of the evidence is based upon the behavior of people in general. However, there is evidence to suggest that scientists act as other people when testing their favored hypotheses.

Two examples of the discrepancy between folklore and fact are provided in the second part of the paper. These are only two of a number of possible examples, but they deal with two important questions. First, do econometric methods provide the most accurate way to obtain short-range forecasts? Second, do complex econometric methods provide more accurate forecasts than simple econometric methods?

The third part of the paper describes the method of multiple hypotheses. This method should help to overcome folklore.

[*] *Journal of Business*, vol. 51, no. 4 (1978), pp. 549–63.

THE PERSISTENCE OF FOLKLORE

Folklore persists because people who hold viewpoints on an issue tend to perceive the world so as to reinforce what they already believe; they look for "confirming" evidence and avoid "disconfirming" evidence. There is much literature on this phenomenon, commonly known as "selective perception."

The tendency for intelligent adults to avoid disconfirming evidence was demonstrated by Wason. He provided three numbers (2, 4, 6) to subjects, and they were asked to determine what rule had been used to generate the three numbers. In order to gain additional information, the subjects were encouraged to generate other series of three numbers. The experimenter provided feedback on whether or not each new series was in agreement with the rule. What happened? The typical subject would think of a rule and then generate series that were consistent with that rule. It was unusual for a subject to try a series that was inconsistent with his own rule. Subjects who were told that their rules were incorrect were allowed to generate additional series. The majority of these subjects maintained the same rule that they had previously but stated it in different terms. (It is like magic; it will work if one can pronounce it correctly!)

In cases where disconfirming evidence is thrust upon people, they tend to remember incorrectly. Fischhoff and Beyth, for example, found that subjects tended to remember their predictions differently if the outcome was in conflict with their prediction.

Wason's studies dealt with situations in which the person had no stake and no prior emotional attachment. When one has invested effort in supporting a particular viewpoint, the tendency to avoid disconfirming evidence would be expected to be stronger. The reward system in science encourages researchers to devote their energies to one viewpoint. The scientist gains recognition by being an advocate of a particular approach or theory. In such a case, the scientist can be expected to avoid disconfirming evidence.

Studies of scientists indicate that they are biased in favor of their own hypothesis. They interpret evidence so that it conforms to their beliefs. For example, in Rosenthal and Fode, experimenters were provided with two equivalent samples of rats, but they were told that one sample was gifted and the other was disadvantaged. In the subsequent "scientific tests," the gifted rats learned tasks more quickly than did the disadvantaged rats.

The above studies dealt with individuals rather than with groups. What happens when group pressures are involved—for example, when someone submits an article to be evaluated by his peers in the "marketplace of ideas"? What happens when learned societies, such as the Econometric Society, are formed to promote the advancement of the science? As the group pressures become stronger, one would expect stronger efforts to avoid evidence that disconfirms the group's opinions. Substantial literature shows how group judgment distorts reality. The study by Asch showed that most subjects would agree with the group that a given line B was longer than another line A, even though the reverse was obviously true.

In fact, the peer review process was studied in an experiment by Mahoney. A paper was sent to 75 reviewers. Some reviewers received the paper along with results that were supportive of the commonly accepted hypothesis in this group. Other reviewers received a copy of the identical study except that the results were reversed so that they disconfirmed the prevailing hypothesis. Reviewers with confirming results thought the study was relevant and methodologically sound. Reviewers with disconfirming results thought the study was not relevant and that the methodology was poor. The confirming paper was recommended for publication much more frequently.

The studies cited above provide only a portion of the evidence. Other relevant studies include Pruitt, Geller and Pitz, Chapman and Chapman, Rosenthal and Rosnow, and Greenwald. This evidence implies that scientists avoid disconfirming evidence. This tendency is stronger when the position is adopted by a group.

It is not surprising then, that great innovations in science have often met with resistance. There is little reason to expect that "modern science" is different. For illustration, one might examine the treatment of Immanuel Velikovsky, a case that is being followed closely by sociologists. This treatment was not the result of a lack of interest or a lack of time; rather it was an active attempt to suppress Velikovsky's theories and to discredit him.

Social scientists are expected to be more prone to group opinion than are physical scientists. Thus, they would experience serious difficulties in adopting new findings. Are econometricians also resistant to innovations? In a critique of what is being done by econometricians, Bassie implies that they are. He claims that econometricians display much conformity to their preconceptions.

Two examples from econometrics are examined below. These examples were selected because they represent an important part in the life of an econometrician—and also because there seem to be discrepancies between folklore and fact. . . .

SHORT-RANGE FORECASTING

Most textbooks on econometrics discuss short-range forecasting. Although seldom stated, the implication is that econometric methods provide more accurate short-range forecasts than other methods. Brown asserted that econometric models were originally designed for short-range forecasting. Kosobud, in a paper on short-range forecasting, referred to ". . . the growing body of evidence on the predictive value of econometric models." In a review of a book on short-range economy-wide forecasting, Worswick said that "the value of econometric models in short-term forecasting is now fairly generally recognized." Various econometric services sell short-range forecasts, and one of their claims is improved accuracy. The press publishes short-range forecasts from well-known econometric models with the implication that these models will provide accurate forecasts.

Survey of Econometricians

In order to go beyond the indirect evidence cited in the preceding paragraph, a questionnaire was mailed to experts in econometrics in late 1975. The survey was based on a convenience sample. Of 56 questionnaires that were sent out, 21 were completed. An additional eight were returned incomplete by respondents who said they lacked the necessary expertise. Thus, replies were received from over 40 percent of the experts. The respondents were from some of the leading schools in econometrics—for example, M.I.T., Harvard, Wharton, Michigan State—and from well-known organizations that sell econometric forecasts. Many of the respondents are recognized as leading econometricians.

The questionnaire asked," Do econometric methods generally provide more accurate or less accurate forecasts than can be obtained from competitive methods for short-term forecasting in the social sciences? Or is there no difference in accuracy?" A set of definitions was also provided.[1]

The results of the survey, presented in Table 1, were that 95 percent of the experts agreed that predictions from econometric models are more accurate.

---

1. These definitions were as follows: "(a) 'Econometric methods' include all methods which forecast by explicitly measuring relationships between the dependent variable and some causal variables. (b) 'Competitive methods' would include such things as judgment by one or more 'experts' or extrapolation of the variable of interest (e.g., by relating the variable to 'time' such as in autoregressive schemes). (c) By 'do,' we mean that comparisons should be made between methods which appear to follow the best practices which are available at the current time. In other words, the methods should each be applied in a competent manner. (d) 'Short-term' refers to time periods during which changes are relatively small. Thus, for forecasts of the economy, changes from year to year are rather small, almost always less than 10 percent. For some situations, however, one-year changes may be substantial. (e) 'Forecasts' refer to unconditional or 'ex ante' forecasts only. That is, none of the methods shall use any data drawn from the situation which is being forecast. Thus, for time series, only data prior to time t could be used in making the forecasts. (f) The 'social sciences' would include economics, psychology, sociology, management, and so on. In short, any area where the behavior of people is involved."

TABLE 1
Survey of Experts on Accuracy of Short-Range
Econometric Predictions
($N = 21$)

Econometric Predictions Rated	Percentage
Significantly more accurate	33
Somewhat more accurate	62
No difference (or undecided)	0
Somewhat less accurate	0
Significantly less accurate	5

Respondents were asked how much confidence they had in their opinion on accuracy. Confidence was rated on a scale from 1 ("no confidence") to 5 ("extremely confident"). (If the question was not clear to respondents, they were instructed to report a low level of confidence.) The average response was about 4. No one rated confidence lower than 3.0. Those who responded with "significantly more accurate" had the highest confidence level.

Another question asked how the respondent would rate himself ". . . as an expert on applied econometrics." Eight respondents rated themselves as "very much of an expert," six as "fairly expert," four as "somewhat of an expert," and two felt that they were "not much of an expert" (there was one nonresponsive on this question). Those who rated themselves as more expert felt that econometric methods were more accurate: Five of the eight who rated themselves as "very much of an expert" felt that econometric methods were significantly more accurate, a rating that was significantly higher than the ratings by the other respondents ($P < .05$ using the Fisher Exact Test).

In general, the survey supported the anecdotal evidence. Experts are confident that short-range econometric predictions are more accurate than predictions from other methods.

Empirical Evidence

Turning to "fact," an examination was made of all published empirical studies that I could find in the social sciences. This survey was conducted primarily by examining references from key articles and by searching through journals. Respondents to the expert survey were asked to cite evidence, but this yielded few replies. Finally, early drafts of this paper were presented at conferences and were circulated for comments over a period of four years; this approach did lead to additional studies. The studies are summarized below.

Christ provided disconfirming evidence on the accuracy of econometric predictions. In the 1951 study, econometric forecasts were better than "no change" forecasts on six occasions and worse on four. These were conditional or ex post forecasts; nevertheless, the results were not encouraging. The reaction to these findings was smiliar to previously mentioned occasions when disconfirming evidence was thrust upon scientists. Two of the discussants for Christ's paper were Lawrence Klein and Milton Friedman. Klein, whose model had been examined by Christ, stated that ". . . a competent forecaster would have used an econometric model . . . far differently and more efficiently than Christ used his model." Friedman, however, was receptive. He said that additional evidence would tend to strengthen Christ's conclusion and that ". . . the construction of additional models along the same general lines [as Klein's model] will, in due time, be judged failures."

Additional evidence on the predictive validity of econometric methods since Christ's papers is described here. Most of these studies are recent. Some are only of a suggestive nature because they compare ex post predictions of econometric models with ex ante predictions from alternative methods. Comparisons between extrapolations and ex post econometric forecasts were made by Kosobud, Cooper, Nelson, Elliott, Granger and Newbold, Narasimham, Castellino, and Singpurwalla, Levenbach, Cleary, and Fryk, and Ibrahim and Otsuki. Extrapolations provided better forecasts than the econometric methods in all studies except Kosobud's and Levenbach's. In Levenbach's, there was a tie for the one-year forecast, and the econometric model was better for the two-year forecast. None of these eight studies claimed to find a statistically significant difference. A comparison between ex post econometric forecasts and judgmental forecasts was carried out by Kosobud, Fair, Haitovsky, Treyz, Su, and Rippe and Wilkinson. Although the econometric forecasts were superior in all but Rippe and Wilkinson, none of these studies reported on statistical significance. However, sufficient data were provided in the Rippe and Wilkinson study to allow for such a test; my analysis of their results indicated that the econometric forecasts were significantly poorer than the judgmental forecasts. Thus, the analyses of 13 ex post studies with 14 comparisons did not provide evidence that econometric methods were superior.

To obtain direct evidence on the short-range predictive validity of econometric methods, a review was made of studies involving ex ante or unconditional forecasts. To qualify for inclusion, a study must have compared econometric and alternative methods where each was carried out in a competent manner. The question of when a method was competently applied created some difficulty. The major effect of this restriction was to rule out studies where the alternative model was a "no-change" extrapolation. Some studies were retained, although the alternative models could have been improved.

In all, 12 studies involving 16 comparisons were found. These studies are summarized in Table 2. The criteria were taken from each study. In other words, they were the most appropriate criteria in the opinion of the researchers who did each study. Efforts were made to test for statistical significance where this had not been done in the published study. In general, serious difficulties were encountered; most of these studies did not provide sufficient data, others failed to use comparable time periods, and still others suffered small sample sizes. The most striking result was that *not one study was found where the econometric method was significantly more accurate.* Nor did the econometric method show any general superiority: Six comparisons showed the econometric method to be superior, three suggested no difference, and seven found that it was inferior.

To guard against biases that may have been held by the author and to ensure that this study could be replicated, two research assistants coded a sample of three studies. The coding was done independently (i.e., the coders did not meet each other) and it was done blindly (i.e., the coders were not aware of the hypotheses in this study). In each of the four comparisons from these studies, there was perfect agreement among the author and the two raters. In addition, five of the ex post prediction studies were coded. The only exception to perfect agreement occurred when one of the coders classified the econometric models as superior to extrapolation in Granger and Newbold. The agreement between the two raters and me on eight out of nine comparisons provides evidence that the ratings were reliable.

The 16 comparisons of predictive validity were in agreement with the 14 ex post comparisons. Econometric forecasts were not found to be more accurate.

SIMPLE VERSUS COMPLEX ECONOMETRIC METHODS

"Progress" in econometric methods appears to be reflected by an increase in complexity in the methods used to analyze data. Leser noted long-term tendencies toward the use of more variables, more equations, more complex functional forms, and more complex interactions among the variables in econometric models. This increase in complexity can be observed by examining various issues of *Econometrica* since 1933 or by examining textbooks. The inference is that, because more complex procedures provide more realistic ways to represent the real world, they should yield more accurate forecasts.

Some researchers imply that complexity will lead to greater accuracy. For example, Suits states ". . . clearly the fewer the equations the greater must be the level of aggregation and the less accurate and useful the result." Of course, not all econometricians believe this. Bassie proposed a

TABLE 2

Accuracy of Econometric Methods for Short-Term Forecasting

Relative Accuracy of Econometric Methods	Source of Evidence	Forecast Situation	Alternative Forecasting Method	Criteria for Accuracy (RMSE = root mean square error; MAPE = mean absolute percentage error)	Test of Statistical Significance
Significantly more accurate (P < .05)	...	...	...	...	...
More accurate	Sims (1967)	Dutch economic indicators	Extrapolation	RMSE	None
	Ash and Smyth (1973)	U.K. economic indicators	Extrapolation	Theil's U	None
	McNees (1974)	U.S. economic indicators	Extrapolation	RMSE	None
	McNees (1974)	U.S. economic indicators	Judgmental	RMSE	None
	Haitovsky et al. (1974, table 7.3)	U.S. economic indicators	Judgmental	Average absolute error	None
	Christ (1975)	U.S. economic indicators	Extrapolation	RMSE	None
No difference	Sims (1967)	Norwegian economic indicators	Extrapolation	RMSE	None
	Ridker (1963)	Norwegian economic indicators	Extrapolation	(Five criteria used)	None
	Christ (1975)	U.S. economic indicators	Judgmental	RMSE	None
Less accurate	Vandome (1963)	U.K. economic indicators	Judgmental	Percentage changes	None
	Vandome (1963)	U.K. economic indicators	Extrapolation	MAPE	Armstrong
	Naylor et al. (1972)	U.S. economic indicators	Extrapolation	Average absolute error	None
	McNees (1975)	U.S. economic indicators	Judgmental	Theil's U	None
	Cooper and Nelson (1975)	U.S. economic indicators	Extrapolation	RMSE/Theil's U	Armstrong
	Liebling, Bidwell, and Hall (1976)	Nonresidential investment	Judgmental	MAPE	None
Significantly less accurate (P < .05)	Markland (1970)	Inventory control	Extrapolation	Coefficient of variation	Armstrong

general rule, "the more a function is complicated by additional variables or by nonlinear relationships, the surer it is to make a good fit with past data and the surer it is to go wrong sometime in the future."

Survey of Econometricians

To gain further information on whether experts believe that increased complexity in econometric models leads to more accurate forecasts, my previously mentioned mail survey asked: "Do complex methods generally provide more accurate or less accurate forecasts than can be obtained from less complex econometric methods for forecasting in the social sciences?—or is there no difference in accuracy?" As shown in Table 3,

TABLE 3
Survey of Experts on Complexity and Accuracy
($N = 21$)

Complex Methods Rated	Percentage
Significantly more accurate	5
Somewhat more accurate	67
No difference (or undecided)	19
Somewhat less accurate	9
Significantly less accurate	0

there was substantial agreement on the value of complexity; **72** percent of the experts agreed and only **9** percent disagreed. The experts were confident in their ratings on the value of complexity. The average confidence level was 4.0 (where 5 = "Extremely confident").

Many factors could affect the relationship between complexity and accuracy. For example, Schmidt, working with psychological data, found simple unit weights to be superior to regression weights for small sample sizes where there were many predictors. Furthermore, the relationship may not be a linear one; that is, complexity up to a modest level might be desirable, and beyond that it could be undesirable.

A specific question asked the experts to make any qualifications they felt important in assessing the relationship. Most respondents did qualify their answers, but it was difficult to find factors that were mentioned by more than one person.

Empirical Evidence

To assess the value of complexity in econometric methods, an examination was made of all published empirical evidence that I could find in the social sciences. Some studies provided indirect evidence on the value of complexity. McLaughlin examined the accuracy of forecasts from **12** econometric services in the United States. These forecasts were made by models that differed substantially in complexity. There were no reliable differences in accuracy among these models: The rankings of accuracy for the models in 1971 were negatively correlated with those for 1972. If there are no reliable differences, then no differences would be found between accuracy and complexity. I reanalyzed data from the study by Jorgenson, Hunter, and Nadiri and found a perfect negative correlation between complexity of the four models (ranked by the number of variables in the model) and the stability of the regression coefficients from one period to the next; this lack of stability for more complex methods would suggest a loss in predictive validity. Friend and Taubman asserted their simple model was superior to more complex models. Fair found little difference between his simple model and the more complex Wharton model in a test of ex post predictive validity.

Direct evidence on the value of complexity was sought by using only studies with ex ante forecasts. Each of the models, whether simple or complex, was done in a competent manner. The results of this literature survey are summarized in Table 4.

To determine whether the coding of the studies in Table 4 was reliable, 8 of the 11 studies (all but Johnston and McNeal, Grant and Bray, and McNees) were independently coded by two research assistants. The coding was blind in that the assistants were unaware of the hypotheses. Discrepancies were noted on only 2 of these studies; one assistant coded Dawes and Corrigan to show that more complex methods were superior, and the other assistant reported complexity to be superior in Wesman and Bennett. The studies in Table 4 suggest that complexity and accuracy are not closely related. No study reported a significant positive relationship between complexity and accuracy. Overall, 7 comparisons favored less complexity and 4 favored more complexity.

The 11 studies that assessed provided validity directly were in agreement with the 5 studies that provided indirect evidence: Added complexity did not yield improvements in accuracy. The empirical evidence does not support the folklore in this area.

MULTIPLE HYPOTHESES: AN ALTERNATIVE RESEARCH STRATEGY

The first part of this paper suggested that econometricians often act as advocates; they attempt to find evidence to support their viewpoint. Furthermore, group opinion is often used to judge truth. Under such conditions, it is likely the beliefs will persist even if unsupported by empirical evidence.

An alternative to the use of advocacy is to adopt the method of multiple hypotheses. Here, each scientist examines two or more reasonable hypotheses (or methods) at the same time. The role of the scientist is to

TABLE 4
Accuracy of Simple versus Complex Methods

Relative Accuracy of Complex Methods	Source of Evidence	Forecast Situation	Criterion for Accuracy	Nature of Comparison	Test of Statistical Significance
Significantly more accurate (P < .05)	...	...	...	...	...
More accurate	Stuckert (1958)	Academic performance	Percent correct	Unit weights versus regression	None
	McNees (1974)	GNP	Theil coefficient; RMSE, mean absolute error	Small versus large models	None
	Grant and Bray (1970)	Personnel	Correlation coefficient	Unit weights versus regression	Armstrong
	Johnston and McNeal (1964)	Medicine	Correlation coefficient	Unit weights versus regression	Authors
No difference	...	...	...	...	...
Less accurate	Dawes and Corrigan (1974)	Academic performance, simulated data, psychiatric ratings	Correlation coefficient	Unit weights versus regression	Armstrong
	Lawshe and Shucker (1959)	Academic performance	Percent correct	Unit weights versus regression	None
	Reiss (1951)	Criminology	Percent correct	Few versus many causal variables	None
	Wesman and Bennett (1959)	Academic performance	Correlation coefficient	Unit weight versus regression	None
	Scott and Johnson (1967)	Personnel selection	Percent correct, correlation coefficient	Unit weights versus regression	None
Significantly less accurate (P > .05)	Claudy (1972)	Simulated data (typical of psychological data)	Correlation coefficient	Unit weights versus regression	Armstrong
	Summers and Stewart (1968)	Political judgments	Correlation coefficient	Linear versus nonlinear models	Armstrong

determine which of the methods is most useful in the given situation. When two or more reasonable hypotheses are studied, it is less likely that the scientist will feel a bias in favor of "his" hypothesis—they are all "his" hypotheses. The orientation of the scientist is changed from one where he seeks to confirm a hypothesis to one where he seeks to disconfirm one or more hypotheses. Because the various hypotheses are tested within each study, there is less need to rely upon the opinions of other experts. The method of multiple hypotheses should help researchers to make more effective use of disconfirming evidence.

Although the method of multiple hypotheses would appear to be less prone to selective perception, and thus superior to the use of advocacy, surprisingly little evidence is available on this issue. This evidence, summarized in Armstrong, provides modest support for multiple hypotheses over advocacy. Most surprising again was the lack of evidence to support advocacy, the research strategy that appears to be most common among social scientists.

CONCLUSIONS

Certain hypotheses about econometric methods have been accepted for years despite the lack of evidence. Ninety-five percent of the experts agreed that econometric methods are superior for short-range forecasting. An examination of the empirical literature did not support this belief: Econometric forecasts were not shown to be significantly better in any of the 14 ex post and 16 ex ante tests. Furthermore, there was no tendency toward greater accuracy over these 30 tests. Similarly, 72 percent of the experts felt that complexity contributed to accuracy, but the examination of the literature did not support such a belief: Complex models were not significantly better in any of the 5 indirect and 11 direct tests.

Thrusting disconfirming evidence upon others provides an ineffective way of changing attitudes. Econometricians are more likely to be convinced by their own studies. The use of the method of multiple hypotheses provides a rational way for econometricians to test their beliefs.

In one sense the situation is encouraging. Twenty-three studies using the method of multiple hypotheses were found (see Tables 2 and 4). These studies are becoming more common; the oldest study was published in 1951 and almost half were published since 1970. This trend in research strategy should be useful in distinguishing folklore from fact.

25. Input–Output Economics*

WASSILY W. LEONTIEF

If the great 19th-century physicist James Clerk Maxwell were to attend a current meeting of the American Physical Society, he might have serious difficulty in keeping track of what was going on. In the field of economics, on the other hand, his contemporary John Stuart Mill would easily pick up the thread of the most advanced arguments among his 20th-century successors. Physics, applying the method of inductive reasoning from quantitatively observed, events, has moved on to entirely new premises. The science of economics, in contrast, remains largely a deductive system resting upon a static set of premises, most of which were familiar to Mill and some of which date back to Adam Smith's *The Wealth of Nations*.

Present-day economists are not universally content with this state of affairs. Some of the greatest recent names in economics–Léon Walras, Vilfredo Pareto, Irving Fisher–are associated with the effort to develop quantitative methods for grappling with the enormous volume of empirical data that is involved in every real economic situation. Yet such methods have so far failed to find favor with the majority of professional economists. It is not only the forbidding rigor of mathematics; the truth is that such methods have seldom produced results significantly superior to those achieved by the traditional procedure. In an empirical science, after all, nothing ultimately counts but results. Most economists therefore continue to rely upon their "professional intuition" and "sound judgment" to establish the connection between the facts and the theory of economics.

In recent years, however, the output of economic facts and figures by various public and private agencies has increased by leaps and bounds. Most of this information is published for reference purposes, and is unrelated to any particular method of analysis. As a result we have in economics today a high concentration of theory without fact on the one hand, and a mounting accumulation of fact without theory on the other. The task of filling the "empty boxes of economic theory" with relevant empirical content becomes every day more urgent and challenging.

* *Scientific American*, vol. 185, no. 4 (October 1951), pp. 15–21. Reprinted with permission.

This article is concerned with a new effort to combine economic facts and theory known as "interindustry" or "input-output" analysis. Essentially it is a method of analysis that takes advantage of the relatively stable pattern of the flow of goods and services among the elements of our economy to bring a much more detailed statistical picture of the system into the range of manipulation by economic theory. As such, the method has had to await the modern high-speed computing machine as well as the present propensity of government and private agencies to accumulate mountains of data. It is now advancing from the phase of academic investigation and experimental trial to a broadening sphere of application in grand-scale problems of national economic policy. The practical possibilities of the method are being carried forward as a cooperative venture of the Bureau of Labor Statistics, the Bureau of Mines, the Department of Commerce, the Bureau of the Budget, the Council of Economic Advisers and, with particular reference to procurement and logistics, the Air Force. Meanwhile the development of the technique of input-output analysis continues to interest academic investigators here and abroad. They are hopeful that this method of bringing the facts of economics into closer association with theory may induce some fruitful advances in both.

Economic theory seeks to explain the material aspects and operations of our society in terms of interactions among such variables as supply and demand or wages and prices. Economists have generally based their analyses on relatively simple data—such quantities as the gross national product, the interest rate, price and wage levels. But in the real world things are not so simple. Between a shift in wages and the ultimate working out of its impact upon prices there is a complex series of transactions in which actual goods and services are exchanged among real people. These intervening steps are scarcely suggested by the classical formulation of the relationship between the two variables. It is true, of course, that the individual transactions, like individual atoms and molecules, are far too numerous for observation and description in detail. But it is possible, as with physical particles, to reduce them to some kind of order by classifying and aggregating them into groups. This is the procedure employed by input-output analysis in improving the grasp of economic theory upon the facts with which it is concerned in every real situation.

The essential principles of the method may be most easily comprehended by consulting the input-output table in figure 1. This table summarizes the transactions which characterized the U.S. economy during the year 1947. The transactions are grouped into 42 major departments of production, distribution, transportation, and consumption, set up on a matrix of horizontal rows and vertical columns. The horizontal rows of figures show how the output of each sector of the economy is distributed among the others. Conversely, the vertical columns show how each sector obtains from the others its needed inputs of goods and services. Since each figure in any horizontal row is also a figure in a vertical column, the output of each sector is shown to be an input in some other. The double-entry bookkeeping of the input-output table thus reveals the fabric of our economy, woven together by the flow of trade which ultimately links each branch and industry to all others. Such a table may of course be developed in as fine or as coarse detail as the available data permit and the purpose requires. The present table summarizes a much more detailed 500-sector master table which has just been completed after two years of intensive work by the Interindustry Economics Division of the Bureau of Labor Statistics.

For purposes of illustration let us look at the input-output structure of a single sector—the one labeled "primary metals" (sector 14). The vertical column states the inputs of each of the various goods and services that are required for the production of metals, and the sum of the figures in this column represents the total outlay of the economy for the year's production. Most of the entries in this column are self-explanatory. Thus it is no surprise to find a substantial figure entered against the item "products of petroleum and coal" (sector 10). The design of the table, however, gives a special meaning to some of the sectors. The outlay for "railroad transportation" (sector 23), for example, covers only the cost of hauling raw materials to the mills; the cost of delivering primary metal products to their markets is borne by the industries purchasing them. Another outlay requiring explanation is entered in the trade sector (sector 26). The figures in this sector represent the cost of distribution, stated in terms of the trade margin. The entries against trade in the primary metals column, therefore, cover the middleman's markup on the industry's purchases; trade margins on the sale of primary metal products are charged against the consuming industries. Taxes paid by the industry are entered in the row labeled "government" (sector 40), and all payments to individuals, including wages, salaries and dividends, are summed up in the row labeled "households" (sector 42). How the output of the metals industry is distributed among the other sectors is shown in row 14. The figures indicate that the industry's principal customers are other industries. "Households" and "government" turn up as direct customers for only a minor portion of the total output, although these two sectors are of course the principal consumers of metals after they have been converted into end products by other industries.

Coming out of the interior of the table to the outer row and columns, the reader may soon recognize many of the familiar total figures by which we are accustomed to visualize the condition of the economy. The total outputs at the end of each industry row, for example, are the figures we use to measure the size or the health of an industry. The gross national product which is designed to state the total of productive activity and is the most commonly cited index for the economy as a whole, may be

FIGURE 1
The Exchange of Goods and Services in the U.S. for the Year 1947

INDUSTRY

Column headings (numbered 1–23 across the top, industry names given diagonally):

1 Agriculture and Fisheries; 2 Food and Kindred Products; 3 Textile Mill Products; 4 Apparel; 5 Lumber and Wood Products; 6 Furniture and Fixtures; 7 Paper and Allied Products; 8 Printing and Publishing; 9 Chemicals; 10 Products of Petroleum and Coal; 11 Rubber Products; 12 Leather and Leather Products; 13 Stone, Clay and Glass Products; 14 Primary Metals; 15 Fabricated Metal Products; 16 Machinery (Except Electric); 17 Electrical Machinery; 18 Motor Vehicles; 19 Other Transportation Equipment; 20 Professional and Scientific; 21 Miscellaneous; 22 Coal; 23 —

(Left-hand axis: INDUSTRY PRODUCING. Printed numeric data columns correspond to purchasing industries 1–18.)

Industry Producing	1	2	3	4	5	6	7	8	9	10	11	12	13	14	15	16	17	18
1 AGRICULTURE AND FISHERIES	10.86	15.70	2.16	0.02	0.19	—	0.01	—	1.21	—	—	0.05	*	0.01	—	—	—	—
2 FOOD AND KINDRED PRODUCTS	2.38	5.75	0.06	0.01	*	*	0.03	*	0.79	*	—	0.44	*	*	*	*	*	—
3 TEXTILE MILL PRODUCTS	0.06	*	1.30	3.88	*	0.29	0.04	0.03	0.01	*	0.44	0.09	0.03	—	0.01	0.02	0.05	0.15
4 APPAREL	0.04	0.20	—	1.96	*	0.01	0.02	—	0.03	—	—	*	*	—	*	*	*	0.10
5 LUMBER AND WOOD PRODUCTS	0.15	0.10	0.02	*	1.09	0.39	0.27	*	0.04	0.01	—	0.02	0.02	0.06	0.06	0.09	0.05	0.05
6 FURNITURE AND FIXTURES	—	—	0.01	—	—	0.01	0.01	—	—	—	—	—	—	—	*	0.01	0.10	0.03
7 PAPER AND ALLIED PRODUCTS	*	0.52	0.08	0.02	*	0.02	2.60	1.08	0.33	0.11	0.02	0.05	0.18	*	0.09	0.04	0.07	0.03
8 PRINTING AND PUBLISHING	—	0.04	*	—	—	—	—	0.77	0.02	—	—	—	—	—	—	0.01	0.01	0.01
9 CHEMICALS	0.83	1.48	0.80	0.14	0.03	0.06	0.18	0.10	2.58	0.21	0.60	0.13	0.12	0.18	0.13	0.08	0.20	0.11
10 PRODUCTS OF PETROLEUM AND COAL	0.46	0.06	0.03	*	0.07	*	0.06	*	0.32	4.83	0.01	*	0.05	0.90	0.02	0.04	0.02	0.03
11 RUBBER PRODUCTS	0.12	0.01	0.01	0.02	0.01	0.01	0.01	*	*	*	0.04	0.05	0.01	*	0.01	0.13	0.03	0.50
12 LEATHER AND LEATHER PRODUCTS	—	—	*	0.05	*	0.01	—	*	—	—	—	1.04	—	—	*	0.02	*	0.01
13 STONE, CLAY AND GLASS PRODUCTS	0.06	0.25	*	*	0.01	0.03	0.03	—	0.26	0.05	0.01	0.01	0.43	0.21	0.07	0.07	0.12	0.19
14 PRIMARY METALS	0.01	*	—	*	0.01	0.11	—	0.01	0.19	0.01	0.01	*	0.04	6.90	2.53	2.02	1.05	1.28
15 FABRICATED METAL PRODUCTS	0.08	0.61	*	0.01	0.04	0.14	0.02	*	0.13	0.08	0.01	0.02	*	0.05	0.43	0.62	0.34	0.97
16 MACHINERY (EXCEPT ELECTRIC)	0.06	0.01	0.04	0.02	0.01	0.01	0.01	0.04	*	0.01	—	—	0.01	0.07	0.28	1.15	0.17	0.63
17 ELECTRICAL MACHINERY	—	—	—	—	—	—	—	—	*	—	—	—	0.01	0.05	0.24	0.58	0.86	0.62
18 MOTOR VEHICLES	0.11	*	—	—	*	—	—	—	—	*	—	—	*	*	0.03	0.03	0.01	4.40
19 OTHER TRANSPORTATION EQUIPMENT	0.01	—	—	—	—	—	*	—	*	*	*	—	*	*	—	—	*	0.01
20 PROFESSIONAL AND SCIENTIFIC EQUIPMENT	—	—	—	—	—	*	0.01	0.03	0.01	—	—	*	*	*	0.04	0.04	0.01	0.07
21 MISCELLANEOUS MANUFACTURING INDUSTRIES	*	0.01	*	0.26	*	0.02	0.01	—	0.03	—	*	0.02	0.01	*	0.02	0.05	0.11	0.02
22 COAL, GAS AND ELECTRIC POWER	0.06	0.20	0.11	0.04	0.02	0.02	0.12	0.03	0.19	0.56	0.04	0.02	0.20	0.35	0.08	0.10	0.05	0.06
23 RAILROAD TRANSPORTATION	0.44	0.57	0.09	0.06	0.14	0.05	0.22	0.07	0.29	0.27	0.04	0.04	0.15	0.52	0.13	0.16	0.07	0.23
24 OCEAN TRANSPORTATION	0.07	0.13	0.01	0.01	0.01	*	0.02	*	0.04	0.09	*	*	0.01	0.08	*	*	*	*
25 OTHER TRANSPORTATION	0.55	0.38	0.08	0.03	0.14	0.04	0.12	0.03	0.10	0.47	0.01	0.02	0.07	0.16	0.03	0.04	0.03	0.07
26 TRADE	1.36	0.46	0.23	0.37	0.06	0.06	0.18	0.03	0.17	0.02	0.05	0.06	0.05	0.36	0.20	0.26	0.14	0.06
27 COMMUNICATIONS	*	0.04	0.01	0.02	0.01	0.01	0.01	0.04	0.02	0.01	0.01	*	0.01	0.02	0.02	0.03	0.02	0.02
28 FINANCE AND INSURANCE	0.24	0.15	0.02	0.02	0.08	0.02	0.02	0.02	0.02	0.13	0.01	0.01	0.05	0.06	0.04	0.05	0.04	0.02
29 REAL ESTATE AND RENTALS	2.39	0.09	0.03	0.10	0.02	0.02	0.03	0.06	0.03	—	0.01	0.02	0.02	0.06	0.03	0.04	0.03	0.02
30 BUSINESS SERVICES	0.01	0.63	0.07	0.10	0.02	0.06	0.02	0.06	0.42	0.04	0.02	0.05	0.01	0.03	0.05	0.09	0.06	0.08
31 PERSONAL AND REPAIR SERVICES	0.37	0.12	*	*	0.04	*	*	0.02	0.01	0.01	*	*	0.03	0.01	0.01	0.01	*	*
32 NON-PROFIT ORGANIZATIONS	—	—	—	—	—	—	—	—	—	—	—	—	—	—	—	—	—	—
33 AMUSEMENTS	—	—	—	—	—	—	—	*	—	—	—	—	—	—	—	—	—	—
34 SCRAP AND MISCELLANEOUS INDUSTRIES	—	—	0.02	—	—	—	0.25	—	0.01	—	0.01	—	0.01	1.11	0.02	0.05	*	—
35 EATING AND DRINKING PLACES	—	—	—	—	—	—	*	—	—	—	—	—	—	—	—	—	—	—
36 NEW CONSTRUCTION AND MAINTENANCE	0.20	0.12	0.04	0.02	0.01	0.01	0.04	0.01	0.04	0.03	0.01	0.02	0.03	0.10	0.03	0.05	0.02	0.04
37 UNDISTRIBUTED	—	1.87	0.30	1.08	0.73	0.27	0.17	0.50	1.49	0.65	0.27	0.27	0.47	0.32	1.14	1.71	0.89	0.41
38 INVENTORY CHANGE (DEPLETIONS)	2.66	0.40	0.12	0.19	*	0.01	0.09	0.03	0.14	0.01	*	0.03	*	0.11	*	*	*	0.01
39 FOREIGN COUNTRIES (IMPORTS FROM)	0.69	2.11	0.21	0.28	0.18	0.01	0.62	0.01	0.59	0.26	*	0.04	0.14	0.62	0.01	0.05	*	0.02
40 GOVERNMENT	0.81	1.24	0.64	0.38	0.34	0.11	0.50	0.34	0.76	0.78	0.11	0.14	0.32	0.82	0.48	0.77	0.40	0.66
41 PRIVATE CAPITAL FORMATION (GROSS)	DEPRECIATION AND OTHER CAPITAL CONSUMPTION ALLOWANCES ARE INCLUDED IN HOUSEHOLD ROW																	
42 HOUSEHOLDS	19.17	7.05	3.34	4.24	2.72	1.12	2.20	3.14	3.75	5.04	1.08	1.20	2.35	5.53	4.14	6.80	3.41	3.39
TOTAL GROSS OUTLAYS	44.26	40.30	9.84	13.32	6.00	2.89	7.90	6.45	14.05	13.67	2.82	3.81	4.84	18.69	10.40	15.22	8.38	14.27

This interindustry table summarizes the transactions of the U.S. economy in 1947, for which preliminary data have just been compiled by the Bureau of Labor Statistics. Each number in the body of the table represents billions of 1947 dollars. In the vertical column at left the entire economy is broken down into sectors; in the horizontal row at the top the same breakdown is repeated.

PURCHASING

FINAL DEMAND

MANUFACTURING INDUSTRIES EQUIPMENT · GAS AND ELECTRIC POWER · RAILROAD TRANSPORTATION · OCEAN TRANSPORTATION · OTHER TRANSPORTATION · TRADE · COMMUNICATIONS · FINANCE AND INSURANCE · REAL ESTATE AND RENTALS · BUSINESS SERVICES · PERSONAL AND REPAIR SERVICES · NON-PROFIT ORGANIZATIONS · AMUSEMENTS · SCRAP AND MISCELLANEOUS INDUSTRIES · EATING AND DRINKING PLACES · NEW CONSTRUCTION AND MAINTENANCE · UNDISTRIBUTED · INVENTORY CHANGE (ADDITIONS) · FOREIGN COUNTRIES (EXPORTS TO) · GOVERNMENT · PRIVATE CAPITAL FORMATION (GROSS) · HOUSEHOLDS · TOTAL GROSS OUTPUT

24	25	26	27	28	29	30	31	32	33	34	35	36	37	38	39	40	41	42						
—	*	*	—	*	*	0.01	—	*	—	—	—	—	0.12	—	—	0.87	0.09	0.17	1.01	1.28	0.57	0.02	9.92	44.26
—	0.01	0.02	*	0.08	0.01	0.03	0.07	0.01	—	—	—	*	0.25	*	0.02	3.47	*	0.42	0.88	1.80	0.73	—	23.03	40.30
0.01	0.05	0.08	0.07	—	0.01	0.01	0.03	*	—	—	*	0.03	*	—	0.01	—	0.05	0.52	0.06	0.92	0.10	0.02	1.47	9.84
0.01	*	*	*	*	*	*	0.02	*	—	—	—	0.02	0.02	*	0.01	0.02	*	0.15	0.21	0.30	0.28	*	9.90	13.32
0.03	*	0.06	0.06	—	0.01	*	0.03	*	—	0.14	*	*	*	—	0.11	0.01	2.33	0.35	0.17	0.17	0.01	0.04	0.07	6.00
0.02	*	—	*	—	—	*	—	*	0.04	0.08	—	—	*	—	—	—	0.20	0.20	0.08	0.03	0.05	0.57	1.46	2.89
0.02	0.08	0.07	*	*	—	*	0.57	*	*	—	*	0.06	0.03	—	0.68	0.06	0.17	0.31	0.04	0.15	0.06	—	0.34	7.90
—	*	—	*	0.04	*	0.02	0.10	0.03	0.21	—	2.45	0.03	0.17	0.01	0.01	0.03	—	0.68	*	0.07	0.16	0.09	1.49	6.45
0.02	0.05	0.17	0.06	0.03	0.01	0.02	0.07	*	*	—	0.01	0.20	0.22	*	0.03	0.04	0.64	1.25	0.30	0.81	0.19	—	1.96	14.05
0.01	*	0.01	0.47	0.27	0.09	0.45	0.20	*	0.01	0.78	*	0.06	0.06	*	0.01	0.01	0.62	0.36	0.06	0.68	0.18	*	2.44	13.67
0.01	*	0.04	*	*	—	0.13	0.06	*	0.01	*	—	0.07	*	—	*	*	0.06	0.47	0.09	0.17	0.02	0.01	0.71	2.82
*	0.01	0.01	*	—	—	*	*	—	—	—	—	0.03	0.01	—	0.01	—	*	0.29	0.11	0.08	0.03	0.02	2.03	3.81
0.01	0.03	0.06	0.02	0.01	*	*	0.04	*	—	—	—	0.02	0.01	—	*	0.06	1.74	0.36	0.10	0.21	0.02	0.01	0.34	4.84
0.43	0.07	0.20	0.05	0.20	—	0.01	—	*	—	—	—	—	*	—	0.15	*	1.19	1.24	0.16	0.77	0.02	—	0.02	18.69
0.10	0.07	0.04	*	0.03	*	0.01	0.06	*	—	—	*	0.03	0.01	—	0.06	0.02	3.09	1.44	0.21	0.39	0.05	0.28	0.95	10.40
0.22	0.03	*	0.03	0.06	—	0.01	0.01	—	0.02	—	—	0.15	*	—	0.07	—	0.51	2.24	0.37	1.76	0.18	5.82	1.22	15.22
0.12	0.03	0.02	0.02	0.04	—	0.01	0.01	0.05	—	—	0.01	0.09	*	—	0.04	—	0.77	1.27	0.25	0.44	0.17	1.75	0.93	8.38
*	—	—	0.01	*	—	0.13	0.02	*	—	*	—	1.05	*	—	0.07	*	0.04	0.67	0.40	1.02	0.15	2.98	3.13	14.27
0.30	—	—	*	0.04	0.08	0.13	—	—	—	—	—	*	—	—	0.01	—	*	0.46	0.02	0.32	1.25	1.20	0.17	4.00
0.02	0.18	0.02	*	—	—	*	—	*	—	—	0.01	0.05	0.18	—	0.01	—	0.02	0.24	0.03	0.18	0.08	0.26	0.62	2.12
*	0.03	0.16	*	*	*	*	0.01	*	—	—	0.15	0.16	0.05	0.05	0.11	0.02	0.03	0.68	0.04	0.19	0.08	0.51	1.89	4.76
0.03	0.01	0.03	1.27	0.44	*	0.09	0.49	0.01	0.06	3.15	*	0.31	0.16	0.05	—	0.22	0.03	0.02	0.03	0.35	0.20	—	—	9.21
0.04	0.01	0.03	0.15	0.41	*	0.06	0.08	*	0.01	0.42	0.03	0.03	0.05	*	0.03	0.25	0.71	0.30	0.08	0.59	0.33	0.27	2.53	9.95
*	*	0.01	*	—	0.22	—	—	—	—	—	—	—	—	—	*	—	—	*	—	1.16	0.31	—	0.10	2.29
0.01	0.01	0.01	0.03	0.19	0.04	0.25	0.31	*	*	0.13	0.03	0.01	0.02	*	0.02	0.10	0.57	0.17	0.04	0.32	0.35	0.10	4.77	9.86
0.07	0.04	0.05	0.05	0.03	0.01	0.42	0.20	0.01	0.04	0.75	0.14	0.37	0.29	0.01	0.09	1.06	2.52	1.01	0.20	1.00	0.05	2.34	26.82	41.66
0.01	0.01	0.01	0.02	0.02	*	0.04	0.33	0.06	0.09	0.06	0.43	0.12	0.07	0.01	—	0.01	0.04	0.08	—	0.04	0.15	—	1.27	3.17
0.02	0.01	0.02	0.05	0.02	0.12	0.30	1.00	*	1.85	0.56	0.02	0.12	0.09	0.03	—	0.07	0.40	—	—	0.14	0.03	—	6.99	12.81
0.02	0.01	0.03	0.05	0.02	0.01	0.15	1.96	0.05	0.21	0.21	0.06	0.71	0.40	0.18	—	0.39	0.08	—	—	—	0.22	0.80	20.29	28.86
0.01	0.05	0.06	0.01	0.02	*	0.03	1.71	0.09	0.14	0.04	0.06	0.12	0.02	0.10	—	0.06	0.13	0.42	—	*	0.04	—	0.18	5.10
*	*	*	0.02	0.11	0.01	0.26	1.42	0.02	0.11	0.03	0.07	0.56	0.08	0.02	0.03	0.23	0.82	1.17	—	—	0.08	0.27	8.35	14.30
—	—	—	—	—	*	*	—	—	0.02	—	—	—	0.09	—	—	—	—	0.16	—	—	5.08	—	8.04	13.39
—	—	—	—	—	—	—	—	—	—	—	—	—	0.01	0.39	—	—	—	0.01	—	0.13	—	—	2.40	2.94
—	*	—	—	—	—	0.04	0.39	0.01	0.11	0.03	0.02	*	*	0.01	—	—	*	0.01	—	0.03	*	—	—	2.13
—	—	—	—	—	—	0.01	—	—	—	—	—	—	0.15	—	—	—	—	—	—	—	—	—	13.11	13.27
0.02	0.01	0.02	0.27	1.12	*	0.13	0.18	0.18	0.03	4.08	*	0.06	0.34	0.02	—	0.07	0.01	—	—	—	5.28	15.70	0.15	28.49
0.34	0.19	0.87	0.25	0.10	0.04	0.03	2.59	0.01	0.71	0.36	0.31	1.13	0.91	0.22	—	0.59	0.43	—	—	—	—	—	—	21.60
0.01	0.05	0.16	*	—	—	—	—	—	—	—	—	—	—	—	0.40	—	—	—	—	0.02	—	—	—	4.43
0.01	0.05	0.14	0.01	0.04	0.50	0.08	—	0.03	0.10	—	—	—	—	*	0.07	—	—	0.01	—	—	1.31	—	1.32	9.52
0.12	0.13	0.19	1.14	0.91	0.26	0.77	3.30	0.44	1.11	4.00	0.21	0.50	0.17	0.32	0.07	1.41	0.47	2.19	0.34	0.83	3.46	0.22	31.55	63.69
1.95	0.90	2.17	5.11	5.70	0.90	6.20	26.42	2.15	7.93	14.06	1.08	8.20	9.41	1.50	—	4.20	10.73	2.27	—	0.85	30.06	—	2.12	223.58
4.00	2.12	4.76	9.21	9.95	2.29	9.86	41.66	3.17	12.81	28.86	5.10	14.30	13.39	2.94	2.13	13.27	28.49	21.60	5.28	17.21	51.29	33.29	194.12	

When a sector is read horizontally, the numbers indicate what it ships to other sectors. When a sector is read vertically, the numbers show what it consumes from other sectors. The asterisks stand for sums less than $5 million. Totals may not check due to rounding.

derived as the grand total of the five columns grouped under the heading of final demand, but with some adjustments necessary to eliminate the duplication of transactions between the sectors represented by these columns. For example, the total payment to households, at the far right end of row 42, includes salaries paid by government, a figure which duplicates in part the payment of taxes by households included in the total payment to government.

With this brief introduction the lay economist is now qualified to turn around and trace his way back into the table via whatever chain of inter-industry relationships engages his interest. He will not go far before he finds himself working intuitively with the central concept of input-output analysis. This is the idea that there is a fundamental relationship between the volume of the output of an industry and the size of the inputs going into it. It is obvious, for example, that the purchases of the auto industry (column 18) from the glass industry (row 13) in 1947 were strongly determined by the number of motor vehicles produced that year. Closer inspection will lead to the further realization that every single figure in the chart is dependent upon every other. To take an extreme example, the appropriate series of inputs and outputs will show that the auto industry's purchases of glass are dependent in part upon the demand for motor vehicles arising out of the glass industry's purchases from the fuel industries.

These relationships reflect the structure of our technology. They are expressed in input-output analysis as the ratios or coefficients of each input to the total output of which it becomes a part. A table of such ratios (figure 2) computed from a table for the economy as of 1939, shows how much had to be purchased from the steel, glass, paint, rubber and other industries to produce $1,000 worth of automobile that year. Since such expenditures are determined by relatively inflexible engineering considerations or by equally inflexible customs and institutional arrangements, these ratios might be used to estimate the demand for materials induced by auto production in other years. With a table of ratios for the economy as a whole, it is possible in turn to calculate the secondary demand on the output of the industries which supply the auto industry's suppliers and so on through successive outputs and inputs until the effect of the final demand for automobiles has been traced to its last reverberation in the farthest corner of the economy. In this fashion input-output analysis should prove useful to the auto industry as a means for dealing with cost and supply problems.

The table of steel consumption ratios (figure 3) suggests, incidentally, how the input-output matrix might be used for the contrasting purpose of market analysis. Since the ultimate markets for steel are ordinarily buried in the cycle of secondary transactions among the metal-fabricating industries, it is useful to learn from this table how many tons of steel at

FIGURE 2

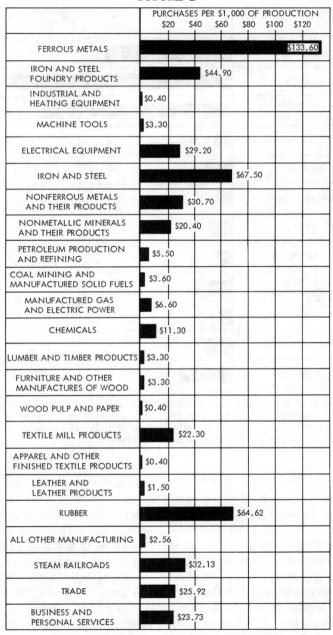

	PURCHASES PER $1,000 OF PRODUCTION					
	$20	$40	$60	$80	$100	$120
FERROUS METALS						$133.60
IRON AND STEEL FOUNDRY PRODUCTS		$44.90				
INDUSTRIAL AND HEATING EQUIPMENT	$0.40					
MACHINE TOOLS	$3.30					
ELECTRICAL EQUIPMENT	$29.20					
IRON AND STEEL			$67.50			
NONFERROUS METALS AND THEIR PRODUCTS	$30.70					
NONMETALLIC MINERALS AND THEIR PRODUCTS	$20.40					
PETROLEUM PRODUCTION AND REFINING	$5.50					
COAL MINING AND MANUFACTURED SOLID FUELS	$3.60					
MANUFACTURED GAS AND ELECTRIC POWER	$6.60					
CHEMICALS	$11.30					
LUMBER AND TIMBER PRODUCTS	$3.30					
FURNITURE AND OTHER MANUFACTURES OF WOOD	$3.30					
WOOD PULP AND PAPER	$0.40					
TEXTILE MILL PRODUCTS	$22.30					
APPAREL AND OTHER FINISHED TEXTILE PRODUCTS	$0.40					
LEATHER AND LEATHER PRODUCTS	$1.50					
RUBBER			$64.62			
ALL OTHER MANUFACTURING	$2.56					
STEAM RAILROADS	$32.13					
TRADE	$25.92					
BUSINESS AND PERSONAL SERVICES	$23.73					

Input to the auto industry from other industries per $1,000
of auto production was derived from the 1939 interindustry table.
Comparing these figures with those for the auto industry in the
1947 table would show changes in the input structure of the
industry due to changes in prices and technology.

FIGURE 3

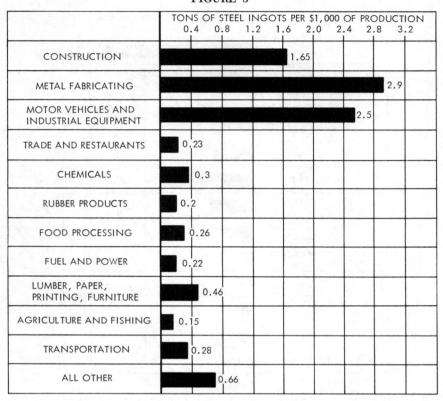

	TONS OF STEEL INGOTS PER $1,000 OF PRODUCTION							
	0.4 0.8 1.2 1.6 2.0 2.4 2.8 3.2							
CONSTRUCTION	1.65							
METAL FABRICATING	2.9							
MOTOR VEHICLES AND INDUSTRIAL EQUIPMENT	2.5							
TRADE AND RESTAURANTS	0.23							
CHEMICALS	0.3							
RUBBER PRODUCTS	0.2							
FOOD PROCESSING	0.26							
FUEL AND POWER	0.22							
LUMBER, PAPER, PRINTING, FURNITURE	0.46							
AGRICULTURE AND FISHING	0.15							
TRANSPORTATION	0.28							
ALL OTHER	0.66							

The output of the steel industry depends heavily on what kinds of goods are demanded in the ultimate market. This table shows the amount of steel required to meet each $1,000 of the demand for other goods in 1939. The current demand for the top three items is responsible for the steel shortage.

the mill were needed in 1939 to satisfy each thousand dollars worth of demand for the products of industries which ultimately place steel products at the disposal of the consumer. This table shows the impressively high ratio of the demand for steel in the construction and consumer durable-goods industries which led the Bureau of Labor Statistics to declare in 1945 that a flourishing postwar economy would require even more steel than the peak of the war effort. Though some industry spokesmen took a contrary position at that time, steel production recently has been exceeding World War II peaks, and the major steel companies are now engaged in a 16-million-ton expansion program which was started even before the outbreak of the war in Korea and the current rearmament.

The ratios shown in these two tables are largely fixed by technology Others in the complete matrix of the economy, especially in the trade and services and households sectors, are established by custom and other institutional factors. All, of course, are subject to modification by such forces as progress in technology and changes in public taste. But whether they vary more or less rapidly over the years, these relationships are subject to dependable measurement at any given time.

Here we have our bridge between theory and facts in economics. It is a bridge in a very literal sense. Action at a distance does not happen in economics any more than it does in physics. The effect of an event at any one point is transmitted to the rest of the economy step by step via the chain of transactions that ties the whole system together. A table of ratios for the entire economy gives us, in as much detail as we require, a quantitatively determined picture of the internal structure of the system. This makes it possible to calculate in detail the consequences that result from the introduction into the system of changes suggested by the theoretical or practical problem at hand.

In the case of a particular industry we can easily compute the complete table of its input requirements at any given level of output, provided we know its input ratios. By the same token, with somewhat more involved computation, we can construct synthetically a complete input-output table for the entire economy. We need only a known "bill of final demand" to convert the table of ratios into a table of magnitudes. The 1945 estimate of postwar steel requirements, for example, was incidental to a study of the complete economy based upon a bill of demand which assumed full employment in 1950. This bill of demand was inserted into the total columns of a table of ratios based on the year 1939. By arithmetical procedures the ratios were then translated into dollar figures, among which was the figure for steel, which showed a need for an absolute minimum of 98 million ingot tons. Actual production in 1950, at the limit of capacity, was 96.8 million tons.

Though its application is simple, the construction of an input-output table is a highly complex and laborious operation. The first step, and one that has little appeal to the theoretical imagination, is the gathering and ordering of an immense volume of quantitative information. Given the inevitable lag between the accumulation and collation of data for any given year, the input-output table will always be an historical document. The first input-output tables, prepared by the author and his associates at Harvard University in the early 1930s, were based upon 1919 and 1929 figures. The 1939 table was not completed until 1944. Looking to the future, a table for 1953 which is now under consideration could not be made available until 1957. For practical purposes the original figures in the table must be regarded as a base, subject to refinement and correction in accord with subsequent trends. For example, the 1945 projection of the 1950 economy on the basis of the 1939 table made suitable adjustments in the coal and oil input ratios of the transportation industries on the assumption that the trend from steam to diesel locomotives would continue throughout the period.

The basic information for the table and its continuing revision comes from the Bureau of the Census and other specialized statistical agencies. As the industrial breakdown becomes more detailed, however, engineering and technical information plays a more important part in determining the data. A perfectly good way to determine how much coke is needed to produce a ton of pig iron, in addition to dividing the output of the blast furnace industry into its input of coke, is to ask an ironmaster. In principle there is no reason why the input-output coefficients should not be entirely derived from "below," from engineering data on process design and operating practice. Thus in certain studies of the German economy made by the Bureau of Labor Statistics following World War II the input structures of key industries were set up on the basis of U.S. experience. The model of a disarmed but self-supporting Germany developed in these studies showed a steel requirement of 11 million ingot tons, toward which actual output is now moving. Completely hypothetical input structures, representing industries not now operating, have been introduced into tables of the existing U.S. economy in studies conducted by Air Force economists.

This brings us to the problem of computation. Since the production level required of each industry is ultimately dependent upon levels in all others, it is clear that we have a problem involving simultaneous equations. Though the solution of such equations may involve no very high order of mathematics, the sheer labor of computation can be immense. The number of equations to be solved is always equal to the number of sectors into which the system is divided. Depending upon whether a specific or a general solution of the system is desired, the volume of computation will vary as the square or the cube of the number of sectors involved. A typical general solution of a 42-sector table for 1939 required 56 hours on the Harvard Mark II computer. Thanks to this investment in computation, the conversion of any stipulated bill of demand into the various industrial production levels involves nothing more than simple arithmetic. The method cannot be used, however, in the solution of problems which call for changes in the input-output ratios, since each change requires a whole new solution of the matrix. For the larger number of more interesting problems which require such changes, special solutions are the rule. However, even a special solution on a reasonably detailed 200-sector table might require some 200,000 multiplications and a greater number of additions. For this reason it is likely that the typical nongovernmental user will be limited to condensed general solutions periodically computed and published by special-purpose groups working in the field. With these the average industrial analyst will be able to enjoy many

FIGURE 4

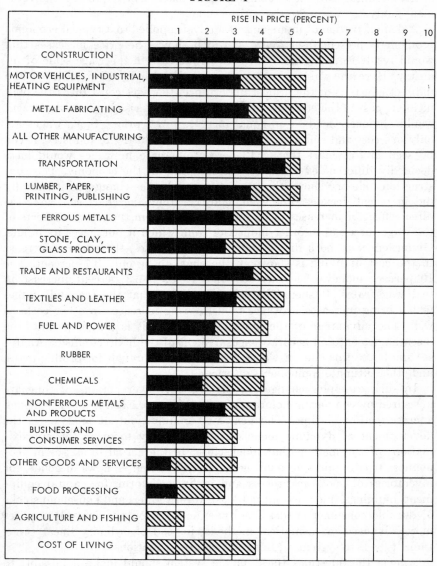

Price increases that would be caused by a 10 percent increase in wages were computed from the 1939 interindustry table. The increases include the direct effect of the rise in each industry's own wage bill (dark bars) and the indirect effect of price increases on purchase from others (striped bars).

of the advantages of the large and flexible machinery required for government analyses relating to the entire economy.

A demonstration of input-output analysis applied to a typical economic problem is presented in figure 4, which shows the price increases that would result from a general 10 percent increase in the wage scale of industry. Here the value of the matrix distinguishing between direct and indirect effects is of the utmost importance. If wages constituted the only ultimate cost in the economy, a general 10 percent rise in all money wages would obviously lead to an equal increase in all prices. Since wages are only one cost and since labor costs vary from industry to industry, it can be seen in the chart that a 10 percent increase in wages would have decidedly different effects upon various parts of the economy. The construction industry shows the greatest upward price change, as it actually did in recent decades. For each industry group the chart separates the direct effect of increases in its own wage bill from the indirect effects of the wage increases in other industries from which it purchases its inputs. Giving effect to both direct and indirect increases, the average increase in the cost of living is shown in the chart to be only 3.7 percent. The 10 percent money-wage increase thus yields a 6.3 percent increase in real wage rates. It should be noted, however, that the economic forces which bring increases in wages tend to bring increases in other costs as well. The advantage of the input-output analysis is that it permits the disentanglement and accurate measurement of the indirect effects. Analyses similar to this one for wages can be carried through for profits, taxes, and other ultimate components of prices.

In such examples changes in the economy over periods of time are measured by comparing before-and-after pictures. Each is a static model, a cross-section in time. The next step in input-output analysis is the development of dynamic models of the economy to bring the approximations of the method that much closer to the actual processes of economics. This requires accounting for stocks as well as flows of goods, for inventories of goods in process and in finished form, for capital equipment, buildings, and, last but not least, for dwellings and household stocks of durable consumer goods. The dynamic input-output analysis requires more advanced mathematical methods; instead of ordinary linear equations it leads to systems of linear differential equations.

Among the questions the dynamic system should make it possible to answer, one could mention the determination of the changing pattern of outputs and inventories or investments and capacities which would attend a given pattern of growth in final demand projected over a five- or ten-year period. Within such broad projections, for example, we would be able to estimate approximately not only how much aluminum should be produced, but how much additional aluminum-producing capacity would be required, and the rate at which such capacity should be installed. The computational task becomes more formidable, but it does not seem to exceed the capacity of the latest electronic computers. Here, as in the case of the static system, the most laborious problem is the assembly of the necessary factual information. However, a complete set of stock or capital ratios, paralleling the flow ratios of all of the productive sectors of the U.S. economy for the year 1939, has now been completed.

This table of capital ratios shows that in addition to the flow of raw pig-iron, scrap, coal, labor and so on, the steel works and rolling mills industry—when operating to full capacity—required $1,800 of fixed investment for each $1,000 worth of output. This would include $336 worth of tools, $331 worth of iron and steel foundry production, and so on down to $26 worth of electrical equipment. This means that in order to expand its capacity so as to be able to increase its output by one million dollars worth of finished products annually, the steel works and rolling mills industry would have to install $336,000 worth of tools and spend corresponding amounts on all other types of new fixed installations. This investment demand constitutes of course additional input requirements for the product of the corresponding capital goods industries, input requirements which are automatically taken into account in the solution of an appropriate system of dynamic input-output equations.

Active experimental work with the dynamic system is under way. Meanwhile the demonstrated power of input-output analysis has thoroughly convinced many workers in the field of its practical possibilities. Of wider consequence is the expectation of theoretical investigators that this new grasp on the facts of the subject will further liberate economics from the confines of its traditionally simplified postulates.

26. The Price of Gasoline: Forecasting Comparisons*

ANTHONY E. BOPP and JOHN A. NERI

The purpose of this article is to compare the results obtained from forecasting the price of motor gasoline using three different methodologies over two different forecast periods. Two of the methodologies are conceptually primitive techniques, a Box-Jenkins (B-J) technique and a simple regression technique. The third method is more complex, an econometric technique. The first two methods are termed *primitive* because, while they can involve complicated statistical procedures, they do not lend themselves to alternative policy analysis and rely on little or no behavioral theory to which their results must conform. They can produce interesting insights into underlying structures, but such structures usually play no role in their statistical formulation. However, they do generate "good" simulations, as demonstrated by I. B. Ibrahim and T. Itsuki and Charles R. Nelson. In fact, Ibrahim and Itsuki and Nelson have demonstrated the excellent B-J capabilities in forecasting GNP components as compared with economic forecasts. Although this paper also compares simulation capabilities, questions of policy assessment are addressed as well as a question of importance at the present: How to forecast gasoline prices? Congress would like forecasts of gasoline prices before it decontrols oil prices. It would not want to decontrol prices if forecasts pointed to "explosively" higher prices (bad politics) and it wants to ensure that prices do not rise faster or higher than economic factors would warrant. It can only test future price increases for "reasonableness" against today's forecast.

There has been a growing interest among economists, forecasters, and others in management science in Box-Jenkins techniques because of their forecasting potential. In an area difficult to simulate, this article shows that the B-J technique produces marginally better forecasts of gasoline prices than an econometrics model for a one-period-ahead forecast; however, for a long-term forecast (18 periods ahead) the econometric technique is far superior. Further it is shown that the B-J technique does not

---

* *Quarterly Review of Economics and Business,* vol. 18, no. 4 (1978), pp. 23–32.

forecast substantially better than a simple regression equation that relies on the forecast of one exogenous variable. Earlier work has either compared an econometric model with a simple regression or with a Box-Jenkins model. This work compares all three simultaneously.

The next section presents a brief description of the problems encountered in forecasting gasoline prices, as well as comparative advantages of the techniques used to make such forecasts, followed by a comparison of the forecast results, and a summary and conclusion.

ESTIMATION METHODS

A basic difficulty in estimating gasoline prices is that gasoline prices were relatively stable from 1960 to 1970, gradually increased from 1970 to 1972, increased exposively from 1973 to the middle of 1974, then oscillated over the second half of 1974. Where would they go in 1975 and 1976? Would there be a gradual increase, a further explosive increase—if they could double, could they quadruple?—or would they return to lower levels? The three forecasting techniques presented are fitted to monthly data from 1960 to 1974 and simulated over the 18-month period from January 1975 through June 1976.

An Econometric Model

The price of gasoline is determined by factors that affect both the supply of and the demand for gasoline. The econometric specification presented here is a reduced form equation from an inventory-price adjustment model used to capture the effects of supply and demand factors. Since gasoline stocks play an important role in the gasoline market, an inventory adjustment model seems appropriate. Following B. T. McCallum, supply, demand, price adjustment, and inventory adjustment equations are first specified and then used to obtain the final reduced form equation for estimation.

Dynamic demand and production equations are specified as follows:

$$Q = a_0 + a_1 {}^* P_g + a_2 {}^* \gamma + a_3 {}^* Q(-1).$$
$$a_1 < 0, a_2 > 0, 0 < a_3 < 1. \tag{1}$$
$$S = b_0 + b_1 {}^* P_G + b_2 {}^* P_C + b_3 {}^* P_D + b_4 {}^* S(-1).$$
$$b_1 > 0, b_2 < 0, b_3 < 0, 0 < b_4 < 1, \tag{2}$$

where Q = quantity consumed of gasoline, million barrels per month as reported by the Bureau of Mines; S = quantity produced of gasoline, million barrels per month as reported by the Bureau of Mines; P_G, P_C, P_D = respectively, wholesale prices of gasoline, crude oil, and distillate, each deflated by the WPI, reported by the Bureau of Labor Statistics; γ = real personal income, billions of dollars, as reported by the Department of

Commerce; and $Q(-1), S(-1)$ = lagged consumption and production.

Thus the quantity of gasoline consumed is assumed to depend upon its own price, income, and a consumption adjustment factor to reflect non-instantaneous stock and behavior adjustments. Production depends upon own-price, crude oil prices, distillate prices (a close substitute in production but not in consumption), and a production adjustment factor.

There are over 80 marketers of gasoline with the largest having less than 7 percent of the sales market. The 20 largest have 80 percent of the national sales market but the regional mix is more diverse. Such facts cannot lead to the conclusion that the gasoline market is atomistic, but they do suggest that a competitive model can be used to explain and predict gasoline prices. If the model does not perform well, then each underlying assumption will be reexamined. Consequently, a competitive price adjustment equation is employed,

$$p^e(+1) - p^e = c(P - P^e),$$
$$0 < c < 1 \tag{3}$$

and a simple linear marginal storage cost function is also used,

$$IC = d_0 + d_1 I,$$
$$d_0 < 0, \text{ and } d_1 > 0 \tag{4}$$

where P^e = expected gasoline price; P = actual price; IC = inventory costs; and I = stock of gasoline, million of barrels, as reported by the Bureau of Mines.

Substituting the foregoing expressions into the market clearing equation,

$$Q = S + I - I(-1) \tag{5}$$

allows for a solution in terms of the price of gasoline. The solution is given by

$$P_G = \alpha 0 + \alpha_1 P_c + \alpha_2 P_d + \alpha_3 P_g(-1) + \alpha_4 I(-1) + \alpha_5 Q(-1)$$
$$+ \alpha_6 S(-1) + \alpha_7 \gamma \tag{6}$$

with a priori, $\alpha_1 > 0, \alpha_2 > 0, \alpha_3 > 0, \alpha_4 < 0, \alpha_5 > 0, \alpha_6 < 0,$ and $\alpha_7 > 0$. This equation was estimated in log form and used to generate the econometric simulation. The estimated parameters and supporting statistics are presented in Table 1. OLS estimates of equation (6) produced a computed h-statistic of 1.25 indicating autocorrelated disturbances. The data were quasi-first differenced and estimated by nonlinear least squares to obtain asymptotically efficient estimators.

Other estimations were tried using various combinations of the right-hand side variables as being jointly determined. When their simulation values showed agreement with the results reported here—often to two decimal places—the simplest specification was adopted and greater confidence was placed in its robustness. All of the signs are correct on a priori

TABLE 1

Variable	Estimated Coefficient	t-statistic
P_o	0.161	2.027
P_d	.202	2.446
$P(-1)$	.504	4.379
$I(-1)$	−.107	−2.454
$Q(-1)$	.007	0.184
$S(-1)$	−.134	−1.999
Y	.151	1.50
Rho	.281	3.50

$\bar{R}^2 = .976$. Standard error of the regression = .018.

grounds and all estimated parameters are significantly different from zero at the 5 percent level except for lagged demand. Since this is an inventory adjustment model, it is reasonable that demand effects are picked up in stock adjustments.

The foregoing specification is rich in policy analysis capability. Not only can the impact of higher crude oil prices and changes in national income be assessed relative to their impact on gasoline prices, but even such seemingly unrelated events as natural gas curtailments can be evaluated relative to the gasoline market. Natural gas curtailments can be expected to push up distillate (heating fuel oil) prices which affect refiners' decisions about relative distillate/gasoline yield levels. It is this policy richness which makes econometric forecasts attractive and difficult—forecast values of exogenous variables are needed.

Note, however, that in order to be consistent a larger model that would also forecast distillate prices should be constructed. One variable in the distillate price equation would be gasoline prices. The solution of the complete model would then simultaneously determine distillate and gasoline prices. In such a model the exogenous effects of cold weather or natural gas curtailments on gasoline prices could be traced. By looking at only one part of such a model—the gasoline price equation—such effects are captured only through exogenous distillate price changes.

A Times-Series Model

The class of time-series model used to forecast gasoline prices follows the methodology of Box and Jenkins. They have shown that all stochastic processes belong to a general class of autoregressive integrated moving average models (ARIMA) with the general form,

$$\phi_p (B) (1 - B)^d z_t = \theta_o + \theta_q (B) a_t \tag{7}$$

where B = the backshift or lag operator, d = the number of differences required to achieve stationarity, $\phi_p(B)$ and $\theta_q(B)$ = polynomials in the

TABLE 2
Autocorrelations: First Differences of the Wholesale Price of Gasoline

			−0.8	−0.6	−0.4	−0.2	0.0	0.2	0.4	0.6	0.8
Lag	1 =	0.615					:*	* *	* *	* *	* *
Lag	2 =	0.465					:*	* *	* *	* *	
Lag	3 =	0.402					:*	* *	* *	*	
Lag	4 =	0.206					:*	* *	*		
Lag	5 =	0.150					:*	* *			
Lag	6 =	0.058					:*	*			
Lag	7 =	0.001					:				
Lag	8 =	−.089					*:				
Lag	9 =	−.034					*:				
Lag	10 =	−.031					*:				
Lag	11 =	0.012					:				
Lag	12 =	0.071					:*	*			
Lag	13 =	0.115					:*	* *			
Lag	14 =	0.055					:*				
Lag	15 =	0.009					:				
Lag	16 =	−.008					:				
Lag	17 =	0.020					:*				
Lag	18 =	0.015					:				
Lag	19 =	−.001					:				
Lag	20 =	0.039					:*				
Lag	21 =	−.008					:				
Lag	22 =	−.007					:				
Lag	23 =	−.016					:				
Lag	24 =	−.066					*: *				

Upper bound on standard error of acf = 0.11

Partial Autocorrelations

			−0.8	−0.6	−0.4	−0.2	0.0	0.2	0.4	0.6	0.8
Lag	1 =	0.615					:****	****	****	****	**
Lag	2 =	0.139					:****				
Lag	3 =	0.116					:****				
Lag	4 =	−.180				*****	:				
Lag	5 =	0.030					:*				
Lag	6 =	−.086					**:				
Lag	7 =	0.012					:				
Lag	8 =	−.056					*:				
Lag	9 =	0.063					:**				
Lag	10 =	−.007					:				
Lag	11 =	0.090					:**				
Lag	12 =	0.058					:**				
Lag	13 =	0.076					:**				
Lag	14 =	−.148					***:				
Lag	15 =	−.070					**:				
Lag	16 =	−.052					*:				
Lag	17 =	0.134					:***				
Lag	18 =	−.007					:				
Lag	19 =	0.016					:				
Lag	20 =	0.038					:*				
Lag	21 =	−.054					*:				
Lag	22 =	−.016					:				
Lag	23 =	−.043					*:				
Lag	24 =	−.078					**:				

lag operator of orders p and q respectively, θ_o = a constant, a_t = a "white noise" disturbance, and z_t = the time series under inspection. On the basis of sample autocorrelations and partial autocorrelations of successive differences of the raw data, an ARIMA $(1,1,1)$ model was identified without a deterministic trend. The autocorrelations and partial autocorrelations are shown in Table 2.

The estimated ARIMA model is

$$z_t = \phi_1 z_{t-1} + a_t - \theta_1 a_{t-1} \tag{8}$$

where $z_t = P_t - P_{t-1}$. P_t = the nominal wholesale price of gasoline used in the econometric model. A test of adequacy of the ARIMA model is provided by use of the Q-statistic.

$$Q = (N - d) \sum_{k=1}^{T} r_k^2 (\hat{a})$$

which is distributed $X^2 (K - p - q)$ under the null hypothesis of white noise residuals. K = the number of computed autocorrelations. For $K = 36$, the computed Q-statistic was 16.6 which is less than the critical value of 21.7 at the 5 percent level, so that the hypothesis of an adequate model cannot be rejected.

The parameter estimates are presented as follows:

Coefficient estimate		t-statistic
ϕ	0.807	2.49
θ	0.238	3.21.

The $\overline{\mathrm{R}}^2$ with the actual series was 0.99.

A Regression Model

Finally a simple regression approach was used to link gasoline prices to crude oil prices. This approach is presented here for two reasons. One is that other comparisons have used it as a naive version against which comparisons can be made. It is so used here in order to benchmark the forecasting power of both the econometric and the Box-Jenkins techniques. A second reason is that, especially in petroleum economics, it is tempting to link product prices directly to crude oil prices. A common linkage is to assume straight cost pass-throughs from crude oil to the product prices. The straight cost pass-through assumption is used here. That is, the following equation was estimated:

$$P_g = a * S_1 + b * S_2 + c * P_c + e, \tag{9}$$

where P_g and P_c = respectively gasoline and crude oil wholesale price indexes and e = an assumed white noise residual. S_1 and S_2 = dummy variables for the months October, November, December, January, February, March, and April (S_1) and May, June, July, August, and September (S_2). Refiners adjust product yields and establish inventory priorities for the heating oil season (S_1) and for the gasoline (S_2) season. The two dummy variables capture the effects of changing the product mix and inventory policy on the gasoline price—crude oil price relationship. OLS produced an estimate of c (crude oil price parameter) of .999 with a standard error of .0178, indicating nearly exact straight cost pass-through. However, OLS produced a computed Durbin-Watson statistic of .5, indicating the presence of autocorrelated disturbances, so a quasi-first differenced equation was estimated directly, producing

	Estimated coefficient	t-statistic
a	−.0688	−4.74
b	−.0474	−4.67
c	.724	5.474
rho	−.396	−1.55.

$$\bar{R}^2 = .976$$

Thus, over the sample period, 1968–74, all three approaches can adequately explain variations in gasoline prices. The next section discusses the results of simulating each approach over 1975 through 1976:6.

SIMULATION RESULTS

Two simulations over 1975 to 1976:6 were performed with each model. One simulation provided one-period-ahead forecasts, the other provided an entire 18-month forecast. Some previous comparisons of Box-Jenkins and econometric techniques had relied solely on the one-period-ahead forecast, asserting that such a simulation is the most favorable one for an econometric method because reliable exogenous variables are then available. However, Box and Jenkins and Nelson show that "diagnostic checking" is an integral part of time-series forecasting: Box-Jenkins type models may need to be respecified frequently as the diagnostic checks indicate. The basic form may remain the same but the parameters must be respecified. Consequently we compared the models over one period ahead and over 18 months.

In order to forecast one period ahead only current values of prices are required for the Box-Jenkins model. For the econometric and regression model it was assumed that real crude oil and distillate prices would increase by 4 percent per year, real income by 3½ percent, gasoline demand and production by 4 percent, and no net change in inventory. For the one-period-ahead forecast some exogenous variables are lagged ones so that actual values were then used. Where current exogenous variables were required, the foregoing growth rates were applied on a monthly basis to get the forecasts for the exogenous variables. For the 18-month forecast, these assumptions were used to generate the set of exogenous variables for the econometric and regression methods. The Box-Jenkins forecast relies on *none* of these assumptions.

Finally note that these assumptions are not "wired in" after the fact. They would have been reasonable ones for late in 1974 and rely on no special insights in macroactivity or energy usage.

Table 3 presents summary statistics for each method for the one-period-ahead forecast and the 18-month forecast.

TABLE 3

Method	R^2	RMSE	Regression Coefficient	Theil U-inequality	Bias	Variance	Covariance
One-period-ahead simulation:							
Box-Jenkins	0.99	0.0098	1.045	0.002	0.24	0.58	0.18
Econometric ...	.96	.0693	1.128	.015	.49	.13	.38
Regression	.85	.097	0.89	.022	.61	.003	.39
Eighteen-month simulation:							
Box-Jenkins	0.52	0.3518	2.264*	0.08	0.8	0.14	0.06
Econometric ...	.82	.2137	1.16	.047	.77	.06	.17
Regression	.78	.082	1.007	.017	.045	.065	.89

* Significantly different from one.

The R^2 shows the squared correlation coefficient for forecast values compared with actuals. All methods have large R^2 for the one-period-ahead simulation, less for the 18-month forecast, and the Box-Jenkins technique has the lowest in the 18-month simulation. The RMSE column shows the root mean square errors of the various methods. The regression coefficient column shows the results of regressing the forecast values on the actual values: only the Box-Jenkins 18-month forecast produces a coefficient significantly different from one, indicating a poor performance. The Theil U-inequalities are presented for the various forecasts as well as the component parts of the forecast error. Note that the order of Box-Jenkins, econometric, regression is preserved on all measures for the one-period-ahead simulations, but generally the order is econometric regression, and Box-Jenkins for the 18-month forecast. The point to be made from inspecting the table is that all of the methods work well for the one-period-ahead forecast with the Box-Jenkins method performing the best—the result of other studies. However, over the 18-month period the Box-Jenkins method's performance falls off drastically while the econometric and the regression approach suffer less from the extended forecast period. Minor points from the table also could be made favoring the econometric approach. The decomposition of the Theil U-inequality shows a large covariance component for the regression method. Large variance or bias components can be corrected by taking larger samples, large covariance components are most troublesome, since they reflect a poor correlation of the forecast with actual values. Finally the forecasts series and the actual series are presented in the appendix. If turning points are counted, then it is found that in the one-period-ahead forecast the Box-Jenkins method captures the two turning points exactly, whereas the econometric method misses each one by a month and shows two false turning points while the regression forecast is much more irregular. An inspection of the actual data starting in 1974:7 shows all of the forecasts to be "reasonable" in the sense that they could be extensions of the irregular movements in 1974 gasoline prices.

When we mentioned the rationale for providing comparisons based on 1- and 18-month forecasts we noted that the Box-Jenkins technique involved diagnostic checking. In a similar vein econometric forecasting involves checking for structural change. However, there are differences. An econometric specification is not altered merely by large changes in the value of exogenous variables. However, such changes are likely to cause a structural change in the Box-Jenkins formulation. An extreme example can be made by noting that econometric equations could allow for persistent declines or persistent increases or persistent fluctuations—all with the same equation. Box-Jenkins formulations are likely to exhibit the need for changing parameter values or changing equation specifications in each case. With respect to the case in question we checked for structural change every six months over the forecast period with the econometric equation and found none, using the Chow test. However, after each six-month interval we found structural change in the Box-Jenkins using the Q-test mentioned earlier. This most likely caused the forecast difficulties with the Box-Jenkins technique found in Table 3. However, when decision makers have to rely on a 18-month forecast, the prospect of revising the forecast 6 months from now is little comfort.

CONCLUSIONS

A number of techniques have been presented to forecast gasoline prices. For policy purposes not only can the econometric technique handle numerous policy scenarios, but it forecasts as well as other methods mentioned lately in the literature. Further, though it has been stated that one-period-ahead forecasts favor econometric methods in comparative studies, this work soundly refutes that notion. It has been shown that the structural viability of econometric methods may in fact favor it in the long run Simulation experts have asserted that econometric methods work well in the short run, but lose predictability over time; perhaps, but no more so than other techniques.

Finally, the Federal Energy Administration (now the Department of Energy) has been hampered by a trigger mechanism pertaining to oil prices. Gasoline, heating fuel, and other oil products have been decontrolled as long as actual prices did not exceed "forecast" prices using simple regression-type models where product prices are related solely to crude oil prices. An econometric method would be far superior in terms of being able to handle extraneous events, such as natural gas curtailments, which would drive up heating fuel prices, which would affect gasoline prices, and which would set off the trigger. A return to a basic econometric model would relieve much of the "triggered" anguish.

APPENDIX

Time Period	Actual WPI0571NS	Forecasts					
		Box-Jenkins		Econometric		Regression	
		1 period	18 period	1 period	18 period	1 period	18 period
1975: 1	2.049	2.066	2.015	2.066	1.928	2.029	2.03
2	2.072	2.083	2.014	2.045	1.911	2.049	2.05
3	2.094	2.100	1.998	2.063	1.965	2.265	2.19
4	2.115	2.118	1.996	2.121	2.084	2.314	2.21
5	2.175	2.174	1.996	2.153	2.140	2.333	2.22
6	2.258	2.255	1.999	2.243	2.179	2.353	2.214
7	2.350	2.345	2.004	2.270	2.279	2.518	2.395
8	2.490	2.483	2.011	2.319	2.273	2.537	2.474
9	2.510	2.533	2.018	2.417	2.244	2.564	2.477
10	2.555	2.546	2.028	2.452	2.274	2.589	2.493
11	2.535	2.526	2.037	2.497	2.243	2.582	2.513
12	2.499	2.488	2.048	2.468	2.160	2.610	2.462
1976: 1	2.477	2.466	2.059	2.431	2.152	2.630	2.22
2	2.466	2.455	2.070	2.402	2.136	2.638	2.34
3	2.413	2.401	2.080	2.392	2.168	2.478	2.417
4	2.385	2.373	2.094	2.393	2.226	2.439	2.428
5	2.399	2.386	2.107	2.376	2.252	2.461	2.438
6	2.487	2.475	2.119	2.375	2.362	2.477	2.448
1974: 7	2.141						
8	2.146						
9	2.158						
10	2.158						
11	2.143						
12	2.043